WITHDRAWN

COMPARATIVE PERSPECTIVES ON RACISM

DAMES

Dansk Center for Migration
og Etniske Studier

**EUROPEAN RESEARCH CENTRE
ON MIGRATION & ETHNIC RELATIONS**

Comparative Perspectives on Racism

Edited by
JESSIKA TER WAL and MAYKEL VERKUYTEN
European Research Centre on Migration and Ethnic Relations
Utrecht University

Ashgate

Aldershot • Burlington USA • Singapore • Sydney

Published by
Ashgate Publishing Ltd
Gower House
Croft Road
Aldershot
Hants GU11 3HR
England

Ashgate Publishing Company
131 Main Street
Burlington
Vermont 05401
USA

Ashgate website: http://www.ashgate.com

British Library Cataloguing in Publication Data
Comparative perspectives on racism. - (Research in
    migration and ethnic relations series)
    1. Racism
    I. Ter Wal, Jessika II. Verkuyten, Maykel
    305.8

Library of Congress Catalog Card Number: 00-131673

ISBN 0 7546 1123 X

Printed in Great Britain by Antony Rowe Ltd.

Contents

List of Figures

List of Tables

List of Contributors

Claudio Bolzman is professor at the Institute of Social Studies where he lectures on migration and intercultural relations. He also lectures in the Department of Sociology, University of Geneva. His research currently focuses on migration experiences, precariousness and different forms of discrimination. His recent publications include: *Sociologie de l'exil*, (Ed. Seismo, Zurich, 1996); *L'altérité dans la société: migration, ethnicité, état* (with H.R.Wicker, A. Wimmer et al., Ed. Seismo, Zurich,1996); *On est né quelque part, mais on peut vivre ailleurs: Familles, migrations, cultures, travail social* (with Pierrette Beday, ed., IES, Genève, 1997).

Malcolm D. Brown is a lecturer in the Department of Sociology at the University of Exeter, England, where he teaches the Sociology of Migration and Racism. His Ph.D., recently awarded from the University of Glasgow, Scotland, was on the construction of Muslim identities in the United Kingdom and France.

Cristiano Codagnone is a lecturer in the Department of Sociology of Bocconi University of Milan, and research associate with the Centre for European Migration and Ethnic Studies (CEMES) with responsibility for the Ethnobarometer Programme jointly organised by CEMES and CSS. His research has recently concentrated on Russian post-Soviet transition, with a particular focus on ethnic and migration issues, and on migration and citizenship issues in Western Europe. Publications include the book, *Questione Nazionale e Migrazioni Etniche: La Russia e lo Spazio Post-Sovietico* (Milan, Franco Angeli-ISMU, 1997), contributions to edited books, and articles in peer-reviewed journals.

Monique Eckmann is a professor at the Institute of Social Studies. She lectures and researches in the field of intercultural relations, anti-racist and intercultural pedagogy and social work. Her recent publications include: *'Das Antirassismus-Telefon: Neue Paradigmen und innovative Praxismodelle im Kampf gegen rassistische Diskriminierung'* in *SozialExtra*, no.9, (Extra Verlag, Wiesbaden, 1997); *A propos du phénomène des Skinheads et du racisme en Suisse* (with Karl Grünberg, Ed.IES, Genève, 1999).

Camil Fuchs is associate professor of Statistics in the Department of Statistics and Operations Research, Tel-Aviv University, Israel, and is president of the Israeli Statistical Association. He is a member of the National Statistical Board, the supervising organisation for the National Bureau of Statistics. He received his Ph.D. in Applied Statistics in 1976, from Tel-Aviv University, prior to which he spent four years as a senior statistical adviser at the Statistical Laboratory, University of Wisconsin-

Madison, USA. Previous appointments include 14 years as director of the Statistical Laboratory, Tel-Aviv University (1982–96). He has published 2 books and over 90 articles in professional journals, in conference proceedings and in research series.

Karl Grünberg is the founder of ACOR. He has published several contributions related to a better comprehension of the past: 'Ouvrages à propos de la politique suisse d'asile durant la Seconde guerre mondiale et actualité des questions qu'ils soulèvent' in *Histoire et société contemporaines*, Université de Lausanne(1995); *La police des étrangers, de l'Ueberfremdung à la politique de trois cercles ou la métamorphose d'une idée fixe*, Cahier N°2, Association romande contre le racisme, Lausanne (1997).

Louk Hagendoorn is professor of Social Sciences at Utrecht University and Academic Director of the *European Research Centre on Migration and Ethnic Relations*. His interests are in the field of inter-group relations, cross-cultural psychology and political psychology. He published on inter-group stereotypes, ethnic conflict and nationalism. He is currently involved in research on racism in the Netherlands and comparative research on ethnic relations in Central Europe, former Soviet countries and the Russian Federation.

Lawrence A. Hirschfeld is associate professor of Anthropology and of Psychology and co-director of the Graduate Program in Culture and Cognition at the University of Michigan. He is author of *Race in the Making: Cognition, Culture, and the Child's Construction of Human Kinds* (MIT Press).

Dirk Jacobs is a research associate at the Katholieke Universiteit Brussel (Catholic University of Brussels) in Belgium, where he is currently doing research on political participation of ethnic minorities in the bi-lingual region of Brussels-Capital. He studied sociology at the University of Ghent (Belgium) and held a research associate position at the Netherlands' School for Social and Economic Policy Research, Utrecht University. His Ph.D. (social sciences, Utrecht University) was on the debate on political participation of foreign residents in the Low Countries. He has published in *Social Compass, Language Problems and Language Planning* and *International Migration Review*.

Ruud Koopmans is a senior researcher at the Department Public Sphere and Social Movements of the Wissenschaftszentrum Berlin für Sozialforschung (WZB). He has published widely on protest and social movements, including *Democracy from Below* (1995), *New Social Movements in Western Europe* (1995), *Acts of Dissent* (1998), and *Paradigmen der Bewegungsforschung* (1998). His current research focuses on the German case of a European comparative research project on Mobilisation over Ethnic Relations Citizenship and Immigration (MERCI).

Hub Linssen is research fellow in the Department of Social Sciences, and the European Research Centre on Migration and Ethnic Relations

(ERCOMER), both within, Utrecht University, NL. His field of interest is the methodology of cross-national comparative research. He has published on nationality stereotypes in Western and Eastern Europe and is currently involved in comparative research on ethnic relations in former Soviet countries and the Russian Federation.

Edwin Poppe is a social psychologist working for ERCOMER and the Department of General Social Sciences, Utrecht University. His research and lecturing activities focus on intergroup relations in Central and Eastern Europe including the former Soviet Union.

Anne-Catherine Salberg Mendoza is a legal adviser and a mediator. She works in both research and FSAR. Her recent publications comprehend: *Les familles monoparentales* (with L. Cardia Vonèche, B.Bastard OFAS, Berne, 1996); *Le glaive, le miroir et l'autre. Expériences de médiations transculturelles en Suisse romande* (with Julien Knoepfler, CLUSE, Neuchâtel, to be published in 1999).

Monica Savulescu-Voudouris is a cultural sociologist, who in 1996 commenced a three year research project on the migration experiences of highly skilled East Europeans who have settled in Western Europe. She has also held positions as visiting professor at the University AI.I. Cuza Iasi, Romania, Universitatea Chisinau, Republic of Moldavia and at the University of Bucharest. Her publications include not only scientific writing, but also several volumes of poetry.

Paul Statham is a senior research fellow in European Political Communications at the Institute of Communications Studies, University of Leeds, UK. His previous appointment was as senior researcher in the department of Public Sphere and Social Movements at the Wissenschaftszentrum Berlin (WZB). He has published academic articles on media, ethnic relations, social movements and Italian politics. He is currently engaged on the British part of a European comparative research project on Mobilization over Ethnic Relations Citizenship and Immigration (MERCI).

Teun A. van Dijk is professor of Discourse Studies at the University of Amsterdam. After earlier work in literary studies, text grammar and the psychology of text comprehension, his research in the 1980s began to focus on the study of news in the press and the reproduction of racism through various types of discourse. In each of these domains, he has published several books. His work has been translated into a dozen languages. His present research in 'critical' discourse studies (CDA) focuses on the relations between power, discourse, and ideology. He holds two honorary doctorates, and is the founder of the international journals *TEXT*, *Discourse & Society*, and *Discourse Studies*, of which he still edits the latter two. He also edited the four-volume *Handbook of Discourse Analysis* and the two-volume introductory *Discourse Studies*. He has lectured in many universities, especially in Europe and the Americas.

Maykel Verkuyten is associate professor in the Department of General Social Sciences, Utrecht University, NL. He has research interests in racism, discrimination and ethnic relations. His current research includes questions on ethnic identity, in particular among young people.

Jessika ter Wal is a Marie Curie post-doctoral fellow at the University of Vienna, Austria. She is a graduate in Italian Linguistics. She completed her Ph.D. thesis on racism and ethnic prejudice in Italian policy and news discourse on immigration at the Social and Political Sciences Department of the European University Institute, Florence, Italy. Her current research interests are racism, political discourse analysis, the extreme right and the historical memory of Nazi-fascism in Italy and Austria. She was responsible for the organisation of the 3rd ERCOMER International conference and has received a grant to co-edit the publication of a selection of the papers presented.

Andreas Wimmer is currently Professor and Director at the Center for Development Research of the University of Bonn. From 1994 to 1999 he was Director of the Swiss Forum for Migration Studies at the University of Neuchatel. He has published works on state building and nationalism, ethnicity and ethnic conflicts, migration, cognitive anthropology, social change, history of anthropology, peasant societies. Regional interests are Mexico and Guatemala, Iraq, and Switzerland.

Acknowledgements

This book is the result of the third international conference, 'New directions in comparative research on racism and xenophobia', of the European Research Centre on Migration and Ethnic Relations (ERCOMER), held in Utrecht in April 1998.

We would like to thank the scholars of different fields who participated in the conference. We also like to express our appreciation to Marieke Blommensteyn, Malcolm Cross, Louk Hagendoorn, Rachel Kress, Hub Linssen, and Lin Lin van Lonkhuyzen for their support in organising the conference and preparing the book.

We are grateful to Routledge for granting permission to use sections of the article 'Explaining Racism and Xenophobia. A Critical Review of Current Research Approaches' in *Ethnic and Racial Studies*, vol. 20 no. 1 pp. 17–41 in Chapter 3 of this book.

Furthermore, our gratitude goes to the organisations that sponsored the conference: the European Commission Directorate-General V, the Royal Dutch Academy of Sciences (KNAW), and the Faculty of Social Sciences at Utrecht University.

Jessika ter Wal & Maykel Verkuyten
Utrecht, May 2000

1 Introduction: Racism in a Comparative Perspective

MAYKEL VERKUYTEN & JESSIKA TER WAL

Racism is a pervasive phenomenon that seems to be gathering force in many parts of the world. The problem of racism is not confined to a particular group, culture or nation. Indeed, in most countries racism is a recurrent and significant social fact. Therefore, comparative understanding and documentation of the multiple manifestations and causes of racism is generally considered of great importance. However, whereas issues of racism and identity are met with increasing political interest and concern, academic research seems to be equipped with disparate conceptual and analytical frameworks. Racism is a problem for which almost everyone has a theory, but no one a clear solution. That there are so many theories can be attributed to a variety of reasons, including the multi-faceted nature of racism itself, as well as differences in disciplinary background, scientific paradigm, political agenda, and the specific social, historical and cultural context. Linked to these are differences in conceptualisation. Racism, prejudice, ethnocentrism, xenophobia, anti-Semitism, ethnicism, stereotyping, differentialism, and Islamophobia, the list exemplifies our point. To be sure, these adjacent or partly overlapping concepts do not refer to the same phenomena. They identify and emphasise particular aspects, processes and articulations as crucial to the study of racism and, accordingly, construct different analytical frameworks.

Here, we will not go into the various meanings attributed to the term racism and the alternatives, nor the relationships between these. This does not mean that we think that conceptual clarity is unimportant. In the wake of post-modernism, there is some sympathy for a definitional looseness and a rejection of prior definitions. It is argued that racist phenomena are contradictory and constantly undergoing transformation, and that therefore a fixing of meanings within tight definitions should be avoided (e.g., Rattansi and Westwood, 1994). However, for the very same reasons a clear understanding of specific contents is imperative. An undefined or inflated concept of racism (or prejudice or xenophobia, etc.) stands in the way of insight and invites muddled thinking. Moreover, it leads to misunderstandings and misinterpretations among scholars.

However, in this introduction we will use the term racism as a general and sensitising concept that refers to the negative portrayal and/or treatment of those defined as 'racial' or ethnic out-groups. We will leave it to the contributors to this book to define and explain the concepts they use. Our focus is on the question of comparative research.

Comparative Research

The phrase 'comparative research' seems to have become the new key for opening doors when raising funds. This is related to the attempts by governments as well as non-governmental and migrant organisations to develop various strategies for combating racism, and such strategies are also initiated at a supra-national level, such as the United Nations and the European Union. Anyone who has ever tried to get money from similar organisations, and increasingly also from national funding agencies, knows that one has more chances when there are four or five countries involved. Aside from obvious political reasons, this preference also seems to rest on more substantial claims; to the effect that comparative research will considerably extend and improve our understanding.

The term 'comparative' has importance not only for fund raising strategies, but also has value and meaning in the social sciences. The phrase 'I am doing comparative research' certainly sounds good and gives the impression that one is looking for broad trends instead of trivial local variations. No wonder, therefore, that many authors are claiming to do comparative research. However, a close look shows that a wide range of activities is labelled 'comparative'. Some of these offer only a selection of studies on various societies, providing no more than the raw material for comparison, while others try to present a more systematic analysis. Indeed, collections of single-country studies about cultural and discursive manifestations of racism do not generally elaborate in detail upon factors and indices for comparison (e.g., Ratcliffe, 1994). Moreover, many publications gather contributions only from the larger Western European countries (e.g., Hargreaves and Leaman, 1995; Miles and Thränhardt, 1995). The greater influence of some national research communities on theorising in an international perspective has evident conceptual limitations.

Systematic comparative analysis appears to be most prolific in social psychological approaches. Such approaches measure features and factors to determine the nature and causes of ethnic prejudice in cross-national settings. This volume offers two analyses of this of less studied geographical areas: former Soviet states, and Central and Eastern Europe. In Chapter 8

Hagendoorn and Linssen compare the effects of group goal attributions on the perception of in- and out-group relations in five former Soviet states. While in Chapter 9 *Poppe* examines the correlation between changes in trait attributions to various ethnic groups, coupling this with shifts in the perception of economic conditions over time.

Comparative studies are to be found in two other areas. One of which produces predominantly policy-oriented studies that chart forms of institutional discrimination (e.g., Bovenkerk, Gras and Ramsoedh, 1995), or evaluate the implementation of anti-discrimination and anti-racist policies (e.g., Wrench, 1996, 1998). The other grew out of political science and concentrates on theorising multiculturalism, migrant integration and citizenship regimes in different societies (e.g., Favell, 1998; Martiniello, 1997; Soysal, 1994). In this volume, contributions by *Jacobs*, and *Koopmans and Statham* are closely linked to this tradition. They bring new material to the discussion by focussing on often neglected aspects of political negotiation and mobilisation around ethnic difference and belonging within different national and legislative settings. Although there are exceptions (Castles and Miller, 1993), this direction has evolved quite independently from the literature on racism. The reasons for this may be various, including the greater difficulty of studying racism comparatively, as well as the politically sensitive status of the concept of racism. In Britain, for example, the critique on the 'race relations' paradigm has moved social and political scientists towards alternative conceptualisations (Miles, 1993).

Scope and Aim of Comparative Research

Comparative research is no doubt important and can be very productive, if only because it confronts people with their tacit assumptions, ethnocentric biases and limitations in knowledge. However, if you think about it more closely then there is something quite familiar in the claim to be doing comparative research. After all is not all research comparative? Indeed, is research that does not compare feasible? Is systematic comparison not the hallmark of the social sciences or even science in general? Of course, to pose these rhetorical questions is to answer them. Epistemologically all understanding is comparative. So why make such a big deal out of 'comparative research'. It seems that it is not so much the element of comparison itself, but rather the unit or the scope of the analysis, and the intended aim of the comparison that is important. Both points are not, however, uncontroversial.

Scope

The scope of the comparison is mostly defined in terms of 'imagined com-munities' such as cultural groups and nations. That is, within the comparative literature there is a tendency to take cultural or national group membership as the unit of analysis. It is interesting to note that an analysis of racism is hardly ever labelled as comparative research when it studies different urban areas in a single city or different majority group members within a region. Typically, cross-cultural and cross-national research is considered comparative. The implicit assumption is that cultural and national differences have a profound, or at least specific, effect on the phenomena one is interested in. Differences of nation and culture seem to be considered of a different kind than, for example, differences in gender, age, social class or area of residence within a culture or country. So comparative research seems to be focused on particular factors, and the basic task of such research consists of identifying circumstances, variables or processes which describe what it is about these groups, cultures or nations that affect the racist phenomena one is interested in. Many studies fail to do this and simply 'compare' nations or groups assuming that there are relevant differences that are used unrestrained in post-hoc explanations.

Moreover, it has been argued that it is no longer possible to take 'societies' as a discrete entity and as a basis for comparison, because they pro-gressively vanish as a result of, for example, global communication (Gabriel, 1998). This then leads to a perspective on general trends and processes, a tracing of similarity rather than difference. More specifically, many scholars have pointed to the risk of reasoning about racism on the basis of observations from within national or cultural units, precisely because these are 'imagined communities'. The risk of reifying notions of 'race' by taking these as the starting points of research has been pointed out repeatedly (Miles, 1989). Moreover, some argue that research which privileges nation or culture as a unit of analysis reproduces essentialist assumptions which the study of racism should, on the contrary, try to challenge (e.g., Lloyd, 1995), for example, by focusing on hybridity (e.g., Caglar, 1997).

As a result, alternative approaches have focused on other entities for comparison. They have for example indicated the means and functions of the intersection of different identity markers of 'race', class, gender, nation, and age in boundary drawing processes (e.g., Anthias and Yuval-Davis, 1992; Lutz, Phoenix and Yuval-Davis, 1995). Another type of research focuses on the observation of the locally specific and differentiated with the aim of showing the impact of 'racism' in concrete processes of community formation and its relations to the state (Solomos, 1987; Solomos and Back, 1996). Post-modernist scholars have shown interest in the construction of 'whiteness' and the processes which render (formerly defined) issues of (in)visibility apparent (Bonnett, 1997; Fine et al., 1997). These studies have provided many valuable insights but most of them have not compared nations or cultural groups.

Aims: Tracing Similarity and Difference

In general, the aim of comparative research is to make a distinction between what is specific and what is general. In other words, its purpose is to identify and account for significant similarities and differences. Every comparative analysis will accept in principle the socioculturally and historically bounded nature of human action. This offers the challenge to do systematic comparisons in order to arrive ultimately at more general processes that transcend particular cultures, groups or societies. For example, in Chapter 8 *Hagendoorn and Linssen* investigate the general functions of trait and goal attribution for a number of ethnic groups in differing social and political conditions. In Chapter 2 *Hirschfeld* examines cross-cultural differences as well as developmental differences between children and adults in showing the nature and origins of the psychological representation of notions of 'race'. In Chapter 3 *Wimmer* argues, from another perspective, that nationalism is a general condition for the emergence of racism in modern societies and refers to numerous examples from a number of countries and regions to sustain this view.

On the other hand, critics regard the aim of identifying general processes as unrealistic and eschew explicit comparisons. They see cultural forms not as external variables influencing social action and processes but as integral and defining parts of these processes. For them culture is not an exogenous factor influencing existing racism but a force that plays a fundamental, constitutive role in the formation and expression of racism itself. Therefore, it would only be possible to determine the content and meaning of racism from within a particular conceptual scheme. Consequently, the possibility for comparative research is then very limited or even absent. In the final analysis, there would be no common measure or cross-framework that could serve as a bridge between different conceptual schemes. However, the acknowledgement and appreciation of differences in racism requires a background of similarity. In order to understand racist phenomena a common point of reference or implicit unit of comparison is necessary.

Assumptions and Objectives

From what we have just said, it follows that there are two comparative research strategies possible. One which starts from the similarities and general principles underlying the multi-faceted expressions of racist phenomena. While the other focuses instead on identifying and accounting for differences in the manifestation of racism(s).

General Principles: Brothers under the Same Skin/One Racism

The first strategy, mentioned above, is based on the assumption that there are general or cross-national characteristics and causes of racism; the 'brothers under the same skin' thesis. Comparative research attuned to this aim is concerned with the basic, or fundamental, processes of social life. It tends to reject implicitly the post-modern conceptions of relativism and contextualisation, promising generalities instead of idiosyncrasies. It implies goals such as testing the generality of existing knowledge and theories, or exploring and explaining variations across societies as to how more general processes are developed and deployed.

(Social) psychology favours a conceptualisation in terms of underlying cognitive and motivational processes, leading to the interpretation that there is *one* racism or *one* prejudice. Indeed, traditionally, (social) psychological theories have stressed the (psychic) unity of human beings. It is assumed that racism or prejudice has a singular nature. Racism may differ considerably in appearance and the way it is expressed but the underlying psychological processes are considered to be the same. At least since Allport (1954) the dominant thinking in (social) psychology has been that racism or prejudice is one thing. Various empirical phenomena are seen as different manifestations or variations of the same racism or prejudice. The differences are considered relatively unimportant in comparison to the essence, which is the generalised negative attitude and its underlying psychological similarities. ·

Allport's and Adorno, Frenkel-Brunswik, Levinson and Sanford's (1950) studies were conducted against the background of 'grand theory' and influenced by a political agenda opposed to prejudice in the post-war world. The aim was to identify general principles, which would allow for unequivocal answers to breach prejudice and racism to be found. This approach, which sees all racism as forms of the same thing, has been criticised for its homogenising effects. This, so the critics argue, removed the specific meanings of racism. The emphasis on cognitive, psychodynamic, and group processes was and still is found to lead to a neglect of detail and content of prejudice. Such research is more concerned with the testing of general theories than with the particularities of groups, cultures or nations. For example, Quillian (1995) uses data from 12 European nations to test the well-known idea that realistic conflict and group threat leads to an increase in prejudice. He is not interested in the circumstances particular to these countries but uses indices such as the percentage of ethnic minority residents and economic prosperity to rank the countries in terms of perceived threat. Or there is Pettigrew and Meertens (1995), who used Eurobarometer survey data from different countries to show that there is an empirical difference between blatant and subtle racism.

Differences: Birds of Different Feather/Racisms

The second research strategy emphasises differences and adopts a 'birds of a different feather' approach. That is, it is obvious that between countries there are many differences that are significant for the study of racism. Comparative research can thus be used to document the specific and unique features of racism in different national or cultural settings, and the specific historical, cultural, political and economic circumstances that give rise to racist phenomena. In the literature there are many claims and arguments about the need to acknowledge important differences between, what are sometimes called, *forms* of racism indicated by the addition of adjectives such as symbolic, aversive, cultural, modern, and new racism (e.g., Barker, 1983; Dovidio and Gaertner, 1986; Wievorka, 1993).

These and other terms are used for conceptualising 'racisms of a different feather'. As a result of similar observations, critical sociology and anthropology have stressed that racism should be conceptualised in the plural. Following post-structuralist and post-modernist claims, uniform and homogeneous conceptualisations of racism are rejected (Goldberg, 1993; Hall, 1991). The concept of a single racism is replaced by that of multifarious cultural and historical formulations, articulations, and formations of racism*s*.

Sociological studies, in particular, have advanced claims, with an emphasis on the historical dimension, about the transformation of racism. That is, how the meaning of racism has shifted from a focus on attitudes and ideas of biological inferiority and cultural incompatibility to various historically and contextually particular articulations of notions of race and racism (e.g., Goldberg, 1992; Solomos and Back, 1994). In general, however, empirical findings of the transformation of contemporary racism in the context of increasingly multicultural societies have led to new conceptualisations with which to account for processes in which specific ethnic groups or identity traits become the target of negative categorisations and evaluations. The examination in Chapter 4 by *Brown* of whether Islamophobia represents a different kind of racism is an example of this approach.

Complementarity

The two research strategies—racism or racism*s*—correspond, to a certain degree, to different disciplinary areas, as well as to different ideological positions and different conceptualisations of racism. These differences are best understood by looking at the attention given to several components or dimensions of racism. While in the first strategy, outlined above, more attention is given to the dimension of individual processes, the formation of stereotypes and ethnic prejudice, in the second the dimension of collective beliefs, identity and social or institutional practices and structures is emphasised. These two research strategies may be analytically distinct, but they hold the potential to enrich and supplement each other. Moreover, they are dependent upon each other.

Many scholars have pointed to the close relations between social structure and practices, on the one hand, and individually held beliefs, on the other. For example, whereas traditional (social) psychology used to conceive of racism as an individual attribute, which was mostly measured in surveys, discursive psychologists and linguists have posed a different aim. They examine the interaction between social structures and processes, on the one hand, and attitudes and opinions, on the other, by focusing on the ways in which these are inscribed in the structures and strategies of naturally occurring discourse (Billig, 1991; Billig, Condor, Edwards, Gane, Middleton, and Alan 1988; Wetherell and Potter, 1992). This analytical discourse approach is aimed at showing the ways in which beliefs become socially shared and reproduced, forming part of more widely shared beliefs, and at common sense ideologies which function to legitimate various exclusionary practices.

Hirschfeld follows a somewhat similar line of thinking, in his Chapter, by linking cognitive processes and cultural constructions. He argues that people are not only inclined to categorise their world as part of their cognitive make-up, but that they also 'learn' to interpret changes in the cultural and social environment and to understand these categories in terms of 'race'. Similarly, in Chapter 5 *Van Dijk* adopts a framework of universal cognitive processes. He argues that these form a fairly solid and stable 'interface' and that people activate this interface when talking and thinking about ethnic relations. At the same time, his theory accounts for the social and political conditions that determine the way in which these discourses are shaped.

There are at least two other arguments for stressing the complementary character of the two research strategies. First, difference entails similarity and vice versa. That is, to say that two things differ from each other implies that they share a common characteristic in terms of which the comparison is meaningful. Thus, a distinction between kinds of racisms is actually based on a comparison within a more abstract category of racism. Similarly, a distinction between racism, prejudice, xenophobia and anti-Semitism is based upon comparisons within a more abstract category such as the construction, portrayal and treatment of a negative 'racial' or ethnic out-group. At the same time, saying that two things are similar requires the implicit acknowledgement of difference. For example, negative evaluations of minority groups are often countered by arguing that we are all humans. However, this stress on common humanity has meaning only in the light of the recognition of group difference. Without difference the claim on similarity is meaningless. In his Chapter *Brown* thus spells out both the differences and similarities between Islamophobia, anti-Semitism and racism, thereby indicating different connotations of the term Islamophobia given in specific national settings. Although he sees an overlap between racism and Islamophobia, when it includes hostility not just towards Islam but also towards Muslims, his aim is to define them as conceptually separate. Applying the notions of similarity and difference in the analysis of the status and meaning of racism leads to different methodological choices. So, similarity and difference are relative terms which presuppose each other. To identify phenomena as different requires identifying the ways in which they are similar, and to claim similarity implicitly acknowledges difference.

Second, the differences between the two research strategies are of course closely linked to different positions in the debate on the philosophy of the social sciences. This debate can be addressed in a number of ways and involves several questions (Fay, 1996). One common distinction is to draw a distinction between a nomological and a hermeneutic approach. The former is committed to seeing particular phenomena as instances of a more general pattern or law. The particular, specific, context is transcended in favour of the general. The interest is in basic processes and causes that are essentially a-historical and a-cultural in nature. Further, the goal is to come up with explanations that take the form of predictions which can be tested empirically. By contrast, a hermeneutic approach emphasises context specificity of phenomena and is interested in the particular for its particularity. The meaning of events and phenomena is considered to be in their social, cultural, and historical circumstances. An explanation is seen as an understanding that implies grasping the social and cultural specificity and describing the historical developments. A particular form or articulation of racism is the result of concrete local, national or historical circumstances. Abstracting from these circumstances would obliterate what is distinctive and illuminating about it. Only by appreciating its distinctiveness can a specific racist phenomenon be understood. The result is an emphasis on description and understanding rather than prediction and explanation.

However, both approaches are not so different as they may appear at first sight. For example, historical analyses are full of causal descriptions that implicitly rest upon some general laws. In these descriptions the grammar of causality, in particular 'because' statements and connectives such as 'since', 'so', and 'as', predominates. An earlier event is thought to produce a subsequent one so that the former is a necessary or sufficient condition for the latter. Both conditions rest on a general law because they assert that whenever a certain event takes place another type of event will occur. In a historical description the intention is to show how the present situation can be explained by examining the past.

Moreover, historical and contextual descriptions are also based upon implicit assumptions about basic human needs and concerns. In order to understand others and their particular world, they must be seen as sharing with us some basic capacities, motives and principles of thought (Fay, 1996). To be intelligible, a description needs a background of similarity and sharing. Without assumptions about common human characteristics we would not be able to assign meaning to the behaviour of others. Similarity is necessary for grasping the uniqueness and distinctiveness of the world of others.

There are similarities or shared characteristics in the different forms of racism as well as many differences. Social scientists may be interested in the unique and particular events as such, or in events as instances of a more general category. For example, a scientist may be interested in the *Front National* as a particular French extreme right wing party or as an instance of extreme right wing parties in general. In the former case the specific historical, economic, cultural and political circumstances in France will be examined. In the latter the focus is on more general circumstances or processes, which may explain such parties' emergence or their growing/lingering electoral success. Both approaches seem valid and valuable, and a combination of the two holds, in principle, the possibility to improve our understanding. Both can be seen as 'part of one general endeavour to explain human activity and the products of this activity. Each provides what the other lacks; only together can they offer a complete picture of what we as humans do and are' (Fay, 1996, p. 175).

These complementary approaches may also improve the adequacy of opposition against racism. Indeed, a frequently observed risk is that strategies aimed at reducing racism are not effective because they aim at either too restricted goals or too generic areas (Goldberg, 1995). That is, a too generic theory or 'solution' (for example, education) may prevent one from grasping the specific nature of and answers to racism in concrete settings, whereas the understanding of a very specific aspect or expression of racism may lose sight of its wider implications.

Making Comparisons

The basic task of comparative research is to replace names of groups, cultures or nations, by circumstances, variables or processes which describe what it is about these groups, cultures or nations that affects the racist phenomena one is interested in. The question however is: how do these factors influence racism? Do they promote the manifestation of racism or determine its essence; do they moderate the degree of racism or mediate its causes? Many studies fail to answer such questions and simply 'compare' nations or groups under the assumption that there are relevant differences. Explanations in terms of power are particularly victim to this, and can lead to tautological research questions. That is, if power is taken as a fixed a-priori given, then the results of research tend to simply confirm this role without further qualification. Rather than comparison what you may end up with is a collection of further evidence useful only for the purpose of an anti-racist critique. However, there are studies which do develop such analytic frameworks. In Chapter 7 *Koopmans and Statham* tease out the factors that influence the manifestation of different forms of mobilisation over ethnic difference and take relevant cross-national differences in citizenship regimes as the starting point and organising principle of the research. This starting point is not immune to criticism, but it makes the comparative dimension explicit from the beginning.

What to Compare

Comparative research raises many questions. For example, there is the question of 'what to compare' or the comparability of phenomena. Let us assume that we are interested in racist violence among urban youth in European cities. Intuitively we would say 'well let's go to different cities and observe, or even measure, racist violence'. The question, however, is what kinds of incidents and behaviours are valid indices. Racist violence seems a clear-cut phenomenon but is actually a name for a specific class of actions, such as the incitement to hatred, the distribution of racist propaganda material, etc. Even in one's own society it is often unclear or disputed what kinds of behaviour should be counted as racist violence.

Another point for discussion is how we should determine whether the level of racism differs between countries. Should we focus on racist incidents, on political extremism, voting behaviour, responses to polls and surveys, media and popular discourse, data on migrant in/exclusion, or perhaps the feelings and experiences of minority groups themselves? The latter possibility is explored in two Chapters of this book. In Chapter 11 *Bolzman, Salberg Mendoza, Eckmann and Grünberg* examine the possibility of using the accounts and evaluations by victims of racist violence as the basis for analysis. Taking the definition of the victims as a starting point, the authors adopt a definition of racist violence that includes verbal violence and institutional discrimination. Then, in Chapter 10 *Savulescu-Voudouris and Fuchs* compare the experience of Jewish identity and anti-Semitic discrimination by minority group members in three different countries. These studies thus allow racism to be viewed from a minority's perspective, which may be considered an indispensable complement to the conventional forms of reporting about the subjects who engage in racist practices, discourse or attitudes. It may indeed provide insight into the recurrence and types of discrimination experienced.

However, in comparative research there are various possible indices that may not have a similar meaning across the countries being studied. It is even possible that we should examine somewhat different types of practices within each society, in order to study the same phenomenon: practices that are considered functionally equivalent. The problem is that the same processes may have different overt manifestations, and also that the same actions may have differing meanings across groups and societies. In Chapter 12 *Codagnone* argues for the importance of such distinctions in the design of a conceptual framework for a project to monitor ethnic relations in different societies. From an empirical perspective, the Chapter by *Koopmans and Statham* shows that different framings in the British and German press coverage of protests by xenophobic movements indicate different conceptualisations of citizenship politics.

Many publications collecting data on racism in various countries are aimed at reporting racism in order to show and account for the increase or variation of racism, with the possibility of elaborating adequate responses to it. For example, indices of voting behaviour, political extremism and polls typically appear in European reporting systems or collections of single country data without initial theory-driven questions being asked (Baumgartl and Favell, 1995; Ford, 1995). The focus on incidents, extremism, and measurable forms of public attitudes and opinions, involves the risk that only specific expressions of racism are generally accepted and known to constitute racism, or an act thereof. Moreover, a focus on racist incidents ensures that counter-racist strategies remain 'responsive' and within the specific sphere of anti-discrimination legislation formulated with individual perpetrators in mind, rather than becoming pro-active in many other spheres of social, political and economic life that affect a group as a whole (Goldberg, 1997).

Conceptual Issues

Comparisons are only useful when that being compared is comparable. One of the key questions here is whether the same concepts can be used in different societies and whether their meaning is similar. In other words, is it relevant that in Britain and the United States the term 'race' is used while it does not feature in several other countries? Perhaps it is (and why then is it relevant); but perhaps it is not. The question of conceptual equivalence, however, is central. The same is true for theoretical concepts such as 'racism', 'nationalism' and 'right wing extremism'. Can these concepts be applied to different societies? For example, Europe and the United States have clearly different histories, patterns of immigration, ethnic minorities and political circumstances.

There are also obvious and important differences between European countries in this regard. In the Netherlands, most academics predominantly claim to study prejudice, stereotypes and ethnocentrism, and to much lesser degree racism. Moreover, when comparing racism in different societies it should be taken into account that due to context-specific criteria ethnic minority groups can be designated on the basis of different criteria as 'blacks', or on the basis of geographical origin, or through the use of legal categorisations. As a result of ethnic identification, the formation of identities and the signification of 'race' may thus also be crucially different from one country to the next (Bovenkerk, Miles and Verbunt, 1991; Miles, 1993; Rath, 1993). In their Chapter, *Koopmans and Statham* refer to these differing definitions in their classification of the citizenship regimes they examine and the related opportunities for political mobilisation on the basis of ethnic difference that arise from these differences. In Chapter 12 *Codagnone* reflects upon the conceptual differences that have to be taken into account when monitoring ethnic relations in Western and Eastern European countries.

In the US, Britain, and France racism is an established part of general and academic discourses. The research paradigms that developed there have influenced the literature on racism in other European countries. For example, in countries with a comparable history of colonialism and immigration such as Britain and France, similar patterns of transformation from the manifestation of a racism of 'inequality' into a racism of 'difference' have been identified (Taguieff, 1988; Wievorka, 1993). However, if the experience of the 'example' countries is taken as a model for analysis or even policy recommendation, there is a risk of failing to recognise the particularity of the context-specific conditions of other countries (cf. Rath, 1993 on the Netherlands and Scandinavian countries). Similarly, the studies on Southern Europe require a context-specific analysis, as for example shown by studies on the Italian case, which reveal differences in terms of history, the greater variety and different position of immigrant communities, and the role of the state (Cole, 1997; Melotti, 1996; Ter Wal, 1997).

It is clear that concepts need to transcend the particular social and historical context in which they emerged in order to possess comparative utility. Only then can the concept help us to understand something about similarities, but also about difference. There is something of a paradox involved here. To compare there must be equivalence, but to compare fruitfully there must be variation in the observed phenomena. The point is that we want differences in some respects and commonalities in others. One way of resolving the difficulty of searching for commonality and difference at the same time is by introducing different 'levels of analysis'. At one level (e.g., racist violence) there can be similarity, but at another level (e.g., racist violence in a particular neighbourhood) there can be a wide variation. For example, ethnic power differences on the national level do not imply a similar pattern on the level of particular urban neighbourhoods (De Jong and Verkuyten, 1996). In another way, social psychology seeks to find notions which could act as mediating factors for sources of ethnic prejudice at the institutional, group and personal level.

However, this notion of 'levels' may also be used to criticise the comparative method. Comparative studies are alleged to produce generalisations at a rather high level of abstraction leading to truisms such as the idea that in times of economic decline there is a tendency for racism to increase. However, several contributions to this volume show how such claims can be tested, qualified and even refuted. In Chapter 9 *Poppe* measures among other things the influence of economic crises and increasing nationalism in Eastern Europe on attributions of morality and competence to different ethnic in- and out-groups. While in Chapter 3 *Wimmer* presents examples which contradict explanations of racism in terms of a realistic struggle over scarce resources, favouring instead explanations of perceived difference mediated by longer historical processes of nation-building. In a different context, *Koopmans and Statham* remark in their Chapter that previous research has not demonstrated any direct relation between levels of deprivation and propensity towards collective action.

How to Compare

In comparative research, data is gathered from particular communities at particular points in time, which raises the question of sampling methods. There are several strategies possible. One can look for similar groups (e.g., majority group members) living in different circumstances, or for similar newspaper reports or parliamentary debates in different countries. But the question of which similarities should always be asked. Therefore, by way of example, in historical discourse analysis it is stressed that contextual analysis and fieldwork should precede the analysis of written or spoken texts (Wodak et al., 1989). However, the question remains, is it sufficient that newspapers from different countries are considered conservative and popular, or that the analysis focuses on parliamentary debates in countries with differing democratic traditions and political constellations? Further, is having the same ethnic background a satisfactory claim of similarity upon which to frame a research question? Or, is it also necessary that there is similarity in, say, educational level, income, and housing?

Of course in explaining racism these may be the factors one is after and should, therefore, show variation, but this does not remove the question 'what is the constant that serves as a basis for comparison'. One can also look for different groups in the same situation (e.g., highly and lowly educated people in the inner city) and try to analyse how these groups react to similar circumstances. But again what are similar circumstances? Do highly and lowly educated people living in the inner city have similar contacts with minorities, and do they have similar resources? Finally, one can try to compare different groups in different situations. In that case, the specific groups or circumstances do not really matter, because the search is for generalities that transcend particularities.

With the first two approaches and with the first in particular, the question of comparative samples is crucial. It has been pointed out by many authors that it is virtually impossible to obtain samples from more than one society which are truly comparable. However, as *Poppe* argues in Chapter 9, in order to make meaningful comparisons the objective should be to obtain samples that differ in some respect relevant to the research question, but are similar enough in other respects. This objective is by no means easy to achieve, but it is at least useful for assessing how much any study fails short of achieving it. One important rule of thumb is that in principle the data collection should not be limited to a single pair of societies or cultural systems (unless it is very clear that these societies are really very similar). Between only two societies there are many differences that could constitute potential rival explanations making it extremely difficult to interpret single-pair comparisons. Single-pair studies are not, however, uncommon. Several studies exist in which it is concluded that there must be universals involved, but only on the basis of similar results among two different ethnic, cultural or national groups.

In addition, an important issue for comparative research is whether we are assessing the same thing, and which techniques should be used. There are numerous questions involved here. For instance, there is the question whether some groups are more familiar with certain techniques (e.g., surveys) than others. It is also possible that there are differences in response bias, a predominance of 'yes' answers or answer patterns based on social desirability, for example, due to different social and politeness conventions in different societies. Furthermore, different groups may react differently to the research and researcher (e.g., trying to please or on the contrary trying to be critical), depending on the ethnic distance or familiarity of the interviewer/researcher, as well as the status and prestige of social science and the political situation. In general the question is whether techniques used have validity and reliability among different groups and in different circumstances.

Moral Issues

Finally, there are the questions of managing such research and the moral responsibility of researchers. If we agree that social and cultural differences have a pervasive influence on people and societies, than we should acknowledge that it also affects ourselves as researchers. Cultural bias and ethnocentrism are never far away. There is always the danger that people in another society are asked questions that are irrelevant to them (but which they answer anyway), and that other issues relevant to them but not to the researcher are not included. The standard solution is to 'de-centre', or to involve researchers from different backgrounds and societies. However, there are many possible models. Other researchers, for example from minority groups, may be used mainly to gain entry to the field and to check the content and language of the questions asked. But they may also be involved in developing leading ideas, relevant concepts and research questions. The particular model chosen has different implications for avoiding biases, but also for the group dynamics in the research team.

The moral issue is a recurrent one when addressing questions of racism. For example, studies may implicitly play a role in sustaining racial categorisations and understandings by taking racial categories for granted. They may render 'race' natural and suggest that 'race' naturally characterises social formation (Goldberg, 1997). Nowadays critique of early prejudice theories is quite common. The once predominant conception of racism as an irrational response on the part of an individual, and thus as an incidental aberration from the norm is considered one-sided at best, and it is now recognised that more 'reasonable' and rational forms of group-based prejudice in various settings of everyday life are contributing to maintain racism (Billig, 1991; Verkuyten, 1997; Wetherell and Potter, 1992). Nevertheless, anti-racist codes and laws drafted by respectable international bodies, and indeed the general understanding of racism in the public sphere, are sometimes built on nothing more than 'common sense' and explanations of racism which draw upon these old assumptions (Czyzewski, 1995).

Existing theories have arisen in particular circumstances which they then reflect (Duckitt, 1992). The specific social and historical contexts in which theories have been developed leave their traces in the questions asked and explanations given. The political context is also important, and may affect theorising even at the conceptual level. Unfortunately, political and ideological debates tend to bias and obstruct the definition and evaluation of anti-racist programmes, either because of divergence itself, or because of the attempt to avoid this by adopting more general or limited, i.e., not racism-specific objectives. The charges against positive action programmes such as 'reverse discrimination', the one-sided attention to overtly racist propaganda or violence, or the introduction of a general discourse against 'social exclusion' are well-documented examples in case (Goodin, 1996). The same concerns can be expressed over the formulation of a new line of studies on ethnic relations, which labels what would have hitherto been termed racism as 'ethnic conflict'.

Earlier we argued that different theoretical paradigms might represent distinctive contributions for the understanding and explanation of racism. However, these paradigms do not only offer different analytical tools but also contain an implicit moral or political position. The choice of an analytical perspective and the use of concepts and research methods are not innocent acts or purely academic matters. Theories, concepts and aspects of research methods carry, usually implicitly, assumptions about the nature of the topic being studied. This distinction is also related to a different practical use of research in terms of reducing or combating the causes for different forms of racism. For example, a conceptualisation of racism in terms of basic cognitive processes or human needs makes racism more or less 'natural' and inevitable, and can thereby function as an excuse for negative attitudes and practices directed at out-groups, thereby withholding support from the feasibility of anti-racist opposition.

Dissatisfied with individualistic approaches, some researchers have shifted attention to the study of racist discourse (see Henwood and Phoenix, 1996). In this volume, the Chapter by *Van Dijk* analyses the features of anti-racist discourse as examples of 'good practice'. Studies of discourse on ethnic issues have in common a critical, anti-racist focus and start from the idea that text and talk about 'race' fulfils interpersonal and wider social and ideological functions. Others, however, eschew the moral commitment of these critical studies because they feel that such partisan viewpoints would compromise objective scientific inquiry and independence (e.g., Favell, 1997).

A critique of the analytical discourse approach is also given by *Jacobs* in Chapter 6. In his view, critical discourse analysis has a 'biased' perspective on ethnic affairs, because it assumes that there is one dominant institutional discourse through which negative ethnic beliefs and opinions are confirmed rather than changed. Such a perspective would for example neglect aspects of political negotiation, positioning and alliance-building that go on in debates about citizenship and voting rights, as well as the existence of majority discourses which aim to improve the position of migrants. Indeed most critical discourse analyses have focused on debates about immigration and asylum law restrictions, while ethnic relations discourses have been primarily used to illustrate negative pre-formulations. In contrast, *Jacobs* combines a pragmatic-linguistic analysis of voting-rights debates with notions gained from political communication and the history of colonialism and 'race' relations, in order to account for different attitudes towards normative models of citizenship.

A final point on moral commitment regards the links between academics and policy making. As mentioned earlier, what we have seen in Europe during the 1990s, is a separation between policy and academic fields dealing with migration and citizenship, on the one hand, and studies on racism, on the other. Both seem to be directed at their own areas of policy links and/or intervention, which are however intrinsically related. This separation is not simply a question of disciplinary boundaries, choice of terminology and areas of interest: it may have important ideological implications.

Conclusion

The foregoing discussion was not intended to be an argument against comparative research on racism. On the contrary, while all the points are valid caveats for comparative research, they do not invalidate the comparative method. They simply point out the relative costs and benefits of comparative research. They also indicate what should be considered and solved when doing comparative research. In general, comparative studies have to be very sensitive to alternative explanations and to the effects of cultural bias in all stages of research. There is an extensive literature on these questions and problems in both anthropology, and cross-cultural and cultural psychology. Indeed, we argue not against comparative research but that scholars undertaking comparative research in the fields of racism and ethnic conflict could use the work that has been done in these fields more systematically.

We want to conclude with six core questions that we view as crucial for conducting and assessing comparative research. They are, in order of relevance:

1) Are the scientific gains to be obtained from comparative research worth the loss of detail about specific societies and communities?
2) What is it about groups or cultural systems that affects the phenomena that is the topic of research?
3) Which and how many units of comparison are necessary to obtain a satisfying answer to the research question?
4) What exactly is the focus of the research question, should it be compared and in what way is it comparable?
5) How is optimal validity and reliability to be guaranteed in making comparisons?
6) How are the results of comparative work interpreted, or what possible alternative explanations are available?

References

Adorno, T. W., Frenkel-Brunswik, E., Levinson, D.J. and Sanford, N.R. (1950), *The Authoritarian Personality*, New York, Harper.

Allport, G. W. (1954), *The Nature of Prejudice*, New York, Doubleday, Anchor Books.

Anthias, F. and Yuval-Davis, N. (1992), *Racialized Boundaries: Race, Nation, Gender, Colour and Class and the Anti-Racist Struggle*, London, Routledge.

Barker, M. (1981), *The New Racism*, London, Junction Books.

Baumgartl, B. and Favell, A. (eds) (1995), *New Xenophobia in Europe*, London, Kluwer Law International.

Billig, M. (1991), *Ideology and Opinions. Studies in Rhetorical Psychology*, London, Sage.

Billig, M., Condor, S., Edwards, D., Gane, M., Middleton, D. and Alan, R. (1988), *Ideological Dilemmas. A Social Psychology of Everyday Thinking*, London, Sage.

Bonnet, A. (1997), 'Construction of Whiteness in European and American Anti-Racism', in P. Werbner and T. Modood (eds), *Debating Cultural Hybridity: Multi-Cultural Identities and the Politics of Anti-Racism*, London, Zed Books.

Bovenkerk, F., Gras, M.J.I., and Ramsoedh, D. (1995), *Discrimination Against Migrant Workers and Ethnic Minorities in Access to Employment in the Netherlands*, International Migration Papers, Geneva, International Labour Office (ILO), Employment Department.

Bovenkerk, F., Miles, R. and Verbunt, G. (1990), 'Racism, Migration and the State in Western Europe: a Case for Comparative Analysis', *International Sociology*, vol. 5, no. 4, pp. 475–90.

Caglar, A. S. (1997), 'Hyphenated Identities and the Limits of "Culture" ', in T. Modood and P. Werbner (eds), *The Politics of Multiculturalism in the New Europe: Racism, Identity and Community*, London, Zed Books, pp. 169–85.

Castles, S., & Miller, M. J. (1993), *The age of migration: international population movements in the modern world*, London, Macmillan.

Cole, J. (1997), *The New Racism in Europe: A Sicilian Ethnography*, Cambridge, Cambridge University Press.

Czyzewski, M. (1995), 'Some Comments on the Research on Tolerance and Intolerance as Presented at the UNESCO Symposium "Tolerance in Transition", Magdeburg, October 14–16, 1995', Unpublished Manuscript, University of Magdeburg.

Dovidio, J.F. and Gaertner, S.L. (1986), *Prejudice, Discrimination and Racism*, New York, Academic Press.

Duckitt, J. (1992), *The Social Psychology of Prejudice*, New York, Praeger.

Favell, A. (1997), 'Citizenship and immigration: pathologies of a progressive philosophy', in *New Community*, April 1997, vol.23, no.2, pp.173–195.

Favell, A. (1998), *Philosophies of Integration. Immigration and the Idea of Citizenship in France and Britain*, Basingstoke, Macmillan.

Fay, B. (1996), *Contemporary Philosophy of Social Science*, Oxford, Blackwell.

Fine, M. et al. (eds) (1997), *Off White. Readings on Race, Power and Society*, New York, Routledge.

Ford, G. (1992), *Fascist Europe: The Rise of Racism and Xenophobia*, London, Pluto Press.

Gabriel, J. (1998), *White Wash. Racialised Politics and the Media*, London, Routledge.

Goldberg, D. T. (1993), *Racist Culture: Philosophy and the Politics of Meaning*, Oxford, Blackwell.

Goldberg, D.T. (1997), *Racial Subjects. Writing on Race in America*, New York, Routledge.

Goodin, R. E. (1996), 'Inclusion and Exclusion', *Archives Europeens De Sociologie*, vol. 37, no. 2, pp. 343–71.

Hall, S. (1989), 'Rassismus als ideologischer Diskurs', *Das Argument*, vol. 31, no. 6, pp. 913–21.

Hargreaves, A. G. and Leaman, J. (eds) (1995), *Racism, Ethnicity and Politics in Contemporary Europe*, Aldershot, Edward Elgar.

Henwood, K and Phoenix, A. (1996), ' "Race" in Psychology: Teaching the Subject', *Ethnic and Racial Studies*, vol. 19, no. 4, pp. 841–63.

Jong, W. de and Verkuyten, M. (1996), 'Urban Renewal, Housing Policy and Ethnic Relations in Rotterdam', *New Community*, vol. 22, no. 4, pp. 689–705.

Lloyd, C. (1995), 'International Comparisons in the Field of Ethnic Relations', in A.G. Hargreaves and J. Leaman (eds), *Racism, Ethnicity and Politics in Contemporary Europe*, Aldershot, Edward Elgar, pp. 31–46.

Lutz, H., Phoenix, A. and Yuval-Davis, N. (eds) (1995), *Crossfires: Nationalism, Racism and Gender in Europe*, London, Pluto Press.

Martiniello, M. (ed) (1995), *Migration, Citizenship and Ethno-National Identities in the European Union*, Aldershot, Avebury.

Miles, R. (1989), *Racism*, London, Routledge.

Miles, R. (1993), *Racism After 'Race Relations'*, London, Routledge.

Miles, R. and Thränhardt, D. (eds) (1995), *Migration and European Integration: The Dynamics of Inclusion and Exclusion*, London, Pinter Publishers.

Pettigrew, T. F., & Meertens, R. W. (1995), 'Subtle and Blatant Prejudice in Western Europe', *European Journal of Social Psychology*, 25, 57–75.

Quillian, L. (1995), 'Prejudice As a Response to Perceived Group Threat–Population Composition and Anti-Immigrant and Racial Prejudice in Europe', *American Sociological Review*, vol. 60, no. 4, pp. 586–611.

Ratcliffe, P. (ed) (1994), *'Race', Ethnicity, and Nation. International Perspectives on Social Conflict*, London, University College of London Press.

Rath, J. (1993), 'The Ideological Representation of Migrant Workers in Europe: A Matter of Racialisation?', in J. Wrench and J. Solomos (eds), *Racism and Migration in Western Europe*, Oxford/Providence, Berg, pp. 215–32.

Rattansi, A. and Westwood, S. (eds) (1994), *Racism, Modernity and Identity: On the Western Front*, Cambridge, Polity Press.

Solomos, J. (1987), *Black Youth, Racism and the State. The Politics of Ideology and Policy*, Cambridge, Cambridge University Press.

Solomos, J. and Back, L. (1995), *Race, Politics and Social Change*, London, Routledge.

Solomos, J. and Back, L. (1996), *Racism and Society*, London, Macmillan.

Soysal, Y. N. (1994), *Limits of Citizenship Migrants and Postnational Membership in Europe*,

Chicago. University of Chicago Press.

Taguieff. P. A. (1988). *La force du préjugé. Essai sur le racisme et ses doubles.* Paris, La Découverte.

Ter Wal. J. (1996).'The social representation of immigrants: the *Pantanella* issue in the pages of La Republica', *New Community,* 22(1), 39–66.

Verkuyten. M. (1997). *'Redelijk Racisme': Gesprekken Over Allochtonen in Oude Stadswijken,* Amsterdam, University Press.

Wetherell. M. and Potter. J. (1992), *Mapping the Language of Racism,* New York, Colombia University Press.

Wievorka. M. (ed) (1993). *Racisme et Modernité,* Paris, La Découverte.

Wodak. R.. Nowak. P.. & Pelikan. J. (1990). *'Wir sind alle unschuldige Täter': Diskurshistorische Studien zum Nachkriegsantisemitismus,* Frankfurt a.M., Suhrkamp.

Wrench. J. (1996), *Preventing Racism at the Workplace, a Report on 16 European Countries,* Dublin, European Foundation for the Improvement of Living and Working Conditions.

2 Making Racial Culture: Children and the Mental Life of a Social Concept[1]

LAWRENCE A. HIRSCHFELD

Introduction

Comparative scholarship on race is almost always coupled with comparative scholarship on rac*ism*. This is not surprising since the two phenomena are empirically so closely linked: all known systems of racial thinking are racist. Still, this move may obscure differences between race, a strategy for partitioning and reasoning about human diversity, and racism the application of that strategy in the service of inequitable systems of power, authority, and resources. Race and racism are neither identical nor necessarily linked, logically speaking. I stress this point because I will argue that race as an idea and racism as a use of this idea differ importantly as to their histories and psychology. In this essay, I will flesh out this observation by exploring three issues: (1) the psychological nature of the idea of race, (2) the way the idea is transmitted from one generation to the next, and (3) its evolutionary origins. I will end by suggesting that the relationship between the idea of race and the practice of racism is indeed contingent, but perhaps not in ways that scholars have typically expected.

The idea of race is part of a broad and comprehensive willingness to categorise events, objects, and living things, a willingness particularly evident in human beings' apparently irresistible impulse to segment and reason about the social world. All humans in all cultures do this. If they did not, human sociality would be impossible. Accordingly, it is no surprise that children also show little difficulty in learning to do this, even children who otherwise have difficulty accomplishing many life-tasks because of impaired cognitive capacities (e.g., children with Down's syndrome or autism) nonetheless recognise basic social categories (e.g., kinship, gender, and relative age) and draw appropriate inferences about them (e.g., recognising that a person's age changes over time but not a person's gender).

Anthropologists, have traditionally interpreted this capacity in terms of the contingencies of social cohesion, protection, and the regulation of authority

23

and power. These contingencies vary considerably from one society to the next. Not surprisingly, anthropologists have documented striking variations in the way different cultures partition the human landscape. In virtue of exposure to a specific culture's social partitions, individuals come to learn—come to represent in their minds—the culturally appropriate system of social classification. Causality here runs from social to individual, from contingent social forces and needs to psychological representations in individual minds. Relatively little attention, unfortunately, has been paid to the way social forces and needs *become* represented in individual minds. This, despite the increasing importance that anthropologists are attributing to the mediating role of representation. For example, Gramsci's influential notion of 'educating consensus' requires that social and cultural forces express themselves as representations of individual relationships in individual minds.

Lack of concern with the role that the mind's architecture and history may play in shaping society and culture is partly traceable to the widely held belief that the task of acquiring and representing social knowledge is trivial. Humans, according to this view, acquire social knowledge when a general capacity to learn encounters a particular social and cultural environment. The conviction that the task is trivial stems from two prior beliefs (1) that an environment saturated with relevant information is both highly redundant and uncluttered in terms of the information it makes available, and 2) that knowledge acquisition is easy since even young children manage to do it.

I contend that neither of these conditions holds. To support this claim, I will review recent research that indicates that the acquisition of social knowledge deploys powerful and specialised cognitive mechanisms that facilitate learning. Put another way, I propose that despite the countless ways that people are sorted into groups, and despite the obvious links between these groupings and the contingencies of social cohesion, protection, and the regulation of power and authority, one strategy for segmenting the social world is both recurrent and privileged *because of its cognitive properties*. I do *not* suggest that cognition directly determines any particular system of cultural belief. Rather, I suggest that cognition plays a critical role in mediating possible cultural outcomes by defining the conditions under which they become stable and can be sustained over time. Thus, I postulate a cognitive device specialised to treat a specific domain of knowledge. This does not mean that the output of this cognitive device is always the same or that it rules out cultural variation. On the contrary, it helps explain cultural variation in terms of the device's diversified range of possible cultural exploitations (see Sperber, 1994).

Despite this emphasis on invariant psychological mechanisms, my goal here is to provide a comparative *cognitive* account of race. I propose to do this not by explicitly or systematically comparing systems of racial and racist thinking across cultures. Rather, I propose to compare the similarities and differences on the one hand, and variation and invariance on the other, that emerge in a particular system of racial and racist thinking. Changes that occur with age as the child's conceptualisation of race crystalises and changes in the way racial systems are represented in individual minds are no less comparative than those implicit in historical or ethnographic accounts. In the same vein, at the end of this essay I propose an evolutionary comparison in which I speculate on how and why *Homo sapiens* came to develop the sorts of minds and the sorts of sociality that gave rise to racial thinking.

I

The empirical focus of this essay is race. Before beginning, a brief comment on the use of 'race' in this essay. Many scholars, in exploring the way humans segment society into groups, distinguish race from ethnicity. Race, in this view, is thought to involve embodied differences—such as skin colour, facial features, hair colour and quality, and so forth. Ethnicity, in contrast, is thought to involve differences in ideation, differences in the habits and traditions that are associated with many groups. I acknowledge that this distinction is not without merit, it helps locate the nature of cultural discourse in any given historical or cultural moment. However the distinction is not principled in the sense that there is no systematic way of distinguishing race from ethnicity *independent of the ideological context in which the distinction is drawn* (Hirschfeld, 1996). For example, during the first decades of the twentieth century in the United States, Jews, Irish, and Italians were not white—while Japanese were. Within a few generations this view had undergone marked change. By the 1950s, Jews, Irish, and Italians had become ethnic groups not racial ones. The notion of 'black' itself serves to illustrate this point. During the period when slaves were imported into the United States, slave traders and buyers paid close attention to the cultural and linguistic differences within Africa that set, what we would call cultural, groups apart from one another. Later, of course, the social fact of slavery caused 'similarities to overwhelm the differences' producing an undifferentiated (and now strictly 'racial') black population (Fields, 1982, p. 145). Given all this, for the purposes of this essay I will not distinguish ethnicity from race.

Although all societies segment humans into (what are assumed to be) 'natural' groups, not all societies deploy the cultural representation 'race'.[2] Other notions of 'natural' groupings are possible, including caste in South Asia, age in many parts of sub-Saharan Africa, and gender virtually everywhere. It is imperative to bear in mind that I am *not* proposing that race or caste capture 'real' *natural* variation—indeed I specifically *deny* it (see

Hirschfeld, 1996). However, the belief that such patterned variation exists is widely accepted and extraordinarily difficult to extinguish not only among the general public, but also among many scientists. Above, I put the word race in scare quotes to signal that I am referring to an idea not a thing. For ease of reading, I will not do so in the rest of this chapter, but the reader should bear in mind the distinction between the concept of race, which is clearly an interesting phenomenon, and race as a biological entity, which just as clearly is not.

Comparative studies reveal considerable variation in the way race is evoked and interpreted. Different cultures and different historic epochs deploy different racial categories and attach different significance to them. The current and supposedly comprehensive census categories used in the United States are black, non-Hispanic white, Hispanic, Asian and other Pacific Islander, and Native American. Still, not long ago the census offered 'Hindoo' and 'mulatto' (indeed several degrees of mulatto admixture were recognised) as possible choices. These categories did not reflect different demographics but different sociopolitical and cultural moments. Ultimately, there are as many ways of classifying race as there are cultures and systems of cultural politics that deploy the concept.

Consider the relationship between an individual's race and that of his or her parents; all systems of race assign individuals to categories on the basis of their parents' race. But this does not mean that a person necessarily belongs to the same race as his or her parents. In some cultures, a person and his or her parents or his or her siblings may belong to different races in virtue of contingent circumstances. In Brazil 'money whitens', an aphorism indicating that a person's race can alter as their financial position does (Harris, 1964). One's race may also oscillate between that of his or her parent's should they each belong to different races. Here again, we encounter significant variation.

In the southern United States prior to the civil war, mixed-race children were assigned to neither parent's race but were considered mulatto, a third race. In many colonial systems a mixed-race child's race was determined by specific acts, depending on which of either parent 'recognised' the child. If he or she was recognised by the colonising parent, he or she was (typically) white; if he or she was recognised by the colonised parent, he or she was not white (Stoler, 1995). Other systems assign mixed-race children specifically to one and only one of the parent's race. Nigerian Moors with white fathers and black (slave) mothers are white and free (Popenoe, 1994). In contrast, in the contemporary United States, mixed-race children almost always belong to the race of the minority parent (Davis, 1991).

This variation aside, some features of racial thinking do recur across cultures (at least in those societies that do deploy a notion of race). Virtually all systems of racial classification assign individuals to one and only one racial category. All assign individuals to categories principally on the basis of their parents' race. All attribute the mutual exclusivity of racial categories and the link between the race of parent and the race of child to 'natural' or biological mechanisms such as birth and inheritance. In short, where it is found, race is invariably an assumption about the nature of the world. The point I am trying to make is that racial assignments, like racial categories themselves, vary widely. At the same time, they remain recognisably similar. Each culture creates its own system for thinking about race, for assigning it, and for resolving racial ambiguity. In this sense there is no single cultural domain of race. On the other hand, non-trivial structural elements of race provide a common theme on which non-trivial variation is played out. The purpose of this essay to account for both this variation and invariance.

II

Let's return to the concept of race in contemporary North America. In the US race is a very troubling phenomenon. I do not mean troubling in its obvious political, economic, and social aspects but in its psychology. The very notion of race triggers unsettling, diffuse, and enduring fears that are particularly manifest when the issue of racial ambiguity arises. Novels, perhaps even more than ethnography, provide striking depictions of this phenomenon. I will turn to two widely read pieces of North American fiction to illustrate.

In 1933, Fannie Hurst published *An imitation of life,* a book so popular that two major films were made of it.[3] In both the novel and the films, a secondary plot line follows the life of the protagonist's daughter, Peola. Although racially 'Black', Peola has light skin and 'European' features. In a moving chapter, Peola returns home after a long absence during which she did not contact her mother. She announces that she has 'passed' as white for the previous five years and that she intends to continue to do so. She further tells her mother that she is engaged to a white engineer and asks that her mother promise never to contact her again.

Her mother, devastated by this news, cautions that her future husband 'will live to curse the day when your lie comes out in your children'.[4] Peola responds that she has been sterilised to prevent the physical potential of her invisible blackness to come out. Hurst seems to accept this as a reasonable solution to an unreasonable or 'unnatural' problem. Among other things, her inability to bear children means that she poses no continuing threat of racial pollution since she will not produce more 'white Negroes', as the novel refers to blacks who pass for white. To be certain that the reader recognises that this potential for racial pollution is excluded (at least from North America), Hurst sends Peola and her husband-to-be to live in Bolivia.[5] The novel offers no challenge to fears of racial contamination; indeed, it exploits them as a plot device.

Fifteen years later, Sinclair Lewis' *Kingsblood royal* was published (Lewis, 1947). A darker vision of race and redemption in the northern Midwest, it tells the story of Neil Kingsblood, a member of a white, wealthy, and privileged family whose life is fundamentally shaken when he discovers that his great-great-great grandfather was black. As others find out, his friends and neighbours recoil from and shun the now black Kingsblood. He loses his job and eventually his home to an attacking mob in the novel's dramatic conclusion. Unlike *An imitation of life*, *Kingsblood royal* directly criticises racial intolerance and prejudice, but like *An imitation of life* it provokes by triggering the notion of racial contamination inherent in the notion of race itself. Both novels thus explore the meaning of race through a lens of racial ambiguity.

Racial ambiguity is, of course, not simply a plot device, it is inscribed in racial practice and racial laws. By convention in the United States, mixed-race children belong to the minority parent's ancestral (or historic) race. Called the 'one-drop of blood rule', this regulation states that if a person has any traceable black ancestry, he or she is black. It is important to keep in mind that two tensions curiously are served by the same rule: one involves racial politics, the other racial biology. The two are fundamentally different. Racial politics are as varied as the political regimes they serve. In the antebellum Deep South, children of interracial couples were neither black nor white, but mulatto. This system of categorisation is almost certainly related to the fact that mullutos occupied a socioeconomic position intermediate between free whites and black slaves. As the need for a structurally intermediate position waned, so did the category. By the end of the civil war children of interracial unions were no longer classified mulatto but black. These political changes speak to the category meaning of being mixed-race. Neil Kingsblood, to return to the novel, is not a target of racial intolerance because he contaminates the biological order but because he contaminates the social one.

The one-drop of blood rule also has a biological meaning, capturing fears of biological pollution. In this sense it reflects a fear of the invisible risks of miscegenation. The racial anxiety in *An imitation of life* centres on the consequences of even small amounts of racial blood. Peola is not afraid that she will be found out because of the way that she looks but because of *invisible* trace of blackness that she can neither shed nor control. The amount is small but the effect powerful. Even a white and a 'white Negro' could, indeed would, have a black child—i.e., a child with black features.

Under both the biological and category readings, the one-drop rule has the same effect: it explains that racial ambiguity is not ambiguous. Black always trumps white. But the way in which this is thought to happen—the mechanism that is thought to *make* it happen—is quite different under the category and biological interpretations. Interestingly, the rule says little *explicitly* about this difference.

III

The one-drop of blood rule is clearly cultural not universal. Indeed, relatively few systems of racial classification employ it. Presumably acquiring the one-drop rule, coming to endorse it, involves attention to the cultural environment, particularly given of the cultural ambiguity, complexity, and abstractness inscribed in it. Accordingly, it is reasonable to expect that acquiring the rule is a major task for the child. Curiously, however, there is no evidence that children are directly taught it. Rather, they seem to *infer* it, largely on their own initiative. Unfortunately, no work has explored *how* children learn to the rule, so there is no basis for determining how they come to draw this inference.

Given this lacunae, I decided to directly examine the question. I set out to know when children learn the one-drop rule and, most importantly given the ambiguity of the rule, *how* they learn it. The research strategy was straightforward. Members of my research group and I asked North American school age children and adults what happens when an interracial couple has a child.[6] As a control, we also asked them about the children of couples of the same race. Adult informants were recruited from undergraduate anthropology classes, school-age children (7-year-olds, second graders and 11-year-olds, fifth graders) were recruited from elementary schools in a predominantly white, middle-class university town.

Subjects were asked to participate in several tasks. In all tasks we showed subjects pictures of four couples: (1) two *same-race couples* consisting of a couple in which both parents are white and a couple in which both parents are black, and (2) two *interracial couples* consisting of a couple in which the father is white and the mother black, and a couple in which the father is black and the mother is white. Two-thirds of the participants were asked to choose among three outcomes represented by category labels or pictures. Half of these subjects participated in the category task. They were asked whether the mixed-race child is 'black', 'white' or 'something else'. The other half participated in a physical appearance task in which they were asked to choose among pictures of three children: one with typically black features, another with typically white features, and another with intermediate features.[7] The remaining third of the subjects participated in a resemblance task in which they were asked to identify how much the mixed-race child resembles each of its parents.

For *same-race couples* in both the category and physical appearance tasks, participants at all ages expected that the mixed-race children would belong to the same race of the parents and would physically resemble them racially. Answers to questions about the *interracial couples* are more interesting. In the category task, second grade children showed no evidence of endorsing the one-drop rule. They predicted that children of interracial couples would be either white or black, with no preference for one over the other. Interestingly, few younger children predicted that the mixed-race child would belong to a third race. It appears that younger children's reasoning was shaped by a race-of-mother strategy, so that if the mother were white the child would be white, and if the mother were black the child would be black. Children in fifth grade, however, preferred one outcome, which interestingly did not correspond to the one-drop rule. They expected the interracial couples' children to belong to neither parents' race. Thus, their judgements are consistent with the system of racial classification, described earlier, found in the Southern United States prior to the civil war. Contemporary adults, in contrast, endorsed the one-drop rule, predicting that the children would belong in the category 'black'.

In the physical appearance task second grade children again chose at random, showing no evidence of favouring a particular strategy for resolving racial ambiguity. Fifth grade children, in sharp contrast to their judgements in the category task, overwhelmingly chose the infant with markedly black features, providing strong evidence that they endorse a physical version of the one–drop of blood rule. Adults, also unlike their judgements in the category task, overwhelmingly selected the intermediate infant, suggesting that they endorse a category interpretation of the rule but not a physical interpretation.

In the resemblance task, in which subjects were asked to rate how much each child would resemble each of their parents, another pattern of reasoning emerged. For the *same-race couples*, all participants thought that a child of a same-race couple would look equally like both parents. For the *interracial couples*, younger children showed no preference. Older children and adults, however, predicted that children of interracial couples would resemble the black parent more than the white parent, indicating in their responses that they support a *physical* interpretation of the one-drop of blood rule.[8]

Taken together, the three tasks converge on the same conclusion. Children come to endorse the one-drop of blood rule sometime between ages 7 and 11. However, what they endorse reflects a singular interpretation of the rule. Initially they interpret it as a question about the biology, the physical features, of race not the category to which a child might be assigned in virtue of his or her parents' race. This is striking inasmuch as these findings also indicate that the adult endpoint is primarily about category membership—the view expressed in *Kingsblood royal*. It would be surprising if otherwise, in that most adults accept that a person's race may be difficult to determine from visual inspection alone—the view expressed in *An imitation of life*. This is not to say that adults completely eschew a biological interpretation. In the resemblance task, adults showed a willingness to endorse a weaker biological interpretation. I say a 'weaker interpretation' because the resemblance task is less direct than either the category or physical tasks. Both the latter are directly about race, either by virtue of the racial categories subjects had to select from or by virtue of the racially-laden pictures that they had to select from. On the resemblance task, we know only that adults and older children believe that the child will resemble the minority parent more than the majority parent, but we do not know what sort of resemblance the subject has in mind (it could be in terms of personality, prowess, etc.).

In short, children learn the one-drop of blood rule just before adolescence. What they learn, however, is neither precisely what adults believe nor what they presumably model.

Of course, it is common to find that the concepts of children and adults differ. If they did not, then there would be no need to speak of learning at all. But in this case, the absence of convergence toward the adult model cannot be attributed simply to the process of learning, at least in the commonsense understanding of this process. In most instances, learning involves developing a *partial* grasp of something about which adult understanding is more comprehensive. In this case, children do not have a partial grasp of the adult version of the one-drop rule. They subscribe to a radically different one.

The problem is all the more mysterious in that it probably does not make sense to talk of an adult endpoint at all—in the way we talk about the adult endpoint when learning calculus. Consider white/Hispanic interracial couples. It is not self-evident that adults, say, in Texas would expect mixed-Hispanic/white children's race to be governed by the one-drop rule. We do know that literature on the rule is almost entirely about black/white admixture and its relationship to the politics of slavery. Anglo/Hispanic relations evolved under quite different historical conditions. Reflecting this, the US census considers 'Hispanic' to be an *ethnicity* not a race. Indeed, the census bureau's recent decision to fold the Hispanic category into questions about race has provoked much controversy. However, when Ken Springer and I repeated the studies, just described, in Dallas, Texas, we found little difference between children's reasoning about white/black and white/Hispanic mixes. Dallas children reasoned, as their Midwestern counterparts had, that black/white couples would have children with typically black features. Springer and I also asked Dallas children about Hispanic/white couples. Surprisingly, given that adult belief is not self-evident, they reasoned about Hispanic/white couples the same way they reasoned about black/white couples. In both cases they apply a biological version of the one-drop of blood rule.

IV

What accounts for all this? What in the environment leads children to expect that mixed-race children will have the physical features of their minority parent rather than a blend of both? It is all the more curious to the extent that the category version of the rule is simpler. Why then do children not learn it first? Why do they endorse the more complex *biological* interpretation?

I have suggested that the cultural environment does not provide sufficient support for the biological interpretation in that we have no evidence that children receive tuition in it. If the cultural environment does not provide sufficient support, where does it come from? I propose another source: the biological reading of the one-drop rule flows from children's prior beliefs about race. These beliefs support the conclusion that race is both a natural and biological phenomenon. As such, the biological version of the one-drop rule need not be taught but emerges *on its own*. Once the child's attention is drawn to the cultural problem of racial ambiguity, the child turns to his or her beliefs about the nature and meaning of race to resolve this ambiguity. Hence how he or she learns it is a function of the knowledge the child brings to the task of learning culture. Children need to be alerted to the problem of racial ambiguity and the outlines of the cultural solutions available. They do not need, however, to be alerted to a biological interpretation. That they bring to the learning task with them.

By proposing that even quite young children assume that race is a natural category of the world, I am *not* suggesting that race is a category of nature. Nor do I suggest that the idea of race springs naturally from the child's mind. In the North American cultural tradition, race is a *natural* property of the world, supposedly inscribed in people's bodies. Of course, this is not the case. Since the disappearance of the Neanderthals, there are no longer subspecies or races of *Homo sapiens*. Yet, with remarkable ease, people can be convinced that race exists and is natural. Where does this commitment to naturalness come from? How is it that the idea is so readily adopted, distributed, and sustained over time?

Sperber (1994, p. 54) provides a conceptual framework in which to set these questions. According to Sperber, to explain culture 'is to explain why some representations become widely distributed...to explain why some representations are more successful—more contagious—than others'. Our question, then, becomes 'Why is a naturalised concept of race such a 'successful' representation?'

The standard account of racial learning provides little help in answering this question. According to this account, race is learned early because it is *perceptually* unavoidable. Neither social nor mental prominence play a role.

Children could hardly avoid learning about race; all they have to do is open their eyes and they discover it. In this view, children attend almost exclusively to surface differences in both *forming* racial categories and *interpreting* them. Hence, being black is initially no more important than being tall. Children learn about being tall and black before they learn about being Republican and French because social groups like black and tall are more visually apparent than social groups like Republican and French.

An implication of this view is that young children possess a fairly impoverished understanding of race, one tethered to outward appearances. Findings from several previous studies lend support to this proposal. For instance, when asked whether a white Canadian child dressed up as an Inuit is an Inuit, most young children answered 'yes' (Aboud, 1988). When asked whether a black child wearing white makeup and a blond wig is black, pre-schoolers responded 'no' (Semaj, 1980).

Several studies I conducted indicate that pre-schoolers are not as fixated by surface appearances as this account stipulates. These studies demonstrate that surface differences neither drive the development of race categories nor do they determine how they are interpreted. Indeed, the findings from these studies indicate that children, rather than having an impoverished grasp, have an enriched, theory-like and surprisingly adult understanding. In one study, meant to assess the extent to which early racial knowledge is linked to perceptual information, my research group examined North American and French children's memory of social categories. We found that, contrary to what the standard view predicts, young children's initial concept of race contains little if any perceptual information. What little visual information young children have is often inaccurate and idiosyncratic (Ramsey, 1987; Hirschfeld, 1988, 1996). In contrast, social categories like gender, occupation, and physique are replete with visual information (i.e., information about what a person of a specific gender, occupation, or physique looks like). In fact, three-year-olds' understanding of race is more abstract than concrete. For instance, they understand that blacks represent an important social grouping despite the fact that it isn't until they are five or six that they are able to identify the physical features associated with being black.

The standard view also predicts that young children believe that race is a superficial property, believing that a person's race can change during his or her life time, as the findings with white children mistakenly identifying other white children for Inuit simply because they are dressed to look like Inuit. These studies asked children about unfamiliar and unnaturally abrupt changes in appearance. This is an exceptional circumstance (except during specific play, such as on Halloween). It is not necessarily the case that under these circumstances children's judgements about race are actually assessed, as opposed to their judgements about abrupt and unnatural changes in appearances. Suspecting that we might reveal a very different pattern of reasoning if we asked about the same transformations in the context of gradual and familiar transformations, we asked young children what can happen to one's race as one grows up (where some aspects of appearance change while others do not) and when the child inherits features from his or her parents (where some physical features of the parents are passed onto the child, while others are not).

This approach seems in principle reliable because previous research shows that even young children have a basic understanding of the transformations associated with the processes of both growth and inheritance. And in fact, the design did provide significant insight into young children's racial concepts. Even three-year-olds expect that a child's race will not alter during his or her lifetime, even if other aspects of morphology do (e.g., physique). They also expect that a child will be the same race as his or her parent, again even if other morphological aspects will not be the same (e.g., physique). In sum, even quite young children demonstrate an elaborate and surprisingly adult-like understanding of race. First, they believe race but not other physical properties to be an inalterable and fundamental aspect of an individual's identity. Second, they believe that race but not other physical properties is inherited and biologically-grounded, expecting that a child is the same race as his or her parents and that the child's race is set at birth. Importantly, this pattern of reasoning is limited to race and possibly gender. Other similarly physical properties are neither immutable, inherited, nor indicative of group identity—even when the properties in question *are* actually immutable, inherited, and informative of group identity (e.g., physique).

V

Let's return to the one-drop rule and why children learn it as they do. From the one-drop study we know that children learn the rule relatively late in middle childhood. Their and the adult versions differ considerably. While the two versions are consistent with each other—they could hardly be otherwise considering that they are both versions of the same rule—children surprisingly learn the more abstract and theory-driven version first. The biological version goes far beyond the information immediately available. The category version, acquired subsequently, is a more straightforward—and in many ways a more salient—cultural representation. As noted earlier, there appears to be little direct public discourse on being mixed-race. What there is focuses more on category identity than biology. Public figures like General Colin Powell, basketball player Grant Hill, and golf marvel Tiger Woods are all popularly identified as black (by category) despite having interracial parents.

Children come to the task of learning the one-drop of blood rule with an elaborate conceptual toolkit. Learners of the rule are already committed to the proposition that race is a biologically-grounded phenomenon, a deep and fundamental, and inalterable property of each individual. It is a commonplace that children rely on prior conceptual knowledge in addressing novel problems. That they should do so when they encounter a novel problem about race is accordingly unsurprising. Given what we know of younger children's biological and essentialist construal of race, it is also unsurprising that the biological version of the one-drop rule trumps the category version.

Still, we know little about why they come to treat racial ambiguity as a problem. We can, however, speculate. As children grow older their perspective on the social world changes. As children move from infancy to toddlerhood, from there to pre-school-age, and from middle-childhood to adolescence, engagement with the social world changes dramatically. As they enter and pass through elementary school, they encounter more and more people who come from increasingly diverse backgrounds. During pre-adolescence peer relations and social identity become progressively entangled. School curricula cover more and more social topics, and in greater depth. Children of this age are probably more likely than younger children to know about Grant Hill and Tiger Wood's family backgrounds. Add to this the racism that saturates contemporary North American society and the decreasing capacity of parents and the community to buffer older children from the effects of this, it is reasonable to expect some version of the one-drop rule to be salient for children of this age.

VI

Prior beliefs steer pre-adolescents toward a biological interpretation of the one-drop rule. What steers young children toward a biological interpretation of race in the first place? How do young children develop a theory-like and elaborate account of race? At present there are few alternatives to the claim that they simply learn it. As we just saw, however, standard learning accounts do not explain why it is that even quite young children learn *so much, so rapidly* about race. A long-dominant presumption in virtually all social sciences (including anthropology) holds that humans are endowed with a general set of learning and reasoning abilities that they bring to bear on any cognitive task, whatever its specific content. On this view, learning a language, a system of kinship, learning marriage preferences and proscriptions, rules of chess or football, all proceed in much the same way and all employ a common set of processes.

Recent research indicates that the notion of a general-problem-solving learning device is deeply flawed. Considerable evidence now indicates that all concepts are *not* acquired in the same fashion. Indeed, from the outset children appear to have access to conceptual resources that allow them to draw inferences far beyond what immediate experience affords (e.g., knowing that one dog barks leads young children to believe that all dogs bark). Evidence from evolutionary theory, developmental psychology, linguistics, and cognitive anthropology lend compelling support to another picture of the mind. Many human abilities are not domain-general but are specialised to handle specific tasks or domains; many cognitive abilities, dispositions, or competencies are *domain-specific*. A number of these are described in the growing literature on domain-specificity. Naive physics is a domain-specific competence that underlies the infant's remarkable abilities to perceive whole objects and make systematic predictions about their movements. Naive psychology is a domain-specific competence that underlies young children's capacity to attribute a person's behaviour to his or her beliefs and desires. Naive mathematics is yet another domain-specific capacity that underlies human infants' ability to distinguish collections of objects according to the number of elements in the collection. (These and other domain-specific competencies are described in Hirschfeld and Gelman, 1994.)

I propose that humans are also equipped with a naive sociology, a domain specific competence that guides the acquisition of social knowledge, and, in particular, knowledge of social *groups*. I further contend that the notion of biologically-grounded race develops out of naive sociology.

VII

Contemporary anthropologists are sceptical of claims that link modern social phenomena, like race, to evolution. With reason. Scientific racism (long a major force in anthropology) and other regrettable attempts to explain *away* cultural phenomena by appeal to evolutionary just-so tales are often wrong and pernicious. Anthropologists have taken the lead in challenging such misuses of the biological and evolutionary sciences. It is critical, however, that we acknowledge that these are *misuses* and cannot be taken as a justification to ignore the biological and evolutionary history of culture.

For example, it is untenable to argue that evolution 'stopped' with the emergence of culture, in significant measure because evolutionary forces have profoundly affected the organisation of the human mind and the specific organisation of the human mind makes culture possible. Each species' nervous system is grounded in biological processes shaped by evolution. On the face of it, this seems self-evident and non-controversial, particularly if we rephrase the claim in terms of other organs. Few doubt, for example, that the human hand with opposable thumbs is a product of natural selection. Few presumably further doubt the link between this and culture: opposable thumbs have given rise to an extraordinary range of new material possibilities, from the effective use of digging sticks to plucking a guitar.

Most of these new material possibilities are shaped by cultural tradition. The same is no less true with mental possibilities. Human infants learn language with remarkable speed and accuracy. No matter how bright they otherwise are, chimpanzees cannot. This is unsurprising once we acknowledge that, in important respects, human cognitive architecture enormously differs from (as well as resembles) that of chimpanzees (or Neanderthals for that matter). Complex aspects of human cognition could hardly have developed outside evolution. This does not mean that all complex aspects of human cognition are given by evolution: Marxism and the auteur theory of cinema are obviously not biological. They are, however, biologically grounded in cognitive competencies that literally render them thinkable.

The notion of an evolved adaptation for acquiring knowledge of race seems, on the face of it, absurd. (This notion about how knowledge develops must be distinguished from the clearly false and pernicious notion that there are distinct human races whose existence reflects an evolutionary progress.) The very idea of race appeared only relatively recently in human history, perhaps as recently as the European age of exploration, certainly too recently to be the product of a biological adaptation. It is implausible, accordingly, that a domain-specific disposition evolved that guides learning about *race*. On the other hand, it is extremely plausible that a domain-specific disposition evolved to guide learning about *social groupings*, given the extraordinary importance group living has for humans.

Two questions pose themselves: first, how would an adaptation to sociality, to inclusionary thinking, underlie a conceptual framework that is fundamentally exclusionary? How do we go from notions about social groupings to notions about race? Second, even if an evolved adaptation for acquiring knowledge about social groupings exists, one which manifests itself in human cognitive architecture, how is it that this adaptation can be invoked to explain a phenomenon that varies greatly from one culture to the next. In short, how can cultural variation emerge out of an invariant, universal cognitive adaptation?

A key to resolving these paradoxes can be drawn from Sperber's (1994) discussion of the relationship between culture and domain-specificity. Domain-specific abilities function to guide learning about objects, events, and relations that were relevant to recurring problems faced, in the case of human beings, during the Pleistocene. When encountering an instance of one of these problems—when something in the environment meets the input conditions of the domain-specific capacity—the capacity is triggered and takes over information processing. For example, to facilitate language processing, the human auditory system automatically filters auditory input so speech is treated by one cognitive system and non-speech by another. In other words, speech meets the input conditions of language processing while a cough does not.

These devices, however, are not perfect. Other environmental stimuli also meet the input conditions of any given domain-specific device, even objects, events, and relations that were *not* part of the evolutionary environment that gave rise to the evolved device. Take as an example, the common phobia the fear of flying. Clearly, a phobia for aeroplane travel did not evolve during the Pleistocene. However, humans have other innate fears that resonate with fear of flying. Most humans are afraid of heights and are uncomfortable in closed spaces. Both common fears can be traced to adaptations to dangers commonly encountered by our ancestral populations—increased and focussed attention when standing on the edge of a cliff (which even infants display) is a good idea. Similarly, claustrophobic anxiety is an adaptative affective state when finding oneself in a confined space (such as a cave). Despite the fact that aeroplane travel was not a part of the environment in which the fear of heights and closed spaces evolved, it nonetheless satisfies the input conditions of these fears.

Sperber's argument is equally valuable in resolving the apparent paradox of varying cultural forms and invariant cognitive architecture. Not all societies have access to air travel. In these societies fear of flying is unlikely. In the same vein, humans have a number of specialised abilities for recognising other individuals, for tracking individual identities. We are fairly good, for example, at recognising someone whom we have not seen for years—and thus has changed considerably in appearance—largely because our face recognising abilities can easily ignore these substantial changes. Many cultural practices exploit this tendency to focus on faces, to remember their specific features, even when the data has degraded (e.g., with age). Masks, face painting, and paintings of faces are quite common. They are also practices that vary considerably in their form and detail from one culture to the next. Yet all involve (all trigger) domain-specific face recognition abilities and all depend on them for ease of memorising and recall. This is not to say that other body parts do not serve as cultural foci—clearly they do (the counting thereof is a good example). Nonetheless, there is special attention to the face in a range of cultural practices, arguably because the face and face-like representation trigger a domain-specific device.

VIII

To return to race. It is generally argued that the concept of race historically emerged during the period of colonial and other overseas encounters, when peoples were encountered whose physical appearance was markedly different from that of colonial voyagers. A sense of the significance of race as 'marvel' comes from expositions in the European and North American metropoles that displayed indigenous, racial-others as novel 'biological specimens' (Rydell, 1984). In this respect, race was essentially a by-product of colonial curiosity and exploitation. The modern concept of race, however, has lost much of this historic specificity and is now generally (mis)interpreted as a 'natural' and general system for partitioning humans into distinct kinds (despite the fact that there is nothing natural or general about any system of racial classification).

I suggest that the modern concept has stabilised and been sustained over time as much because of cognitive as cultural and historical factors. A domain-specific folk sociology guides children to spontaneously adopt specific social representations. Race satisfies the input conditions of this disposition, even if it is not an input condition for which the device was 'designed'. Although I do not have the space here to specify the specific input conditions that race satisfies, I can briefly sketch what they are *not*. There has been considerable speculation about why humans live in groups and what cognitive mechanisms may have evolved to facilitate group living. A number of evolutionary explanations have been proposed, most involving the positive consequences of reciprocal systems of social exchange, a hallmark of human sociality (Wrangham, 1980; Lévi-Strauss, 1949). Other researchers have focussed on issues of competition and risk. In this light, race and other xenophobic beliefs have been explained as adaptations to predation, particularly that by other humans, adaptations which (1) facilitate recognition of members of other groups (Shaw and Wong, 1989; Van den Berghe, 1981) and (2) promote biases that favour members of one's own group over members of other groups (Fishbein, 1996; Reynolds, Galger and Vine, 1987; Van den Berghe, 1981).

This latter proposal assumes that a major task of human group-living is to avoid dangers posed by other humans, particularly those from other groups. Clearly this argument has merit, after all humans are probably the only species that preys upon its own kind. However, this approach may overestimate the dangers of human group predation, particularly when the prototype is assumed to be *tribal* predation in which discrete, bounded and internally homogenous cultural, political, and linguistic groupings enter into conflict and competition with each another. There is good reason to be sceptical of this Hobbesian view of aboriginal existence. Many first-contact reports stress the fluidity of 'tribal' boundaries and the relative ease with which people moved across them (Fried,

1975). Indeed, the notion of discrete tribal entities may fundamentally distort the relationship between human groups. As Lévi-Strauss (1964) so elegantly demonstrates, a much more likely image is that of micro-cultural foci that transform from one to the other over time and space, not mini-nation states with vigilantly maintained borders and radically distinct cultural traditions.

Recognising and understanding the composition of human groups may well have little to do with avoiding danger. Rather, knowledge of groups may serve to facilitate exchange and alliance formation. This is as important *within* a cultural entity as *between* them. One of the most striking aspects of human society is the number and variety of human group affiliations available, even within the smallest and most simply-organised locale. Groups based on gender, age-grade, kinship, trade, and marriage not only exist, but cross-cut each other, compete for each individual's allegiance, and are invoked constantly in everyday life. Given this complexity, fluidity, and the possibility for multiple allegiance, a child capable of focussing attention on the range of groups that exist, their nature, and their scope would have an advantage over a child with less-well developed capacities. By the same token, a child able to disentangle the dense web of affiliation and alliance found in everyday circumstances would be advantaged over a child less able to carryout this sort of 'analysis'. In short, an innate competence for rapidly and accurately parsing the social environment and assessing the importance of a particular affiliation at any given moment would confer an adaptive advantage on anyone possessing it.

However, as small-scale populations developed into larger and more localised political and economic units, and as competition between units increased, predatory human groups did become a central part of the human landscape. Under these conditions, a competence whose initial purpose was to identify groups and naturalise some (because a 'natural' group has precedence in coalition-building over more contrived groups) became a powerful mechanism for creating radical and 'natural' difference, not 'natural' commonality, since these units were now truly separated in time and space by cultural and particularly political frontiers. In short, the concept of race emerged as a consequence of a competence to promote not inhibit the scope of sociality. Admittedly, this consequence, ironically, has little substantive connection to the problems for which the competence was selected. The race concept emerged as political, economic, and material conditions changed. These changes triggered the innate device—met its input conditions. In doing so, concepts that bore little resemblance to those initially selected-for emerged.

Conclusion

There is much more to the evolutionary account, and, as I cautioned earlier, what I have presented here is not a coherent evolutionary argument but a sketch of what the argument might look like. My hope is that it is sufficiently plausible to persuade the reader that the problem of explaining racial concepts requires that we acknowledge and explore cognitive and evolutionary as well as cultural conditions. Indeed, I hope to have persuaded the reader that explaining culture means explaining how cultural representations not only emerge, but are selected for and sustained. This does not discount the roles of culture and power.[9] Representations are selected because they are present in a particular cultural environment. A domain-specific device cannot attend to, act on, or elaborate representations with which the organism does not come in contact. Without the existing representations, children and adults could not act on them.

The concept of race is found only in cultures in which race is part of the ambient cultural environment. Specific representations of race vary across cultures because each cultural environment guides children to a specific range of possible groupings. In some cultural environments this includes race. But in other cultural environments children are guided to other possible ways of grouping people, reflecting the specific historical contexts in which these cultures' colonial encounters occurred. In concluding *Race in the making* (Hirschfeld, 1996), I speculated that it is plausible, perhaps likely, that children in South Asia, guided by the same domain-specific disposition, find 'caste' more biological than 'race'. While we do not know if race is less salient than caste to South Indian children, Mahalingham (1998) presents evidence that caste is indeed essentialised and naturalised much as race is in European and North American societies. I also speculated that children in some East-African societies may find 'age-grades' more biological than either 'race' or 'caste'. In all such cases, that certain social categories are more readily learned contributes to the social and cultural stability of these categories. The work remains to be done.

Young children develop a hyper-biologised notion of race not simply because they learn it. Rather, to borrow Chomsky's (1988) bon mot about language acquisition, race is not something the child does, but something that happens to the child. Race 'happens' as a complex of cultural and cognitive events converge. A domain-specific disposition is triggered by a cultural arti-fact not originally a function of the disposition's evolution. Cultures contain a massive number of representations but few are sustained for very long. Those that are sustained do so either as a result of substantial, often institutional effort—as with higher mathematics—or in virtue of their resonance with human cognitive architecture. Race, I maintain, is a prime example of the latter.

Many may have difficulty accepting that cognition and cognitive development play such a crucial role in the maintenance of a cultural form that is so blatantly linked to the unequal distribution of power and authority. The argument may seem more plausible if we take a less politicised example. Given their cognitive architecture children spontaneously adopt certain cultural representations but find others more difficult to acquire. Cultural representations that meet the input conditions of domain-specific capacities stand a better chance of being sustained over time than cultural representations that do not.

Consider creole languages. When colonial, commercial, and other forces bring populations together in linguistically unfamiliar contexts, a common result is the emergence of a pidgin language—a cobbled and often limited language of which no one is a native speaker. Sometimes children are raised within a pidgin-speaking environment. As a result pidgin serves as input to the language acquisition process. When this happens what children eventually speak is not a pidgin but a creole language. Unlike pidgins, creoles are natural and fully-elaborated languages. The reason that pidgins transform into creoles is that children are equipped with a language acquisition device—an evolved adaptation for learning language—that once triggered produces as output fully articulated creole despite the fact that input to the device was contingent and linguistically incomplete (Bickerton, 1990).

I contend that the concept of race is a social counterpart to creole languages. Clearly race would not be created outside specific cultural and political environments, but just as clearly it would not be sustained in the absence of human cognition, specifically a specialised competence for acquiring knowledge of the social world. Moreover, it would not be sustained without *children* who are integral to the maintenance of its fundamental qualities. Race is not naturalised simply because it serves specific political and economic purposes. It serves these purposes—more accurately it is recruited to serve them—because of the specific cognitive properties it possesses. In short, race is recruited by systems of inequitable power, authority, and resource distribution because it is so easily thinkable, readily sustained across time and space, and—most of all—quickly learned.

Notes

1   Versions of this paper were presented at the Department of Anthropology, University of California, Santa Barbara and the Institute of Psychiatry, University of London. This

version has benefitted from the comments of various members of those audiences, to whom I am most grateful, particularly Leda Cosmides, Isaac Marks, and John Tooby. I also wish to thank Ann Stoler for comments on earlier drafts of this essay.

2   By 'race' I mean the *belief* , commonly encountered in North America and northern Europe, that there exists (1) patterned variation in obvious inborn features of appearance (e.g., skin and hair colour), (2) patterned variation in less obvious inborn traits, predilections, and potentials (e.g., intellectual capacity, athletic prowess, etc.), and (3) a causal link between (1) and (2).

3   The first film, with Claudette Colbert, Louise Beavery, and Warren Williman, and directed by John M. Stahl, was released in 1934. The second, starring Lana Turner, John Gavin, and Sandra Dee and directed by Douglas Sirk, was released in 1958.

4   The original text 'translates' this phrase, indeed of the mother's speech, into a degraded, supposedly 'Negro' register. The linguistic constructions are crude, simple, and clearly meant to be demeaning. I prefer not to follow the same practice and have altered the quotes.

5   The second film made from the novel is uncomfortable with even this degree of subtlety. In the film, Peola marries into a white family as she so deeply wants. She remains, however, terrified that her 'real' race will be discovered. The terror is realised at the moment of her child's birth when she frantically and clumsily tries to discover whether the infant is black. Her husband, convinced by her actions that the child is not his, leaves her. Rapidly the dream existence which she wanted crumbles. The 'message' is clear: race is a fundamental and biological aspect of a person's identity. Regardless of Peola's physical appearance, the 'seed' of her 'blackness' remains intact.

6   Unless stated otherwise, participants in all studies described in this essay live in a small college town in the Midwest of the US. The population is largely white. About 15 per cent is minority, mostly black. No attempt was made to determine the race of participants in the studies, hence no analyses by race of participant were conducted. Justification for this decision as well as detailed descriptions of the studies can be found in Hirschfeld (1995).

7   The intermediate choice was produced by morphing the stimuli-drawing of the typically black child and that of the typically white child.

8   In addition to the main tasks just described, several control tasks were conducted to rule out the possibility that the children's responses could be interpreted in other ways. For example, we looked at their expectations about the inheritance of hair colour, we found that children who believe that interracial couples will have offspring with black features expect that those of parents whose hair colour is different will have an intermediate shade of hair colour. This, and other control studies, strongly support that claim that children *are* reasoning about race in the tasks described in the body of the paper, not simply the inheritance of dark and light physical properties.

9   For a discussion of this approach from several viewpoints, see *Ethos*, vol. 25 no. 1, 1997.

References

Aboud, F. E. (1988), *Children and Prejudice*, Basil Blackwell, New York.

Bickerton, D. (1990), *Language and Species*, University of Chicago Press, Chicago.

Chomsky. N. (1988), *Language and the Problems of Knowledge: the Managua Lectures*, MIT Press. Cambridge, MA.

Davis. F. (1991), *Who is Black?: One Nation's Definition*, Pennsylvania State University Press, University Park, PA.

Fields. B. (1982), 'Ideology and race in American history', in J. Konsserf and S. McPherson (eds), *Region, Race, and Reconstruction*, Oxford University Press, Oxford.

Fishbein. H. (1996), *Peer Prejudice and Discrimination: Evolutionary, Cultural, and Developmental Dynamics*, Westview Press, Boulder.

Fried. M. (1975), *The Notion of the Tribe*, Cummings, Menlo Park, CA.

Harris. M. (1964), *Patterns of Race in the Americas*, Norton, New York.

Hirschfeld. L. (1988), 'On Acquiring Social Categories: Cognitive Development and Anthropological Wisdom', *Man*, vol 23, pp. 611–638.

Hirschfeld. L. (1995), 'The inheritability of identity: Children's understanding of the innate potential of race', *Child Development*, vol 66, no. 5 pp. 1418–1437.

Hirschfeld. L. (1996), *Race in the Making: Cognition, Culture, and the Child's Construction of Human Kinds*, MIT Press, Cambridge, MA.

Hirschfeld. L. and Gelman, S. (1994), *Mapping the Mind: Domain Specificity in Cognition and Culture*, Cambridge University Press, New York.

Hurst, Fannie (1933), *Imitation of Life*, Harper & Brothers, New York.

Lévi-Strauss. C. (1949), *Les structures elementaires de la parenté* [The elementary structures of kinship]. Presses universitaires de France, Paris.

Lévi-Strauss. C. (1964), *Le cru et le cuit* [The raw and the cooked], Plon, Paris.

Lewis. S. (1947), *Kingsblood Royal*, Random House, New York.

Mahalingam, R. (1998), 'Essentialism, Power and Representation of Caste: A Developmental Study', doctoral dissertation, Department of Psychology, University of Pittsburgh, Pittsburgh, PA.

Popenoe. R. (1994), 'Racism in the Sahara desert: skin color, caste, and paternity among Arab-Berber Moors', Paper presented at the annual meeting of the American Ethnological Society, Santa Monica.

Ramsey. P. (1987), 'Young Children's Thinking about Ethnic Differences', in J. Phinney and M. Ratheram (eds), *Children's Ethnic Socialization: Pluralism and Development*, Sage, Beverley Hills.

Reynolds. V., Galger, V. and Vine, I. (1987), *The Sociobiology of Ethnocentrism: Evolutionary Dimensions of Xenophobia, Discrimination, Racism, and Nationalism*, Croom Helm, London.

Rydell. R. (1984), *All the World's a Fair: Visions of Empire at American International Expositions, 1876–1916*, University of Chicago Press, Chicago.

Semaj. L. (1980), 'The Development of Racial Evaluation and Preference: A Cognitive Approach', *The Journal of Black Psychology*, vol. 6, pp. 59–79.

Shaw. R. and Wong. Y. (1989), *Genetic Seeds of Warfare: Evolution, Nationalism and Patriotism*, Unwin Hyman, Boston.

Sperber. D. (1994), 'The modularity of thought and the epidemiology of representations', in L. Hirschfeld and S. Gelman (eds), *Mapping the Mind: Domain Specificity in Cognition and Culture*, Cambridge University Press, Cambridge.

Stoler. A. (1995), *Race and the Education of Desire: Foucault's History of Sexuality and the Colonial Order of Things*, Duke University Press, Durham.

Van den Berghe, E. (1981), *The Ethnic Phenomenon*, Elsevier, New York.
Wrangham, R. (1980), 'An Ecological Model of Female-bonded Primate Group', *Behaviour*,
    vol. 75, pp. 262–300.

3 Racism in Nationalised States: A Framework for Comparative Research

ANDREAS WIMMER

There is perhaps no other research field in the social sciences that is more politicised than discussions on the recent rise of racism. Many researchers actively promote such politicisation because according to a widely shared opinion '...the efficacy of a theory about race and racism is to be assessed in terms of the ways in which it renders possible resistance to racism', as Goldberg (1993, p.41) has put it. It would certainly be naive to believe that one could remove oneself completely from this arena of conflicts. Even simple and apparently purely pragmatic definitions of racism and xenophobia do imply a certain political perspective. It is, to borrow an epidemiological metaphor, in the cracks of the small details that the bacteria of ideology take hold.

Despite this, I stick to the pre-post-modern, thus modern, idea that it is not only possible to examine social scientific propositions with regard to their political implications and hidden messages, but also with regard to their empirical plausibility. Added to which, I still hold the currently rather unfashionable conviction that it is precisely this element which distinguishes scientific discourse from others such as political discourse. Statements about the relative validity of an explanation are what can be expected from such a strategy of argumentation, not, as Popper would have it, a decisive experiment allowing a theory to be 'falsified' (cf. Wimmer, 1995a, ch. 2).

In what follows I would first like to discuss the four most prominent explanations concerning xenophobia and racism found in the social science literature and confront them with the results of empirical research. The four models derive from rational choice theory, functionalism, sociobiology and discourse theory respectively.

Building on this, I wish to propose an alternative analytical perspective. In the Weberian view I will try to develop, xenophobia and racism are interpreted as an extreme form of nationalism, a consequence of the ordering of the modern world according to the principle of the nation-state. In which for the first time, notions of political legitimacy were fused with the idea of ethnic solidarity. Distinctions based on racial and/or ethnic markers were thus transformed into powerful elements of political discourse and practices of exclusion. In my view, future comparative research should be based on a deeper understanding of this relation between racism and political modernity. Some possible lines along which such a comparative research programme might be developed will be discussed in the final section.

It may be useful to define the concepts of xenophobia and racism before starting the discussion (see Miles, 1991, pp. 93–103; 1993, ch. 3; Taguieff, 1988). Five different ideological constructions of the relation between 'us' and 'them' can be distinguished. Together they form the repertoire of tropes from which modern discourses of exclusion are constructed. First, the fear of being 'inundated' by foreigners and estrangement from one's culture (fears of inundation). Second the idea that mixing different cultural or biological 'entities' is harmful (phobia of interbreeding and creolisation). Third, that the marks of certain biological or cultural 'characteristics' are so 'profound', that they cannot be changed during the lifetime of an individual or history of a group (idea of impregnation). Fourth, a hierarchisation of the different entities in which one's own group comes first. Finally, the perception of a zero sum game between foreigners and 'ourselves'. In my opinion, this allows xenophobia and racism to be viewed as two points on a continuum of ever more exclusionist discourses. Fears of inundation, phobia of interbreeding and the perception of a zero sum game constitute a xenophobic worldview. Biological and 'cultural' racisms are additionally characterised by a hierarchic organisation of groups and the idea of impregnation.

Rational Choice Theory

According to one thesis xenophobia and racism stem from an intensive rivalry between migrants and *autochthons*. From the perspective of established inhabitants migrants compete for residential space and working opportunities especially when jobs and cheap housing are scarce, such as in times of economic crisis (for Germany: Von Freyberg, 1994 and Castles, 1987; for the Netherlands: Van Amersfoort, 1982; for the USA: Olzak, 1993). According to these authors, racist or xenophobic discourse helps to legitimate one's position in the struggle over scarce resources. The theoretical core of this argument is often a model of rational decision making (see Banton, 1983; Hechter, 1986, Van Den Berghe, 1997). The thesis thus takes the xenophobic vision of a wave of job seeking foreigners at face value which is not to say that it is an implausible one.

However, if we consider this diachronically, we realise that xenophobic fears of foreign domination are not anymore virulent when wages drop or unemployment rises—both indicators of intense competition in the job market. The Swiss case illustrates this point fairly well. An *Überfremdung*, a surplus of foreigners, was first 'diagnosed' in the 1880s. Complaints were heard from the working class of competition from Italian immigrants, from the Swiss-French about the political influence of Bismarck's Germany over their Alemannic countrymen, and from the bourgeois Swiss-Germans about the number of German workmen and journeymen (Imhof, 1993). There were even riots, as well as pogrom-style evictions of Italians in the Outer Sihl district, in Zurich towards the end of July 1896 (Hoffmann-Nowotny, 1992, pp. 79f.; compare for similar events in other European countries Lucassen, 1995). However, this first wave of fear of foreign domination occurred in a time of modest but steady economic growth (Ritzmann et al., 1995).

The same applies for the second wave, which occurred round 1917 (Romano, 1990). Data on real wages for this period are also available, and show that significant increases were recorded in the building and industrial sector (Ritzmann et al., 1995). Moreover, the percentage of foreigners in the residential population reached its peak in 1914 and dropped continuously after that, from 15.4 per cent to about five per cent at the beginning of World War II. Although direct competition for jobs may also have diminished during this period, the *Überfremdung* remained high on the political agenda until the mid-1930s (Romano, 1990). When voices hostile to foreigners rose again in the mid-1960s both the GNP and real wages were on the increase (until 1970), and full employment prevailed for a further decade.

However, one could object that such aggregate data say little about the competition in specific industries or regions. Unfortunately studies which measure competition selectively are still very rare. Indeed one of the most comprehensive and methodically reliable is a study by Olzak (1993), in which she set out to demonstrate that the ethnic conflicts and pro's tests in the USA between 1876 and 1914 could be explained by a competition model. Comparing the frequency of ethnic disputes, as reported in the press, with various measures of competition (occupational segregation, economic depression, state of workforce training, immigration rates, etc.), Olzak demonstrated that the immigration rate, which in this period attained its historic peak, had no influence on the amount of ethnic conflicts and protests. But the proportional change in these rates did have an effect (Olzak, 1993, pp. 78f.).

On closer examination, however, Olzak's study refutes rather than verifies the competition thesis: changes in immigration figures had no significant influence on the level or frequency of conflicts with *immigrants* (almost exclusively white at the time) but rather with those categorised as black or Chinese. Conflicts with 'blacks' amounted to 55 per cent; those with white immigrants to only 30 per cent (Olzak, 1993, pp. 77, 83), even though only approximately 200 000 'blacks' moved into the industrialising North between 1890 and 1910, and thus became competitors for the indigenous residents there (previous figures were insignificant). Paltry figures when compared with the one million people *a year* who immigrated—mainly from Central, Southern, and Eastern Europe between 1890 and 1914. At the same time, occupational segregation of 'blacks' increased while that of immigrants receded.[1] Thus direct competition between long-time residents and 'blacks' slackened while that with immigrants *intensified*.

An analysis of the data at the city level also shows that the degree of occupational segregation of immigrants had a greater statistical impact on violence against those regarded as 'black' than on the foreigners themselves, while the degree of occupational segregation of 'blacks' did not significantly influence the assaults on them. On the other hand, the percentage of 'blacks' in a residential population correlated with the acts of violence against them, while the proportion of immigrants did *not* coincide with the level of hostility toward them (Olzak, 1993).

Another line of criticism could be developed on the basis of a large number of studies from social psychology and sociology. In their overwhelming number they teach us that 'negative attitudes' towards foreigners do not prevail especially among people who are unemployed[2] nor among those who fear the loss of their job (Hoskin, 1985, pp. 14f.; Silbermann and Hüsers, 1995, pp. 73–6), or who worked alongside foreigners (Hoffmann-Nowoltny, 1973, p. 87; Silbermann and Hüsers, 1995, pp. 60–3).[3] It should also be noted that, at least since World War II, *real* competition for jobs between native- and foreign- born has been rather limited. Among economists, to be sure, intense discussion persists if immigrants replace or supplement the indigenous work force. However, Rürup and Sesselmeier (1993, p. 289) conclude in their overview that the supplementation thesis must be viewed 'as the more relevant and until now the clearly better corroborated' (for Switzerland see Ritschard, 1982; for the USA see Borjas, 1990; Tapinos and Rugy's (1994) review of various studies comes to the same conclusion).

Incidentally, the simple competition thesis also fails to account for the xenophobes' motivation, although rational choice theory refers to this specifically. Thus analyses of Swiss voting results show that in acceptance of more restrictive immigration laws or rejection of improved legal status for foreigners, fear of labour market competition plays a less significant role than generalised fears of loss of social status and identity (Linder, 1993, p. 157). Similar motives also stir up racist football fans, such as those in London's East End (Cohen, 1991, pp. 323ff.).

It follows from this that the intensity of hostile feelings towards immigrants or ethnic minorities does not depend on the degree of labour market competition. It seems that xenophobia and racism are based on perceptions of equality and difference, of legitimate and illegitimate competition (Bélanger and Pinard, 1991) that cannot be deduced from the structures of competition in the labour market.

While this proposition runs contrary to much sociological and economic writing on xenophobia and racism, it seems to be widely accepted in social psychology. However, social psychologists rarely go beyond this point in the story (see Poppe, and Hagendoorn and Linssen in this volume), while the true challenge consists in understanding the dynamics behind the inclusion of *specific* groups within the sphere of legitimate competition or, conversely, why competition from certain *other* groups is perceived as unfair (see e.g., Windisch, 1978).

Functionalism and Sociobiology

According to a theses equally widespread at present, though no longer in academic circles, racism and xenophobia are seen as consequences of a clash of incompatible cultures. In contrast to immigrants from Southern or Eastern Europe those from the Third World are seen as incapable of assimilation. They come, as one well known European researcher has put it, from societies with a 'mainly agrarian and often semi-feudal or feudal structure...which internally is still in part strongly oriented to tribe and clan, perhaps equipped with religions which have not experienced the Reformation and Enlightenment'. In addition to this 'cultural incompatibility', low educational qualifications and professional experience are also blamed for the new immigrant's inability to integrate into the class structure of the host society, and therefore for his or her consequent ghettoisation as a marginalised sub-proletariat. It is not only the immigrant but also those culturally or even racially different who are, to follow this view, also favourite targets of xenophobic sentiments that spread in times of social crises (Hoffmann-Nowotny, 1992, pp.74, 22f., 24 and 25).

Thus, according to this functionalist view, it is the minorities' inability to integrate into the structure and culture of the host society that gives rise to the majority population's xenophobia. This, in turn, forces minorities to close their ranks, feeding perceptions of cultural difference and so on.

Immigrants of the most varied ancestry have heard this cultural incompatibility argument repeatedly during the course of history and have often proved it false. The following passage is taken from a work of no less than Thomas Jefferson. It refers to the immigration of Germans to the USA during the eighteenth century and deserves to be quoted at length:

> It is for the happiness of those united in society to harmonise as much as possible in matters which they must of necessity transact together...Every species of government has its specific principles. Ours perhaps are more peculiar than those of any other in the universe. It is a composition of the freest principles of the English constitution, with others derived from natural right and natural reason. To these nothing can be more opposed than the maxims of absolute monarchies. Yet, from such, we are to expect the greatest number of emigrants. They will bring with them the principles of the governments they leave, imbibed in their early youth; or, if able to throw them off, it will be in exchange for an unbounded licentiousness, passing, as is usual, from one extreme to another. It would be a miracle were they to stop precisely at the point of temperate liberty.   (Jefferson, 1972, pp. 84f.)

The Irish and Polish immigrants of the nineteenth century were in the eyes of the British officials equally as incapable of assimilation (Miles, 1982). The same holds true for Irish, Jewish and Italian newcomers during the high-water mark of mass immigration to the United States in the early decades of this century. There is ample evidence that native-born whites perceived these immigrants as racially distinct from themselves and incapable of assimilation and that such perceptions blossomed into full-blown racist theorising during that period (Higham, 1970; Jacobson, 1998). Finally, in an official report from the 1960s, Swiss officials considered Italian migrants security risks because they had 'an entirely different attitude towards the state and the community'. Especially the poorer and uneducated among them were found to be traditionally 'more or less hostile to state power' (cited in Hoffmann-Nowotny, 1992, p. 81). Despite these fears the Germans, Irish, Jews and Italians in the US, as well as the Irish in Great Britain, and the Italians in Switzerland (Hoffmann-Nowotyn and Hondrich, 1982) were able to integrate themselves into their 'host' society. Xenophobic feelings against them have largely disappeared (for the case of the Italians, see Hoffmann-Nowotny Bösch, Romano and Stolz, 1997).

One could retort as follows, giving the functionalist argument a sociobiological overtone. The fear that cultural incompatibility will lead to discrimination against immigrants, ghettoisation and outbursts of xenophobic hatred has indeed been falsely expressed at times. But it applies precisely if '*objective* cultural distance' is actually too great or when 'racial barriers' divide immigrant and native-born, which has not been the case in the examples given above. Three examples can be given to contradict this reformulation.

After the independence of Indonesia, several hundreds of thousands of individuals of 'mixed descent' migrated from the former colony to the Netherlands over a short period of time. Although public opinion and governmental experts regarded them to be culturally completely different, not blessed with a 'Protestant work ethos', they could not be refused entry because they possessed Dutch citizenship. Thanks to a remarkable social work effort, these immigrants were so completely integrated into the Dutch labour market and dispersed through mixed residential areas that by the mid-1970s they were no longer clearly discernible as a minority group (Van Amersfoort, 1982, ch. 7).[4] The question remains open as to under which conditions such a result can be expected and, if this one example is reason enough to push for compulsory assimilation as a policy as well as the allocation of the necessary means to implement it. What the example does demonstrate is that considerable 'objective cultural distances' and degrees of 'racial distinctiveness' can be overcome simply by defining a group of immigrants as 'belonging' to the national 'we' and thus entitled to be cared for by the state. Racism as an extreme form of ethnocentrism is by no means an 'inevitable' outcome of the confrontation of culturally and/or racially clearly discernible populations, as some sociobiological approaches imply (van den Berghe, 1978).

My second example is taken from the history of immigration to the United States. Chinese labourers migrated from California to the Mississippi delta in the 1870s. There they joined free blacks as part of the 'coloured' agricultural labour force in the race-segregated society of the American South. The Chinese immigrants and their children managed gradually to cross the racial divide by distancing themselves socially from blacks and adopting distinctive elements from southern white culture (Loewen, 1971).

As a last example, I refer to Brazil (see Banton, 1983, ch. 3). Despite the recent criticism of the myth of Brazilian racial democracy (Skidmore, 1993), it has been shown that a mixed-race population does not necessarily segregate or have to organise itself in a racially defined hierarchy. The contrast to the US is impressive enough: There, even with upward social mobility, 'blacks' find themselves again in *black* ghettos—this time in the suburbs (Alba and Logan, 1993). Incidentally, studies on segregation in the USA also make it clear that this is due less to 'cultural distance' than to rejection by the white middle class. After all, in the case of Asian immigrants a spatial desegregation occurs concomitant with their upward social mobility—a phenomenon independent of the degree of cultural assimilation (Alba and Logan, 1993). Again the *perception* of incompatibility and unbridgeable cultural distance must be explained: What leads to segregational behaviour if the 'objective' cultural or 'racial distinctiveness' between *autochthons* and immigrants are not the decisive factors?

A final argument is of a rather theoretical nature. A static and essentialist definition of culture, as was characteristic of social anthropological discourse until the 1960s, still forms the basis for the conception of cultural incompatibility (see the critique by Castles, 1993). Yet in the meantime it is considered to be outdated in this discipline, with discussion focusing on individual and sub-cultural variability, and the processual character and strategic adaptability of cultural practice (compare Wimmer, 1996b).

These critical remarks should in no way be taken to refute the considerable orientation problems that can be experienced, especially by first generation immigrants, due to cultural differences, nor that the presence of immigrants can cause confusion, fear, and defensive reactions among the longer established inhabitants. The issue is only to what extent the degree of cultural difference is responsible for the intensity of rejection. In view of the evidence of the vastly differing abilities of various immigration countries to 'absorb' immigrants from other cultures or 'races', we can conclude that the perception of difference and menace is not directly linked in a straightforward way to objective differences between members of a society. Again, the real task rests in discovering the mechanism which could account for the perception of certain groups at certain points in time and in certain places as foreign while they are perceived as familiar in other circumstances.

Discourse Theory

In the approach that dominates the field of discussion at the moment, at least in the disciplines of sociology and anthropology, this critique is radicalised to its extremes. The analytical relevance and even the empirical existence of cultural differences are simply denied. According to a number of discourse theories currently *en vogue*, it is no longer the immigrants and their characteristics who are focused upon but the discourse of those who speak of them. The discursive construction of unbridgeable cultural or racial otherness helps to exclude the immigrants and ethnic minorities from the core social group and to establish domination over them.

Above all it is those in official or semi-official positions of power who create this discourse of exclusion and self-empowerment, and institutionalise it in multicultural social work or in immigration policies. In this way the consequences of their own politics are made invisible because the cultural difference of the immigrants is made to bear the blame for their exclusion and impoverishment while xenophobia can be explained as cultural conflict. At the same time a definition of the social situation can be imposed which makes the 'immigration problem' responsible even for the general crisis in political legitimacy and for economic difficulties. 'Ethnics' are categorised as different and are separated, through administrative and discursive practices, from the 'general' population, although they largely share the same culture of mass consumption (Radtke, 1990). As a consequence a 'sociogenesis of ethnic minorities' takes place (Dittrich and Radtke, 1990; Bukow, 1992).

These discursive practices represent a breeding ground, so the argument goes, in which normal, everyday racism as well as politically-organised right wing extremism can thrive. The multicultural idea that every culture should be allowed its place to flourish is open to reinterpretation as the right of *autochthons* to defend their culture and homeland against the threat of cultural creolisation (for France, see Silvermann, 1992; for the Netherlands, Van Dijk, 1991; for Great Britain, Solomos, 1988).

In the aftermath of the British study by Robert Miles (most recently, 1993), 'racist' immigration discourses and administrative measures in France (Silvermann, 1992), the Netherlands (Schuster), and Australia (Castles, 1993) have been examined. Critics of the multicultural social policy of the United Kingdom (Anthias and Yuval-Davis, 1992), the Netherlands (Essed, 1992), Sweden (Ålund), Germany (Radtke, 1990), New Zealand (Wetherell and Potter, 1993), and Australia (Castles) orient themselves on this theoretical perspective.

We owe an important insight to such analyses: official or semi-official discourse offers a structure of opportunity to which immigrant groups can relate (compare the sample case of Padilla, 1986), as much as groups hostile to them can. To be sure, these opportunities are not always perceived—or, if so, perhaps with completely different political consequences than the ones intended. Individual groups can promote their own views, contrary to the intentions of the entire publishing, political, bureaucratic, and economic elite of a country. The 'ethnic revival' in the US, for example, directed itself *against* the 'melting pot' model of the majority population and the state apparatus. The same can be shown for ethnic movements in the United Kingdom (Werbner, 1996) or Mexico (Wimmer, 1993).

Additionally the majority's perception of basic social problems can develop independently from those held by the national elites. Swiss history for example shows very clearly that the change in official immigration policy and discourse towards a more restrictive model around 1970 occurred only as a *reaction* to nationalist and xenophobic social movements that had first developed among unionised members of the working class (Wimmer, 1998).

The Dutch case illustrates this point even more clearly. Rath (1993) has shown that Dutch official discourse on immigration and the integration of 'ethnic minorities' cannot be interpreted as 'racist', if one takes the two minimum requirements for a definition of racism to be an acceptance of cultural or racial hierarchy and an anti-assimilationist stance. Nevertheless, there have been racist and xenophobic political movements in the Netherlands just as in other European countries.

Thus reality effects are not only to be attributed to the discourses of those groups holding the power to define official social categories.[5] Instead, what must be analysed are the conditions under which these discourses spread within a population and are perceived as credible. The converse is also to be expected: that official views and policies only react to public sentiments and grassroots protest movements. If, however, institutionalised discourses are credited à la Foucault with quasi-magic power and if the concept of society is limited to that of the field of discourses, the conditions for the formation of such social movements—of majorities and minorities—vanish from sight (see Wimmer, 1991). To present such an analysis of discursive shifts, we therefore have to take into consideration the non-discursive conditions that influence the acceptance of different points of view, classifications, and problem-definitions.

Struggling over Collective Goods

In order to develop a political economy of racist discourse, we first have to understand how notions of culture and identity are intertwined with the political structures of modern societies. It is my aim to show in this section that racism and xenophobia are directly linked to the basic characteristics of the nation-state, the key political institution of modern societies. Racism and xenophobia are a consequence of the bundling of the interests and ideas of the members of the nation-state in a way that produces highly integrated communities within the modern world society. This certainly does not imply that xenophobia—for example in the form of anti-Judaism—did not exist before the rise of the nation-state (see the following section). It does mean, however, that xenophobic discourses of exclusion can only have gained the degree of legitimacy and political power that they have had in modern times, because politics is seen as a matter of representing an ethnically defined people in whose interests the state is supposed to act.

The formation of nation-states can thus be analysed as a process of social closure—to use a term of Max Weber's again. Let me briefly mention three aspects of this process of closure, a symbolic, a legal and a political one, before addressing the relationship between this process and racist social movements in more detail.

First, in the late nineteenth century Benedict Anderson's now proverbial 'imagined' community came into being, that is the conception of a community sharing a common origin, historical experience, and political destiny. In Switzerland, for example, this representation centres on a story of common descent from mythic pastoralists and peasants, united in the struggle for freedom and grouped around a heroic alpine landscape (see Marchal and Mattioli, 1992).[6] Such imaginings implied a new relationship towards territoriality: The immediate surroundings of a settlement, bound by relations of friendship, kinship, and profession, were no longer the horizon for expectations of solidarity. The quasi-familial idea of mutual bonds and assistance was extended to the national group.[7] The limits of state territory now formed the line beyond which the world of insecurities and dangers began.

The second point is even more important: The new order not only created an imagined community of the kind just described, but also a real community of interests. Still, at the beginning of the last century, all inhabitants of a territory were members of the 'union of citizens' without regard to their linguistic affiliation or cultural origin. The rights of citizenship lapsed after permanent emigration. Beginning in the 1850s, however, citizenship and national membership were fused and the principle of residence was replaced by life-long membership in the club of citizens (for Germany, see Franz, 1992; for France, Withol de Wenden, 1992; for a comparison of the two countries, Brubaker, 1992). The nation-state became the unit within which, after a long period of internal warfare and revolutionary upheavals, citizens were granted the right to freedom of trade within the national boundaries, equality before the law, democratically based socio-political participation, and, finally, varying social rights along the lines of a liberal, constitutional and welfare state society (see Marshall, 1950; de Swaan, 1993; Lucassen, 1995). From here on the rights of participation and solidarity appeared as the collective wealth of a nation and the state as its guardian. In other words, the institution of citizenship can be interpreted as a form of social closure (Brubaker, 1992, ch. 1; Wimmer, 1996a).

The third aspect of the formation of the nation-state is the process of political closure along national lines. Contrary to that of multicultural empires like the Austro-Hungarian monarchy or the Osmanian sultanate, the political process in modern nation-states became and is still highly ethnicised. Access to state power and access to services of the new bureaucracy were restricted to those who could show themselves to be part of the national community. An administrative or military ruling class of 'ethnic others', like the Mamelukes or the Janissaries, became unthinkable; the rule of French-speaking lords over German-speaking peasants was now seen as a scandal (compare Kappeler, 1992) because the only legitimate form of government had become the rule of like over like (Geertz, 1977; Kedourie, 1988). The ideal of popular sovereignty and the claim to national self-determination were inter-twined in the political thinking of the nineteenth century nationalist movements. These became the twin principles of the modern nation-state. Seen together, the symbolic, legal and political closure along national lines had the effect that state, culture, and territory are now perceived as belonging to the members of the nation (see Handler, 1991; Malkki, 1990). The state and its territory are owned by the people who have been united into a national community of generalised solidarity.

Why has this nationalistic self-image and the political institution of the nation-state been so successful? According to the argument followed here, the nation-state does not appear as a functional necessity of highly differentiated societies (contrary, e.g., to Gellner, 1991). Nor does it automatically result from the rise to power of the bourgeoisie—as Marxists would have it. Rather, it is to be interpreted as the outcome of a successful compromise of interests between different social groups: an exchange of the guarantee of political loyalty for the promise of participation and security. Similarly, the institutional arrangements of the nation-state, a constitution, rules to resolve conflicts, a specific shaping of political and social rights, etc., are negotiated between different interest groups and thus reflect the balance of power between them and their varying capacities to enforce their vision of society.

Of course this social compact between elites and various component elements within society developed only gradually in the course of a long and painful history of struggles over inclusion and exclusion. It is significant that racist constructions were initially used as ideological tools to legitimate the marginalisation of peasant and proletarian sections of the society, and were not directed against non-national 'others' until a later stage of the institutionalisation of the nation-state, as Robert Miles (1993, ch. 3) has recently shown. This process of gradual inclusion

> ...facilitate[d] the ideological identification of certain social strata within the sub-ordinate classes (which are defined as belonging and therefore as having a natural right of access to scarce rights and resources) with the institutions responsible for the organisation of production and distribution of material resources and political rights (i.e., with capitalists and the institutions of the local and the national state).   (Miles, 1993, p. 102)

Periodically this institutional arrangement and the nationalistic self-image associated with it runs into a crisis; the 'social contract' breaks down because the balance of forces between the different groups has changed during the course of economic and political developments. The space available here does not allow for detailed discussion, but perhaps a reminder is necessary that that this does not happen *because* of higher immigration rates. Clear signs of times of crisis are rising rates of suicide and criminality, as well as the appearance of social movements which try to enforce their vision of the future.[8]

One of these projects for the future consists of revitalising the national community by insisting on the right of the 'legitimate owners' of the state and territory to a privileged seat in the theatre of society. During times of intensified social conflicts and general disorientation, appeals for national solidarity aim to safeguard the rights and privileges of the *autochthons* that the state is supposed to protect. Whoever has the shortest or most marginalised history of participation in the formation of the nation-state— immigrants or ethnic minorities who have been excluded from the mainstream of national history—appears as an additional threat to the now precarious social union. In the eyes of the xenophobes there is a zero-sum game to be played out for the right to the collective wealth gained by joint work and suffering, a fight for the institutionalised promises of solidarity.

The 'others' become strangers, intruders in an ideal community of nation or race—the true causes, even, of the break-up of this communal harmony and therefore those responsible for the many insecurities that the future seems to bring. A kind of 'moral panic' spreads, to borrow a term from Goode and Ben-Yehuda (1994), the fear of a chaotic breakdown of the social world triggered by the released flood of foreigners. When the 'presumption of loyalty' (Weber) is abandoned, the cultural distance to the strangers seems to become insurmountable and competition for jobs and housing is seen as illegitimate and unfair—independently, as we have seen, from objective cultural distances and the structural segregation in the labour market.

Rather, it is especially those groups seen as traitors to the national political project who are hardest hit by xenophobic exclusion, as is today the case with Muslim minorities stereotyped as fundamentalists. Immigrant groups with high unemployment rates or asylum seekers also become targets of xenophobic hatred, because they seem to hinder the state in its true task, namely to look after the well-being of its 'owners' (compare Willems, 1995: pp. 517f.). Social workers, liberal big business, advocates of a multicultural society and the state who is seemingly unwilling to take action are seen as traitors to the common national cause (see the case study in Göran, 1991).

In the radicalised, racist versions of this vision the 'people' therefore have to take things into their own hands and stop the 'others' from 'invading' one's territory. A Manichean view of a fight between the morally superior 'nations', 'cultures' or 'races' and the barbarian ones is developed. Since neither accommodation nor assimilation is seen as a desirable or possible solution to this conflict, every measure to segregate the groups involved and to restore the morally sanctioned hierarchy between them becomes legitimate, even acts of violence or overt discrimination.

Such a xenophobic or racist way of interpreting the social crisis does not appeal equally to all members of a society. Shifts in social status and the many intricate balances of power threaten the prestige and socioeconomic standing of some groups more than others. It is these downwardly mobile groups that are most likely to resort to such methods of ensuring a future because they seem more dependent on mechanisms of solidarity orgainsed by a nation-state.[9] With the current accelerated growth of the tertiary sector, and especially of the information industry, along with the corresponding decline of other economic sectors (see Klauder, 1993), this scenario holds most true for those with weak educational backgrounds. There are many studies on the social distribution of xenophobic attitudes (Hoffmann-Nowotny, 1978, pp. 88, 103, 105, 108; Wagner and Schönbach, 1984; Becker, 1993; Linder, 1993; Mugny et al., 1991; Willems, 1995) and of the composition of the electorate of xenophobic right wing parties (Niedermayer, 1990, pp. 572, 576; Betz, 1991, pp. 12f.; Winkler, 1994) that have shown this.

Similar conclusions can be drawn from the analysis of past waves of xenophobic movements. The most advanced research has been done on the rise of the National Socialist Workers Party in Germany. Falter (1991) found that it was the established Protestant middle classes and the rural proletariat who formed the foci of support for the Nazis' political programme. Both groups were clear victims of the industrialisation process and were threatened by a loss of social standing.

In the eyes of such groups the territorial dimension of the national community is of special importance (Waldmann, 1989); solidarity at the borough or village level becomes a mini-model of the nation. The physical presence or visibility of foreigners in these social spaces—and especially their integration in local schools and communal institutions—nurtures perceptions of invasion, inundation, and existential rivalry in times when the social contract ruptures and promises of a future become rare assests (see the case studies of Cohen, 1991; de Jong, 1989).[10]

Xenophobic and racist perceptions of social reality therefore do not become acute because they are strategically instrumental in a fight for scarce jobs or housing. Neither does it make much sense to interpret them as a result of a culture clash caused by migratory movements across countries and continents. Nor are they mere radicalisations of the institutionalised discourse of exclusion and devaluation that political and administrative elites generate in order to overcome deficits in political legitimacy.

According to the hypothesis I am developing, xenophobia and racism are linked in a much more fundamental way to the basic principles of modern societies. They are the result of basing collective identities, participatory rights and of organising the political process on the idea of a national community. In other words, xenophobia and racism are an integral part of the institutional order of the nation-state or as Etienne Balibar so elegantly expresses it, they are 'an inner complement of nationalism and always exceed it' (Balibar, 1988, author translation).

Perspectives for Comparative Research

This is, of course, merely an outline of an explanatory approach, and not an elaborated theory already founded in empirical detail, although I have included as much empirical research as possible in order to establish a comparative base for the argument presented here. The theoretical outline, on the other hand, could just as well be used as a guideline for the design of future comparative research.

A theory, according to which racism and xenophobia perform an integral function in the modern nation-state opens up three different axes of comparison. First, a systematic study of the emergence of xenophobic and racist discourses during the process of nation-state formation could tell us much about the difference between pre-modern and modern forms of exclusion and inclusion. Whereas older forms were based on sacred hierarchies of status groups without clear territorial connotations, the new ones are constructed around the horizontal distinction between territorialised ethnic or national groups (cf. Wimmer, 1996c). Consequently, in pre-modern empires the most crisis-ridden, dangerous and thus most zealously protected 'border' was the one between the palace of the nobles and the rest of the town or village. In the new order of nation-states, however, it is the frontiers between national territories that become the focus of an almost ritualised fear of social disorder (cf. Wilson and Donnan, 1998).

According to the inner logic of these distinctively modern forms of exclusion, the stranger within the national territory becomes even more dangerous then the one lurking on the other side of the frontiers, he or she is the demonised the fifth column secreted within one's group. While the stranger 'out there' has become the object of systematised negative stereotyping and the enemy of innumerable nationalist wars (cf. Wimmer, 1997), the stranger within has been the target of the innumerable waves of xenophobia that have swept most Western countries since at least the middle of the nineteenth century.

We would expect racist forms of discrimination and exclusion to flourish exactly at that moment when groups hitherto excluded from the national 'we' gain full citizenship status and thus access to the collective goods of the nation. Two of the most virulent and violent forms of racism, those against Jews and 'blacks', seem to correspond to this hypothesis. Before the formation of modern nation-states, Jews and 'blacks' were, in law and in practice, relegated to the bottom of the social hierarchy. They were so on the basis of the distinction between Christian and non-Christian and between civilised and non-civilised peoples respectively. It is only after the abolishment of slavery and after the so-called emancipation of the Jews, thus after their inclusion into the community of citizens, that modern forms of racist discrimination and hatred have developed against both groups (cf. Geiss, 1988). Future research from such a historical and comparative point of view would surely lead to a revision of the hypothesis and to a much richer and more finely textured account of the relations between racism/xenophobia and political modernity.[11]

Apart from such an analysis of long-term historical change, shorter periods within the modern epoch could be focussed on for comparative research. Xenophobic attitudes spread into and retreat from the public sphere, evicting or giving way to other vehicles for enacting the national drama: the developmentalist optimism of the 1950s and 60s for example, or the *fin de siècle*-songs of national decay. Such cycles of expansion and contraction have been traced empirically using, for example, longitudinal media content analysis (Imhof, 1996). The task for future research would consist of relating these waves of xenophobic discourses to indicators for downward and upward social mobility. According to the theory outlined here, a clear correlation should be discernible between the degree of status loss and the penetration of the public sphere by xenophobic discourses. This relationship would certainly not be a straightforward one, because it is mediated by the formation of social movements and the various degrees of access these have to the sphere of public representations (see Statham and Koopmans, ch. 7).

The second dimension of a comparative research programme would consist of country or regional comparisons. Two possible research strategies come to my mind. The first one would consist of a comparison of the main targets of xenophobic discourses of exclusion. One could ask, for example, why Muslim communities apparently face more xenophobic rejection in France then they do in the Netherlands. According to the approach developed here, which group is perceived as a danger to the national community would depend on the model of social cohesion around which a national community has been imagined (cf. Schiffauer, 1993). In France, where the nation is conceptualised along republican ideals of democracy, militant Islam with its blending of religion and politics can easily be portrayed as the antithesis to the very *raison d'être* of the French nation-state. In the Netherlands, the nation has, since the emancipation of the catholic groups, been imagined (and organised) as a collection of various, religiously defined social pillars. Hence adding another non-Christian pillar to the Dutch constitutional state does not seem to be an insurmountable difficulty (cf. Mahnig, 1998).

Such comparative perspectives could equally be developed on a regional level. Cole (1997) has shown, for example, that Sicilian members of the working class feel devalued and discriminated against by their fellow countrymen from the North; this explains their rather distant attitude towards the encompassing notion of Italianness and their astonishing openness towards other 'humble people' arriving from abroad. In other words, working class Sicilians do not feel part of the national contract that has developed around the central state and have consequently held on to other, non-nationalised discourses of belonging (as do other sections of Italian society, albeit for other reasons). A similar study among Northerners from the same social background (or among Sicilian workers that emigrated to the North) would be of great interest. In any case, much more comparative research based on rigorous methodology and data analysis is needed in order to understand the logic according to which racist and xenophobic discourses are applied to and shifted around the various possible targets

As a second strategy of regional comparison, we should try to compare the *degrees* of xenophobic rejection between different countries or regions within countries. Why is xenophobia a more common reaction in Rotterdam than in Amsterdam, as Chris Husband asked during the conference of which this collection is the record? Why, in the recent Eurobarometer questionnaire, did Belgian citizens choose, far more so than any other participating country, to place their crosses in those boxes that researchers take as indicators for xenophobia? According to the theory of xenophobia as ultra-nationalism, these differences should again be explained by the relative degree of downward social mobility in different regions and countries. The strategy of assuring one's future by an appeal to the national community, excluding those perceived as a threat to its hyper-familial bonds of solidarity, only makes sense for those who see a dark future and are thus prepared to defend their privileges as members of the core national group. Regions of heavy de-industrialisation, such as the port city of Rotterdam, especially when compared to the thriving 'global city' of Amsterdam, or Germany's *neue Länder* (Castner and Castner, 1992) which suffered a collective loss of status and security after their exposure to market mechanisms, are therefore supposed to be centres of xenophobic activity. It is interesting to emphasise, as the case of the *neue Länder* so clearly does, that these mechanisms seem to work independently of demographic processes such as those measured by immigration rates or percentage of foreign born (weather naturalised or not). However, these are mere hypothesis that would have to be corroborated by solid cross-national and cross-regional comparisons—a research strategy that has, astonishingly enough, not yet been developed in this field.

Table 3.1 summarises the possibilities for future comparative research that flow on from the approach outlined in this chapter. It is obviously a very ambitious programme. Most of the questions asked require data still lacking, cross-nationally valid indicators have yet to be developed, historical archives have yet to be scoured. Not to mention the usual difficulties of comparative research, where *ceteris* constantly refuse to be *paribus* and where we easily get lost in contextualisations and historical specifications.

Table 3.1   Possibilities for Future Comparative Research

Unit of comparison	Object of comparison	Hypothesis
Same society, different periods in time	Epochal shifts in discourses of exclusion (pre-modern to modern)	The process of nation-state formation changes main discourses of exclusion (from hierarchical, non-territorialised ideologies of exclusion to vertical, territorialised forms based on ethnic/racial distinctions)
		Access to citizenship by groups considered to be outside the national community results in xenophobic/racist rejection of these groups
	Fluctuations in success of xenophobic/racist discourses (in modern societies)	Xenophobic attitudes spread when processes of downward social mobility take on momentum
Same time, different societies or sub-societies	Target group of racist and xenophobic discourses of exclusion	Targets depends on the model of social cohesion around which the national community is imagined and institutionally organised
	Different degrees of success of xenophobic discourses	Racist and xenophobic discourses are more readily accepted and reproduced where processes of downward social mobility are strong (e.g., in de-industrialising regions)

At present, much writing on racism and xenophobia comes close to witch hunting in areas most of us had until recently considered to be safe: liberalism's racist shadow was exposed (Goldberg, 1993); multiculturalism was deconstructed until its neo-racist bones lay bare to the sun (Essed, 1992); most recently anti-racism was dismantled as a mirror-image of racism (Taguieff, 1996), to list but a few. Racism seems to lurk behind every corner in the post-modern labyrinth of thought, and thus its locus and focus are nowhere. Going beyond this literature of denouncement implies a change of strategy and of reasoning, away from the deconstruction of texts, allusions to hidden meanings, and the revelations of opaque structures, and towards an empirically dense and argumentatively solid research on a comparative basis. If this will lead us not only to a better intellectual understanding of the dynamics underpinning the production of racist and xenophobic discourse and practice, but also to a new and more effective way of countering them, it would be more than we ever could have hoped for.

Notes

1   Olzak, 1993: p.94, footnote; ch.8 for the period between 1870 and 1880; ch. 9 for the entire period.

2   Falter (1991, ch. 8.2) reached this conclusion in his analysis of voting behaviour during the rise of the National Socialists in Germany. The lower the rate of unemployment in a region, the more success they had at the polls. In areas with high unemployment, on the other hand, the Communist Party proved very popular.

   A questionnaire by Sinus (1983, cited in Heitmeyer 1992: p. 45) measuring unemployed German youths' perception of competition appears to produce results contrary to my thesis. The percentage of officially or unofficially unemployed youths believing that foreigners took jobs was round the 20 per cent mark, approximately double that of employed youths. However, the figures for those youths that consider this belief to be wrong support my thesis: 36 per cent of the short-term unemployed versus 29 per cent of their employed peers. Thus there is no clear connection between unemployment and the perception of illegitimate competition.

   Heitmeyer (1992, p. 52) also provides a table (based on Baethge et al. 1980 and Rosen 1985) clearly showing that there is no linear connection between youth unemployment and the number of terrorist acts committed by right wing extremists in the Federal Republic of Germany.

3   Hoffmann-Nowotny's extensive Swiss study from the late 1960s, provides empirical data against the thesis that the degree of labour market competition determines the level of hostility to foreigners. Between 1950 and 1960 skilled and unskilled workers faced a quadrupling in the ratio of foreigners to themselves (to 39 per cent). However, they expressed comparable levels of workplace discrimination to that of professional workers (about 46 per cent), who experienced the same quadrupling but only to a total of 6.8 per cent. Further, only 28 per cent of skilled workers pleaded for sharp discriminatory measures

even though the percentage of foreigners in the total workforce during the course of the decade doubled (excluding seasonal workers, to 28 per cent; 40 per cent if including them) (Hoffmann-Nowotny, 1973, pp. 48, 48f, 118f.).

4   Van Amersfoort found that the geographical and social structural dispersion of the Dutch-Indonesians effected their dissolution as an ethnic group, a view recently criticised by Willems et al. (1990).

5   Those producers of public discourse *par excellence*, journalists, are not immune to this. A quantitative content analyses of the Swiss press (Küpfer 1994) acquitted the profession of charges of one-sided or even xenophobic coverage. The contributions most hostile to foreigners were found in the 'Letters to the Editor' section. Only the popular newspaper *Der Blick* tends to report, in line with the views of this section of the paper, often on acts of violence committed by those seeking asylum. Van Dijk's (1991) assertion of a systematic derogation of foreigners in the media is reduced in the case of the Swiss press to the fact of negative coverage, which is characteristic of the media system in general.

6   Other metaphors of national communities are discussed in Alonso 1994: pp. 382–4; Kapferer 1989.

7   For homogenisation of the space of identification, see Gellner 1991; for France, Weber 1976; for corresponding efforts in Switzerland, see Bendix 1992.

8   See Wimmer 1995b, on this terminology for the analysis of social change and a corresponding model of the historical developments in Mexico from the 17th century to the present. For a more detailed theory of crisis causation see Bornschier, 1988.

9   One very strong statistical correlation corroborates this thesis. That of the relationship between many people's perception as to the career opportunities available to them coupled with their desire for social mobility on one hand, with, on the other, a perception of being overrun by foreigners, of losing their national particularity, and an approval of work practices discriminatory to foreigners. The higher a person rates their own professional group's future chances, as well as his or her ability to achieve their desired upward mobility, the less he or she will feel, or support, that listed in the previous sentence. 'Estimated future opportunity is notably more significant than a person's professional position in determining the degree of xenophobic attitude a person may have' (Hoffmann-Nowotny 1973, pp. 89, 120; see also the results of the Eurobarometer, 1998 dedicated to attitudes towards foreigners; however, Silvermann and Hüsers 1995, pp. 63–7 found only a weak correlation between xenophobia and the estimation of one's future economic opportunities).

There are studies showing that it is more those who *fear* a downgrading, an economic and social marginalisation or have cause to fear it who are attracted by right wing populism or radical politics. (Kalinowsky et al., 1985, cited in Heitmeyer 1992, p. 54; Niedermayer 1990, pp. 573f.). Winkler (1994, p. 83) cites a German study by Veen, Lepszy, and Mnich which shows Republican voters are deeply uncertain about the future, although he also cites the studies of Roth as well as Falter and Schumann which do not confirm this finding.

Yet the correlation between the perception of future opportunity and fear of being overrun by foreigners appears clearly at the aggregate level. Studying the period 1966–67, Liepelt (1967, cited in Heitmeyer 1992, p. 52) established a clear inverse correlation between the index of private economic expectations in Germany and the election potential of the right

wing radical NPD (*Nationale Partei Deutschlands*).
A study of the winners of the modernisation of the 80s and 90s, lends support to this thesis. It included professional service sector employees, whose 'cosmopolitan self-image' made them—according to the authors, who had set out to prove otherwise—'resistant' to right wing ideologies. Some 113 of the 118 respondents even found multiculturalism exciting and favoured the motto 'Foreigners welcome!'(Grimm and Ronneberg 1994, pp. 106, 123)

10 However, this territorial aspect should not be over estimated. Racism can exist where the percentage of foreigners is insignificant (see the Polish 'anti-Semitism without Jews' or the marked xenophobic tendencies in Germany's eastern as opposed to its western states, Castner and Castner 1992) or where they are hardly identifiable as such (e.g., the Nazi hunt for assimilated Jews who were considered especially dangerous).

11 Compare with that of the history of philosophy, Goldberg, 1993.

References

Alba, R.D. and Logan, J.R. (1993), 'Minority proximity to whites in suburbs: An individual-level analysis of segregation', *American Journal of Sociology*, vol. 98, no. 6, pp. 1388–1427.

Alonso, A.M. (1994), 'The politics of space, time and substance: State formation, nationalism, and ethnicity', *Annual Review of Anthropology*, vol. 23, pp. 379–405.

Anthias, F. and Yuval-Davis, N. (1992), *Racialized Boundaries. Race, Nation, Gender, Colour and Class and the Antiracist Struggle*, Routledge and Kegan Paul, London.

Balibar, E. (1988), 'Racisme et nationalisme', in E. Balibar and I. Wallerstein (eds), *Race, nation, classe. Les identités amiguës*, Editions la Découverte, Paris.

Banton, M. (1983), *Racial and Ethnic Competition*, Cambridge University Press, Cambridge.

Becker, H. (1993), 'Einstellungen zu Ausländern in der Bevölkerung der Bundesrepublik Deutschland', in B. Blanke (ed.), *Zuwanderung und Asyl in der Konkurrenzgesellschaft*, Leske and Budrich, Opladen, pp. 141–150.

Bélanger, S. and Pinard, M. (1991), 'Ethnic movements and the competition model: Some missing links', *American Sociological Review*, vol. 56, pp. 446–457.

Bendix, R. (1992), 'National sentiment in the enactment and discourse of Swiss political ritual', *American Ethnologist*, vol. 19, no. 4, pp. 768–790.

Betz, H.-G. (1991), 'Radikal rechtspopulistische Parteien in Westeuropa', *Aus Politik und Zeitgeschichte*, no. 44, pp. 3–14.

Borjas, G. J. (1990), *Friends or Strangers: The Impact of Immigrants on the U.S. Economy*, Basic Books, New York.

Brubaker, R. (1992), *Citizenship and Nationhood in France and Germany*, Harvard University Press, Harvard.

Bukow, W.-D. (1992), 'Ethnisierung und nationale Identität', in Institut für Migrations- und Rassismusforschung (ed.), *Rassismus und Migration in Europa*, Argument-Verlag, Hamburg, pp. 133–146.

Castles, S. (1987), *Migration und Rassismus in Westeuropa*, EXpress Edition, Berlin.

Castles, S. (1993), 'La sociologie et la peur de "cultures incompatibles". Commentaires sur le rapport Hoffmann-Nowotny' in M.-C. Caloz-Tschopp and M. Fontolliet Honore (eds), *Europe: montrez patte blanche: les nouvelles frontieres du "laboratoire Schengen"*, Centre Europe-Tiers Monde, Geneva, pp. 370–384.

Castner, H. and Castner T. (1992), 'Ausländerfeindlichkeit bei Jugendlichen. Hilfe durch Kontakte und Begegnungen', *Das Parlament* of Dec 11 1992, no. 51, pp. 34–36.

Cohen, P. (1991), 'Wir hassen die Menschen, oder: Antirassismus und Antihumanismus', in Uli Bielefeld (ed.), *Das Eigene und das Fremde. Neuer Rassismus in der Alten Welt?* Junius, Hamburg, pp. 311–336.

Cole, J. (1997), *The New Racism in Europe: A Sicilian Ethnography*, Cambridge University Press, Cambridge.

De Jong, W. (1989), 'The development of inter-ethnic relations in an old district of Rotterdam between 1970 and 1985', *Ethnic and Racial Studies*, vol. 12, no. 2, pp. 257–278.

De Swaan, A. (1993), *Der sorgende Staat. Wohlfahrt, Gesundheit und Bildung in Europa und den USA der Neuzeit*, Campus, Frankfurt.

Dittrich, E. and Radtke, F.-O. (eds) (1990), *Ethnizität. Wissenschaft und Minderheiten*, Westdeutscher Verlag, Opladen.

Essed, P. (1992), 'Multikulturalismus und kultureller Rassismus in den Niederlanden', in Institut für Migrations- und Rassismusforschung (ed.), *Rassismus und Migration in Europa*, Argument-Verlag, Hamburg, pp. 273–387.

Falter, J. W. (1991), *Hitlers Wähler*, C.H. Beck, München.

Franz, F. (1992), 'Das Prinzip der Abstammung im deutschen Staatsangehörigkeitsrecht', in Institut für Migrations und Rassismusforschung (ed.), *Rassismus und Migration in Europa*, Argument-Verlag, Hamburg, pp. 237–246.

Geertz, C. (1977), 'The judging of nations. Some comments on the assessment of regimes in the new states', *Archives Européennes de Sociologie*, vol. 18, no. 2, pp. 245–261.

Geiss, I. (1988), *Geschichte des Rassismus*, Suhrkamp, Frankfurt.

Gellner, E. (1991), *Nationalismus und Moderne*, Rotbuch, Berlin.

Goldberg, D.T. (1993), *Racist Culture. Philosophy and the Politics of Meaning*, Blackwell, Oxford.

Goode, E. and Ben-Yehuda, N. (1994), *Moral Panics. The Social Construction of Deviance*, Blackwell, Oxford.

Göran, R. (ed.) (1992), *Encounter with Strangers. Refugees and Cultural Confrontation in Sweden*, Lund University Press, Lund.

Grimm, S. and Ronneberger, K. (1994), 'Weltstadt und Nationalstaat. Frankfurter Dienstleistungsangestellte äussern sich zur multikulturellen Gesellschaft', in Institut für Sozialforschung (ed.), *Rechtsextremismus und Fremdenfeindlichkeit. Studien zur aktuellen Entwicklung*, Campus, Frankfurt, pp. 91–128.

Handler, R. (1991), 'Who owns the past? History, cultural property, and the logic of possessive individualism', in B. Williams (ed.), *The Politics of Culture*, Smithsonian Institution Press, Washington, pp. 63–74.

Hechter, M. (1986), 'Rational choice theory and the study of race and ethnic relations', in J. Rex and D. Mason (eds), *Theories of Race and Ethnic Relations*, Cambridge University Press, Cambridge, pp. 264–279.

Heitmeyer, W. (1992), *Rechtsextremistische Orientierungen bei Jugendlichen. Empirische Ergebnisse und Erklärungsmuster einer Untersuchung zur politischen Sozialisation*, Juventa, Weinheim.

Higham, J. (1970), *Strangers in the Land: Patterns of American Nativism, 1860–1925*, Atheneum, New York.

Hoffmann-Nowotny, H.J. (1973), *Soziologie des Fremdarbeiterproblems. Eine theoretische und empirische Analyse am Beispiel der Schweiz*, Enke, Stuttgart.

Hoffmann-Nowotny, H.J. (1992), *Chancen und Risiken multikultureller Einwanderungsgesellschaften*, Swiss Council on the Sciences Report no. 119, Swiss Council on the the Sciences, Bern.

Hoffmann-Nowotny, H.J. and Hondrich, K.O. (eds) (1982), *Ausländer in der Bundesrepublik*

Deutschland und der Schweiz. Segregation und Integration: Eine vergleichende Untersuchung, Campus, Frankfurt.

Hoffmann-Nowotny. H.J., Bösch, A., Romano, G. and Stolz, J. (1997), *Das "Fremde" in der Schweiz – 1969 und 1995. Eine Replikationsstudie*. Institute of Sociology, final report of the NF-funded research project "Das Fremde in der Schweiz", Institute of Sociology, Zurich.

Hoskin. M. (1985), 'Die öffentliche Meinung in der Bundesrepublik Deutschland und die ausländischen Arbeitnehmer', in Marita Rosch (ed.), *Ausländische Arbeitnehmer und Immigranten – Sozialwissenschaftliche Beiträge zur Diskussion eines praktischen Problems*, Beltz-Verlag, Weinheim, pp. 31–60.

Imhof, K. (1993), 'Nationalismus, Nationalstaat und Minderheiten. Zu einer Soziologie der Minoritäten', *Soziale Welt*, vol. 44, no. 3, pp. 327–357.

Imhof, K. (1996), 'Die Semantik des Fremden in sozialen Krisenphasen', in H.-R. Wicker et al. (eds), *Das Fremde in der Gesellschaft. Migration, Ethnizität und Staat*, Seismos, Zurich, pp. 199–214.

Jacobson. M.F. (1998), *Whiteness of a Different Color. European Immigrants and the Alchemy of Race*, Harvard University Press, Cambridge.

Jefferson, T. (1972/1787), *Notes on the State of Virginia. Edited with an Introduction and Notes by William Peden*, Norton, New York.

Kapferer. B. (1989), 'Nationalist ideology and a comparative anthropology.' *Ethnos*, vol. 53, nos 3/4, pp. 161–99.

Kappeler. A. (ed.) (1992), *The Formation of National Elites. Comparative Studies on Governments and Non-Dominant Ethnic Groups in Europe, 1850–1940, vol. VI*, New York University Press, Dartmouth.

Kedourie. E. (1988), 'Ethnicity, majority and minority in the Middle East', in M. Esman and I. Rebinovitch (eds), *Ethnicity, Pluralism and the State in the Middle East*, Cornell University Press, Ithaca, pp. 25–31.

Klauder. W. (1993), 'Die künftige Veränderung des Beschäftigungsprofils: Prognosen zum Arbeitsmarkt', in B. Blanke (ed.), *Zuwanderung und Asyl in der Konkurrenzgesellschaft*, Leske and Budrich, Opladen, pp. 79–96.

Küpfer. R. (1994), '… darunter zwei Asylbewerber'. *Eine quantitative Inhaltsanalyse von Schweizer Tageszeitungen zur Asylthematik*, UNESCO, Bern.

Linder. W. (1993). 'Migrationswirkungen, institutionelle Politik und politische Öffentlichkeit', in W. Kälin and R. Moser (eds), *Migrationen aus der Dritten Welt. Ursachen – Wirkungen – Handlungsmöglichkeiten*, Haupt, Bern, pp. 147–164.

Loewen. J. (1971), *The Mississippi Chinese: Between Black and White*, Harvard University Press, Cambridge.

Lucassen. L. (1995), *The Great War and the end of free migration in Western Europe and the United States (1880–1920)*, Unpublished paper for the workshop "Regulation of Migration", Nijmengen University, December 14 and 15.

Mahnig. H. (1998), *Integrationspolitik in Grossbritannien, Frankreich, Deutschland und den Niederlanden: eine vergleichende Analyse*. Forschungsberichte des Schweizerischen Forums für Migrationsstudien No 10, Swiss Forum for Migration Studies, Neuchatel.

Malkki. L. (1992), 'National geographic: The rooting of peoples and the territorialization of national identity among scholars and refugees', *Cultural Anthropology*, vol. 7, no. 1, pp. 24–44.

Marchal. G.P. and Mattioli, A. (eds) (1992), *Erfundene Schweiz. Konstruktionen nationaler Identität*, Chronos, Zurich.

Marshall. T.H. (1950), *Citizenship and Social Class*, Cambridge University Press, Cambridge.

Miles. R. (1982), *Racism and Migrant Labour: A Critical Text*, Routledge and Kegan Paul, London.

Miles, R. (1991), *Rassismus: Einführung in die Geschichte und Theorie eines Begriffs*, Argument-Verlag, Berlin.

Miles, R. (1993), *Racism After 'Race Relations'*, Routledge and Kegan Paul, London.

Mugny, G., Sanchez-Mazas, M., Roux P. and Pérez, J.A. (1991), 'Independence and interdependence of group jugments: xenophobia and minority influence', *European Journal of Social Psychology*, vol. 21, pp. 213–223.

Niedermayer, O. (1990), 'Sozialstruktur, politische Orientierung und die Unterstützung extremrechter Parteien in Westeuropa', *Zeitschrift für Parlamentsfragen*, vol. 21, no. 4, pp. 564–582.

Olzak, S. (1993), *The Dynamics of Ethnic Competition and Conflict*, Stanford University Press, Stanford.

Padilla, F. (1986), 'Ladino ethnicity in the city of Chicago', in Susan Olzak and Joane Nagel (eds), *Competitive Ethnic Relations*, Academic Press, New York, pp. 153–172.

Radtke, F.-O. (1990), 'Multikulturell – Das Gesellschaftsdesign der 90er Jahre?', *Informationsdiens zur Ausländerarbeit*, vol. 4, pp. 27–34.

Rath, J. (1993), 'The ideological representation of migrant workers in Europe: A matter of racialisation', in John Wrench and John Solomos (eds), *Racism and Migration in Western Europe*, Berg, Oxford, pp. 215–232.

Ritschard, R. (1982), 'Die makroregionale Verteilung ausländischer Arbeitskräfte in der Schweiz und der Bundesrepublik Deutschland', in H.-J. Hoffmann-Nowotny and K.-O. Hondrich (eds), *Ausländer in der Bundesrepublik Deutschland und der Schweiz. Segregation und Integration: Eine vergleichende Untersuchung*, Campus, Frankfurt, pp. 195–254.

Ritzmann, H. et al. (1995), *Historische Statistik der Schweiz*, Chronos, Zurich.

Romano, G. (1990), 'Mehr Fremde – mehr Fremdenangst? Bemerkungen zu einer gängigen Argumentation', *Asylon* (Bundesamt für Flüchtlinge), vol. 6, pp. 2–7.

Rürup, B. and Sesselmeier, W. (1993), 'Einwanderung: die wirtschaftliche Perspektive', in F. Balke et al. (eds), *Schwierige Fremdheit. Über Integration und Ausgrenzung in Einwanderungsländern*, Fischer, Frankfurt, pp. 285–304.

Schiffauer, W. (1993), 'Die civil society und der Fremde – Grenzmarkierungen in vier politischen Kulturen', in F. Balke et al. (eds), *Schwierige Fremdheit. Über Integration und Ausgrenzung in Einwanderungsländern*, Fischer, Frankfurt, pp. 185–199.

Silbermann, A. and Hüsers, F. (1995), *Der 'normale' Hass auf die Fremden. Eine sozialwissenschaftliche Studie zu Ausmass und Hintergründen von Fremdenfeindlichkeit in Deutschland*, Quintessenz, München.

Silvermann, M. (1992), *Deconstructing the Nation. Immigration, Racism and Citizenship in Modern France*, Routledge and Kegan Paul, London.

Skidmore, T.E. (1993), 'Bi-racial U.S.A. vs. multi-racial Brazil: Is the contrast still valid?', *Journal of Latin American Studies*, vol. 25, pp. 373–386.

Solomos, J. (1988), *Black Youth, Racism and the State: The Politics of Ideology and Policy*, Cambridge University Press, Cambridge.

Taguieff, P.-A. (1988), *La force du préjugé. Essai sur le racisme et ses doubles*, Editions la Découverte, Paris.

Taguieff, P.-A. (1995), *Les fins de l'antiracisme*, Michalon, Paris.

Tapinos, G. and Rugy, A. de (1994), 'The macroeconomic impact of immigration: review of the literature published since the mid-1970s', in SOPEMI, *Trends in International Migration: Annual Report 1993*, OECD, Paris, pp. 157–177.

Van Amersfoort, H. (1982), *Immigration and the Formation of Minority Groups; The Dutch Experience 1945–1975*, Cambridge University Press, Cambridge.

Van Den Berghe, P. (1978), 'Race and ethnicity: a socio-biological perspective', *Ethnic and Racial Studies*, vol. 1, no. 4, pp. 101–111.

Van Den Berghe, P. (1997), 'Rehabilitating stereotypes', *Ethnic and Racial Studies*, vol. 20, no. 1, pp. 1–16.

Van Dijk, T. A. (1991), *Racism and the Press*, Routledge and Kegan Paul, London.

Von Freyberg, T. (1994), 'Ausländerfeindlichkeit am Arbeitsplatz. Zur Untersuchung ethnischer Konflikte zwischen deutschen und ausländischen Beschäftigten', in Institut für Sozialforschung (ed.), *Rechtsextremismus und Fremdenfeindlichkeit. Studien zur aktuellen Entwicklung*, Campus, Frankfurt, pp. 129–166.

Wagner, U. and Schönbach, P. (1984), 'Links between educational status and prejudice: Ethnic attitudes in West Germany', in N. D. Miller and M. B. Brewer (eds), *Groups in Contact*, Academic Press, Orlando, pp. 29–52.

Waldmann, P. (1989), *Ethnischer Radikalismus. Ursachen und Folgen gewaltsamer Minderheitenkonflikte am Beispiel des Baskenlandes, Nordirlands und Quebecs*, Westdeutscher Verlag, Opladen.

Weber, E. (1976), *Peasants into Frenchmen: The Modernisation of Rural France 1800–1914*, Stanford University Press, Stanford.

Werbner, P. (1996), 'Essentialising essentialism, essentialising silence. Debates on ethnicity and racism in Britain', in H.-R. Wicker, J.-L. Alber, C. Bolzman, R. Fibbi, K.Imhof, and A. Wimmer (eds), *Das Fremde in der Gesellschaft. Migration, Ethnizität und Staat*, Seismos, Zurich, pp. 309–332.

Wetherell, M. and Potter, J. (1993), *Mapping the Language of Racism: Discourse and the Legitimation of Exploitation*, Columbia University Press, New York.

Willems, H. (1995), 'Right-wing extremism, racism or youth violence? Explaining violence against foreigners in Germany', *New Community*, vol. 21, no. 4, pp. 501–523.

Willems, W., Cottaar, A. and Van Aken, D. (1990), 'Indische Nederlanders. Van marginale groep tot succescolle migranten?', in D. van Arkel et al. (eds), *Van Ost naar West. Racisme als Mondiaal Verschijnsel*, Ambo, Baarn, pp. 34–149.

Wilson, T.M. and Donnan, H. (1998), *Border Identities. Nation and State at Internatinal Frontiers*, Cambridge University Press, Cambridge.

Wimmer, A. (1991), 'Was macht Menschen rebellisch? Über die Entstehungsbedingungen von sozialen Bewegungen', in E. Berg, J. Lauth and A. Wimmer (eds), *Ethnologie im Widerstreit. Kontroversen über Macht, Markt und Geschlecht in fremden Kulturen*, Trickster, Munich, pp. 289–310.

Wimmer, A. (1993), 'Ethnischer Radikalismus als Gegennationalismus. Indianische Bewegungen im sechsten Jahrhundert nach Kolumbus', in P. Gerber (ed.), *500 Jahre danach. Zur heutigen Lage der indigenen Völker beider Amerika*, Rüegger, Chur, pp. 127–149.

Wimmer, A. (1995a), *Die komplexe Gesellschaft. Eine Theorienkritik am Beispiel des indianischen Bauerntums*, Reimer, Berlin.

Wimmer, A. (1995b), *Transformationen. Sozialer Wandel im indianischen Mittelamerika*, Reimer, Berlin.

Wimmer, A. (1996a), 'L'État-nation – une forme de fermeture sociale', *Archives Européennes de Sociologie*, vol. 37, no. 1, pp. 163–179.

Wimmer, A. (1996b), 'Kultur. Zur Reformulierung eines ethnologischen Grundbegriffs', *Kölner Zeitschrift für Soziologie und Sozialpsychologie*, vol. 48, no. 3, pp. 401–425.

Wimmer, A. (1996c), 'L'héritage de Herder. Nationalisme, migrations et la pratique théorique de l'anthropologie', *Tsantsa. Revue de la Société Suisse d'Ethnologie*, vol. 1, pp.4–18.

Wimmer, A. (1997), 'Who owns the state? Understanding ethnic conflict in post-colonial societies', *Nations and Nationalism*, vol. 3, no. 4, pp. 631–665.

Wimmer, A. (1998), 'Binnenintegration und Aussenabschliessung. Zur Beziehung zwischen Wohlfahrtsstaat und Migrationssteuerung in der Schweiz des 20. Jahrhunderts', in M. Bommes and J. Halfmann (eds), *Migration in nationalen Wohlfahrtsstaaten. Theoretische und vergleichende Untersuchungen*, IMIS, Osnabrück, pp 199–221.

Winkler, J. (1994), 'Die Wählerschaft der rechtsextremen Parteien in der Bundesrepublik Deutschland 1949 bis 1993', in W. Kowalsky and W. Schroeder (eds), *Rechtsextremismus. Einführung und Forschungsbilanz*, Westdeutscher Verlag, Opladen, pp. 69–87.

Windisch, U. (1978), *Xénophobie? Logique de la pensée populaire*, L'age d'homme, Lausanne.

Withol De Wenden, C. (1992), 'Fragen der citoyenneté', in Institut für Migrations- und Rassismusforschung (ed.), *Rassismus und Migration in Europa*, Argument-Verlag, Hamburg, pp. 229–236.

4 Conceptualising Racism and Islamophobia

MALCOLM D. BROWN

Introduction

This chapter examines the conceptual distinctions and overlaps between racism and Islamophobia, and some key issues for comparative research. Earlier debates about the definition of racism, though unresolved, may have become stale. So racism may be considered an ideology premised on somatic differences and a negative judgement about one or more racialised groups, or an assertion of incompatibility between different culturally-defined groups, or a confusion of biological givens with social and historical processes. Furthermore, we may choose to emphasise the conceptual unity of racism, or its diversity. Either way, the relationship with Islamophobia is of increasing sociological and political importance. Although the term is relatively recent, Islamophobia is an expression of something that is deeply ingrained in European history, and which today is significant at the level of international politics and the situations of Muslim communities in Western Europe.

The three sections of this chapter address different reasons for asserting that this is an important topic. In the first of these sections, entitled 'Islamophobia, Orientalism and Religious Prejudice', I look at the historical significance of Islamophobia in the dual context of Orientalist representations of Islam, which date back centuries, and the contemporary significance of Islam in international politics. That the category 'Muslim' is still being racialised, and that this identification of 'Muslim' with 'Arab' or 'Pakistani' is part of a neo-Orientalist homogenising discourse which creates an amalgam of Muslims, Arabs, fundamentalists, extremists and terrorists can be seen by looking at the areas of overlap between Islamophobia and racism. In recent European history, the definition of Bosnian Muslims as an ethnic group was a pretext for 'ethnic cleansing', and it was claimed that this was necessary to prevent the establishment of an Islamic fundamentalist state which would become a base for the Islamisation of Europe.

I also suggest that there is a possible comparison between Islamophobia and anti-Semitism, as both are based on some form of opposition to a group that is defined in religious *and* ethnic terms. In addition, there have been, in

73

both cases, historical variations in the relative importance accorded to the religious and ethnic dimensions. Anti-Semitism *qua* racism has largely succeeded anti-Semitism *qua* religious hatred, but Islamophobia is still articulated in religious terms, perhaps increasingly so. Indeed, the medieval image of the 'Moor' or 'Saracen' was arguably more racialised than the contemporary image of the Islamic fundamentalist, or terrorist, who is both 'out there' and uncomfortably 'close to home', like an 'enemy within'.

In the second section, 'Examples of Islamophobic Discourse', I examine some examples of Islamophobic discourse, and draw attention to another important reason for making the conceptual distinction between Islamophobia and racism, which is the danger of conceptual inflation. Phenomena such as the 'ethnic cleansing' of Bosnian Muslims necessitate a conceptualisation of Islamophobia which goes beyond the racism paradigm. Islamophobia should be seen as a (passive) fear or (active) hatred of Muslims, rather than an ideology as such, though it does find ideological expressions. As many Muslims perceive themselves to be a transnational, multi-ethnic community (*ummah*)—a perception that can be objectively verified—it is necessary to make an analytical distinction, between racism and Islamophobia, reflecting the distinction between a racialised *ethnie* and a religious group which may become racialised, but whose alleged differences are not primarily biological or somatic. It is in making this analytical distinction that the conceptualisation of racism and Islamophobia needs to be developed and clarified.

One way in which this can be done is indicated in the third section on comparative issues. That Islamophobia and racism can be examined in a comparative perspective is important, because it points to the differing contexts in which Islamophobia is articulated (or some of the effects of cultural differences across Europe), and the common relationship between Islamophobia, state education and the politics of integration or multiculturalism. If the relationship between Islamophobia and cultural or differential racism is taken into account, it then becomes clear that some reactions to the Rushdie affair in Britain, and the *affaire du foulard* (the headscarf affair) in France, alleged a cultural and ideological incompatibility between Western and Islamic values, sometimes to the extent of characterising Islam as inferior and archaic. In these cases, differential racist and Islamophobic discourses were mixed, and sometimes barely distinguishable, even though, as I have argued, the analytical distinction must be made.

Islamophobia, Orientalism and Religious Prejudice

The Coining of the Term 'Islamophobia'

The term Islamophobia was coined in the late 1980s, and first used in print in 1991, in the American journal *Insight*, which stated: 'Islamophobia also accounts for Moscow's reluctance to relinquish its position in Afghanistan, despite the estimated $US300 million a month it takes to keep the Kabul regime going.'[1] While there is a prominent fear of Islam in the international political arena, and this is by no means confined to Moscow, the relationship with domestic Islamophobia has contributed to the gradual (and still very partial) acceptance of the term in British media discourse. This has come about mainly through articles by academics such as Akbar Ahmed, Yasmin Alibhai-Brown and Tariq Modood (who had used the term Muslim-phobia in the 1980s), and letters by some activists. The first reference to Islamophobia that I have found in a British newspaper was in June 1994, in a letter to *The Times* from the Bangladeshi High Commissioner in London. He wrote:

> I suspect that Islamophobia, under the guise of fundamentalist scaremongering, is being deliberately promoted in the overseas media, in order either to divert attention from socio-economic unrest in their own countries or to search for an 'enemy' following the collapse of communism.[2]

Shortly afterwards, the term started to be applied to Muslims in Britain. Responding to an article by Suzanne Moore, a letter in *The Guardian* argued:

> If Suzanne Moore had written 'All religions are not the same. People kill each other over these beliefs. Let's not pretend that Judaism is a cosy little belief system...' there would have been an immediate, and wholly justified, outcry from the Jewish community. Anti-Semitism, though regrettably far from dead, is at least no longer acceptable in Britain. But in fact she wrote it of Islam. And Islamophobia is alive and well. Prejudiced talk about Muslims and Islam is widespread, not just from the far right but also from mainstream politicians and commentators of both right and left, including secular liberals such as Ms. Moore.[3]

Although the term Islamophobia has frequently been used in academic journalism, it has also been used by Muslims to describe their own situation, and this has fed gradually into wider media discourse. An example is the *Glasgow Herald*'s report of a speech by the late Kalim Siddiqui, leader of the Muslim parliament, in which he was reported as saying 'a wave of Islamophobia was sweeping the country'.[4] However, the identification and critique of Islamophobia still seems to be a marginal discourse in the British media.

Orientalism and the Historical Emergence of Islamophobia

Although the term Islamophobia is part of a marginal discourse, although it does not (as far as I am aware) exist in another European language, and although the term is relatively recent, it expresses something which is not only significant at the level of contemporary politics (national and international), but which is deeply ingrained in European history. In this sense, Islamophobia is an adaptation of Orientalism, a concept most famously associated with Edward Said's (1995) critique, *Orientalism*. His thesis is that the Orient was a Western creation and a tool of Western hegemony, and that a dualism of Orient and Occident has been constructed, since at least the eleventh century, through a comprehensive Western discourse (popular, literary, journalistic and academic), the academic discipline of Oriental studies, and a system of colonial institutions. What they had in common was that they presented the Orient as fundamentally different from the West, essentially inferior to the West, and as homogeneous and unchanging.

Islam was perceived as one aspect of this incompatible, inferior and homogeneous Orient, and reinforced this perception. Abdallah Laroui (1990) shows that Western and Arabo-Islamic thought have had a great deal in common at various points in history, but that the historical interactions have led each culture to be more and more clearly defined *vis-à-vis* the other, establishing and consolidating a dualism of the West and Islam. He writes:

> Europe, Arabness (*Urupa, 'Uruba*); each word refers here to a cultural tradition, in whose formation geography, economics, psychology, state organisation, language and religion have concurred, without any one of these elements ever having been the sole determinant...In each case, it is a question of a cultural tradition being developed over centuries through a combination of relatively constant facts and events which impose irreversible choices. Century after century constant structures and fortuitous, irreversible events have combined to form two highly individualised traditions.[5]   (Laroui,1990, p.155)

The confrontation between Western and Arabo-Islamic cultures had a number of important effects, one of which Laroui identifies as complementarity (*complémentarité*). The dynamic of complementarity emerges when two antagonistic societies are faced with the same problem. Where solutions a and b are available, and one society chooses a, the other *must* choose b (or choose not to find a solution at all):

the dynamic of complementarity has presided over the choices which Arabs and Europeans have made for the past millennium, in domains as varied as theology (trinitarianism versus unitarianism), metaphysics (immanence versus transcendence), aesthetics (figuration versus abstraction), military strategies (infantry versus cavalry), architecture (the open house versus the closed house), urban planning (orthogonal streets versus concentric streets); I have not cited clothing, washing, or food, which everyone can detect immediately.[6]

(Laroui, 1990, p.156)

Thus, Laroui seems to arrive at the Orientalist paradigm, whereby Islam and the West are defined as dualistic opposites, albeit by a different route from Said. Although negative discourses about the barbarian Other from the East can be identified in the Greco-Roman period, and a perception of Islam as heretical or schismatic is almost as old as Islam itself,[7] the real Oriental-Occidental dualism was established with the crusades, a period in which Europe was still in the aftermath of the Great Schism between the Western ('Catholic') and Eastern ('Orthodox') churches, and a common enemy made it possible to preserve the unity of Christendom, at least in the collective imagination. This is perhaps the beginning of Islamophobia's entrenchment in Western culture and *doxa*.

Moving on some eight-hundred years, if the Orient had been perceived as homogeneous and unchanging, the modern emergence, diffusion and partial success of anti-colonial movements demonstrated that it was neither. It had changed from the days of overt hegemonic colonialism, and it was beginning to fragment into nation-states, sometimes in conflict with each other. So there was a shift from a sensual stereotype of the Orient, to a discourse of Islamic fundamentalism, fanaticism, and oppression of women. What remained the same, however, was that the West considered itself intellectually superior to the Orient. Such discourses of superiority became particularly marked when Muslim communities began to establish themselves in Western Europe. Although there had been such communities for centuries, the period in which classic colonialism ended (symbolised by the independence of India in 1947 and of Algeria in 1962) marked the beginning of large-scale migration from the former colonies to the West, and this migration was part of a process by which the West maintained its power over the Orient. The Orient was no longer defined geographically, but as a group of people, a society, a culture, and a system of values, of which religion was a part.

The Comparison with Anti-Semitism

The most obvious conceptualisation of Islamophobia, then, is as a form of religious prejudice (though its tangible expressions go beyond mere prejudice, which is in itself somewhat elusive and hidden). Religious prejudice is older than racism, but the two can be compared, and they do overlap, as the example of anti-Semitism demonstrates. Anti-Semitism, or something like anti-Semitism, has also existed in Europe for centuries. The medieval legend of the wandering Jew, condemned to wander the earth forever for striking Christ as he carried the cross, was a cruel reality for the Jewish people. Thomas Aquinas wrote that 'they are subject to perpetual servitude and their goods are at the disposition of the ruler', and the fourteenth-century flagellants blamed the Jews for plague, calling for them to be killed as an act pleasing to God (Southern, 1970, pp.17, 308). This religious persecution is movingly and instructively recounted by the Catholic theologian Hans Küng:

> In the Imperial Constantinian Church what had been pre-Christian, pagan anti-Judaism was given a 'Christian' stamp...[T]he situation of the Jews became even more difficult, particularly after the high middle ages. Jews were slaughtered in Western Europe during the first three crusades and Jews in Palestine were exterminated. Three hundred Jewish communities were destroyed in the German Empire from 1348 to 1349; Jews were expelled from England (1290), France (1394), Spain (1492) and Portugal (1497). Later came the horrifyingly virulent anti-Jewish speeches of the elderly Luther. Persecution of Jews continued after the Reformation, there were pogroms in Eastern Europe, and so on. It must be admitted that, during these periods, the Church probably slew more martyrs than it produced. All of which is incomprehensible to the modern Christian.   (1978, p.168)

There are three points which can be made from this. First, the form of 'anti-Judaism' changed from pre-Christian to Constantinian Christian—in both cases it was part of an overall state doctrine. Second, there is a link between anti-Judaism and the proto-Islamophobia of the crusades. Third, there is a religious dynamic to earlier anti-Judaism which is 'incomprehensible' within a contemporary religious framework. This is because, as pre-Christian anti-Judaism gave way to Constantinian anti-Judaism, so religious anti-Judaism gave way to a secular anti-Semitism. Leon Poliakov reached the conclusion that the religious form of anti-Judaism gave way—due to the secularisation associated with the French revolution—to an anti-Semitism articulated in terms of racial conflict. However, all that had changed was the justification for hatred, not the hatred itself. As Poliakov (1975, pp.458–9) asserts: 'The conflict was regarded as racial, but if contemporaries formed an imaginary image of a Jewish race, they did so because a theologically condemned caste already existed.'

Thus, there was a racialisation of 'Jewishness'. But does a parallel racialisation occur with Muslims? Certainly, the category 'Muslim' is often racialised, but, apparently, so was the medieval image of the 'Moor' or 'Saracen'. The Jews have been seen as 'a people'; can we say the same about Muslims? The concept of the *ummah*, which I cited in the introduction to this chapter, implies a trans-national, multi-ethnic community. In other words, it implies that Islam is world-wide, and not the property of a particular ethnic group. But it also emphasises the community of Muslims, or imagined community of people who perceive themselves as having something in common, and a responsibility to one another. Thus, the idea of the *ummah* and that of the nation are remarkably similar.

The Characteristics of Islamophobia

As I have argued, the term Islamophobia is new, but it expresses something which is much older. It is this link between the origins and contemporary expressions of Islamophobia which have given rise to the term, as a result of a consciousness of the religiously-defined Other, and a growing awareness of the reality of Islamophobia, whatever term may be used. According to the Runnymede Trust's recent paper on the subject, Islamophobia, like Orientalism, involves a perception of Muslim culture as inferior to Western culture, and this perception is expressed in the following ways:

1. That Muslim cultures mistreat women, but that other religions and cultures have outgrown patriarchy and sexism.
2. That Muslims co-opt religious observance and beliefs to justify political and military projects, but that such fusing of spiritual and temporal power is not pursued in societies influenced by other religions.
3. That they do not distinguish between universal religious tenets on the one hand and local cultural mores (for example, those of rural Pakistan) on the other, but that a similar failure to distinguish between universal faith and local culture does not occur in other religions.
4. That they are literalist in their interpretation of scriptures, but that analogous literalism is found only on the fringes of other faiths.
5. That they have difficulties in sending representatives to meet external bodies, but that issues of political representation and legitimacy are unproblematic in other religions.
6. That they are compliant and unreflective, but that other religions and societies have their healthy internal debates and diversity.

(Commission on British Muslims and Islamophobia, 1997, p.7)

The juxtaposition of Muslims with other religions, cultures and societies clearly underlines and undermines the stereotypes involved. However, the perceptions of Muslim culture as inferior to Western culture are rarely, if ever, expressed in the form indicated. Certainly, it is often asserted that Muslims mistreat women, use religion to justify political and military projects, confuse religion and culture, interpret the Qur'an literally, face problems of political representation and legitimacy, and are compliant and unreflective. However, the reverse is not usually explicitly asserted regarding the West. The implication is either forgotten, or it is toned down to something like: 'Women are mistreated in the West, but not as much as in Muslim cultures.' Nevertheless, the juxtapositions do indicate some characteristics of Islamophobia, which are expressed systematically as eight main features of what are called 'closed views of Islam':

1. Islam seen as a single monolithic bloc, static and unresponsive to new realities.
2. Islam seen as separate and other—(a) not having any aims or values in common with other cultures (b) not affected by them (c) not influencing them.
3. Islam seen as inferior to the West—barbaric, irrational, primitive, sexist.
4. Islam seen as violent, aggressive, threatening, supportive of terrorism, engaged in a 'clash of civilisations'.
5. Islam seen as a political ideology, used for political or military advantage.
6. Criticisms made by Islam of 'the West' rejected out of hand.
7. Hostility towards Islam used to justify discriminatory practices towards Muslims and exclusion of Muslims from mainstream society.
8. Anti-Muslim hostility accepted as natural and 'normal'.

(Commission on British Muslims and Islamophobia, 1997, p.5)

These are intended to distinguish Islamophobia from legitimate debate, disagreement and criticism of Islam. Disagreement with the theological bases of Islam (belief in the unicity of God, in God's self-revelation through the Prophets and the Holy Books, and in the concept of accountability at the Last Judgement) does not in itself constitute Islamophobia, nor does criticism of what some Muslims perceive to be the cultural and political consequences of Islam. This is an important point as it distinguishes Islamophobia from racism—the concept of legitimate debate with a racialised group hardly makes sense (though disagreement with the dynamic of racialisation does).

It should be noted that some features of this 'closed view of Islam' are also characteristic of what Aziz Al-Azmeh (1996) calls 'neo-Afghanism', a Muslim discourse explicitly linked to 'Islamic fundamentalism'. For example, in such discourse, Islam is perceived to be monolithic, static, unresponsive and separate, and any deviation from this is regarded as *bid'a* (literally 'innovation', with connotations of heresy). In other words, it is concerned with a 'pure' and 'authentic' Islam. Criticisms of this 'closed view of Islam' are not necessarily

Islamophobic. Indeed, they are often made by other Muslims, Al-Azmeh among them.

Examples of Islamophobic Discourse

The systematic nature of the above statements about 'closed views of Islam' and Islamophobic perceptions of Muslim culture as inferior to Western culture, means they are somewhat general and divorced from the empirical situations in which Islamophobia is expressed. In order to compliment that approach, I would like to examine some specific, empirical, concrete examples of Islamophobic discourse, which help us to understand the diversity of Islamophobia, and the possibilities for international comparisons.

An Example of Religiously-Motivated Islamophobia

In October 1995, members of a group for Muslim-Christian dialogue in the Lille area of France received the following hand-written note in the post:

> Lambersart Anti-Islamic centre,
> 96 rue de l'abbé Lemire,
> 59130 Lambersart.
>
> The Qur'an is a web of absurdity, a complete heresy. Islam is a religion of imbalance. Only the Gospel is the source of truths. Mrs Raimonde Debeir, 96 rue de l'abbé Lemire in Lambersart, offers a reward of 1 000 francs to an Islamist if he converts to the Gospel. May someone tell him![8]

One way in which Islamophobia is expressed is by claiming that Islam is inferior to other religions or worldviews, in this case Christianity. So the particularity of this example of Islamophobic discourse lies in its motivation, which is clearly religious. However, it is not uncommon for people to think that their own religion or worldview is superior to others—in many cases, this is why people have a particular religion or worldview, and this would constitute a legitimate disagreement with Islam, not Islamophobia *per se*. Clearly, it would not be useful to say that believing strongly in something other than Islam constitutes Islamophobia. But here there is an *explicit* attempt to *denigrate* Islam *in particular*, presumably because the writer feels that Islam constitutes a significant threat to Christianity. This belief comes from a particular understanding of contemporary sociopolitical realities, not from theological conviction, which is why it does seem to cross the line between a legitimate criticism of Islam and an instance of religiously-motivated Islamophobia.

If further evidence for this analysis is needed, the writer claims that the Gospel is the only source of truth, leading to the logical (in terms of her argument) conclusion that Islam, like other religions, is mistaken. So far, her argument is theological, not Islamophobic. However, she does not stop there. She also claims that Islam, in particular, is characterised by absurdity, heresy, and mental instability. In addition, the bounty of one '1 000 francs' is offered to an 'Islamist', rather than a 'Muslim'. This is probably an unconscious confusion of the two terms, but the common association of 'Islamist' with 'terrorist' is still invoked here, and this plays on people's fears, undermining attempts of Muslims and Christians (to whom the letter was sent) to achieve mutual understanding.

The 'Islamalgame'

This common association, between Islam and terrorism, exists throughout the West, though it is expressed and analysed in a particularly lucid way in France. This is undoubtedly due to the history of French colonialism, the contemporary politics of immigration, and the civil war in Algeria. The classic example of this *Islamalgame*, as it has come to be known, must be the headline which appeared in *France-Soir* six days after the bombing of the Port-Royal RER station in Paris on 3 December 1996. It read: '37 *Beurs* judged: The Trial of the Moroccan Commandos Opens in Paris, 6 Days after the RER Bomb Attack.'[9] The mixing of nationality, immigration, urban 'social problems', terrorism in France, armed conflict in Morocco, and the fear of 'Islamic fundamentalism' is revealing. The *Beurs* are associated in the popular imagination with the *banlieues* (large peripheral housing estates of major cities), with overtones of social deprivation, unemployment, crime, drugs, and violence. These same *banlieues* are perceived as a fertile recruitment ground for the preachers of an '*Islam de rupture*'.[10] In addition, their nationality is an issue of struggle—they are born in France, of North African origin. Thus the headline is illustrative of the conflict between the *jus solis* and *jus sanguinis* principles of nationality, as well as the fear, exploited by the *Front National*, of immigration. Moreover, the article was about the trial of a group of *Beurs* for terrorist offences in Morocco that had nothing to do with the RER bomb attack to which the headline refers. However, the assumption that the RER attack was the work of 'Islamic fundamentalists', and the perception that conflict in North Africa (which itself conflates the quite different situations in Algeria and Morocco) is solely or mainly about 'Islamic fundamentalism', were grounds for putting the two together. The use of the words '*Beurs*', '*commandos du Maroc*' and '*l'attentat du RER*' indicates a fear of fundamentalism, violence, and cultural incompatibility, and the danger of 'their problems' being exported 'over here' as a result of migration.

The Danger of 'Conceptual Inflation'

There is a direct connection between such Islamophobic, or 'Islamalgamic', discourse, and the anti-immigration racism of the *Front National*, or, by extension, the extreme right in other European countries. However, there is no clear expression of racism in Madame Debeir's letter, nor is there a direct attack on Muslims, as opposed to Islam. To give the writer the benefit of the doubt, she is making a point similar to that made by Fay Weldon, in her response to the Runnymede Trust document which accused her of Islamophobia. *The Independent on Sunday* reported her reaction as follows:

In 1989, soon after the Ayatollah Khomeini declared a *fatwa* against Salman Rushdie for writing *The Satanic Verses*, Fay Weldon published *Sacred Cows*, a pamphlet critical of the fundamentalist interpretation of the Koran. The authors of the [Runnymede] pamphlet say that her writing helped to demonise Islam and they quote the following passage: '[The Koran is] food for no thought. It is not a poem on which society can be safely or sensibly based. It gives weapons and strength to the thought police'…'The piece they quote seems to be a perfectly valid comment to make about either the Bible or Koran. I feel outraged and besmirched that these peaceful and apt words have been used in this way,' Ms. Weldon said…'Are they seriously arguing that Islamophobia is the same as racism? Officially Britain is a Christian culture—who goes to church these days? I say hooray for Muslims and down with Islam. The mullahs have done everyone a great disservice.' [11]

It seems from this that we should recognise two kinds of Islamophobia: a hostility to Islam which becomes a hostility towards Muslims; and a hostility towards Islam without hostility towards Muslims. In principle, it may be more helpful to use Islamophobia to denote hostility towards Islam, and Modood's earlier term Muslim-phobia to denote hostility towards Muslims. However, Islamophobia appears to be the term we are stuck with, and it does have the virtue of indicating that there is a degree of fluidity between hostility towards Islam and hostility towards Muslims. Furthermore, it may not be useful to use the label 'Islamophobia' to represent hostility towards Islam without hostility towards Muslims. This is because there seems to be a danger of 'conceptual inflation' (to use Robert Miles's term), which leads to such a broad definition of Islamophobia that it becomes difficult to subject it to critique. The first kind, which is clearly Islamophobic, seems to have more in common with racism, because it is directed against people, rather than against an idea.

An Example of Islamophobia Motivated by Racism

In some cases, there is a common expression of racism and Islamophobia, in which the conceptual distinction is not reflected in the actual discourse. Here, as an example, three statements published on the world-wide-web by a Danish group:

> Why could a World religion like Islam be invented in the poor desert part of the Middle East? Why not in the more densely populated Egypt or Iraq or Iran? Perhaps because the barbarian populations have some unspoiled quality, that makes them open to new chances. Mohammed took in what was fitting his people from Jew-dom, Christianity and Mongolian warfare.

> Our democratic and enlightened aristocratic tradition makes us advanced and valuable people to the world. We have little to learn and much to lose by mixing our people with what may be environmental (not genetic) half-apes.

> The 'black school' we call the old church school where rote-learning was top priority. We support Moslem schools which are worse—learning the Koran in a dead Arab language. We should use less money on the immigrants and it should aim at integration, not aim at supporting their crusade against us. [12]

The particularity of such discourse lies in the explicit mixing of racism and Islamophobia. The first statement characterises Muslims as inferior, backward 'noble savages'. The second asserts that Muslims and Westerners are incompatible, and proposes a programme of isolation, a kind of racist quarantine rather than apartheid (and a clear example of Taguieff's *racisme différentialiste*). The third statement adds to this a perception that the inferior and incompatible Other is constituting a direct threat to 'us'. This is an extreme example insofar as it explicitly mixes racism and Islamophobia, but various forms of the statements cited are not confined to this group's website.

Comparative Issues

The different types of Islamophobia identified in the previous section of this chapter raise some issues for comparative research between countries, as well as between Islamophobia and racism. The fear or hatred of Muslims is expressed through a variety of discourses, some of which are specific to one country, while others exist across Europe. (In North America, Islamophobia may still be a minor discourse—although it is common to identify Islam with international terrorism, this conflation does not yet seem to have significantly affected discourses about Muslims in North America.)

Islamophobia and Politico-Religious Systems

An example of the widely differing contexts in which Islamophobia is articulated can be seen by comparing the establishment status of Christianity in Britain, the system of *laïcité*[13] in France, and the traditional Dutch pillarised model. These affect the situations in which Muslim communities live in Europe. In addition, these three models are highly complex: England has an established church, the Church of England, but there are no established churches in Scotland, Wales or the north of Ireland; *laïcité* does not affect Alsace or Lorraine, and there are connections between the state and religious bodies, for example, the state role of *Notre Dame de Paris*, or, until recently, the involvement of the French government in appointing the rector of the *Mosquée de Paris*; and, in the Netherlands, the system of pillarisation[14] has been documented as having declined (see Rath, Meyer and Sunnier, 1997). So, there are differences within countries, which indicates that there are further possibilities for comparative research *across* and *within* nation-state boundaries. This also emphasises that these political boundaries are not unproblematic when it comes to comparative research.

State Education and the Politics of Integration

The place of Islam in state education, and political discourse on integration (or multiculturalism) are issues relevant across Europe. The Danish group, cited above, certainly linked the two. Jørgen Nielsen (1995) has argued that the educational sphere is a major arena in which such representations of Islam are developed. Comparing the Rushdie affair and the *affaire du foulard*, he writes:

> The 'affairs' exposed tensions between ideological secularists in the political and cultural establishments of Europe, the bearers of the culture of the nation-state, and those who saw religion as having an active and critical role to play in public life. Above all, issues of the education of children were central: were they to be educated into a national culture, or did parents have the right to determine the nature of their children's education?   (Nielsen, 1995, p. 158)

On the politics of integration, Christopher Husbands (1995) addresses 'the issue of Muslim assimilability and Muslim responses to it' in Britain, France and the Netherlands. He suggests that there is a link between Islamophobic discourse and the extent of 'moral panics' about the national identity of the country in question. This link is certainly not a direct correlation; nevertheless, a strong link between the two phenomena may be a heuristic hypothesis with which to begin comparative research on the relationship between racism and Islamophobia.

Definitions of Racism

In order to systematise a conceptualisation of what racism and Islamophobia have in common, where they influence and constitute each other, and where they must be kept conceptually separate, I shall try to identify and classify the diverse definitions of racism. Michel Wieviorka (1995, p.37) makes a useful distinction between three dimensions, or referents, of the term 'racism', which can be paraphrased as: (a) prejudices, opinions and attitudes; (b) behaviours and practices of discrimination, segregation and violence; and (c) racism as a cognitive doctrine, public discourse or political ideology. Social scientific definitions of racism tend to take the third dimension as a starting point, so racism is essentially an ideology that *manifests* itself in political programmes, exclusionary practices, violence, or prejudice. Even then, there is no real consensus about how the ideology of racism should be defined, and although the debates of the 1980s may have become stale, they remain unresolved. So racism may be an ideology which holds that human beings are separated by somatic criteria into different 'racial' groups, and which implies a negative judgement about one or more of these groups. Racism may be an ideology which holds different groups to be incompatible, even if they are culturally defined and, in theory, equal. Or racism may be an ideology which takes social and historical processes, and assumes that they are biological givens. These three views are associated with Robert Miles (1989), Pierre-André Taguieff (1987), and Martin Barker (1981), respectively.

Perhaps part of the problem is the chameleon-like nature of racism. It is capable of changing its appearance, while retaining the same essence. The problem is exacerbated by the appearance of racism being more than super-ficial. Taguieff's vicious circle of racism and anti-racism should alert us to this. There is a heterophobic racism, a hatred of the racially-defined Other, which is opposed by a heterophilic anti-racism, an appreciation of the Other. In reaction to this, a heterophilic racism emerges, which also appreciates the Other—so much does it appreciate the Other that it seeks to maintain the Otherness of the Other and avoid any mixing between Self and Other. But this is still racism. It, in turn, is opposed by a heterophobic anti-racism which rejects the idea of difference in favour of universality, something particularly relevant to France (Taguieff 1987, p.38, *et passim*).

Aspects of Islamophobia vis-à-vis Definitions of Racism

It is difficult to discern from this what the irreducible essence of racism is, or even if there is one. I will leave that problem to others, since I am discussing the matter in order to compare it with a definition of Islamophobia. I have already defined Islamophobia as religious prejudice. In one sense, it is narrower than this definition would suggest, because it refers solely to prejudice against Muslims. In another sense, it is broader, because it can refer to more than prejudice. The Runnymede Trust define it as 'referring to dread or hatred of Islam—and, therefore, to fear or dislike of all or most Muslims' (Commission on British Muslims and Islamophobia, 1997, p.1). They identify four separate, yet overlapping, interconnected and mutually reinforcing aspects of Islamophobia (though it should be emphasised that *causal* relations cannot be taken for granted): prejudice, discrimination, exclusion and violence. Prejudice is expressed in everyday conversation and in the media. Discrimination exists in the provision of services, notably health and education, and in employment practices. Exclusion from management and responsibility, and even, employment occurs, also from politics and government. Finally, Muslims are subject to violence, in the forms of verbal abuse, vandalising of property, and physical assaults (Commission on British Muslims and Islamophobia, 1997, pp. 11–12).

There are three aspects of this definition that allow comparison with the, previously listed, definitions of racism. First, Islamophobia is defined *primarily* as a hostility towards Islam, rather than Muslims, though it must manifest itself (secondarily) as hostility towards Muslims. The thing to note is that hostility towards Muslims is strictly secondary. Thus, although Islamophobia is not defined as *being* an ideology, it is defined *in terms of* ideology, or *with reference to* ideology, as is racism. In other words, Islamophobia is defined as being in opposition to an ideology, whereas racism is defined as being an ideology in its own right.

Second, the different aspects of Islamophobia mirror two of Wieviorka's dimensions of racism: prejudices, opinions and attitudes; and behaviours and practices of discrimination, segregation and violence. However, there is no mention of Islamophobia as a cognitive doctrine, public discourse or political ideology. On the other hand, this does not mean that such an ideology does not exist, though it is difficult to say where it exists, or who articulates such an ideology.

Third, it is theoretically possible to conceptualise Islamophobia in terms of Taguieff's vicious circle. This starts with a (heterophobic) Islamophobia, or a hatred of the Muslim Other. A heterophilic critique of Islamophobia, like the Runnymede report, emerges in response to this. Such a critique 'acknowledges that Islam is distinctively different in significant respects from other religions and 'the West', but does not see it as deficient or as less worthy of esteem', and argues that Islamophobia 'prevents non-Muslims from appreciating and benefiting from Islam's cultural, artistic and intellectual heritage, and from its moral teachings' (Commission on British Muslims and Islamophobia, 1997, pp.6, 12). This, in turn, reinforces a kind of heterophilic Islamophobia (though this term is an oxymoron, so 'heterophilic Orientalism' may be preferable) which values the Otherness of Islam and of Muslims, seeks to maintain this Otherness, and exclude the constituted Other from consideration as 'one of us'. Finally, the critical response to this, seen, for example, in Edward Said's work, is one which rejects this principle of Otherness, shows it to be a social construction rather than a natural or quasi-natural division between human beings, and emphasises the heterogeneity of Muslim and Western cultures.

Conclusion

Racism and Islamophobia have certain aspects of their definitions and expressions in common, though their origins are more complicated. It can be said that they both originate from representations of the Other, but so do other forms of prejudice, such as sexism or homophobia. Among those things which racism and Islamophobia have in common are that: (a) both are defined primarily with reference to ideology; (b) both are constituted by prejudices, opinions and attitudes, and by behaviours and practices of discrimination, segregation, and violence; and (c) both can be conceptualised in terms of a vicious circle of heterophobia and heterophilia.

The most obvious answer to the question of how racism and Islamophobia influence and constitute each other is that 'Muslims' are subject to racialisation. What happens here is that another criterion of difference is added on to the religious criterion in order to emphasise the perceived incompatibility between 'white', 'Christian', 'European' Westerners and 'Muslims'. Yet this is not a dominant discourse of Islamophobia, except perhaps in the United Kingdom (though even this is open to controversy). In any case, the religious criterion can also be added on to the 'racial' one, and this is something which happens increasingly. In some ways, it seems as if the medieval image of the 'Moor' or 'Saracen' was more racialised than the contemporary stereotype of the fanatical, misogynistic terrorist who quotes the Qur'an in support of authoritarianism and violence.

Yet the most difficult question which I have sought to address in this chapter is not what racism and Islamophobia have in common, nor where they influence and constitute each other. It is the question of how they must be kept conceptually separate, which is particularly important when it comes to clarifying and applying the term Islamophobia in comparative research. Islamophobia does not follow a dynamic of racialisation, yet it can make use of racialisation in order to emphasise and confirm the alleged incompatibility of the Muslim Other. Similarly, racism does not focus on religious incompatibility, but religious differences can be used to underline the alleged incompatibility, even inferiority, of the racialised Other. Perhaps, and here I conclude, the difference is this. Racism is essentially an aspect of modernity, albeit an unwelcome aspect. Islamophobia is an anachronism in the modern world, but it is still there. It may be possible to struggle against those aspects of modernity which divide and defile humanity, racism among them. But the very anachronism of Islamophobia may mean, paradoxically, that it is here to stay.

Notes

1   *Insight*. 4.2.91. p.37.

2   *The Times*, 28.6.94, p.21.

3   *The Guardian*, 27.9.94, p.21.

4   *Glasgow Herald*, 1.4.96, p.10.

5   'Europe, arabité (*Urupa*, '*Uruba*); chaque mot réfère ici à une tradition culturelle dans la formation de laquelle ont concouru la géographie, l'économie, la psychologie, l'organisation étatique, la langue, la religion, sans que jamais un de ces éléments ait été le seul déterminant...Dans l'un et l'autre cas, il s'agit d'une tradition culturelle élaborée à travers des siècles par l'action conjuguée de données relativement constantes et d'événements qui imposent des choix irréversibles. Siècle après siècle se combinent structures constantes et événements contingents irréversibles pour former deux traditions bien individualisées'. *All French to English translations are my own.

6   'Le fait de complimentarité a présidé aux choix qu'ont fait au cours d'un millénaire Arabes et Européens dans des domaines aussi variés que la théologie (trinitarisme contre unitarisme), la métaphysique (immanence contre transcendence), l'esthétique (figuration contre abstraction), l'art militaire (infanterie contre cavalerie), l'architecture (maison ouverte contre maison fermée), urbanisme (rues orthogonales contre rues concentriques); je ne cite pas le costume, la toilette, la cuisine, la maintien que chacun peut encore détecter du premier coup d'œil'.

7   Here, I am assuming that Islam began with the Prophet Muhammad (570–632 CE), though Muslims would insist that he was the last of the Prophets, and that Islam is as old as humanity itself.

8   This letter has a number of errors in spelling and grammar, but I have reproduced it as written. The original French text is as follows:
'Centre anti-islamique de Lambersart, 96 rue de l'abbé Lemire, 59130 Lambersart
Le coran est un tissu d'inepties, une hérésie complète. L'islam est une religion de déséquilibre. Seul l'évangile est source de véritées [sic].
Madame Raimonde Debeir, 96 rue de l'abbé Lemire à Lambersart offre une prime de 1000.00 francs à un islamiste si il se converti à l'évangile. Qu'on se le dise!'

9   '*Beur*' is a slang expression for the children, born in France, of migrants from North Africa, coined by the *beurs* themselves as an alternative to the pejorative, even racist, *raton* or *melon*. This was a front-page headline in *France-Soir*, 9.12.96. The original, French text reads: '37 Beurs jugés: Le procès des commandos du Maroc s'ouvre à Paris, 6 jours après l'attentat du RER'.

10 The term '*Islam de rupture*' is used by Philippe Aziz (1996).

11 The *Independent on Sunday*, 2.3.97, p.10. The first addition is my own.

12 All three extracts were copied, on 6 March 1998, from the no longer accessible webpages, respectively: www.glistrup.com/desert.htm
www.glistrup.com/osmanic.htm
www.glistrup.com/koran.htm

13 '*Laïcité*' refers to the separation of Church and state in France.

14 'Pillarisation' in the Netherlands refers to a social structure in which each group, religious, politcal etc., had its own political, social, and cultural organisations.

References

Al-Azmeh, A. (1996), *Islams and Modernities*, Verso, London.
Aziz, P. (1996), *Le paradoxe de Roubaix* [The Paradox of Roubaix], Plon, Paris.
Barker, M. (1981), *The New Racism*, Junction Books, London.
Commission on British Muslims and Islamophobia (1997), *Islamophobia: A Challenge for Us All*, Runnymede Trust, London.
Husbands, C.T. (1995), ' "They Must Obey Our Laws and Customs!"': Political Debate About Muslim Assimilability in Great Britain, France and The Netherlands', in A.G. Hargreaves and J. Leaman (eds), *Racism, Ethnicity and Politics in Contemporary Europe*, Edward Elgar, Aldershot, pp. 115–30.
Küng, H. (1978), *On being a Christian*, Collins, Glasgow (originally published as *Christ sein*, R. Piper & Co. Verlag, Munich, 1974).
Laroui, A. (1990), *Islam et modernité* [Islam and Modernity], Editions Bouchene, Algiers.
Miles, R. (1989), *Racism*, Routledge, London.
Nielsen, J.S. (1995), *Muslims in Western Europe*, Edinburgh University Press, Edinburgh.
Poliakov, L. (1975), *The History of Anti-Semitism* (vol. 3), Routledge and Kegan Paul, London (originally published as *Histoire de l'antisémitisme*, Calmann-Lévy, Paris, 1968).
Rath, J., Meyer A. and Sunier, T. (1997), 'The Establishment of Islamic Institutions in a De-Pillarizing Society', *Tijdschrift voor economische en sociale geografie* [Journal of Economic and Social Geography], vol. 88, pp. 389–95.
Said, E.W. (1995), *Orientalism: Western Conceptions of the Orient*, Penguin, London.
Southern, R.W. (1970), *Western Society and the Church in the Middle Ages*, Penguin, London.
Taguieff, P.-A. (1987), *La force du préjugé* [The Strength of Prejudice] La Découverte, Paris.
Wieviorka, M. (1995), *The Arena of Racism*, Sage, London (originally published as *L'espace du racisme*, Editions du Seuil, Paris, 1991).

5 Ideologies, Racism, Discourse: Debates on Immigration and Ethnic Issues

TEUN A. VAN DIJK

Aims

This paper studies some of the ideological properties of political discourse on immigration and minorities in contemporary Europe. It combines results of my current work on the theory of ideology (Van Dijk, 1998a) with those of an earlier large project on the discursive reproduction of racism (Van Dijk, 1984, 1987, 1991, 1993a). More specifically, the framework of this discussion is an international project, directed by Ruth Wodak[1] and myself, which examines and compares the way leading politicians in seven EU countries speak and write about immigration and ethnic issues.

Although there are obvious contextual differences between immigration, 'race' relations, and hence between talk about these issues in the various countries, the overall theoretical framework for their analysis is essentially the same. This framework, which will only be briefly summarised here, combines elements from the following multidisciplinary triangle: (a) an elite theory of racism as a form of ethnic dominance and inequality, (b) a socio-cognitive approach to (racist, nationalist) ideologies and other social representations, and (c) a complex multi-level analysis of text and talk in context, in general, and of parliamentary debates, in particular.

Thus, although the examples analysed in this paper are taken from a debate in the British House of Commons on asylum seekers, it is assumed that many of the properties of this debate may also be found in immigration debates in other western European countries. Earlier analyses and comparisons of debates on immigration and ethnic issues in Western Europe shows that there are differences of style (e.g., in the UK, France and Germany, MPs may interrupt, heckle and shout, which is much less the case in Spain and the Netherlands), and of nationalist rhetoric (especially in France), but that the main topics, argumentation strategies and especially the standard arguments (topoi) against immigration are very much comparable (Van Dijk, 1993a).

91

Another difference exists between countries where immigration has been taking place for some decades now (the UK, France, the Netherlands), and the countries where immigration is a more recent phenomenon (Italy, and especially Spain). In the first group of countries, issues of affirmative action, integration, minority policy, and other topics related to multicultural societies are more prominent. In the latter countries, the main topic and concern of talk is still often that of new immigration and their reception and integration. In the countries where large-scale immigration goes back several decades, there are also MPs who belong to immigrant communities (see also Hargreaves and Leaman, 1995). Common to nearly all countries is the current preoccupation with a 'flood' of asylum seekers, a topic common to many debates in most western European countries.

Discourse and Racism

The issue to be theoretically dealt with here is the relations between ideology, racism and discourse. My first thesis about these relations is that *both* racism and ideology are prominently reproduced by social practices and especially by discourse. I am interested in these processes of societal reproduction and how exactly text and talk are involved in such processes. More specifically, from a more critical perspective, I want to know how discourse reproduces systems of dominance and social inequality, such as racism. That is, the broader framework of my investigation is the type of analytical discourse research now commonly designated as *critical discourse analysis* or CDA (Fairclough, 1995; Fairclough and Wodak, 1997; Van Dijk, 1993b).

This way of framing my problem entails that I do not equate racism with ideology, as is often done in the literature (Miles, 1989). Racism does have an ideological basis, but cannot be reduced to it alone. As a form of dominance and social inequality, racism also needs to be defined in terms of various types of social practice, such as discriminatory discourses and other acts of interaction, at the micro-level. At the same time it requires analysis at the macro-level, through analysis of institutional arrangements, organisational structure, and group relations of power abuse (for details, see the vast literature on the social and institutional dimensions of racism, e.g., Essed, 1991; Feagin and Sikes, 1994; Marable, 1995; Omi and Winant, 1994; Solomos and Wrench, 1993; Van Dijk, 1991, 1993a; Wellman, 1993).

Although I do analyse ideologies in terms of the social cognitions of social groups, other social representations are also involved in this cognitive domain of analysis, such as knowledge, opinions or attitudes (such as prejudices) (Dovidio and Gaertner, 1986; Fiske and Taylor, 1991; Farr and

Moscovici, 1984; Spears, Oakes, Ellemers and Haslam, 1997). Moreover, whereas this is true for groups, I finally also needed what I term *mental models* of individual group members in order to be able to account for individual discourses and acts of discrimination, and hence for personal variation in the social system of racism.

In sum, racism is a complex system of social inequality in which at least the following components are combined:

a) ideologically based social representations of (and about) groups
b) group members' mental models of concrete 'ethnic events'
c) everyday discriminatory discourse and other social practices
d) institutional and organisational structures and activities
e) power relations between dominant white and ethnic minority groups.

Without this complex, multidisciplinary framework it is impossible to understand many of the structural and functional properties of talk in western European parliaments, as I analyse it below. Not only is it necessary to describe what parliamentarians say in such debates, and how they do so, but also *why* these political elites speak the way they do, and what functions such properties have in the overall system of racist inequality characterising western European societies and their ideological underpinnings.

However, space limitations allow only the highlighting of some of these features of racism and its reproduction, namely the relations between racist cognition (ideologies, representations and models) on the one hand and (political, parliamentary) discourse on the other.

Ideology

The multidisciplinary theory of ideology that inform this analysis of parliamentary debates, is markedly different from prevailing, largely sociological, political-economic and philosophical approaches (see Larraín, 1979; Eagleton, 1991). Instead of using vague notions such as 'prevailing ideas', 'belief systems', or '(false) consciousness', as they are used in the traditional literature, I propose to found a new theory of ideology based on a more explicit socio-cognitive theory, in which ideologies are first defined as fairly general and abstract mental representations which govern the shared mental representations (knowledge and attitudes) of social groups. Second, the societal dimension of the theory makes explicit which groups, group members, or institutions, are actually involved in the formation, confirmation, reproduction, or change of such ideologies. As is the case for the reproduction of racism, I assume, for instance, that specific elite groups, such as politicians, journalists, teachers, scholars, and their institutions, are greatly involved in this process of ideological reproduction. Third, as suggested above, I assume that these societal (and historical) processes of ideological formation and change are enacted by group members through social practices in general, but especially in many forms of institutional talk and text (for detail, see Van Dijk, 1998a).

To summarise this complex theory of ideology as a form of social cognition, I highlight the following main points (see Figure 3.1); some details will be elaborated later where I deal with racist ideologies and discourse.

(1) An ideology is a type of *belief system* (Seliger, 1976). This implies that they should be characterised in cognitive terms, and not be confused with, or reduced to, social practices or discourses, or societal structures of any kind. One may however say that such practices or discourses are expressions or enactments of underlying ideologies.

(2) Ideological belief systems, however, are at the same time *social,* and defined for *social groups,* and hence are forms of shared, societal cognition (Fraser and Gaskell, 1990). Although individuals, as group members, may have ideologically based opinions, ideologies as such are not individual.

(3) Unlike classical theories of ideologies, I do not assume that ideologies are limited to 'dominant' classes, groups or formations; dominated groups may have, for example, ideologies underlying their resistance to domination. Under specific social conditions, *any social group* or social movement may develop an ideology.

(4) In addition to organising the shared social representations and social identity of a group, ideologies control *intra-group action* and cooperation, as well as *inter-group perception and interaction* of group members.

(5) Ideologies are not just any kind of socially shared belief systems, but should be located at a more fundamental or basic level. They are less specific than, for instance, social attitudes (e.g., about abortion, the death penalty, or immigration), but form the *'axiomatic'* basis of numerous attitudes and much knowledge (about various social domains) as shared by group members.

(6) I distinguish between *group knowledge,* that is, beliefs held to be true by a group according to its own truth criteria, and the more general, culturally shared knowledge that is taken for granted, undisputed, and generally (and discursively) presupposed, across groups, within a given culture or historical period. I call this latter kind of knowledge *common ground* knowledge. Of course, what counts as 'knowledge' within one group may be seen as ideologically based beliefs from the perspective of another group. Similarly, common ground beliefs may, and generally will, alter over time (and may even be reduced to the knowledge of specific groups), whereas the knowledge of specific groups (e.g., scholars) may later enter the common ground.

(7) The essential distinction between group knowledge and cultural common ground knowledge allows us to distinguish between ideological and non-ideological beliefs in a given culture. Thus, contrary to most other approaches, I hold that beliefs which are taken for granted and undisputed within a given culture are by definition not ideological *within that culture* (they may, of course, later or from another perspective be seen as ideological). In informal terms: ideologies presuppose competition, conflict, struggle, or differences of opinion and knowledge between groups.

(8) Ideologies are themselves constituted by *basic propositions* that represent what is good or bad for the group. They are, thus, based on the *values* and *norms* that each social group develops or borrows from more general cultural values (freedom, liberty, autonomy, truth, reliability, etc.).

(9) Virtually neglected in traditional approaches, a socio-cognitive theory of ideology also focuses on the *internal structures* or *organisation* of ideologies. Discursive and experimental evidence suggests that ideologies tend to be *polarised*, e.g., as propositions about Us and Them, as is also suggested by the 'conflictual' or 'competitive' social basis of ideologies.

(10) I go on to assume that ideologies are organised by a *fixed ideological schema* gradually learned and applied by social actors during their socialisation and identification with various social groups. Categories in this schema are, e.g., membership criteria, typical actions, goals, norms and values, group position (relations with other groups), and specific group resources. These categories and their contents are some kind of group *self-schema*, defining the basics of their 'socio-cognitive' identity.

(11) Ideologies along with the knowledge and attitudes they control are general, social, and shared by group members. However, ideological practices and hence discourses are engaged in by *individual group members* and in specific social situations, and are therefore unique. To describe and explain that uniqueness, I therefore need a cognitive interface between social representations of groups and real action, the text or talk of individual social actors, namely *mental models*. These models are subjective representations (in episodic memory) of specific events or situations in which or about which social actors communicate or act (Johnson-Laird, 1983; Oakhill and Garnham, 1996; Van Dijk and Kintsch, 1983).

(12) Because mental models not only feature biographical representations of personal experiences but also *instantiations of shared social representations*, ideologies may indirectly influence mental models. Because such 'biased' mental models are the cognitive structures on which social practices and discourse are based, this brings me, finally, to an explicit way of relating ideology with text and talk.

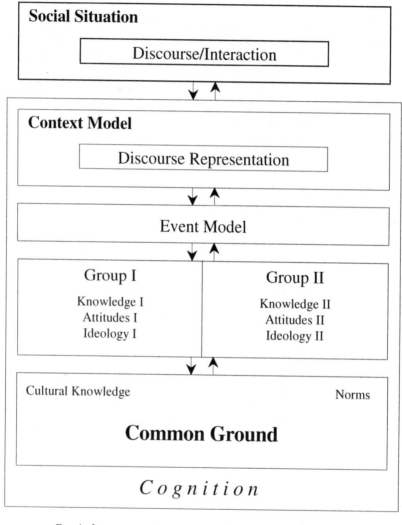

Figure 5.1   Political Discourse and Political Cognition

(13) Discourse is not only based on mental models of events that people think or speak about, but also on mental models of the *communicative situation* in which they speak, write, read or listen (Van Dijk, 1998b). It is this personal, subjective representation of the relevant features of the social situation that defines the notion of *context*. In other words 'semantic' event models and 'pragmatic' *context models* together give shape to the contents and variable structures of a discourse in production or to their appropriate understanding in comprehension. Since context models may also be ideologically influenced (e.g., in the ways interacting participants are represented as own or other group members), also contextually controlled structures of discourse may be ideologically based.

Taken together, this provides the cognitive basis for a theory of contextualisation.

Racist Ideologies

Given this theoretical framework, it is possible to make the next step, and examine the nature of racist ideologies (for some earlier studies, see Barker, 1981; Guillaumin, 1973; Jager, et al., 1998; Yeboah, 1988). How do the main properties of ideologies distinguished above specifically apply to a theory of racist ideologies? Again, I merely summarise the main features (and problems) of such a theory.

(1) Since, by definition, each ideology must be shared by a social group, racist ideologies would be based in the group of *racists*. For several reasons, however, this group is not only ill-defined, but its identification would also imply a clear distinction between racists and non-racists, a distinction which is highly problematic. Moreover, this group is hardly self-defined as such. I therefore prefer to speak of racist practices that some members of a group (e.g., white Europeans) may engage in more or less frequently or intensely. In other words, the social basis of racist ideologies is a problem that requires further analysis.

(2) For the same reason, the definition of the *ideological self-schema* of 'racists' is problematic, because racists seldom identify themselves as such. However, even when not self-categorised as racist, this self-schema may feature the following categories: (a) *membership devices*: by color, 'race' or nationality, e.g., 'We white people', 'We Dutch people', etc.; (b) *activities*: racist practices/discourse (talking negatively about minorities, discrimination, differentiation, exclusion, inferiorisation and problematisation etc.); (c) *goals*: 'Keeping them down and out.'; (d) *values*: e.g., the purity and priority of the own group; (e) *position*: superiority and dominance over Others; (f) *resources*:

'our' territory, space, nation, and white color, and preferential access to all social resources.

In other words, for those group members (e.g., white Europeans) who have an ideology featuring these categories and their related propositions, one would say they have a racist ideology (whether or not they identify with such a group or self-define themselves as such).

(3) Racist ideologies govern other shared social representations, and especially *racist attitudes*, prejudices, etc. (Dovidio and Gaertner, 1986; Spears, Oakes, Ellemers and Haslam, 1997). These attitudes are negative opinions on (the role of) minorities in various social domains: immigration, housing, welfare, work or education. Given the structure of the ideological schema above, thus, we may expect that for each of these domain we find specific opinions such as keeping Them out of the country, the neighborhood, the job, etc. or assigning priority to ourselves in situations in each of these domains.

From Racist Cognition to Racist Discourse

As suggested before, these underlying racist ideologies and ideologically controlled ethnic/racial prejudices may finally be expressed in text and talk. For concrete news reports, everyday stories, or discussions about specific cases, this will occur on the basis of ideologically controlled mental models, that is, by biased definitions of the situation (for concrete case studies, see Jäger, 1992; Wetherell and Potter, 1992; Van Dijk, 1984, 1987, 1991, 1993; Wodak, Nowak, Pelikan, Gruber, de Cillia and Mitten, 1990). Ideological propositions may also be expressed directly as generic expressions about Us and Them in other discourses, especially those of politics, scholarship and education. Us and Them may be the prototypical form for racist propaganda.

Given these underlying structures, and those of specific contexts that may favor or prohibit them (the same people will speak differently about the Others in different situations), we may expect overall interactional, pragmatic, semantic and stylistic strategies that select or emphasise positive information about Us, and negative information about Them (or avoid negative information about Us and positive information about Them). The effects of these ideologically based strategies of positive self-presentation and negative Other-presentation may be observed at all levels of discourse structures in text and talk. Conversely, these 'biased' discourse structures may in turn lead to the desired biased mental model about ethnic events or general representations about ethnic minorities among the recipients. Note again, though, that, both in production and in comprehension, this process of 'racist discourse processing' is also a function of *context*. Social domain, setting, situation, other participants as well as their roles and goals, among other things, may favor, modify or block racist text or talk.

Parliamentary Debates

Parliamentary debates are also partly defined by their complex, institutional context. Indeed, people sometimes say something very similar in other genres (in e.g., a school textbook, the classroom, or the media), for instance, about immigration, but only when uttered in the context of a congress or parliament will such discourse be part of a political debate.

Many of the structures of a political debate are a function of the context: Chair-controlled allocation of speaking time, duration and order, as well as interjections; the reading of prepared speeches; a strict etiquette of address; formalised rules of interjection; as well as overall strategies of persuasion, and the polarisation between government and opposition speakers.

According to my theory and analysis, parliamentary debates are, by definition, ideologically based. MPs do not speak as individuals but as group (party) members. Parties are the quintessential ideological groups, because party formation is largely ideological. This (theoretically) implies that contributions to a debate are a function of the ideology of the party as interpreted by the speaker. In other words, the social representations of MPs are one of the cognitive categories that form part of a context (that is, of a context model).

This is not merely an analytical category, but also a practical, group member's category. Not only will MPs express (intentionally or not) their ideologically based mental models of a particular event (e.g., the immigration of asylum seekers), but other MPs (and the public) will typically hear such discourse as 'partisan' and hence as ideological. Conversely, parliamentary discourses may also contribute to the changes of context, such as the relations between groups, for example, between government and opposition parties.

I will show that even such variable forms as those controlled by the context may have an ideological basis, much the same as for the variation between the emphasis on Our good actions as opposed to Their bad ones. Indeed, as mental models, contexts by definition inherit some of the ideological orientations of the group with which the speaker identifies (e.g., MP, Conservative, male, white, Western, middle class, representative of a specific region, etc.). Such ideological mental models will, therefore, also control the 'ideological' structures of a discourse. Members of dominant elite groups, for instance, may use specific language forms to derogate dominated minority groups or to highlight their own expertise, credibility, moral standing or status, as well as doing the same for their constituents, their fellow MPs or the media.

Semantics

Members of a parliament engage, then, in parliamentary debates constrained by the context models they have for each specific session of parliament. They do so first by selecting or constructing relevant propositions from the event models, that is, of all they know about an issue, such as the immigration of a specific group of asylum seekers. Of course, given the severe time constraints, only small fractions of event models may be relevant for expression. Generally speaking, each selection of meaning should be a function of the political aims, rules or strategies that define a debate. Among other things, they should enhance the role and prestige of the speakers or their parties. Thus, polarisation of 'content' may be the result. Moreover, both the global and the local meanings of a discourse should be a function of the politico-ideological aim of the debate as a whole, such as legislating on immigration restrictions.

The global topics of parliamentary debates are often stereotypical (see also Reeves, 1983; Van Dijk, 1993a): (a) Some social or political phenomenon has been noted, and will now be defined according to the ideology of the speech participants, usually as a *problem*. Such problem-definitions of the situation may also apply to current policies (or Bills of law) of the government. (b) The (usually negative) *consequences* of such events (or policies) will be 'spelled out' if no appropriate action (policy, legislation) is taken. (c) Government parties or, more critically, opposition parties will positively or negatively deal with current policy and action. After examining the problems associated with such actions in the past, or conversely having blasted the policies of the opponents, they will make proposals and argue for an expedient policy, extolling the beneficiary consequences of new policies or laws or of the actions recommended by an MP. At this stage, other MPs may intervene or interrupt, and participate in the ensuing debate.

The semantic macro-structures (thematic structures) that organise such debates are (mentally) selected from event models providing a speaker's definition of the situation. In principle, these main topics are selected from the high-level propositions of the speaker's models, but in some cases, for contextual (political) reasons, lower level 'details' may be focused on, for example, when these are detrimental to the opponent(s) (the government and/or opposition party, or a particular politician). Such 'biased' definitions of the situation (event models) are based on attitudes and hence are ideological; indeed, the contextually monitored selection of main topics of a debate may also be ideologically controlled. For example, if current or proposed legislation harms asylum seekers, anti-racist speakers may apply their anti-racist ideologies and attitudes to call such legislation 'racist'. This may also apply to apparently irrelevant details, such as with whom an MP has been seen having lunch.

In general, then, ideological topic selection in most discourse, and even more so in parliamentary discourse, will involve the selection of any topic that contributes to the formation of positive models and social representations of the ingroup, and negative ones about the outgroup (that is, the opposition or the outgroup(s) under discussion, for instance, asylum seekers).

An Example

Let us examine a concrete example. On March 5, 1997, a debate on asylum seekers was held in the British House of Commons. The debate was initiated by Mrs. Teresa Gorman (Conservative MP for Billericay, Essex), who sets out to speak about what she defines in her own words as:

> the particular difficulties faced by the London boroughs because of the problems of asylum seekers. (P1)

As expected, a phenomenon (arrival of asylum seekers) is introduced, defined as a problem, and its consequences for Us are highlighted. Note that the ambiguous phrase 'problems of asylum seekers' for her clearly means 'the problems caused by asylum seekers'. Her speech in no way expresses any understanding for the problems *experienced* by asylum seekers.

Other *topics* (macro-propositions) that control her speech are:

a) We should distinguish between genuine and bogus asylum seekers.
b) A recent document found that asylum seekers cost 200 million pounds per year.
c) London ratepayers should not have to pay for this.
d) Many asylum seekers are illegal immigrants.
e) Previous legislation [by the Conservative government] cut benefits and thus halved the number of bogus asylum seekers.
f) Current proposals for legislation [by the Labour opposition] aim to reverse these measures, and will cause massive immigration of asylum seekers.
g) Recent court decisions have resulted in many millions of extra expenditure for London borough councils.
h) Some illegal immigrants cost the taxpayer a lot of money.
i) Some illegal immigrants are involved in crime.
j) Especially the borough of Westminster has to pay a lot for everyday living costs of asylum seekers.
k) Contrary to what is sometimes said, people in Westminster are not very rich.
l) Elderly people should not have to pay for the up keep of illegal asylum seekers.
m) Some bogus asylum seekers are 'playing the system'.
n) This is a national problem, and these costs should be paid nationally.

o) Many people in Westminster have below average incomes.
p) Asylum seekers go through many appeals against deportation.
q) The opposition should be serious and not change current legislation.

Further reduction of these topics would globally define the topics of her speech as:

A) Many asylum seekers are bogus and break the law.
B) We (Westminster) have no money to pay for them.
C) The law that reduced the number of bogus asylum seekers should not be abolished.

It is obvious from this example that the selection of topics is ideological, and controlled by racist attitudes about asylum seekers (from outside of Europe) being bogus, frauds, and criminals. Throughout her speech thus, also at the local level, Mrs. Gorman will enumerate examples and engage in descriptions that are negative about asylum seekers.

However, following the positive ideological self-image, she presents Us first as MPs who should uphold current law, second as caring representatives of a constituency (Westminster), and third, more implicitly as (white) English threatened by massive immigration ('this would open the floodgates again').

Part of the strategy of positive self-presentation is in the form of a number of pity-moves, in which poor elderly (British) people are contrasted with bogus asylum seekers who 'play the system'. The racist nature of her speech (as the next speaker also points out) is exclusively based on a focus on a few negative examples, and the whole orientation towards asylum seekers as causing problems and difficulties, costing lots of money, or entering the country illegally.

Her main Labour opponent, Jeremy Corbyn (Islington South, a seat in London) on the other hand, speaks from the position of an anti-racist, humanitarian ideology. The topics of his speech include:

a) We should think about why people seek asylum.
b) The Geneva Convention guarantees people a safe place.
c) Britain has few asylum seekers compared to other countries, especially outside of Europe.
d) It is an exaggeration to say that we have too many asylum seekers.
e) Asylum seekers, who already have terrible experiences, now also have these in Britain, for instance, gained from the immigration authorities and the police.
f) Seeking asylum is becoming increasingly difficult.
g) Many people, also Conservative MPs, have negative opinions about them.

h) (Replying to interruption) People seek asylum like those who fled from Nazi Germany. It is nonsense not to admit them.

i) Asylum seekers are destitute and should be able to live during appeal processes.

j) We should listen to the terrible experiences of asylum seekers.

k) Many regimes (also 'democratic' ones in Eastern Europe) violate human rights.

l) (After an interruption by Mrs. Gorman claiming that over 90 per cent of asylum seekers are not genuine) Some 'democratic' regimes violate human rights and thus cause people to flee, for example, Kurds from Turkey or people from (the) Ivory Coast.

m) Many people here do not listen to the terrible stories of asylum seekers.

n) In Britain many asylum seekers are put in prisons.

o) Many asylum seekers are badly treated.

p) That there has been a hunger strike by asylum seekers shows that their problems are serious.

q) This is a blemish on the Human Rights record of Britain.

r) Asylum seekers should be helped and respected.

s) The Government's regime creates serious problems for asylum seekers.

t) Many (e.g., Churches) have been protesting against imprisonment of asylum seekers.

u) Why does the British government not protest against human rights violations in many countries?

Obviously, these topics derive from a definition of the situation (a mental model) of asylum seekers in Britain that is ideologically opposed to that of the previous speaker. Instead of presenting asylum seekers in a bad light, their plight is highlighted, and the British authorities and Government are criticised for their policies and actions. The basic ideological and attitudinal propositions expressed here deal with the imperative of international law, with Human Rights principles, and with humanitarian principles to help those in need. The main value expressed here is that of solidarity with the oppressed. The complex attitude that inspired the mental model being conveyed here features propositions about how asylum seekers are tortured and otherwise persecuted by oppressive regimes; how in this country they are badly treated by immigration authorities and police, as well as being put in prison; and how they need financial support to live. The specific model of the current situation features further details about specific countries, and specific events (a hunger strike) and examples of bad treatment.

That is, the selection of topics is largely controlled by an ideologically based model and general social representations organised by anti-racist and humanitarian ideologies, as they are usually associated with a more progressive (Labour) position.

Local Semantics

Ideologies not only monitor the overall, global meaning (or topics) of discourse, but also their more local meanings, as they are actually expressed in, and implied by a debate's words and sentences. Again, in the racist contribution to this debate, we may thus expect to find many concrete examples of negative Other-presentation.

A first move of this strategy is to properly define or *categorise* the relevant sub-groups, namely as 'bogus' asylum seekers and as genuine ones respectively (numbers indicate paragraphs from which the examples are taken):

> There are, of course, asylum seekers and asylum seekers (P2)
> Genuine asylum seekers…[vs.]…economic migrants…benefit seekers on holiday (P2–3)[2]
> alleged asylum seekers (P16)
> Genuine applicants…are frustrated and suffer from delayed applications because of those who are not genuine (P47)

We see in the last example that the negative presentation of 'bogus' asylum seekers is enhanced by emphasising how they hurt genuine ones. This is also part of the strategy of positive self-presentation, because it implies first that 'We' are not simply against (all) asylum seekers, and secondly that We care for the 'genuine' asylum-seekers.

Once the 'bogus' asylum seekers are properly defined, identified and categorised, the speaker will proceed to describe who the bogus asylum seekers are and what they do, thereby focusing first on the problems and difficulties They create, and what they cost Us:

> [difficulties]…because of the problems of asylum seekers (P1)
> the burden of expenditure that those people are causing (P3)
> £200 million a year cost…[that] would again become part of the charge on the British taxpayer (P6)
> The problem of supporting them (P8)
> She cost the British taxpayer £40,000 (P14)
> at the expense of the British public (P14)
> an enormous financial burden on the tax payers (P15)
> [they have to be housed in] expensive accommodation (P16)

Note the important strategy of creating a pitiful image of poor, old ratepayers, in order to emphasise that these cannot share the burden, a populist move which also enhances the problematic nature of immigration, and further contributes to the positive self-image of the speaker as caring for poor old people. Note also the semantic ploy of using presuppositions. That immigrants cause difficulties It is not asserted as a debatable opinion, but simply presupposed as a fact.

The next move in the strategy of negative Other-presentation, appears in the following examples, where the Others are seen to break 'Our' norms, if not the law.

> [A man from Romania] He has never done a stroke of work in his life (P22)
> [they] are milking the social services (P23)
> playing the system...addicted to the social services (P24)
> racket of evading our immigration laws (P7)
> I am sure that many of them are working illegally, and of course work is readily available in big cities (P8)
> She was arrested, of course, for stealing (P14)
> or to do a bit of work on the black economy (P18)

Note that where the speaker refrains from (over)generalising, she uses vague quantifiers such as 'many'. Obviously, the attributes focused on here are consistent with prevailing stereotypes and prejudices about Others (especially non-Europeans): They are lazy, They cheat, They abuse Our system, They work illegally and They steal. Basically, They violate Our laws and morals. That is, racist ideologies articulate evaluations in relation to Our values, and will derogate the Others as fundamentally different from Us: They are inconsistent with whatever We stand for.

On the other hand, positive self-presentation of the (British) ingroup may be observed in the following example, of which the first, positive part introduces a *disclaimer*:

> The Government are keen to help genuine asylum seekers, but... (P7)

Apart from emphasising the good We do for Them, part of this strategy of positive self-presentation is a move that *euphemises* Our less positive actions:

> To discourage the growing number of people from abroad (P2)

Severe restrictions on immigration and institutional harassment of asylum-seekers are thus mitigated by the word 'discourage'.

Another well-known move in the strategy of positive self-presentations is what we may call the move of *apparent empathy*. Here the speaker seems to show positive feelings about a group, but (as is usual with disclaimers) this is followed by '*but*' and a statement that implies something negative about Them:

> I understand that many people want to come to Britain to work, but there is a procedure whereby people can legitimately become part of our community. (P4)

Note that in this example another ideology is emerging, namely that of legalism: Whatever happens, the law must be respected, including the rules and regulations of immigration. This formulation also implies that when the Others break those laws, We can legitimately take action against Them.

To avoid allegations of bias, speakers routinely engage in the well-known *apparent negation* disclaimer, which begins by denying a negative self-characteristic, but continues negatively about Them:

> I did not say that every eastern European's application for asylum in this country was bogus. However... (P46)

The point of analysing these semantic moves is to show that all properties of meaning of a discourse may be affected by some ideological component of event and context models. Positive self-presentation applied to speakers and their groups is a strategy that is based on context models, and aims at managing the impression speakers make on recipients. Thus, avoiding an impression of being racist can only be explained in terms of social representations and ideologies speakers have about racism—representations which may, of course, be inconsistent with those of a critical recipient or analyst, who may see such denials of racism precisely as a marker of racist speech.

Anti-Racist Ideology

Note that what has been argued for local semantics as controlled by racist ideologies, also applies to the influence of anti-racist, humanitarian, and other progressive ideologies. Here, instead of negative Other-presentation, one would expect to find various moves of *positive Other-presentation*, as well as genuine empathy with and sympathy for asylum seekers:

> It is a major step for someone with legitimate fear to seek refuge in exile (P34)
> They are now living [a] life of virtual destitution (P41)
> I wonder whether those who make decisions on refusing people asylum...have ever taken the trouble to sit down and listen to the stories of the people who have

been tortured and abused (P52)
It is difficult for people to talk about torture experiences (P53)
Hon. Members should stop and think for a moment about the circumstances of
those who come to this country seeking asylum (P55)

Similarly, various semantic functional relations are to be expected, such as
the provision of more general examples, for instance, about the terrible plight
of asylum seekers:

[No MP] has been woken up by the police at 4a.m., taken into custody (P34)
If one has grown up in Iraq and has always been completely terrified of anyone
wearing any type of uniform (P35)
areas of oppression (P39)
summarily imprisoned...beaten up etc. (P40)
We should consider the experiences of people who have fled countries (P40).
[in the Ivory Coast] they crushed trade unions and they crushed student
opposition, sending troops into various universities (P50)

Note that these examples are not merely expressions of knowledge about
the horrors asylum seekers have lived through. They are also selected and
formulated as a function of underlying ideologies and social representations,
for instance, critical ones about the police, the military, or oppressive regimes.
Harassment, imprisonment, beatings, and crushed oppositions are part and
parcel of the social representations of oppressive groups or institutions, as
organised by a progressive, anti-racist or humanitarian ideology. Such negative
representations may also be relevant for self-critical discourse about Our
people, institutions or country:

In the United Kingdom there has been a systematic erosion of people's ability to
seek asylum (P36)
The UK, for example, prides itself on its close relationship with Turkey, yet...
(P49)
Almost uniquely among European countries, this country routinely puts in prison
people who seek asylum (P54)
In this country, people who say that get routine abuse from Home Office
Ministers and Conservative Members (P55)
The Government's regime on asylum seekers is creating a serious situation (P57)

Note though that the ideological polarisation between Us and Them in
these anti-racist examples is not between Us-English and Them-Foreigners,
but presupposes a split within the ingroup itself. The speaker is not merely

exercising self-critique, but criticising ideological Others, namely Conservatives. The political implications of such ideologically based accusations are obvious when conveyed by a Labour speaker attacking a previous Conservative speaker.

As is the case in racist negative Other-presentation, also the Conservative Others in anti-racist talk are represented as violating basic rules, norms, principles or values, such as the norm (in fact: a law) that asylum seekers cannot be sent back, the norm not to have close relationships with oppressive regimes (a corollary of a democratic ideology), that innocent people should not be put in prison, that power abuse by the authorities is wrong, and so on. In other words, from another perspective, such anti-racist discourse presents the Conservative Others as violating the Moral Order, specifically all the principles of Human Rights. In the following examples, several of these principles are formulated even more explicitly:

> I suggest that he [the MP] start to think more seriously about human rights issues (P38)
> [on benefit rights] Not to do so is a gross abuse of individual human rights (P39)
> democracy does not always follow multi-party elections (P49)
> Is that how a democratic Government should behave? (P50)
> Attitudes towards asylum seekers need to be changed (P56)
> Routine imprisonment should end (P56)
> I hope that we shall recognise that we should have a slightly more humane approach towards asylum seekers in this country (P57)
> Europe must stop its xenophobic attitude towards those who seek a place of safety here and adopt a more humane approach (P58)
> Where is the outright condemnation from the Government of the denial of human rights in...It seem[s] more interested in trade and selling arms to those regimes than in defending human rights (P59)

Although specifically applied to the present, British, situation, these are examples that could easily be drawn, almost directly, from anti-racist and democratic social representations and ideologies. That is, they are generic statements, and not specific ones based on unique personal mental models. Apart from being critical statements, these examples are, at the same time, moral imperatives and exhortations. Finally, such critique may, of course, explicitly address the Others in terms of racist accusations:

> There also has been a vindictiveness against asylum seekers—it has been parroted in this debate by some Conservative Members—which has been promoted by some newspapers, particularly the Daily Mail (P36)

The Hon. Lady seems to have moved on a bit from the cant and prejudice that she produced in her earlier speech.

Rhetoric

What is true for semantics also holds for 'rhetorical' semantic figures. Generally, emphasising and de-emphasising meanings are rhetorical operations conventionalised as figures of speech such as metaphor, hyperbole, euphemism, and the like. It is, then, not surprising that the choice of such semantic figures of speech is also controlled by underlying ideological models, social representations, and ideologies.

Thus, in order to emphasise the threat of immigration, the speaker will hyperbolically refer to opening the floodgates (P6). Similarly, the negative characteristics attributed to the Others may be enhanced by specific *metaphors*, such as:

> they are milking not only the taxpayers but the caring services (P23)
> They are simply parasites (P24)

Especially the implicit comparison of outgroups with threatening or disgusting animals, like parasites in the last example, is a standard meta-phorical way to derogate minorities, and was also a familiar ploy in Nazi propaganda about the Jews.

Such metaphors are not merely discursive, rhetorically persuasive ways of expressing properties of mental models. They may be associated more deeply with thought and judgment. If minorities or Others are thus associated with properties of animals, we may assume that also the social representations about minorities are connected to representations of animals. This may imply that in racist ideologies, the Others are basically also represented as less human, so that attitudes and specific models about minorities will tend to be associated with the appropriate animals: If asylum seekers are seen as a threat, they may be thought of in terms of threatening animals, and if they are seen as 'living off us', then parasitic animals may be the appropriate cognitive association. In other words, ideologies may influence the very thought processes that underlie discourse.

Another well-known rhetorical ploy found in discourse on immigrants and minorities is the *numbers game*: the use of figures to speculate about the number of new people entering the country. Often used by the press, its further rhetorical function is usually the same as that of hyperbole, i.e., by emphasising the numbers of immigrants (or what they cost) their threatening or problematic nature may be enhanced:

> There are about 2000 families...the cost is estimated to be 2 million a year...but for London as a whole...£140 million a year (P10).
> Over 90 per cent of people who claim asylum turn out not to be genuine (P47)

In sum, throughout the discourse, and at all levels, structures, strategies and moves are all geared towards the most effective expression and persuasive communication of ideologically based mental models and social representations. Whatever else may be said, the overall strategy is to present the Others, or their arrival and immigration, in a negative light.

The choice of these negative characteristics may be ad hoc, and tied to a unique model, but often it is controlled by the contents of ideological stereotypes, prejudices and ideologies. The same is true for the representation of Us, or the relation between Us and Them. For instance, also in this speech, We (or at least some of Us) are represented as victims of the asylum seekers, and more generally, if the 'flood' of asylum seekers does not threaten to drown us, they are, at the very least, a financial burden to us.

All these meanings derive from socially shared representations about minorities and immigrants, and are not merely the unique, contextually specific constructions of an individual speaker. And since many recipients share these representations, such discourse will also be eminently recognisable, and thus very likely to coincide with and the ethnic prejudices and ideologies that recipients may already have, or otherwise persuasively contribute to their development.

The same is true, *mutatis mutandis*, for the representation of the Others (the Conservatives) in dissident, anti-racist text and talk. Violating human rights and the moral order will be similarly emphasised. In the following concrete example, metaphor, hyperbole, and comparison are used to emphasize the negative actions and policies of the Conservative Government:

> Britain has among the smallest number of asylum seekers of any European country (P33)
> Many people sought asylum from Nazi Germany (P38)
> History shows that unless we stand up for human rights (P59)

Argumentation

Of the many properties of parliamentary discourse, argumentation structures are paramount. That ideological positions are defended and attacked can be seen in the discursive moves which are made, some of which have already been examined above in terms of semantic or rhetorical structures. Globally, the Conservative argument is that the uncontrolled immigration of the many 'bogus' asylum seekers places a financial burden on the community, and that therefore the current restrictions should remain in place. Conversely, the Labour argument is that international legal, and moral imperatives do not allow us to prohibit asylum seekers to enter the country, and that therefore the restrictive law should be changed.

These global arguments and conclusions are supported, more locally, by a host of specific arguments. These provide, for example, evidence that many asylum seekers are indeed 'bogus', abuse the system, and break the law, as well as why (London) councils cannot bear the financial burden, or, conversely, that those refugees applying for asylum are doing so legitimately. Similarly, restrictions on immigration are judged untenable on account of basic moral principles of human rights, as well as international law. Where the Conservative argument makes a rational appeal to practical consequences, lack of money, as well as more principled arguments that 'our' poor and elderly should not bear the brunt of the cost of taking care of asylum seekers. Again, these arguments all derive from general social representations of asylum seekers, oppressive regimes, the elderly, and so on.

More specifically, we find *argumentational moves*, characteristic of discussions about immigration, on both sides of the debate (sometimes critically categorised as fallacies). Thus, both main speakers will have recourse to arguing by authority. The Labour speaker supports his argument with recourse to the moral authority of, e.g., Amnesty or the Churches:

the opportunity to read the papers from Amnesty International or from Helsinki Watch (P42)
The Churches Commission for Racial Justice... (P58)

On the other hand, the Conservative speaker refers to the conclusions of a bipartisan (and hence not-partisan) committee that established the costs of receiving asylum seekers.

Similarly, both speakers will make *appeals to the emotions* of the recipients by starkly emphasising the situation of those they speak for, viz., the elderly, poor tax payers, and asylum seekers, respectively:

Many of these people live in old-style housing...They are on modest incomes. Many of them are elderly...with a little pension from their work. They pay their full rent and for all their own expenses (P21)
I wonder whether those who make decisions on refusing people asylum...have ever taken the trouble to sit down and listen to the stories of the people who have been tortured and abused (P52)

A typical fallacy of racist argumentation is to generalise from single examples, as also the Conservative speaker does when she gives concrete examples in order to claim or imply that asylum seekers are lazy, or criminal:

> [A man from Romania] He has never done a stroke of work in his life (P22)
> She was arrested, of course, for stealing (P14)
> Similarly, racist discourse will attribute negative characteristics to Others, typically by arguing from impressions and not evidence:
> I am sure that many of them are working illegally, and of course work is readily available in big cities (P8)

Conversely, the anti-racist speaker will typically resort to the *ad hominem* argument of accusing the conservative speaker of racism.

These few examples of argumentational moves (there are many others not dealt with here), also show that the nature of argumentation is ideologically controlled. It is true that, whatever the ideological position of speakers they may have recourse to the same types of moves and strategies. Both sides of a debate may exaggerate, use populist arguments, appeal to emotions, or invoke authorities when arguing. In that respect, argumentation, just like other discourse structures, is ideologically neutral. However, the specific contents being chosen for arguments and conclusions are obviously ideologically based, for example when the Conservative speaker sets out to prove that asylum seekers break the law and our norms, or when she argues that poor 'ratepayers' should not have to pay for 'able' asylum seekers.

On the other hand, there are also argumentational strategies and moves that, as such, appear to be more typical (though seldom exclusively so) of conservative, progressive, racist or anti-racist speakers. Racist discourse typically engages in unwarranted generalisations from individual negative examples of an immigrant breaking the law or violating Our norms. Thus, a fallacy is the argumentational counterpart of the 'cognitive' fallacy of generalising from models to social representations, as is the case for prejudice formation. Conversely, anti-racist discourse may resort to *ad hominem* arguments, attacking speakers as racists instead of arguing against their positions.

Conclusions

This paper has explored some of the relations between discourse, racism, and ideology. Within the framework of a new theory of ideology, I have argued that ideologies should be properly analysed in terms of social cognition, and may be defined as the basic structures which organise the social representations of a group. In this respect, ideologies differ from the general, culturally-shared common ground of undisputed knowledge and attitudes. Ideologies may be represented in terms of ingroup self-schemata, featuring categories that define the basic characteristics of a social group, such as their membership criteria, activities, goals, norms, values, relations to specific other groups, and resources. Ideologies, and the social representations organised by them, may become specific in mental models of concrete events and situations, which in turn are the basis of discourse and other social practices.

Racism has often been defined in terms of (racist) ideologies. However, I argued here that this would be a reduction of the more complex notion of racism as a system of social inequality and dominance. This system has both a mental-level of analysis and reproduction, featuring racist ideologies and social representations of a group, as well as a social-level of analysis, featuring everyday discriminatory interaction and discourse, on the one hand, and group relations and institutions, on the other. As is the case for other ideologies, also racist ideologies are largely (though not uniquely) reproduced by text and talk.

These ideas were applied in a succinct analysis of a debate in the British House of Commons, in order to show that many properties of such political discourse are controlled by underlying ideological models and social representations. I emphasised, though, that this is only the case in a particular context, where I defined 'context' as a mental model of the discursively relevant properties of the communicative situation. For instance, the context here defined the nature and the aims within the specific genre of a parliamentary debate, the intentions of the speakers, and ultimately the political functions of the turn-taking, structures, meanings and other characteristics of the debate.

Ideological positioning occurred at all levels of discourse, for instance, in the choice of topics, local meanings, disclaimers, implications and presuppositions, descriptions, metaphors, hyperbole, and argumentation. The overall strategy in the speech of racist speakers is to focus on the negative characteristics of the Others, and to represent Us as the victims of these Others. Anti-racist discourse on the other hand, will focus on the plight of the asylum seekers, and on fundamental norms, laws and principles of human rights, and hence has a basically moral slant. Thus, we see how fundamental prejudices occur in racist discourse, in topics as well as in other structures, about non-European immigrants as being lazy, criminal, cheating, untrustworthy, etc., and can be marshaled to argue against less severe immigration law. Anti-racist speakers on the other hand, make extensive use of humanitarian, human rights ideologies, operate with positive attitudes about asylum seekers, and negative ones about conservatives, as may be expected.

My main point was thus, to show what racist ideologies are and how they may be expressed in discourses of social and political interaction, and how racist ideologies may thus be propagated and reproduced in society.

Notes

1   Ruth Wodak is Professor of Applied Linguistics at the University of Vienna.

2   All omissions and additions to the text of each MP's speech are mine. The text is from Hansard. The numbering given at the end of each line is my own.

References

Barker, M. (1981), *The New Racism*, London, Junction Books.
Dovidio, J.F. and Gaertner, S.L. (eds) (1986), *Prejudice, Discrimination, and Racism*, Orlando, FL. Academic Press.
Eagleton, T. (1991), *Ideology. An Introduction*, London, Verso.
Essed, P. (1991), *Understanding Everyday Racism: An Interdisciplinary Theory*, Newbury Park, Sage.
Fairclough, N. (1995), *Critical Discourse Analysis. The Critical Study of Language*, London, Longman.
Fairclough, N.L. and Wodak, R. (1997), 'Critical Discourse Analysis', in T.A. Van Dijk (ed.), *Discourse Studies. A Multidisciplinary Introduction. Vol. 2, Discourse as Social Interaction* (pp. 258–284), London, Sage.
Farr, R.M. and Moscovici, S. (eds) (1984), *Social Representations*, Cambridge, Cambridge University Press.
Feagin, J.R. and Sikes, M.P. (1994), *Living with Racism. The Black Middle-Class Experience*, Boston, MA, Beacon Press.
Fiske, S.T. and Taylor, S.E. (1991), *Social Cognition*, New York, McGraw-Hill.
Fraser, C. and Gaskell, G. (eds) (1990), *The Social Psychological Study Of Widespread Beliefs*, Oxford/New York, Clarendon Press/Oxford University Press.
Guillaumin, C. (1973), *L'idéologie raciste. Genèse et langage actuel* (Racist ideology. Genesis and actual language), The Hague, Mouton.
Hargreaves, A.G. and Leaman, J. (eds) (1995), *Racism, Ethnicity, and Politics in Contemporary Europe*, Aldershot, Edward Elgar.
Jäger, S. (1992), *BrandSätze. Rassismus im Alltag* ('Brandsätze'—Inflammatory Sentences/Firebombs. Racism in everyday life), DISS-Studien, Duisburg, DISS.
Jäger, S., et al. (1998), *Der Spuk ist nicht vorbei. Volkisch-nationalistische Ideologeme im offentlichen Diskurs der Gegenwart* [The Ghost hasn't gone. Volkisch-nationalist ideologemes in contemporary public discourse], Duisburg: DISS.Johnson-Laird, P.N. (1983), *Mental Models: Towards a Cognitive Science of Language, Inference and Consciousness*, Cambridge (New York), Cambridge University Press.
Larraín, J. (1979), *The Concept of Ideology*, Athens, University of Georgia Press.
Miles, R. (1989), *Racism*, London/New York, Routledge.
Oakhill, J. and Garnham, A. (eds), (1996), *Mental Models in Cognitive Science. Essays in Honour of Phil Johnson-Laird*, Hove (Sussex), Psychology Press.

Omi, M. and Winant, H. (1994), *Racial Formation in the United States. From the 1960s to the 1990s,* London, Routledge.

Reeves, F. (1983), *British Racial Discourse. A Study of British Political Discourse about Race and Race-Related Matters,* Cambridge, Cambridge University Press.

Seliger, M. (1976), *Ideology and Politics,* London, Allen & Unwin.

Solomos, J. and Wrench, J. (eds) (1993), *Racism and Migration in Western Europe,* Oxford, Berg.

Spears, R., Oakes, P.J., Ellemers, N. and Haslam, S.A. (eds) (1997), *The Social Psychology of Stereotyping and Group Life,* Oxford, Blackwell.

Van Dijk, T.A. (1984), *Prejudice in Discourse: An Analysis of Ethnic Prejudice in Cognition and Conversation,* Amsterdam/Philadelphia, J. Benjamins Co.

Van Dijk, T.A. (1987), *Communicating Racism: Ethnic Prejudice in Thought and Talk,* Newbury Park, CA, Sage.

Van Dijk, T.A. (1991), *Racism and the Press,* London/New York, Routledge.

Van Dijk, T.A. (1993a), *Elite Discourse and Racism,* Newbury Park, CA, Sage.

Van Dijk, T.A. (1993b), 'Principles of Critical Discourse Analysis', *Discourse and Society,* vol. 4, no. 2, pp. 249–83.

Van Dijk, T.A. (1998a), *Ideology. A Multidisciplinary Study,* London, Sage.

Van Dijk, T.A. (1998b), 'Towards a Theory of Context and Experience Models in Discourse Processing', in H. Van Oostendorp and S. Goldman (eds), *The Construction of Mental Models during Reading,* Hillsdale, NJ, Erlbaum.

Van Dijk, T.A. and Kintsch, W. (1983), *Strategies of Discourse Comprehension,* New York, Academic Press.

Wellman, D.T. (1993), *Portraits of White Racism,* Cambridge, Cambridge University Press.

Wetherell, M. and Potter, J. (1992), *Mapping the Language of Racism: Discourse and the Legitimation of Exploitation,* New York, Harvester-Wheatsheaf.

Wodak, R., Nowak, P., Pelikan, J., Gruber, H., de Cillia, R. and Mitten, R. (1990), *"Wir sind alle unschuldige Täter". Diskurshistorische Studien zum Nachkriegsantisemitismus* ("We are all innocent perpetrators": historical discourse studies in postwar anti-Semitism), Frankfurt/Main, Suhrkamp.

Yeboah, S.K. (1988), *The Ideology of Racism,* London, England, Hansib.

6 Giving Foreigners the Vote: Ethnocentrism in Dutch and Belgian Political Debates

DIRK JACOBS

Over the last decade political sociologists have paid increasing attention to the theoretical and empirical links between migration, the dynamics of citizenship, and processes of inclusion and exclusion (see Hammar, 1990; Brubaker, 1992; Bauböck, 1994; Soysal, 1994; Martiniello, 1995; Oommen, 1997; Favell, 1998). Cross-national comparison has been central to all these studies. At first sight, such comparative research appears a relatively easy endeavour—one merely has to assess to what extent the relevant characteristics and dynamics of (at least two) countries are divergent or similar. However, *in practice*, it usually turns out to be a much more difficult task, one confronting the researcher with a substantial number of theoretical and methodological problems. The complexity increases if, *at the same time*, the aim is to compare the importance of racism or ethnocentrism in political debates and policy concerning migrants across these countries. I will discuss some of the potential pitfalls of such an undertaking using a number of 'classic' approaches in the area of political citizenship. To do so I will examine the parliamentary debates on enfranchisement of foreign residents in the Netherlands and Belgium during the 1980s, focusing, necessarily, on nitty-gritty politics and on related processes of polarisation. Finally, I will draw attention to the importance of colonial history and its influence on conceptions of national identity and state-citizenship in the Netherlands and Belgium.

Enfranchisement at the Municipal Level

The Constitution of Belgium and the Netherlands stipulates that, as a rule, voting rights are linked to nationality. Therefore, the definition of the 'nation' in nationality legislation determines who can participate in the system of representative democracy and who cannot. Those categorised as 'foreign', as non-nationals, may not vote. This mechanism raises a fundamental problem. Indeed, once the gap between 'the people' (as a legally bounded nation) and 'the population' (all inhabitants regardless of legal status) widens numerically—due to, for example, immigration—the abstract narrative of popular sovereignty becomes an increasingly unstable one upon which to base a state's existence. In 1970, 7.2 per cent of the Belgian population did not possess Belgian nationality. In 1995, this figure was 9.1 per cent. In the Netherlands 1.6 per cent of the Dutch population were non-nationals in 1970, a figure which had increased to 4.9 per cent by 1995. No wonder, then, that political participation of foreign residents has been the subject of (parliamentary) debate in these countries since the early 1970s. This debate is now an unavoidable one for countries all over Europe, where non-nationals form a substantial part of the population. All the more so considering the centrality of modern democratic ideologies to the Western European political landscape.

Understanding this debate, its outcomes, and the importance racism and ethnocentrism have had in shaping policy in the different nation-states, is an intriguing task. Take the Netherlands and Belgium, two countries with almost similar nationality legislation, yet in the Netherlands non-national residents gained the vote at the municipal level in 1985, while this was impossible in Belgium until 1998.[1] How can we explain this difference? These seem to be simple research questions. But appearances can be deceptive. How should we assess the importance of ethnocentrism in the debate and its policy outcome. But appearances can be deceptive.

Critical Discourse Analysis?

If one starts by defining the lack of voting rights for non-national residents on all levels as a form of (latent) racism—as Rath asserts Castenmiller and Brants do (Rath, 1990, p. 140)—then one can easily illustrate how this latent racism (and ethnocentrism) is being reproduced at the level of debate. Tracing several discursive mechanisms used to oppose the enfranchisement of non-national residents is not difficult. There are abundant examples of dubious statements on foreigners and multiculturalism expressing racist—or at least xenophobic and ethnocentric—tenets in defence of the principle of membership. But what can we learn from this? One would be able to show that there are some discursive mechanisms which *possibly* contribute to the reproduction of a system of racism (or white hegemony or ethnocentrism). However, taking into account the large number of studies on the discursive reproduction of racism and ethnocentrism (see Van Dijk, 1993; Ter Wal, 1998), this would be old news at best. Moreover, 'all' that could be achieved would be to denounce the whole debate as reproducing a system of citizenship reliant on domestic closure. In doing so, one would be forced to focus on stable elements over the course of the debate, disregarding fluctuations and changes. Formulating a meaningful answer to the research question using critical discourse analysis (CDA) becomes quite difficult in these circumstances. One could answer the question of why state-citizenship is used as the basic criterion for (national) voting rights in the Netherlands and Belgium. If allegiance to the principle of membership is to be seen as a form of latent or disguised elite-racism, one can trace and denounce patterns thereof in both countries. It becomes more complicated, however, to give an answer for why it was possible to enfranchise non-national residents at the municipal level in the Netherlands in the 1980s while this was impossible in Belgium. One would then have to accept the possibility that there are gradations of elite-racism, that there is less (or a more moderate form of) elite-racism in the Netherlands than in Belgium and that this is what explains differences in policy outcome. Or, that there is elite-racism in the parliamentary debate on national voting rights in the Netherlands, but not in the debate on municipal enfranchisement. The dominant ideology thesis (see Abercrombie, Hill and Turner, 1980), a central tenet of most forms of CDA, especially in the work of Van Dijk, does not, however, allow such variations at the level of theory.[2] At best, in the Brubaker, R. (1992) framework of Van Dijk, local enfranchisement of non-national residents could be seen as an alternative strategy which *appears* to tackle the dominant framework but in fact just strengthens hegemony. In other words, whatever the decision on municipal voting rights, elite-racism would remain the underlying mechanism along with ethnocentrism and white hegemony. This, however, would still not explain why different choices were made in the Netherlands and Belgium on the issue of local franchise. Perhaps Yasemin Soysal's (1994) theoretical framework on post-national membership can help us out here.

Post-National Membership?

Post-war European states have been increasingly granting non-national residents the same social, economic, and civic rights to which their citizens are entitled. Hammar (1990) and Brubaker (1990) have depicted these changes as an expansion of the scope of citizenship on a territorial basis: in entitlement to rights, the principle of residence has augmented the principle of membership. As a result, the legal status of non-national residents and nationals has become increasingly similar all over Europe. Heisler and Heisler (1991) have suggested this process is the result of the developing welfare state's internal logic of expansion; social and economic rights have been granted to non-nationals following the development of the welfare system as a universalistic system redistributing social goods (within territorial boundaries). Indeed, in order for the welfare state to be successful as a means towards social stability, it must treat every inhabitant equally regardless of nationality.

However, according to political sociologist Yasemin Soysal (1994) the transformation of citizenship has been of a much more profound nature than a merely territorial expansion. She rejects those explanations attributing the changes in citizenship law to the emergence of the welfare apparatuses. In her opinion 'there is nothing inherent about the logic of the welfare state that would dictate the incorporation of foreigners into its system of privileges' (Soysal, 1994, p. 138). Instead, she claims the extension of rights to migrants is the result of the more profound rise of the narrative of universal personhood. In her opinion universal human rights have over the years 'replaced' national rights, as the basis of legitimacy for individual rights in the post-war era. Soysal claims that justifications for the state's obligations to foreigners have moved beyond the scope of the nation-state itself (Soysal, 1994, p. 142). 'Personhood' has become a central legitimating category over 'nationhood'. She accounts for this discursive revolution by referring to two interrelated lines of historical development. On the one hand there has been increasing globalisation and an emergence of transnational political structures which has complicated nation-state sovereignty and jurisdiction (Soysal, 1994, p. 144). While, on the other hand, there has been the emergence of universalistic rules and conceptions, formalised and legitimated by a multitude of international codes and laws, which have ascribed universal rights to individuals regardless of their nationality (Soysal, 1994, p. 145). In sum, citizenship has obtained a totally new 'post-national' character. Soysal stresses this 'post-national citizenship confers upon every person the right and duty of participation in the authority structures and public life of a polity, regardless of their historical and cultural ties to that community' (Soysal, 1994, p. 3).

According to Soysal, the rise of this post-national narrative led to the rapid extension of rights to migrants. Foreign residents are thus increasingly granted access to civil, social, economic and political rights. The acquisition of political rights is, however, somewhat more problematic. Reversing the Marshallian sequence, political rights are only given to non-national residents after civil and social rights have been granted. Furthermore, only local voting rights are extended to non-nationals. Soysal claims that this is due to the symbolic meaning which the right to vote carries in terms of popular sovereignty and the codification of political rights at a time when the nation-state was at its ideological apex (Soysal, 1994, p. 131). Nevertheless, she concludes that all over Western Europe 'rights, participation and representation in a polity, are increasingly matters beyond the vocabulary of national citizenship' (Soysal, 1994, p. 165). She is eager to claim that 'in a world within which rights, and identities as rights, derive their legitimacy from discourses of universalistic personhood, the limits of nationness, or of national citizenship, for that matter, become inventively irrelevant' (1994, p. 162). In view of this conclusion it seems that Soysal relies on the inevitability of voting rights being granted to migrants in due time (Klopp, 1995, p. 781). But can one claim, as Soysal (1996, p. 21) does, that 'rights, participation and representation in a polity, are increasingly matters beyond the vocabulary of citizenship'? And does this perspective help us to compare different policies in different countries and to compare the importance of ethnocentrism in the debates leading to these policies?

At first glance one could answer yes to these questions. Indeed, one could examine to what extent the universalistic, post-national narrative is now embedded in several countries, and in what way this has been obstructed (or not) by the phenomenon of ethnocentrism in political debates. Hypothetically ethnocentrism would be weaker in Dutch and stronger in Belgian politics, thus accounting for the different degree of development and importance of the post-national narrative. This narrative would be stronger in the Netherlands, thus accounting for local enfranchisement of non-national residents. However, what is problematic in Soysal's model is that it does not give us a framework with which to understand and analyse precisely *how* this works. Her model does not help us assess the timing of the development of the post-national model, nor does it take public debate and politics sufficiently into account to be able to explain policy change. In addition, national frameworks and traditions seem to be of little importance in her view of the development of post-national membership. But even leaving aside the problem of conceptual weakness on the link between the post-national narrative and actual policy-development, one should stress that the empirical data do not support Soysal's model either. Focusing on the issue of voting rights alone, her perspective cannot help us to understand, in a straightforward way, why there is local, but not national, enfranchisement in the Netherlands and neither of these (yet) in Belgium. In earlier work (Jacobs, 1997) I have shown that local enfranchisement of non-national residents in the Netherlands has not been the result of the rise of the post-national narrative. With the introduction of municipal enfranchisement of non-nationals the principle of state-citizenship has indeed been partly replaced by the principle of residence, but this happened in such a way that the vocabulary of the nation-state was not fundamentally challenged—rather it was strengthened.

Cultural Idioms of Nationhood?

With regard to the aforementioned importance of national frameworks and traditions, the American sociologist Rogers Brubaker (1992) takes a totally different perspective to Soysal in his book *Citizenship and Nationhood in France and Germany*. Brubaker starts from the postulate that each country has its own particular 'cultural idioms', 'national styles of thought', on nationhood and citizenship. These idioms have historical roots and deeply structure the debate on immigration and integration policy. As such, they actually make the existence of a post-national discourse *à la Soysal* unthinkable. Brubaker focused on France and Germany. He states that in France the nation has been seen as unified around a common political project and future since the revolution of 1789. In Germany, Brubaker contends, the nation has always been seen as a unity of common descent and culture. He suggests that these idealistic views on nationhood were brought into the respective citizenship laws and reproduce themselves constantly as crucial rhetorical devices in any debate on citizenship and integration. As such, they structure the current debates on incorporation of migrants.

It should be noted that Brubaker's approach in studying citizenship and nationhood can be criticised as suffering from a teleological imperative. He starts with the observation that France and Germany have totally different laws on nationality and then tries to trace the historical reasons for this difference. This in my opinion could lead to a bias in which the importance of contingency is *ab initio* excluded and stereotypical ideas on countries are fostered. This being said, Brubaker's model does, however, seem to allow us to understand the existence of cross-national differences in policy; basic principles of immigration policy can be seen as the result of cultural idioms. But does his approach allow easy comparisons of particular differences in the debates leading to these policies? I would argue that it does not. To stick to France and Germany, the framework of cultural idioms in itself cannot help us to explain the disenfranchisement of migrants in both countries. Indeed, in both these countries with, according to Brubaker, completely different cultural idioms, foreigners do not, in principle, hold voting rights.

But let us suppose, for the sake of argument, that the framework of cultural idioms can be used to understand the dynamics of debate on the political rights of migrants, accepting at the same time that it cannot directly explain policy outcomes. Indeed, one could claim that the disenfranchisement of foreigners is 'normal' for all nation-states regardless of their cultural idiom, precisely because this would be one of the basic tenets of any nation-state's ideological base. Perhaps, then, one should accept that there is always a reluctance towards enfranchisement to start with. One could even accept that this would not have to completely do away with the explanatory value of cultural idioms in studying political rights of non-residents. Plausibly, some cultural idioms leave more options open for partial enfranchisement of non-residents than others. This being said, it could well be just a 'coincidence' that the very different cultural idioms of both France and Germany do not allow partial enfranchisement. And, that this does not necessarily have to hold for the cultural idioms of other countries.

Returning to the Netherlands and Belgium, it could well be that the Dutch cultural idiom *did* and Belgian cultural idiom *did not* support partial enfranchisement. Some have, indeed, claimed that enfranchisement of non-national residents in the Netherlands is due to a typical Dutch cultural idiom. In this scenario the Netherlands is and always has been a 'tolerant' country, combining a system of pillarisation with openness for other communities (see Zahn, 1989; Van Thijn, 1997). Tolerance, in this story, has been the main characteristic of Dutch culture right back to the seventeenth century. Precisely this cultural idiom is what made local enfranchisement of non-national residents possible (Hisschemöller, 1988, p. 43). Belgium, in contrast, has always had a very intolerant political culture, distrustful of other communities and limiting itself to rigid pillarisation and political patronage. Additionally, the multi-national character of the state limits any possibilities for the constituent cultures to reach a consensus on the issue of integration of foreigners. Hence, enfranchisement of non-nationals is unthinkable. These contrasting grand narratives are fashionable and intriguing, tempting even, to use as explanations for the different policy responses. One could also assess to what extent the cultural idioms and political cultures are ethnocentric in character. But once again, we are easily confronted with a potential teleological pitfall if we adopt such a perspective. Claiming that a particular policy is the result of a noble tradition or a malign cultural idiom is one thing, providing clear empirical evidence for a causal link between a (postulated) political-cultural tradition and policy outcomes is a completely different story. Indeed, empirical analysis of the argumentation and discourses used in the parliamentary debates on voting rights in the Netherlands and Belgium turns out to lead to the conclusion that the dynamics of the debates are in fact very similar in both countries. Rhetorical references to the principle of tolerance clearly appear more frequently in Dutch than in Belgian debates. But the concept of tolerance never holds pole position in the argumentations used by the politicians of either country. In addition, there is no clear pattern demonstrating that the *topos* of tolerance (or the acceptance of cultural diversity) is any more prevalent as a basic conceptual source of argumentation in the Netherlands than in Belgium. In practice, one would have to reconstruct the argumentation, disregarding the obvious similarities and emphasising the differences, in order for them to appear the result of clear-cut tolerant or intolerant political-cultural traditions. In sum, the idea of stable cultural idioms is empirically untenable and mainly seems to reproduce stereotypes, at least if it is used in rigidly, reducing actual discussions to political cultures.

Bringing Debate and Politics Back into the Limelight

In a nutshell, the fundamental problem of the approaches of Soysal and Brubaker is that they rely on the assumption that clear-cut patterns of thought, debate, and argumentation are translated directly into policy outcomes. It is indeed tempting to start off from the premise that there is one stable and dominant idiom or framework for thought in every historical phase and for every typology of countries (as Soysal and Brubaker have done). In my opinion, one must, however, hold in mind that dominance is in essence an unstable fact, which has to be constantly reproduced in political debate. At certain stages one idiom or framework can indeed be evidently dominant. One should take care, however, not to assume *a priori* that this gives enough reason to think the same idiom or framework will continue to be, or has been, dominant before as well. In general, one talks about 'dominance' to argue that there often are long term patterns at work even though, at some minor intermediary stages, there appears to be a rupture in the short term. This generates the analytical reflex to temporarily disregard exceptional situations which do not fit into the dominant framework. If this happens systematically, one is confronted with an analytical bias. Much work using the theoretical-interpretative concept of 'dominance' unknowingly feed this bias. In the end, these perspectives 'merely' find what they were looking for, thus reproducing stereotypes or prejudices. The same pitfall is present when falling back on most forms of CDA. Critical discourse analysis often begins with the theoretical postulate that the social order is sustained by the discursive reproduction of dominant ideologies which win the top-down consent or acquiescence of many. It is tempting to postulate the existence of a dominant ideology (e.g., racism, white hegemony) *a priori* and to then trace, unveil and denounce 'signs' of the 'reproduction' of ideological domination in discursive activities. The problem is, however, that this can only render 'proof' in a circular manner that there is such a thing as a dominant ideology in 'reality' to begin with. This sometimes leads to analytical myopia, a strong fixation on processes of reproduction coupled with a limitation to the study of stability. Indeed, the priority lies in discovering and denouncing the dominant ideology otherwise haunting society as a mysterious ghost.

To avoid these problems, I use (Jacobs, 1998a) a different research strategy to that common to many current forms of CDA (such as in Van Dijk, 1993). In addition, I have tried to do more than trace just one dominant discourse in debate or reconstruct one typology of policy formation, as in the approaches looking at post-national membership (Soysal, 1994) or cultural idioms (Brubaker, 1992). For theoretical and methodological reasons, I deliberately chose not to search for one dominant ideology which 'shapes' and 'structures' the debate (and then assess to what extent it is racist or ethnocentric). What I did look into was the role which different frames (discourses³)—representing and constructing reality—have played over time in the debate, and have tried to hint at the explanation for these fluctuations. In doing so, I have presumed that no single ideology (as a worldview) 'controls' the debate, but that we are in fact confronted with an ongoing struggle between different ideologies (both as political narratives and worldviews) articulated to various degrees in public statements. The debate is thus seen as a struggle between a range of discourses, and policy outcomes are seen as the result of coalitions made between the political actors using the same or a similar set of discourses (see Hajer, 1993, p. 45; Rose and Miller, 1992, p. 175). Policy is then the result of the creation of networks (of politicians) around discourses which make certain phenomena understandable in a similar language and logic, constructing goals and fate in a similar direction (Rose and Miller, 1992, p. 184). In other words, by starting with the premise that there are different discourses which should be traced and analysed, actual debate and politics are brought back into the analysis. In CDA and the approaches of Soysal and Brubaker, actual debate and politics often seem to be of no real significance. I see this as a serious flaw and that, far from being neglected, the nitty-gritty of politics (related to electoral competition) should be a key topic for study. I therefore opted for an inductive research strategy. It is only once the dynamics of (the discourses in) the debate can be charted in this way, that the importance of racism and ethnocentrism can be assessed.

To empirically trace the discourses used in the debate, I used the grounded theory method (Glaser and Strauss, 1967; Strauss and Corbin, 1990) as a procedure for qualitative text analysis, combined with the insights of linguistic pragmatics (Blommaert and Verschueren, 1994). The corpus of texts was systematically analysed on two levels: the layer of explicit argumentation was charted using the grounded theory method, while the implicit layer (linguistic transformations) was analysed using the discourse analysis toolkit of linguistic pragmatics. The argumentation clusters (of statements) found with this double-layered analysis are the discourses. I postulated that a particular discourse is used by a politician or a political faction to enforce a specific standpoint on the issue being discussed. This normally happens in order to influence policy in accordance with their own political opinions, although one should not rule out that there can also be more pragmatic-electoral motives involved—sometimes a politician merely wants to improve his or her profile within the electorate, hoping to gain or retain support from certain groups of voters. However, in order to study the dynamics of the debate, it is far more important to study the importance and significance of a discourse than to focus on intentions—which are not traceable. One can state that the importance of a discourse depends on the extent to which a politician can gain support within the parliamentary arena for a specific perspective on reality. In the Dutch and Belgian cases, no single political faction—due to the lack of a majority—is able to dominate parliament, and the different parties must therefore cooperate and attune their respective discourses. In such a situation, the importance of a discourse is assessed by looking at the way in which the political actors try to build discourse coalitions (Hajer, 1993). What matters here is that these coalitions consist of a set of actors who share and defend (or seem to do so) the same social construct(s) as the basis for coordination of discursive elements in one seemingly coherent narrative. At moments of decision making, policy (changes) will, of course, be determined by the narrative in which the discourse-coalition's central political actors are participating at that moment. Since enfranchisement necessitates a constitutional amendment, the creation of a (exceptionally) broad consensus between left and right wing parties is unavoidable. It should be noted that all political actors, from both sides, must be willing and able to combine their political interests and ideological narratives into one story line favouring the enfranchisement of non-national residents.

When examining the data, the grounded theory method led, somewhat surprisingly, to the observation that both the Dutch and Belgian debates could be best reconstructed in a two-dimensional space, each represented by a question (for an elaboration of this point see Jacobs, 1998a). The first is, whether barring non-national residents from voting or standing for election represents a democratic deficit. The second is, do certain conditions need to be fulfilled to have a viable multicultural society in which migrants participate (where possible or desirable) in the political process and whether or not this necessitates certain demands be made of non-national residents (and/or nationals of ethnic minorities). The answers to these two basic questions constitute the most important discursive fields in the course of the debate on political integration of foreigners in the Netherlands and Belgium. Indeed, using these two dimensions nearly all statements in the debates can be examined against each other in one (imaginary) space, thus providing an adequate means of condensing the debate. One can postulate that in the development of parliamentary debate these two dimensions are at the threshold of the argumentational struggle over this issue. It is at the intersection of these two dimensions that distinct discourses have been created concerning enfranchisement of non-nationals. I distinguished, analytically and empirically, four major discourses which, to borrow Stephen Castles' (1994) terminology, I have labelled *assimilationist exclusionary, assimilationist inclusionary, pluralist inclusionary* and *segregationist exclusionary.* Although they are not exclusively linked to certain (clusters of) political parties, they are in general clearly connected to specific positions in the political spectrum. The *segregationist exclusionary* discourse is used by extreme right wing parties, the *pluralist inclusionary* discourse is used foremost by left wing parties, while the *assimilationist exclusionary* discourse is primarily used by right wing parties. The *assimilationist inclusionary* discourse is used by both left wing and right wing parties, although more often by the latter.

In the *assimilationist exclusionary* discourse, that non-nationals are disenfranchised is not regarded as a democratic deficit. That non-nationals cannot vote is considered self-evident in the system of nation-states. Moreover, those non-national residents who wish to vote should opt for naturalisation. However, in this discourse, naturalisation is only possible once a person is sufficiently assimilated. In its most radical form, the 'newcomer' is only allowed to adopt state citizenship if this equals 'melting' into the receiving nation (conceptualised as a community of common culture) to the point of indistinction. In contrast, in the *assimilationist inclusionary* discourse, that (large) parts of the population do not posses voting rights *is* regarded as a democratic deficit. Non-national residents should obtain or be granted citizenship, or rights as close to this status as possible, in order to decrease or avoid this deficit. However, at the same time certain conditions required to create a viable *de facto* multicultural society (in which migrants can participate politically) should be taken into account. A minimum level of cultural assimilation is obligatory. The state has an important responsibility in this process: it should 'educate' and 'mould' non-national residents into rational citizens just as it does with nationals. The granting of voting rights could in a way be instrumental in achieving this. The aim is to integrate migrants into the political community, which at the same time requires a high degree of cultural assimilation from the migrants. In the *pluralist inclusionary* discourse, that (large) parts of the population do not have voting rights is also viewed as a democratic deficit. In addition, it is believed that non-national residents need not meet any specific demands for the society to be a viable multicultural one in which migrants can participate politically. In this discourse, migrants are admitted to the political community, while the maintenance of those cultural differences seen as unproblematic is accepted. In the *segregationist exclusionary* discourse, that non-nationals do not have the vote is not considered a deficit. The creation of a viable multicultural society is thought impossible. Ethnicised groups should at best be segregated and 'foreign elements' should, in the worst case scenario, be expelled or destroyed. This discourse has a clear ethnocentrist and racist tenet.

It is striking that these same basic discourses were at the heart of the political debate in both countries. For reasons of space, I cannot elaborate on this issue here, but I do want to stress that this can be explained *post facto* when focusing on parallel historical developments influencing the formation of the discourses (see Jacobs, 1998a, pp. 268–69). The outcomes of the debate, however, were different due to the possibility or impossibility of constructing discourse coalitions in favour of enfranchisement within the respective political fields at specific strategic moments of the debate.

Since left wing parties in general tended to support enfranchisement of foreigners (see Rath, 1990), the positions taken up by the right wing parties were crucial in this event. The importance of ethnocentrism in these political debates can best and most easily be assessed in a comparative set-up. One should examine the way in which 'traditional' political parties have positioned themselves in relation to the extreme right wing parties and to what extent polarisation (a phenomenon leading to populism) has occurred on the migrant issue, influencing the formation of discourse coalitions. Indeed, since the discourses used in the debates are the same in both countries, it does not make a lot of sense to merely discuss the xenophobic or ethnocentric tenet of these discourses as such. In addition, focusing on the extremist positions in the debate is not very informative because the actors using them hardly ever attain a position of veto during coalition bargaining (Immergut, 1992). It is much more interesting to look into how the formation of specific coalitions around the basic discourses is influenced by electoral competition and ideological competition (of traditional parties with extreme right wing parties) and to what extent the struggle between and with the basic discourses has been accompanied by polarisation (or not).

The Enfranchisement of Foreign Residents Debate in the Late 1970s and Early 1980s

In 1985, after more than ten years of parliamentary debate, non-national residents (of more than five years) were granted municipal voting rights in the Netherlands (see Jacobs, 1998b). This policy change was the result of the creation of a (temporary) 'hybrid' discourse containing elements from different political narratives combined into one discourse coalition. When, in the 1970s, a left wing government proposed partial enfranchisement of non-nationals using *pluralist inclusionary* as well as an *assimilationist inclusionary* discourse, the right wing parties (especially the right wing liberals) objected strongly, clutching on to an *assimilationist exclusionary* discourse. However, in 1977, after gaining office, they unintentionally changed their position in response to terrorist activities by Moluccan youngsters[4] (see Steijlen, 1996, pp. 161–65). Indeed, once the Moluccan violence had placed the wider ethnic issue on the national agenda, the right turned to an *assimilationist inclusionary* discourse which could (and would) be combined with the *pluralist inclusionary* discourse that the left had been using on the issue. It was envisioned as a symbolic act with which the government could appear to be taking action on the societal position of non-nationals (especially Moluccans). From then onwards both the right and left supported local enfranchisement, making an effort to avoid open conflict on the issue. This led, eventually, to a change in the constitution and electoral legislation.[5] At the same time, a significant extension of *ius soli* was introduced to the Dutch nationality legislation. The introduction of these changes was assisted by a secret agreement between all but the extreme right wing parties to keep debate on the issue to a minimum, thus providing the extreme right with little chance to gain ground with their *segregationist exclusionary* discourse.

The opportunity for a discourse coalition on the issue of partial enfranchisement of non-national residents did not arise in Belgium. During the 1970s left wing advocates of the enfranchisement of non-nationals had lobbied the political parties using a *pluralist inclusionary* discourse. At the turn of the decade the left wing government had promised to take up the issue using *an assimilationist inclusionary* discourse, while the right, using an *assimilationist exclusionary* discourse, had opposed the idea of enfranchisement in general. Soon thereafter political instability caused the left wing pro-enfranchisement government to be replaced by a right wing government. Hoping to attract votes in competition with extreme-right wing parties in the city of Brussels, the Wallonian right wing liberals of the time turned from an *assimilationist exclusionary* discourse to implicit anti-migrant discourses (flirting on the edges of *segregationist exclusionary* discourse). They forced the other parties in the right wing coalition government to drop the issue of enfranchising non-national residents even if they were still undecided. This blocked the possibility of setting up a discourse coalition in favour of enfranchisement. Instead, in a discourse coalition combining the *assimilationist inclusionary* discourse and the *assimilationist exclusionary* discourse, *ius soli* was introduced to Belgian nationality legislation, partly in order to counter demands for enfranchisement of non-nationals. It is important to note that it was in the same bill introducing *ius soli*, that limitations to residence for non-nationals in the city of Brussels were brought in. Thus the highly debated illegal practices of the then mayor of the Brussels' municipality Schaarbeek, Roger Nols, were no longer merely condoned but even institutionalised. Nols had been refusing to allow non-EU-migrants to register as resident in the local area under his jurisdiction. This illegal practice was thus transformed into official policy for a number of Brussels' municipalities. In this climate, all traditional political parties (the left wing ones included) gradually withdrew their more pro-migrant polices, fearing the growing electoral appeal of the extreme right wing parties. The right wing liberals' adoption of elements of the extreme right wing's positions had thrown a mantle of improved credibility and *salonfähigkeit* over what was previously unacceptable. This in turn extended the process of polarisation on the migrant issue and at the same time shifted the spectrum of possible stances towards that of restriction. In the long-run, this led to further electoral success for the extreme right (especially the Vlaams Blok in Flanders). As such, the fear of the 'white backlash' turned into a self-fulfilling prophecy (compare Bourdieu, 1998, p. 23).

Explaining the Differing Importance of Polarisation in the Debate on Enfranchisement

I have argued that the debate on local enfranchisement should not be studied by looking for 'the' dominant discourse affecting policy outcomes, but that one should reconstruct the debate as a struggle with different discourses and look into which discourse coalitions were at the basis of policy outcomes. When comparing Belgium and the Netherlands, it was striking that although the same basic discourses were used, the dynamics of the debate in each country differed. In the previous section I stressed the crucial difference between the debates of each country, stating that in the Netherlands an explicit effort not to polarise was made (thus locking extreme right positions out of the debate), while in Belgium polarisation occurred. In this way, stances that could legitimise or strengthen (latent) racism and ethnocentrism were consciously avoided in the Dutch debate, while the Belgian debate was partly transformed into an electoral struggle over the anti-migrant vote. This had a crucial effect on the formation process of the discourse coalitions which led to the respective policies of both countries. The challenge is now, of course, to explain the importance of this difference in the effect of polarisation (and the emergence of a racist, or ethnocentric, 'undercurrent') on the relevant policy outcomes.

The American political scientist Gary Freeman (1995) claimed that in all liberal-democratic states which are not traditional immigration countries, there is a strong consensus among the political elites to neutralise the issue of immigration in politics and exclude anti-migrant or racist positions from the main-stream political forum. According to Freeman the elite has an anti-populist ethos and is much more sensitive to the interests and perspectives of groups that profit from immigration—groups which largely overlap with existing lobbies—than to the interests and perspectives of those who see immigration as a threat. Combined with the inherent inclusionary logic of liberal-democracy, states will adopt liberal policies towards non-national residents despite the apparent resistance of the general public. Freeman, however, does not take into account the importance of electoral (and ideological) competition on the immigration issue nor the discursive struggle in the debate on integration (compare Brubaker, 1995). As Rath (1990, p. 142) has pointed out, the possibility of enfranchisement of non-nationals only arises if the major political parties do not clash on the issue of equal rights for foreigners. Once anti-migrant parties gain in popularity and/or traditional parties engage in competition to conquer the anti-migrant vote, the chances for enfranchisement diminish steadily. This statement seems to be correct to a large extent. In contradiction to Freeman's vision the political elite is not at all reluctant to engage in populist rhetoric and polarisation around the migrant issue, as was clearly the case in Belgium. A key question here is why traditional parties allow themselves to engage in these kind of malign strategies (or not).

In my opinion, electoral competition and polarisation around the migrant issue is not so much to do with the proportion of migrants actually present. A threshold of tolerance is not what is at work here. I see more of a link with the *voluntary* choice politicians make as to whether or not to play upon the general public's latent xenophobia (which has a structural foundation in socio-economic competition and is linked to a historical-cultural inertia of the construction of a national identity). In the Netherlands traditional political parties chose not to begin a populist-xenophobic political adventure due to an explicit desire to counter the growth potential of extreme right wing political parties. In Belgium a different attitude was adopted. In the early 1980s the right wing liberals chose, in Brussels, to go to the people with an anti-migrant election platform. Instead of counter-attacking extreme right wing ideas, xenophobic positions were normalised which in turn created a fertile basis for further extreme right wing growth.

I claim that these differences are less to do with cultural idioms but are, on a level of explanation that exceeds, without excluding, voluntarism, related to the influence the character of immigration has on the debate on integration. I specifically want to emphasise the importance of the colonial history and its relationship to concepts of national identity and state-citizenship in the debate on integration, and especially the debate on enfranchisement in the 1980s.[6]

Belgium has had a relatively short but very intensive period of colonial history, of which there is little evidence on the streets of Belgium. During and after the colonial period it was made almost impossible for autochthonous inhabitants of Congo, Rwanda and Burundi to come and live in Belgium. In addition, black (former) Belgian subjects were simply refused Belgian citizenship. Using a legal, in effect racial, distinction between Belgian citizens and (former) Belgian subjects, black subjects were not allowed to become a part of the Belgian nation. This was different in the Netherlands. From 1892, in the Dutch-East-Indies (Indonesia) there was a similar racial distinction in citizenship between Dutch citizens and Dutch subjects. However, in the Dutch-West-Indies (the Netherlands Antilles) and Suriname a similar distinction was deemed unnecessary due to the smaller population involved. After the independence of Indonesia, racial differentiation, between citizens and subjects, citizenship was abolished. Black inhabitants of the Netherlands Antilles and Suriname were, as Dutch citizens, entitled to relocate to the Netherlands where they enjoyed the same rights as the autochthonous Dutch citizens. When Suriname was granted independence in 1975, its inhabitants were given the option to keep their Dutch state citizenship if they moved to the Netherlands before the day of independence. Immigration to the Netherlands (and the linked maintenance of Dutch citizenship) was far from promoted for black citizens but, equally, it was not hindered. Indeed, there were no remaining legal grounds with which to allow only white Surinamese inhabitants to 'return' to the Netherlands and thus keep their Dutch citizenship. This led to a situation in which the Netherlands became increasingly 'coloured' despite *ius sanguinis* remaining the basic principle for the acquisition of nationality.

As a result, before *ius soli* was introduced in both countries in the mid 1980s, it still made some sense in Belgium to discursively present the nation as being in essence an ethnically homogeneous white community, while it made far less sense to do so in the Netherlands. Black Dutch people of Antillian or Surinamese descent were *de jure* citizens of the Netherlands. *Ius sanguinis* as the basic principle of Dutch nationality law, did not allow an overlap between the legal distinction of citizens and foreigners on the one hand and racial categorisations on the other, as was the case in Belgium. Consequently, the topics of racism, antiracism and discrimination gained a different political importance in each country, with obvious implications for integration debates, in particular the debate on enfranchisement of non-national residents. In the Netherlands, racism posed an immediate threat for a significant part of the nation, i.e., the migrant electorate. This enhanced the sensitivity of the political elite to the problem of discrimination. Racism and discrimination were more readily seen as an internal and shared problem than was the case in Belgium. In addition, this stimulated efforts towards an inclusive immigration policy. Indeed, immigration affected the very heart of the Dutch national narrative. A side effect of this was that it prevented the formation of quasi-racist positions in the debate on enfranchisement of non-nationals. The distinction between citizens and foreigners was not synonymous with that of ethnic difference. If ethnic difference were to be used to argue against the enfranchisement of non-nationals, this could be easily countered by referring to the Dutch nationals of Surinamese or Antillian descent who already had voting rights. Anti-racism and anti-discrimination became thus topics that could quickly be mobilised in the debate on integration in general and the debate on enfranchisement of non-nationals in particular. Xenophobia and extreme right wing politics were seen as a shared internal threat. In Belgium, on the contrary, racism was an issue seen more as a problem of relations between Belgians and foreigners than an internal Belgian problem that affected a part of the electorate or questioned the Belgian nation. Anti-racism and anti-discrimination were not as successful as counter arguments raised in debates on ethnic difference between state citizens and foreigners. For a long time, one could assume that no 'coloured' Belgians suffered from racism; only foreigners could be 'coloured', and thus potential victims of racism. One could, given the bi-cultural character of Belgian society, wonder why discrimination did not evolve into a topic of political debate. Indeed, one could argue that linguistic conflict within Belgium and the multinational character of the Belgian state should have formed the basis for an increased openness to anti-discrimination and anti-racism. It could be argued that Flemish and Walloons would be all too familiar with what discrimination is, due to the internal Belgian conflict and that from this experience, both communities should be able to feel solidarity with non-nationals. One should, however, keep in mind that the linguistic conflict in Belgium has hardly been identified by those concerned as arising from ethnic tensions or racism (for a view to the contrary see Vandeweyer, 1998). The *de facto*—albeit decreasing—bilingualism of the population, the specific position of Brussels and the extensive (historical) internal migration has prevented the *Belgo-Belgian* conflict from being easily translated into ethnic terms. One should not forget that, by way of example, many, if not the majority, of Wallonian inhabitants of Brussels refuse to identify themselves as Walloons in their conflict with the Flemish community; Walloons live in Wallonia, not in Brussels. Racism has not been and is not seen as an 'internal' Belgian issue.

In short, one can state that the two countries' divergent immigration histories have affected the debate on enfranchisement of non-nationals in the 1980s in an indirect way due to the different significance of the issue of racism for each country. And, that this was linked to the form of incorporation of non-white people in each nation. For the Dutch case, specific attention must furthermore be drawn to the particular case of the Moluccans. As noted earlier, the historical debt of honour Dutch society has towards the Moluccans, worked in favour of voting rights for non-nationals. For historical and moral reasons it could not be demanded of the Moluccans that they take up Dutch nationality even though it was thought that they should have as close to equal rights with Dutch citizens as possible. Moluccan terrorism only strengthened this conviction. An unexpected consequence was that the gap between citizens and non-nationals was not as great in the Netherlands as in Belgium. Furthermore, the specific situation of the Moluccan community was the direct cause for an integration policy based on a multicultural model in which cultural differences were accepted as a fact and seen as a potential basis for emancipation.[7] Despite the fact that the Dutch polity was at the same time portrayed as a culturally homogeneous entity.

The situation with the Moluccans is also useful for explaining the difference between the situation in the Netherlands and that in France. One could say that France, just like the Netherlands, has experienced a 'colouring' of its nation, due to the possession of state-citizenship by inhabitants of (former) colonial areas as Algeria and the DOM/TOM (*Départements et Territoires d' Outre Mer* [French Overseas Territories], Martinique, Guyana, Réunion, Guadeloupe, New Caledonia, etc.). There are, however, some important differences to be noted which explain why this has not prevented polarisation on the issue of immigration in France in the 1970s and 1980s.

First, France has, for historical reasons, a specific republican vision on state-citizenship in which assimilation as a virtue and goal is a central element and in which *ius soli* is, at least in theory, the basic principle of nationality legislation (see Brubaker, 1992). This has made it possible to assess the legitimacy of the possession of state citizenship with the criterion of adaptation. Which has led to debate on the difference between *Français de souche* and *Français de papier*, the questioning of *ius soli* and, hence, to polarisation over integration-policy, all without needing to frame the debate in *explicitly* racial terms. Whereas, in the Netherlands, the only clear cause of the 'colouring' of the nation was the 1892 introduction of *ius sanguinis* mentioned earlier. Criticism of this was only possible in explicitly racial terms which, due to the excesses of Nazism, was taboo. Moreover, Suriname had been granted independence in 1975 precisely because the leftist government, Den Uyl, wanted to remove the stain of colonialism (Eppink, 1998, p. 234). Hopes for a model decolonisation combined with the Dutch leftist government's wish to maintain a progressive image left no room for any stance even slightly resembling racism.

Second, in France the republican differentiation between French citizens and foreigners had, and has, absolute priority, denying any room for gradual distinctions between *citoyens* and foreigners. Racism should, as an internal problem within the nation, be strongly resisted. However, in France this could not stimulate a more moderate view on the division and difference between state citizens and non-nationals, because there was no group which the French state wished to include as a part of the nation without demanding that its members take-up French citizenship. The exceptional position of the Moluccans in the Netherlands and their particular history in relation to the Dutch state, led to the recognition of a special kind of foreigner, a hybrid category in between that of the national and that of the genuine foreigner. This facilitated a moderated perspective on the division between nationals and foreigners and made it possible to implement a multicultural integration policy without having to relinquish the fiction of an ideal culturally homogeneous political community.

Conclusion

Policy changes do not have to be the result of a genuine compromise at the level of argumentation or the dominance of one specific type of reasoning, but may just as easily be the result of an 'ad hoc' discourse coalition. No single discourse or ideology completely 'controls' and 'structures' the debate. It is therefore not advisable to begin with a framework that allows nothing more than the revelation and condemnation of a single dominant discourse. Furthermore, such approaches do not allow cross-national comparison of the importance of ethnocentrism (or racism) in debate and policy, while *at the same time* explaining why particular policy outcomes can be very different in different countries. As an alternative strategy, debate and policy should be analysed as the result of a struggle between (and within) different discourses and ideological narratives in the political field. Although discourses as separate entities shape the course of the debate (and the possibilities for position-taking within it), the political actors can (and do) strategically use them in creating (temporary) discourse coalitions. In the end, policy is the result of the creation of networks (of politicians) around specific discourses which make certain phenomena understandable in a similar language and logic. As such, discourses (and the extent to which their affinity allows alliances to be built around them) are important in causing, and concomitantly, in helping us to understand policy developments. The specific discourse coalitions leading to policy-outcomes, in which the discourses are mobilised, have to be related to the logic of the political field at several stages of the controversy chosen as the object of study. Inter-party electoral and ideological competition and the process of coalition-bargaining are crucial factors in this process. To assess the importance of ethnocentrism in debate and politics in different countries, one should focus on the degree of polarisation on migrant issues, along with its link to inter-party electoral and ideological competition. The challenge for international comparison becomes, then, the explanation of the differences in electoral competition and the varying levels of polarisation in the debates on migrant issues. Here, colonial history, and its relations to ideas on national identity and state-citizenship, was integral to an understanding of the differences between Belgium and the Netherlands. Perhaps other historical events or traditions are of greater importance in other countries in structuring electoral and ideological competition over the migrant issue. Whatever the exact factors may be, it is crucial to link interpretations based on grand narratives about citizenship to the socio-logic of the political field in general and the analysis of nitty-gritty politics in particular.

Notes

1 Since 1985 all non-nationals resident for five years in the Netherlands, may vote in municipal (local-government, as opposed to national or provincial) elections. In 1996, the five year condition was abolished for EU-citizens (in compliance with the Treaty of Maastricht). In October 1998 the Belgian constitution was adapted in order to make it possible for non-nationals to vote in municipal elections. EU-citizens will be able to vote in Belgian local (municipal) elections in October 2000. Other foreign residents will be able to participate in local elections in the year 2006, at the earliest.

2 It should be noted, however, that some critical discourse analysts, such as Norman Fairclough, Margaret Wetherell and Jessika ter Wal, have questioned the dominant ideology thesis and explicitly try to take change and counter-discourses into account.

3 Here a discourse is defined as a relative, bounded set of claims, images and tropes through which meaning is given to reality in reference and in opposition to other discourses (see Ellingson, 1995, p. 107; Hajer, 1993, p. 45; Bourdieu, 1991, p. 185).

4 After granting Indonesia independence, the Netherlands had to provide asylum to Moluccans (and their families) who had fought alongside the Dutch in the colonial army against the nationalist rebels. For a long period of time the Moluccan community had to live out their exile in quite unfavorable conditions (despite repeated promises of improvement from successive Dutch governments). This led to serious tensions and, in the end, to terrorism. The most spectacular terrorist activities were the highjakings of a train and of a primary school during the election period of 1977.

5 The entire process took nearly eight years, since any modification of the constitution is a time-consuming activity, inertia is institutionally assured (see Jacobs, 1998a; Jacobs, 1998b, pp. 354–55).

6 I merely want to discuss the situation in the 1980s. It should be noted that the processes leading to polarisation (or not) in the Netherlands and Belgium around the immigration issue are quite different in the 1990s (see Jacobs, 1998a, pp. 250–53).

7   It is often claimed that the system of pillarisation is the cause for the categoral policy for
ethnic minorities and the Dutch multicultural model (Entzinger, 1994, p. 404; Bousetta,
1997, p. 219). I want to stress that the 'Moluccan factor' is an important intermediary
link. Indeed, Belgium has also had (and to a certain extent still does have) a system of
pillarisation, but this did not lead to the creation of a multi-cultural model for
incorporation of migrants.

References

Abercrombie, N., Hill, S. and Turner, B. (1980), *The dominant Ideology Thesis*, Routledge,
London.
Bauböck, R. (1994), *From Aliens to Citizens. Redefining the Status of Migrant in Europe*,
Avebury, Aldershot.
Blommaert, J. and Verschueren, J. (1994), 'The Belgian migrant debate', *New Community*, vol.
20, no. 2, pp. 227–251.
Bourdieu, P. (1991), *Language and Symbolic Power*, Polity Press, Cambridge.
Bourdieu, P. (1998), *Contre-feux*, Liber, Paris.
Bousetta, H. (1997), 'Citizenship and Political Participation in France and the Netherlands:
Reflections on Two Local Cases', *New Community*, vol. 23, no. 2, pp. 215–232.
Brubaker, R. (1990), 'Immigration, Citizenship and the Nation-State in France and Germany: A
Comparative Historical Analysis', *International Sociology*, vol. 5, no. 4, pp. 378–407.
Brubaker, R. (1992), *Citizenship and Nationhood in France and Germany*, Harvard University
Press, Cambridge.
Brubaker, R. (1995), 'Comments on Modes of Immigration Politics in Liberal Democratic
States', *International Migration Review*, vol. 24, no. 4, pp. 903–908.
Castles, S. (1994), 'Democracy and Multicultural Citizenship. Australian Debates and their
Relevance for Western Europe', in R. Bauböck (ed), *From Aliens to Citizens. Redefining
the Status of Migrants in Europe*, Avebury, Aldershot, pp. 3–27.
Ellingson, S. (1995), 'Understanding the Dialectic of Discourse and Collective Action: Public
Debate and Rioting in Antebellum Cincinnati', *American Journal of Sociology*, vol. 101,
no. 1, pp. 100–144.
Entzinger, H. (1993), 'L'immigration aux Pays-Bas: du pluriculturalisme à l'intégration' in M.
Wieviorka (ed), *Racisme et modernité*, La Découverte, Paris, pp. 400–415.
Eppink, D. (1998), *Vreemde buren. Over politiek in Nederland en België*, Contact, Amsterdam.
Favell, A. (1998), *Philosophies of Integration: Immigration and the Idea of Citizenship in
France and Britain*, Macmillan, London.
Freeman, G. (1995), 'Modes of Immigration Politics in Liberal Democratic States', *International
Migration Review*, vol. 24, no. 4, pp. 881–902.
Glaser, B. and Strauss, A. (1967), *The discovery of Grounded Theory: Strategies for Qualitative
Research*, Aldine, New York.
Hajer, M. (1993), 'Discourse Coalitions and the Institutionalization of Practice: The Case of
Acid Rain in Great Britain', in F. Fischer and J. Forester (eds), *The Argumentative Turn in
Policy Analysis and Planning*, UCL, London, pp. 43–76.
Hammar, T. (1990), *Democracy and the Nation State*, Avebury, Aldershot.
Heisler, M. and Heisler, B. (1991), 'Citizenship – Old, New and Changing: Inclusion, Exclusion
and Limbo for Ethnic Groups and Migrants in the Modern Democratic State' in J.
Fijalkowski, H. Merkens and F. Schmidt (eds), *Dominant National Cultures and Ethnic
Minorities*, Free University of Berlin, Berlin.

Hisschemöller, M. (1988), 'Kiesrecht voor niet-Nederlanders (1970–1980), Bestuurs- en beleidstheorieën achter de discussie rond een non-issue', *Beleid en Maatschappij*, vol. 15, no. 1, pp. 32–44.

Immergut, E. (1992), 'The Rules of the Game; the Logic of Health Policy-Making in France, Switzerland and Sweden' in S. Steinmo and K. Thelen (eds), *Structuring Politics. Historical Institutionalism in Comparative Analysis*, CUP, Cambridge, pp. 58–89.

Jacobs, D. (1997), *Migrants and Political Citizenship. Soysal's Model of Postnational Membership and the Dutch Debate over Voting Rights for Foreign Residents*, paper presented at the workshop 'Citizenship and the Transition of European (Welfare) States' of the 25th Joint Sessions of the European Consortium for Political Research, Bern, 27 February–4 March.

Jacobs, D. (1998a), *Nieuwkomers in de Politiek. Het parlementair debat over kiesrecht voor vreemdelingen in Nederland en België (1970–1997)*, Academia Press, Gent.

Jacobs, D. (1998b), 'Discourse, Politics and Policy: The Dutch Parliamentary Debate about Voting Rights for Foreign Residents', *International Migration Review*, vol. 22, no. 2, pp. 350–374.

Klopp, B. (1995), 'Book Review. Limits of Citizenship', *American Journal of Sociology*, vol. 101, no. 3, pp. 779–781.

Martiniello, M. (1995), *Migration, Citizenship and Ethno-National Identities in the European Union*, Avebury, Aldershot.

Oommen, T. (1997), *Citizenship and National identity. From Colonialism to Globalism*, Sage, London.

Rath, J. (1990), 'Voting Rights' in Z. Layton-Henry (ed), *The Political Rights of Migrant Workers in Western Europe*, Sage, London, pp. 127–157.

Rose, N. and Miller P. (1992), 'Political Power Beyond the State: the Problematics of Government', *British Journal of sociology*, vol.43, pp. 173–205.

Soysal, Y. (1994), *Limits of Citizenship. Migrants and Postnational Membership in Europe*, University of Chicago Press, London.

Soysal, Y. (1996), 'Change Citizenship in Europe: Remarks on Postnational Membership and the National State', in D. Cesarani and M. Fulbrook (eds), *Citizenship, Nationality and Migration in Europe*, London, Routledge.

Steijlen, F. (1996), *RMS, van ideaal tot symbool. Moluks nationalisme in Nederland 1951–1994*, Het Spinhuis, Amsterdam.

Strauss, A. and Corbin, J. (1990), *Basics of Qualitative Research; Grounded Theory, Procedures and Tactics*, Sage, London.

Ter Wal, J. (1997), *The Reproduction of Ethnic Prejudice and Racism through Policy and News Discourse. The Italian Case (1988–1992)*, Dissertation, European University Institute, Florence, Italy.

Vandeweyer, L. (1998), 'Het verschil tussen Germanen en Latijnen. Bron van anti-Belgicisme?' in M. Beyen and G. Vanpaemel (eds), *Rasechte wetenschap?Het rasbegrip tussen wetenschap en politiek voor de Tweede Wereldoorlog*, Acco, Leuven.

Van Dijk, T. (1993), *Elite Discourse and Racism*, Sage, Newbury Park.

Van Thijn, E. (1997), *Ons kosteljkste cultuurbezit. Over tolerantie, non-discriminatie en diversiteit*, oratie, Rijksuniversiteit Leiden, Leiden.

Zahn, E. (1989), *Regenten, rebellen en reformatoren, een visie op Nederland en de Nederlanders*, Contact, Amsterdam.

7 Political Claims-Making against Racism and Discrimination in Britain and Germany

RUUD KOOPMANS & PAUL STATHAM

Introduction

Recent increases in migration flows and the growing size of ethnic minority populations have made migration and citizenship into one of the most contentious policy areas in 1990s Europe. As migration and citizenship are so intimately related to questions of national identity and sovereignty—which are already challenged by the combined pressures of economic and cultural globalisation and political transnationalisation—they have become hot topics for public debate. In addition to the politicisation of migration and citizenship within institutional politics, groups and organisations mobilising either for, against, or on behalf of migrants and their interests have entered the political scene. Nowhere is this more apparent than in France, where the xenophobic *Front National* seriously threatens the traditional right. Extreme right and xenophobic mobilisation has become an important feature of political life in other countries too, taking the form of ethnonationalist parties (France, Belgium, Austria), mass public attacks on minorities and asylum seekers (Germany), or more diffuse forms of racial violence (Britain). Racist violence and the rise of xenophobic parties have in turn provoked counter-mobilisation from anti-racist groups, sometimes involving the attacked minorities themselves, but often dominated by members of the majority ethnic group acting on behalf of migrants and minorities. In recent years, anti-racist movements have mobilised large numbers of people across Western Europe, notably in France, where *SOS racisme* played an initiating role for anti-racist movements elsewhere in Europe, including Germany, where the wave of racist attacks in the early 1990s provoked one of the largest mass movements in the history of the Federal Republic. Finally, migrants and minorities themselves, who for much of the post-war period could be considered passive objects of 'guest-worker' and labour-supply policies, have come to play an increasingly important political role. In some countries, such as post-colonial Britain and the Netherlands, which are committed to a 'multicultural' model of integration,

139

migrant organisation has been actively stimulated by the authorities in an effort to involve them in the policy process.

To note that migration and citizenship have become a central field of political contention is hardly original. What is surprising, however, is that the literature has not adequately taken up these developments by adopting theoretical and methodological perspectives geared to analysing this new quality of migration, citizenship, and ethnic relations as a field of political mobilisation. Several scholars have recently pointed out the lack of collective action and social movement perspectives relative to the wealth of research on structural, demographic and policy aspects of immigration and ethnic minorities (Rex, 1994; Solomos and Back, 1995). In this chapter, we want to develop a collective action perspective on political contention over migration, citizenship, and ethnic relations. We shall focus on a broad range of forms of such contention which, we denote as collective 'claims-making'. This includes not only forms of protest such as demonstrations and political violence—the traditional focus of social movement studies—but also more routine forms of intervention in the public sphere such as public statements or political decisions.

We will begin by discussing and combining two theoretical approaches— political opportunity and framing—with which important advances have been made in comparative analyses of social movements in the last decade. We then specify how this theoretical perspective can be applied to the analysis of contention over migration and ethnic relations by drawing on cross-national differences in national identity and modes of citizenship and migrant incorporation. After a brief discussion of our methodological approach, we then move on to our empirical analysis, which consists of two parts. In the first part, we present data on the most important characteristics of claims-making in the broad field of migration and ethnic relations in Britain and Germany. This provides a contextual setting for a more detailed analysis of claims-making in the sub-field of anti-racism and anti-discrimination, which forms the second part of our empirical analysis. We will show that the nature of claims-making in this field differs fundamentally between Britain and Germany, regarding both the issues that are central, and the actors involved as claimants and addressees of demands.

Opportunity and Framing Approaches to Political Mobilisation[1]

In contrast to classical perspectives which followed the Durkheimian tradition and defined social movements as unreflective, semi-automatic responses to the strain and discontent produced by social change (e.g., Le Bon, 1960; Kornhauser, 1959), resource mobilisation theory emerged from the late 1960s onwards (e.g., Zald and Ash, 1966; Oberschall, 1973; McCarthy and Zald, 1977). This perspective builds on rational choice theory and the conviction that the 'wretched of the earth' do not always rebel, and it stresses the active role of social movement entrepreneurs and organisations in mobilising their constituencies. The focus of resource mobilisation theory on factors internal to movement organisations led to a relative neglect of the relationship between movements and macro-level political contexts as an explanatory variable for mobilisation. In response to this shortcoming, the concept of a 'political opportunity-structure', gained ascendance from the 1980s onwards (McAdam, 1982; Tarrow, 1994; Kriesi, Koopmans, Duyvendak and Giugni, 1995). The political opportunity approach builds on the findings from the seminal historical work of Charles Tilly (e.g., Shorter and Tilly, 1971; Tilly, Tilly and Tilly, 1975; Tilly, 1978) which demonstrated that periods of widespread popular mobilisation coincided with crises of political authority and increased dissent among the political élite, and that—contrary to classical assumptions— macro-processes such as industrialisation and urbanisation did not directly affect levels of mobilisation. For Tilly, crises within the political context, that typically occur at times of defeat in war or economic recession, constituted opportunities for collective mobilisation by challengers from below. Extending this insight to cross-national comparative research, the idea is that differences in levels of mobilisation are not a direct outcome of national differences in patterns of modernisation, but are mediated by a country's particular structure of political institutions and its configuration of power relationships.

The concept of 'political opportunity-structure' has been applied, both longitudinally and cross-nationally, for the constraining and facilitating role of institutional structures and power configurations in relation to the potential for mobilisation by social movements. Tarrow (1994), for example, identifies four dimensions that define the potential for mobilising a challenge to a political system: the stability of political alignments; formal channels of access to the political system; availability of allies in the polity; and intra-élite conflict. Kriesi et al. (1995) and Duyvendak (1995), applied a similar perspective cross-nationally, and were able to successfully argue that the low level and radical forms of mobilisation by new social movements in France relative to other western European countries, is related to the closure and centralisation of French political institutions and to the entrenched dominance of traditional left-right cleavages within the party system.

Applying these political opportunity insights to the issue-domain of migration and ethnic relations politics, we might expect that, in a diachronic perspective, mobilisation over such issues is most likely to emerge during crises of political regulation, when the political authorities are internally divided on migration and minority issues and unable to agree on adequate solutions. From a comparative perspective, we might expect that national differences in xenophobic, anti-racist and minority mobilisation are linked, first, to the way in which these movements' concerns are incorporated in, or excluded from, mainstream politics, and, second, to the channels of access that such movements have for promoting their demands. This is the basic approach that we advocate here. However, we argue that it is also necessary to refer to another body of recent social movement research, namely the 'framing and political discourse' approach,[2] which adds a degree of qualitative sensitivity to the political opportunity approach by referring to the content and nature of the claims that are made by challengers in different settings.

Frame analysis draws on symbolic interactionism, in particular Goffman (1974), and the constructivist school in the sociology of social problems (e.g., Hilgartner and Bosk, 1988). Where the resource mobilisation and political opportunity perspectives emphasise the strategic and material dimensions of mobilisation, the framing perspective focuses instead on the symbolic and discursive dimensions. By doing so it reminds us that discontent, resources, and opportunities are not simply 'out there' in the external world, but have to be cognitively defined and constructed, i.e., 'framed' through action (e.g., Snow, Rochford, Worden, and Benford, 1986; Gamson and Modigliani, 1989; Snow and Benford, 1992). Social movement organisers have to define issues and problems as collective concerns, identify causes, present solutions, and make the actors and institutions which are supposed to implement them publicly visible. In addition, they have to convince their potential adherents that collective action is a necessary and a potentially successful means towards these ends. This process is made more difficult by competition within the public sphere. Movement organisers have to be more convincing than other actors, such as counter-movements, and other civil society actors and public authorities, who promote alternative definitions of the situation and policy proposals.

Unfortunately, the framing perspective has thus far been applied mainly in an 'ad hoc' and descriptive way, and has not produced clear hypotheses about the effects of framing on levels and forms of collective action (Benford, 1997). This is the main point of Koopmans and Duyvendak (1995), whose analysis of anti-nuclear movements in several European countries shows that, although the movements had very similar argumentation strategies, the groups which were more successful in influencing public opinion, were those active in countries such as the Netherlands, where the movement faced favourable institutional opportunities for preventing the construction of nuclear plants. In France, on the other hand, where all the major parties were firmly behind nuclear power and few opportunities for juridical intervention were available, levels of rejection of nuclear energy actually declined among the public during the 1980s, contrary to the prevalent trend across Europe (Nelkin and Pollak, 1981; Kitschelt, 1986). This example shows that the success of discursive efforts depends not just on the 'quality' of the argumentation in the framing strategies deployed by the collective actors, but on their 'fit' with hegemonic discourses and on the institutional opportunities for inserting challenger-frames into the process of policy formation and implementation.

Following the insights of the framing and political discourse approach, we argue that it is necessary to systematically analyse the semantic contents of claims made by collective actors in the public domain. The important question is how one can insert this dimension of public discourse within a political opportunity perspective. The approach that we advocate here, follows in the wake of recent research which has emphasised the need to combine and integrate the insights from opportunity and framing perspectives more systematically (McAdam, McCarthy and Zald, 1996; Diani, 1996; Koopmans and Statham, 1999a; Statham, 1998). If one takes on board, as we consider necessary, that only perceived realities can affect collective action, then it follows that attention should be focused on the type of opportunities that are rendered publicly visible. These manifest opportunities may be derived directly from characteristics of political systems. This is clearly the case for the more stable aspects of political culture and institutions, for which the opportunities and constraints have been internalised by the citizenry in a learning process that extends across several generations. Thus French citizens have learnt that they will achieve little if they direct their demands at impotent peripheral authorities instead of at the all-powerful centre in Paris. Similarly, British citizens know that given the country's electoral system, the formation of a new political party is not a very effective means to promote change—an important factor explaining the electoral weakness of the British extreme right.

In addition to these more stable institutional and cultural dimensions, there are more volatile dimensions of political opportunities, and this is where the discursive realm plays a crucial role. For example, dissent among the political élite becomes perceived as an opportunity for mobilisation only when it enters the public sphere, instead of remaining limited to cabinet meetings, parliamentary committees or other non-public arenas. When élite dissent enters the public sphere, a process in which the mass media plays a special intermediary role, political discourse may develop powerful dynamics of its own, through processes of contagion, amplification, and escalation. Such dynamics become even more significant when other collective actors from civil society are drawn into taking positions on the conflict, either as 'third parties' or protagonists.

In our view, challengers attempting to mobilise their claims in the public sphere are more likely to be successful, depending on their ability to achieve three strategic aims: visibility, resonance, and legitimacy. First, the collective actor and its aims must be rendered publicly *visible*. Many challenges simply fail, because they do not cross the first hurdle of being reported by the media, or they are able to mobilise only ephemeral or local-level public attention. Second, to have an impact the mobilised challenge must provoke public reactions from other actors, i.e., it must *resonate* and carry the contention to a wider public. Even public claims that are reported in the media remain inconsequential if no one reacts to them, and political business continues as usual. Third, no matter how much visibility and resonance a challenge achieves, it will only achieve a level of success when it becomes a *legitimate* contention. This means that an actor needs to achieve 'legitimacy' for itself and its claims by resonating positively in the reactions of other actors, who express at least partial support by acknowledging that something has to be done about the problem.

We argue that this insight regarding the importance of the visibility, resonance, and legitimacy of mobilised claims in the public discourse is likely to be most fruitful when situated within a political opportunity approach. Indeed, the political discourse dynamics for a contested issue-field may be seen as constituting a set of *discursive opportunities*, that determine which of the strategic political demands made by movements are more likely to achieve visibility, resonance, and legitimacy in the public sphere. This discursive dimension extends the institutional focus of the traditional concept of political opportunities, to bring cultural and discursive elements of issue-fields back into consideration as variables for shaping collective action. Equally, by combining discursive and institutional dimensions of political opportunities, we redress the present indeterminacy in framing literature, by demonstrating why some framing efforts succeed in mobilising a public constituency, whereas others, no less elaborate or consistent in any objective sense, fail to do so. By combining the discursive and institutional dimensions of political opportunity, we are in a better position to disentangle the connections between dominant perceptions of national identity embedded in the institutional politics of migration and ethnic relations, e.g., in different national policies and legislation for including/excluding minorities, and the contents and levels of demands which collective actors are able to mobilise in the public domain.

National Modes of Citizenship as Opportunity-Structures for Mobilisation[3]

Some aspects of political opportunity-structures can be considered relevant for the mobilisation of any social movement, independently of the substantive nature of the political field in which the movement acts. Thus, the British 'first-past-the-post' electoral system favours majority parties and constrains the opportunities of social movements to push for change through the formation of challenging political parties, regardless of whether it is the extreme right, ethnic minorities, or the ecology movement. Similarly, the strong position of sub-national, and particularly regional authorities in federal states, like Germany, affects the mobilisation patterns of all collective actors when compared to the political centralisation of countries like Britain. However, it should also be noted that for some movements, for example, the ecology movement, the degree of spatial division of power may be more relevant than it is for others, in this case the peace movement.

Nonetheless, it is important to specify the institutional and discursive opportunities relevant for each particular field of political contention; what is relevant within the field of migration and ethnic relations is not 'per se' relevant to the politics of gender and sexuality, let alone industrial relations. For the specification of relevant dimensions of the opportunity-structure within the field of migration and ethnic relations, we can fruitfully draw on contemporary debates about the different national modes of incorporation and ways of attributing citizenship which exist in European countries.

The important comparative work of Rogers Brubaker (1992) draws attention to the ongoing divergence of the German and French legal and policy regimes for incorporating non-nationals within a system of social and political rights. Brubaker's approach emphasises what for us is the discursive dimension of ethnic relations politics, namely that a state's legal definition of citizenship bears a distinct embedded cultural imprint of nationhood, and that these deeply embedded national self-definitions of citizenship continue to shape the divergent political responses of nation-states to migrants. Thus he explains the continually higher naturalisation rates in France relative to Germany, by the greater openness toward accepting new members of the French *jus soli* tradition of citizenship, where citizenship is a territorial birthright, compared to the more exclusive German *jus sanguinis* tradition, where citizenship is based on an ethno-cultural belonging to the nation. Brubaker, however, overstates the importance of the signification process and the conception of nationhood in defining access to citizenship and political inclusion, and understates the material importance of citizenship rights for the incorporation of migrants. In the wake of Brubaker's research, a considerable number of scholars have applied more contextual approaches that take the different citizenship configurations of nation-states as the explanatory variable for political responses to the incorporation of ethnic difference (e.g., Castles and Miller, 1993; Castles, 1995; Smith and Blanc, 1996; Ireland, 1994; Favell, 1998).

A considerable degree of consensus has built up regarding the different 'modes' of national political responses for incorporating ethnic difference. The determinants for the degree and form of inclusiveness/exclusiveness of a national politics for incorporating ethnic difference can be defined along two dimensions of citizenship: first, the criteria for formal access to citizenship; and second, the cultural obligations that this access to citizenship entails.

The first dimension relates to the distinction between an ethno-cultural and a civic-territorial basis of criteria for attributing full citizenship to minorities or migrants. Here the ethno-cultural can be seen as the more 'closed', and the civic territorial the more 'open' opportunity-structure for minorities and migrants to gain access to full national citizenship and the political leverage that this may entail. Of course, for xenophobic and extreme right groups the evaluation of opportunities derived from these modes of citizenship is exactly the reverse. When the civic notion of a citizenship that is inclusive towards minorities is firmly embedded in a country's institutions and public discourse, the extreme right will find it difficult to assert its ethno-nationalist frame in the public sphere. However, this does not necessarily mean that a situation where the ethnic notion of citizenship is strongly rooted in institutional politics this situation favours high levels of xenophobic mobilisation. On the contrary, if exclusive policies with regard to migrants are already backed and implemented by institutional actors, there is little need for potential voters, adherents, or activists to lend their support to a xenophobic party or movement organisation. From this we deduce, that the most favourable conditions for xenophobic mobilisation will occur, when conceptions of citizenship are ambiguous between more exclusive and more inclusive elements, or when the political élite are internally divided on issues of citizenship and national identity. Such forms of ambiguity and dissent among the élite are precisely what many European countries have experienced since the 1980s, perhaps the most dramatic example being Italy in the early 1990s, and as a consequence political opportunities have opened up for the rise of xenophobic challengers (Koopmans and Kriesi, 1997; Koopmans and Statham, 1999a).

The nature and extent of the respective challenges also depends on the second dimension of citizenship and migrant incorporation: this relates to the distinction between assimilationism and cultural pluralism, which differ in the degree of cultural homogeneity and allegiance which a state requires when granting citizenship to new members. Here assimilationist approaches present a more 'demanding' variant for including ethnic or religious difference, where countries require a full conversion to the dominant national culture as the single and unitary ideological focus of belonging and membership. In contrast other societies allow a degree of cultural pluralism within the definition of national belonging, which produces a more 'accepting' variant for including ethnic or religious difference within national politics. Translated into the language of opportunity-structures, this implies that minorities will find it easier to constitute themselves as independent collective actors and to assert claims for cultural and group rights in pluralist systems. Whereas, in assimilationist regimes such as France, mobilisation will be facilitated across ethnic boundaries on the basis of universal 'Republican' values and a common identification as 'immigrants'.

Regarding the opportunities for mobilisation of anti-immigrant groups, we expect these to be generally more favourable in regimes where there is a lack of consensus among the political élite relating to the dominant model. Thus, if the assimilationist model is successful in its own terms by absorbing immigrants into the majority culture and integrating their material interests into cross-ethnic forms of political organisation such as the labour unions, then the assimilationist model may be resistant to anti-immigrant mobilisation (Wieviorka, 1996). However, the decline of such forms of political integration, coupled with the shifting patterns of migration towards groups whose cultural difference is more 'resistant' to assimilatory pressures—the main example being Islamic minorities—has caused a crisis in the assimilationist model. This has given rise to contradictory responses among the political élite. French politics has shifted between recognition of some form of multiculturalism (cf., the French discussion on the *droit à la différence*—the right to difference), and taking steps towards an ethno-cultural exclusion model in order to exclude those migrants deemed 'unwilling to assimilate' from full citizenship rights. As argued above, the political opportunity perspective suggests that such ambiguities, uncertainties, and contradictions regarding questions of citizenship and national identity provide a particularly fertile ground for the intervention of xenophobic groups into national politics and the public sphere. This is not to say that the multicultural model is immune to such challenges. Once more, the crucial question is whether such an incorporation regime is internally consistent and based on a consensus among the political élite, which again will be most likely if the model is successful on its own terms. When the presupposition of multiculturalism—namely that the recognition of cultural difference is ultimately the best way to guarantee social equality and peaceful relationships between different ethnic groups—begins to crack, which may be evident in the persistent socioeconomic marginalisation or 'minorisation' (Rath, 1991) of minorities, and ethnic strife and competition at the local level, then there is a high likelihood that xenophobic groups will profit from the ensuing destabilisation of the official mode of incorporation.

When one combines the two dimensions of access to citizenship and notions of national identity that we have discussed, it becomes possible to identify the three main 'modes' of national politics for ethnic relations: *ethno-cultural exclusionism; civic assimilationism;* and *multicultural pluralism.* In the real world, the ethno-cultural exclusionist mode of ethnic relations politics is most closely approximated by the example of Germany. The German politics of migration and ethnic relations continues to be shaped by an ethnic conception of nationhood. Thus ethnic German immigrants (*Aussiedler*) newly arrived from Russia and Eastern Europe, have a constitutionally guaranteed right to full citizenship rights on the basis of their hereditary link to the German people (*deutsche Volkszugehörigkeit*). By contrast, second and third generation Turks born and educated in Germany, face relatively high barriers to political inclusion. As the official naturalisation guidelines put it unambiguously: 'The Federal Republic of Germany is not a country of immigration; it does not have the intention to increase the number of German nationals by way of naturalisation' (Hailbronner and Renner, 1998, p. 864). *Aussiedler* do not count as immigrants here. Although the ancestors of some of these groups migrated from the territory of what is now Germany hundreds of year ago, they are considered 'returnees', who may even receive compensation for part of the cost of migrating to Germany (the so-called *Rückkehrkosten-zuschuß*).

By contrast, France is the European country which is closest to the civic assimilationist mode of ethnic relations politics. In France, the state is loathe to accept cultural pluralism within its national ideology, but in contrast to Germany, full rights to citizenship are obtained by birth within the national territory, and naturalisation is relatively easy for first generation migrants. However, the French state expects its citizens in return to place allegiance to the Republic prior to any religious, ethnic or cultural allegiance. This embodiment of French republicanism as a secular religion has placed high barriers to collective mobilisation by minority groups on the basis of shared ethnic or religious identity, indeed such forms of organisation have been allowed by the state only since 1981.

The third mode of ethnic relations politics is at odds with the mono-culturalism of Germany and France. Multicultural pluralist variants of ethnic relations politics are represented—albeit in different forms—by Britain, the Netherlands and Sweden in the European context. Here the state not only gives relatively easy access to citizenship by way of naturalisation or territorial birth, but actually recognises former immigrant groups as 'ethnic minorities' with their own special group rights. For example, in Britain, state bodies sponsor and promote equal treatment of 'racial minorities' in the labour market. The Commission for Racial Equality (CRE) is a state-funded institution which issues guidelines relating to the practices that private and state institutions should employ to avoid non-intentional discrimination against minorities. It also campaigns to uphold, implement and extend the framework of Race Relations and equal opportunities legislation that is already in place in Britain. Local authorities also play a role, by allocating funding for special provision to minorities, and regional and local equality councils act as local-level 'watchdogs' for ethnic minorities. Ultimately though, even within multicultural incorporation regimes such as that of Britain, the degree of cultural pluralism tolerated is limited by the extent to which special group rights are allowed to challenge the primacy of universal civic rights. The move by some British local governments in the 1980s to interpret equal treatment in the labour market as a need for 'positive action' recruitment policies to redress past discrimination was met with strong opposition.[4]

Britain and Germany represent cases of two different modes of incorporating migrants and minorities, which are based on equally divergent conceptions of citizenship and nationhood. As we show in the empirical analysis, this has important consequences for the actors and substance of claims-making in the migration and ethnic relations field.

Reconstructing Political Claims-Making from Newspaper Reports[5]

Our research strategy attempts to combine the quantitative rigour of recording collective actions with a qualitative sensitivity to the discursive elements of the claims made by the actors. For cross-national comparison, the core data source has been retrieved from one national newspaper for each country. The selected newspapers, *The Guardian* for Britain and the *Frankfurter Rundschau* for Germany, have a similar political affiliation (centre-left), and are broadsheet newspapers with a reputation for a consistent and detailed coverage of the topic. Reports relating to the topic were collected from the sections of the newspaper reporting national daily events, omitting editorial and commentary sections, for three editions (Monday, Wednesday and Friday) of the six which appear each week. It should be made absolutely clear at this point, that we have also applied this method to other newspapers in order to control for biases in the primary newspaper source.[6]

For coding, the primary unit of analysis for 'claims-making' is the reported act. This follows in the methodological tradition of protest event analysis from social movement research (Rucht, Koopmans and Neidhardt, eds, 1998), and not that of many media content analyses which take the article as the unit of analysis. Our coded acts may either be a protest event (demonstration, riot, arson, etc.) or a conventional action form (public statement, press conference, policy decision, etc.). It is worth emphasising, that we do not code the opinions and claims made by the author of the news article, we are interested only in the acts and claims that are attributed to 'third parties'. We code all acts within the ethnic, racist/extreme right, and anti-racist mobilisation fields, plus all acts by all actors in the issue-fields of asylum/immigration, ethnic relations, anti-racism and xenophobia that occur on the national territory. Important variables refer to actor types; action forms; the size, target and intensity of protest mobilisation (where present); and the actor on whom demands are made (addressee). Regarding the semantic contents of the claims, these are coded for the political aims and/or causal frames (where present). The different claims made by one actor in relation to a specific act are coded as part of the unitary act, and in cases where several demands are expressed, these are coded with the first as the first political aim, the second as the second political aim, and so on. As well as using a highly detailed category system, we attempt to store the discursive contents of claims, where this is feasible and necessary by retrieving the original speech of the claim present in the original text.

The resultant database has a high level of flexibility. As we shall shortly demonstrate, it is suitable for macro-level analyses of general issue-fields for cross-national research, and can also provide detailed information on a particular actor or movement and its strategic location within the national issue-field.

Political Contention over Migration and Ethnic Relations in Britain and Germany: General Characteristics

To put into context the more detailed analysis of claims-making about anti-racism and anti-discrimination that we present in the next section, it is helpful to take a look at some of the central characteristics of the broad field of migration and ethnic relations. Table 7.1 gives an impression of the distribution of claims-making in our two countries across four broad issue-fields. A first notable finding is that there are more than five times as many claims recorded in Germany than in Britain. This difference may be partly due to differences in reporting styles between the newspapers chosen in the two countries. Compared to the *Guardian*, the *Frankfurter Rundschau* tends to report larger numbers of events in less detail. However, judging from our experience with the two newspapers in the context of another project (Koopmans, 1996a), the difference in Table 7.1 seems much too large to be merely a methodological artefact. Thus, the politics of ethnic relations, citizenship and immigration seems to be a more important field of political contention in German politics in the 1990s than is the case in Britain.

The first row in Table 7.1, 'immigration politics' includes general immigration issues such as border controls and illegal immigration, and issues relating to asylum seekers, refugees and other specific immigrant groups, such as the *Aussiedler* in Germany. The relative importance of this issue-field does not differ much between Britain and Germany, although within the category there is a relatively strong emphasis in Germany on the issue of asylum, which may be seen as a result of the fact that Germany was much more strongly affected by the post-1989 wave of refugees from Eastern Europe than Britain.

Whereas 'immigration politics' deals with the regulation of immigration, the next two rows in the table refer to issues regarding the position of resident migrants and their integration into the host society. The category 'minority rights and integration politics' refers to claims regarding the political, social, and cultural rights of resident minorities, and to (actual or perceived) problems with their integration, for example, the issue of minority crime. Such issues are clearly more prominent in the British public debate than in Germany. Britain's official commitment to racial equality and a form of multiculturalism provides both institutional channels of access, and discursive resonance and legitimacy to claims referring to minority rights. By contrast, Germany's view of migrants as foreigners does not facilitate such types of claims-making.

In the third political issue-field, 'anti-racism and anti-discrimination', which we analyse in more detail in the next section, the issue of contention is not so much the minorities themselves and their rights and integration, but their treatment by the host society and its institutions. It is clear that this issue-field is of almost equal importance in both countries. However, as we shall see, this apparent similarity hides important differences in the types of anti-racism and anti-discrimination issues that are central in the two countries.

Finally, we distinguish a field that we label 'xenophobic politics', referring to undifferentiated rejections of migrants and minorities, that do not in themselves refer to any substantive policy issues. This includes statements and slogans like 'Germany for the Germans' or 'rights for whites', and violent attacks on minorities. Although they constitute a relatively small minority in

Table 7.1   Distribution of Claims over Migration and Ethnic Relations by Issue-Field, 1990–1995 (Per Cent)

	Germany	Britain
Immigration politics	41.1	38.3
Minority rights and integration politics	8.0	18.2
Anti-racism and anti-discrimination politics	40.0	41.4
Xenophobic politics	10.9	2.1
Total	**100.0**	**100.0**
N=	5 396	1 024

both countries, xenophobic claims were clearly more frequent in Germany. One should be careful in interpreting this finding as proof of a greater virulence of xenophobia in Germany. First, our data cover only overt forms of xenophobic claims-making and not the privately held views of citizens, which may well contain as many elements of xenophobia in Britain as in Germany. Second, in so far as we measure overt claims, we must take into account that the selection process by which such claims are made publicly visible by the media may well differ importantly between Germany and Britain. Due to its historical past in the Nazi period, acts of xenophobia have a high societal resonance in Germany. As a result, attacks by Germans on foreigners probably have a much higher likelihood of being considered newsworthy by journalists in Germany, than equivalent acts have in Britain. In how far this may explain the differences in Table 7.1, in whole or in part, is not easy to determine and would be a subject for a paper of its own. However, for our present analysis we may simply take the result at face value. Real or perceived, xenophobic claims and violence play a more prevalent role in the German public sphere than in Britain, and this has important consequences for the types of anti-racist and anti-discrimination claims-making that occur in the two countries.

Tables 7.2a and 7.2b shift the focus to the actors involved in claims-making over migration and ethnic relations. The first columns in each table show the percentage shares of different actors in the overall claims-making in the field. Without going into too much detail, we want to highlight several important findings which demonstrate the relevance of opportunity-structures in shaping the patterns of claims-making. First, the relative importance of different state and party-political actors reflects the different nature of the institutional structure and culture of German and British politics. Thus, the relatively centralised nature of the British polity is reflected in the marginal role played by regional and local political actors. Second, legislative actors play a more important role in British politics, which is linked to the legitimacy and power British MPs derive from their direct mandate from the electorate as representatives of constituencies. By contrast, political party organisations are much more important in Germany, because of both the strong role given to political parties in the German constitution and the fact that the German system of electoral representation attributes more importance to votes for party lists than for individual candidates. Another noteworthy finding with regard to actors within institutional politics is the marginal role played in both countries by transnational actors such as the UN and the EU. Since migration is among the fields where globalisation tendencies have progressed furthest, this indicates that thus far globalisation does not seem to have significantly eroded the primacy of the nation-state as a political actor.[7]

A striking finding regarding movement-like collective actors is the large difference between Germany and Britain with regard to the role played by ethnic minority organisations and groups, on one hand, and xenophobic and extreme right groups, on the other. While ethnic minorities play a marginal role as actors in the German public discourse (less than seven per cent of all claims), they are responsible for one fifth of the claims made in Britain (19.8 per cent), making them the single most important actor in the field. Thus, public debate in Britain is not just *about* minorities, but it is also to an important extent shaped *by* them. Again, this is again related to Britain's relatively inclusive ethnic relations policies, which not only generally enhance the visibility, resonance, and legitimacy of minority organisations and claims, but also provide minority actors with substantive channels of access to political and legal decision-making, through provisions laid down in the Race Relations Act, and other supplementary laws relating to anti-discrimination and equal opportunity. In addition the British state provides concrete support, funding and sponsorship for ethnic minority organisations, in particular through the Commission for Racial Equality (CRE) at the national level, and associated bodies and local government funding at the regional and local levels.

Whereas ethnic minority mobilisation remains weak in Germany, xenophobic and extreme right groups play a much more important role than in Britain. Most of this claims-making by the extreme right takes the form of violent attacks against minorities, and in particular against asylum seekers. This violence was related to a favourable opportunity-structure in the years 1991–1993, when a very controversial debate on asylum policies dominated the German political and media agendas (Koopmans, 1996b).

The second columns of Tables 7.2a and 7.2b give an impression of where the different actors are substantively situated in the public debate, by presenting the average 'valence' of claims made by each actor category. To compute these valences, we assign a score of –1 to each claim: if it supports xenophobic groups; and/or calls for a restriction in the numbers or rights of migrants/minorities; and/or is carried by a physical attack on ethnic minorities. Conversely, a +1 score is given to claims: if they are directed against racism, discrimination and xenophobic groups; and/or call for the extension or defence of the rights of migrants/minorities. Ambivalent and neutral statements are given a score of 0. The Tables show the resulting average position scores of different actors, within a discursive space running from –1 (for actors whose claims are exclusively anti-minority or xenophobic) to +1 (for actors whose claims are exclusively pro-minority or anti-xenophobic). By arranging the position scores in an ascending order we get an impression of the 'discursive distances' between the claims-making of different actors.

Not surprisingly and in accordance with the idea of social movements as challengers, we find that movement-like actors occupy the extremes of the discursive space. On the 'anti-minority' side, we find extreme right parties such as the British National Party (BNP) and the National-Democratic Party of Germany (NPD), and diverse extreme right and racist groups, including Neo-Nazi organisations, loosely organised skinhead groups and xenophobic youth gangs. On the other side of the discursive spectrum, we find anti-racist groups

Table 7.2a   Actors in Claims-Making over Migration and Ethnic Relations: Percentage Share in Total Claims-Making and Average Valence of Claims, Germany, 1990–1995

	Share of Total Claims %	Average Valence[*]
Racist and extreme right groups and organisations	4.5	–0.84
Youth groups	2.3	–0.58
Unknown actors	9.1	–0.21
National government	8.5	0.12
Regional and local governments	14.7	0.24
National political parties	11.6	0.26
Regional and local political parties	5.8	0.41
State executive bodies	0.7	0.44
Judiciary	4.4	0.44
Police and security agencies	2.1	0.47
Federal legislative	3.2	0.49
Employers' and business organisations	0.7	0.55
Miscellaneous organisations and groups	3.7	0.56
State executive bodies for migration/minority issues	2.0	0.57
Media	0.7	0.59
Supranational institutions (EU, UN)	0.6	0.61
Foreign governments	0.7	0.62
Churches	3.3	0.75
Regional and local legislative bodies	1.4	0.77
Scientific and cultural organisations	2.1	0.77
Unions and professional organisations	3.2	0.80
Antiracist, human rights and pro-minority organisations	5.4	0.91
Minority and migrant organisations and groups	6.7	0.93
Radical left groups	2.6	1.00
Total/overall average	**100.0**	**0.34**
N=	5 396	

[*] –1=anti-minority/racist; 1=pro-minority/anti-racist; 0=neither pro- nor anti-minority/racist.

and ethnic minority organisations in both countries. However, Tables 7.2a and 7.2b make it absolutely clear that in contrast to extreme right groups, anti-racists and minorities operate in a much more supportive environment. The near 'discursive allies' of anti-racists and minorities include not only other relatively marginal actors such as the radical left in Germany, and human rights organisations in both countries, but also established civil society institutions such as the labour unions and the churches.

Table 7.2b   Actors in Claims-Making over Migration and Ethnic Relations: Percentage Share in Total Claims-Making and Average Valence of Claims, Britain, 1990–1995

	Share of Total Claims %	Average Valence*
Racist and extreme right groups and organisations	2.3	−0.92
National government	13.8	−0.34
Police and security agencies	4.7	−0.21
Regional and local legislative bodies	3.1	−0.09
Regional and local political parties	0.3	−0.08
Regional and local governments	1.3	−0.08
Unknown actors	2.8	−0.07
Foreign governments	0.3	0
Employers' and business organisations	1.5	0.07
National political parties	1.3	0.15
Supranational institutions (EU, UN)	0.8	0.38
Media	2.2	0.43
State executive bodies	2.0	0.50
Judiciary	7.2	0.53
National legislative	12.5	0.55
State executive bodies for migration/minority issues	4.1	0.71
Miscellaneous organisations and groups	0.8	0.75
Minority and migrant organisations and groups	19.8	0.75
Churches	1.3	0.77
Scientific and cultural organisations	3.7	0.87
Unions and professional organisations	2.6	0.89
Anti-racist, human rights and pro-minority organisations	11.6	0.95
Total/overall average	**100.0**	**0.42**
N=	1 024	

* −1=anti-minority/racist; 1=pro-minority/anti-racist; 0=neither pro- nor anti-minority/racist.

Moving from the extremes to the centre of the discursive space we encounter those actors who can be qualified as 'members' of the polity. However, far from a unified 'vested interest alliance', we find a broad range of positions, sometimes coming very close to those of challenging social movement groups. This becomes especially clear if we differentiate government, legislative, and party actors by party political affiliation. In Germany, a very interesting case in point is the position of the Bavarian Christian Democrats, the CSU, who actually occupy a very similar position (–0.40; 2.7 per cent of all claims) as the extreme right *Republikaner* party in its anti-minority stance (–0.38; 0.9 per cent).[8] The CSU openly states that it aims to prevent the establishment of a political party to its right—a strategy which has thus far been quite successful. Table 7.2a suggests that this success was achieved by occupying the *Republikaner* party's public discursive space, i.e., by absorbing an important part of the extreme right's demands on minorities and migrants. To a lesser extent the same may be said of the British Conservative Party (–0.32; 17.7 per cent), although their position is clearly further away from that of the BNP (–0.86; 0.7 per cent). In the British electoral system, which disadvantages small parties, it is probably not necessary for the Conservatives to move very far to the right in order to absorb the electoral threat of the BNP. Conversely, unlike the *Republikaner* party, the BNP does not have much incentive to adopt more moderate positions since its electoral prospects are bleak anyway.

On the other side of the spectrum, we can see that anti-racist and minority groups can also count on support for their claims from within the political system. In Britain, the Labour Party (+0.71; 9.6 per cent)—which incidentally returns several 'black' Members of Parliament from constituencies with high minority populations—comes out clearly in favour of migrants and minorities, while in the German case this holds for the Liberal FDP, the Free Deomocratic Party (+0.64; 4.8 per cent), and for the Greens (+0.79; 4.1 per cent). State executive bodies dealing with migration and minority issues, such as the CRE in Britain and the Federal and regional Foreigners' Commissioners (*Ausländerbeauftragten*) in Germany, are another important ally, within the state apparatus, of anti-racists and minority groups. Conversely, the British Liberals' position (–0.09; 2.2 per cent) is more ambivalent, and the same is true for the German Social Democrats, the SPD (+0.37; 14.0 per cent), and even more so for the Christian Democrat CDU (+ 0.08; 10.1 per cent).

These Tables, 7.2a and 7.2b, simplify the positioning of actors within the field of migration and ethnic relations by supposing that we are dealing with a one-dimensional discursive space. However, as Table 7.3 shows, there are significant differences in the average valence scores, depending on the sub-field we are dealing with. In both countries we see the same hierarchy. Among the three substantive policy related issue-fields,[9] average scores are lowest in both countries for immigration issues, followed by minority rights and integration, and then anti-racism and anti-discrimination. In other words, new immigration finds less support in the public sphere than the extension of rights to already established legally resident migrants. More clearly still, public claims-making in both countries strongly opposes racism and discrimination. Surprisingly perhaps, this rejection of racism and discrimination is more unequivocal in Germany than in Britain. As we see in the next section, this is related to the different substantive content of this field, which is dominated by more controversial issues in Britain than in Germany.

Table 7.3   Average Valence of Claims on Immigration and Ethnic Relations by Issue-Field, 1990–1995[*]

	Germany	Britain
Immigration politics	0.20	0.32
Minority rights and integration politics	0.34	0.41
Anti-racism and anti-discrimination politics	0.85	0.59
Xenophobic politics	–1.00	–1.00
Overall average	**0.34**	**0.42**
N=	5 396	1 024

[*]–1=anti-minority/racist; 1=pro-minority/anti-racist; 0=neither pro- nor anti-minority/racist.

Distinguishing between these issue-fields also allows a more precise identification of the discursive position of actors in both countries. Only the extreme right occupies a consistent anti-minority position in all fields. Conservative parties, as well as the police and security agencies tend to occupy negative positions with regard to immigration and minority politics, but do not differ significantly from other actors in their rejection of racism and xenophobic violence. What we see here is a 'law and order coalition', which calls for the repression of xenophobic groups while simultaneously problematising crime, political extremism, illegal immigration, and 'misuse' of the right to asylum among ethnic minorities and migrants. Other actors, such as the SPD, in Germany, come out clearly in favour of an extension of rights for resident minorities, but take positions on immigration and asylum issues that are often close to those of the conservatives. Finally, minority and anti-racist organisations, along with their supporters such as the labour unions and the churches, occupy a consistent pro-minority position. As a consequence, the size and composition of pro-minority and anti-minority coalitions differ by issue-field and few actors can be simply classified as pro-minority or anti-minority on all counts. With these general characteristics of claims-making over immigration and ethnic relations in the two countries in mind, we can now proceed to a more detailed analysis of the field of anti-racism and anti-discrimination.

Claims-Making in the Anti-Racism and Anti-Discrimination Field

Most societal actors in liberal democratic societies reject racism and discrimination as normatively objectionable. Even sections of the extreme right may agree with this at a general level. Disagreement quickly mounts, however, when specific forms of racism and discrimination are discussed, when social and political sources of racism and discrimination and those responsible are identified, and when policy solutions are needed. On this level there may be a wide divergence not only between the views of individuals, but between the views of whole societies on what are the central issues of racism and discrimination.

Regarding the politics of anti-racism in Britain and Germany, a first difference concerns the terminology used. Apart from the radical left fringe, no one in Germany uses the term 'racism'. Instead, Germans talk about 'hostility towards foreigners' (*Ausländerfeindlichkeit*). 'Race' is generally absent from the political discourse on ethnic relations in Germany: 'race relations' or 'racial equality' are concepts which do not have a German equivalent. This is a result of the the fact that the language of race is strongly identified with the Nazi regime. Distinguishing people on the basis of race or colour is therefore considered to be illegitimate and dangerous, even if it is done for the purpose of promoting racial equality. It should be noted that such reservations with regard to the use of racial categories are perhaps most pronounced in Germany, but can also be found in many European countries which experienced occupation and the extermination of their fellow citizens on racial grounds. In a broader comparative perspective, it is perhaps the dominance of racial terminology in the Anglo-Saxon world that is exceptional, rather than Germany's strong reservations with regard to this way of framing the problem of xenophobia and discrimination.[10] If in the following, we talk about racism and anti-racism, we should keep in mind that in the German context we are referring to the contention over *Ausländerfeindlichkeit*, and this is not exactly the same as racism in the British case.

With this caveat in mind, we refer now to Table 7.4, which gives an overview of the substantive type of claims that were made in the anti-racism and anti-discrimination field. We have distinguished three main categories of claims. These are differentiated by the degree to which racism and discrimination are seen: either as a structural phenomenon, which has its source in the power structures and culture of the state and other societal institutions (*institutional racism and discrimination*); or as a problem that resides in the public's prejudices and the activities of xenophobic and extreme right wing groups (*societal racism and discrimination*). Between these two categories of claims, we distinguished a third hybrid category—*institutional responses to discrimination and racism*. This is where the state institutions themselves are not seen as the cause of racism and discrimination, but where

Table 7.4 Type of Claims in the Anti-Racism and Anti-Discrimination Field (Per Cent)

	Germany	Britain
Institutional discrimination and racism	**4.9**	**44.3**
Institutional discrimination general	–	12.7
Employment/labour market discrimination	–	9.4
Social service provision discrimination	–	5.4
Judiciary/legal system racism	–	1.2
Police racism	1.4	7.1
Mainstream politics racism	3.5	8.5
Institutional responses to discrimination and racism	**12.1**	**21.2**
Policy effectiveness & implementation re: discrimination	–	7.3
Judicial/legal system responses to discrimination/racism	0.7	5.2
Police responses to discrimination/racism	6.3	8.5
Politicians responses to discrimination/racism	5.1	0.2
Societal discrimination and racism	**83.0**	**34.5**
General	31.4	4.1
Tolerance/solidarity/protection of minorities	9.4	11.1
Education/community solutions	3.5	0.2
Vergangenheitsbewältigung (dealing with the past)	2.0	–
Counter-mobilisation	6.7	1.7
Repressive measures against racists/extreme right	19.9	7.1
Anti-racist claims	1.1	0.9
Physical Attacks on extreme right	3.9	0.4
Miscellaneous claims relating to public racism/discrimination	5.1	9.0
Total	**100.0**	**100.0**
N=	2 158	424

the problem is identified as the inadequate or ineffective ways in which the state and politicians take issue or deal with racism, discrimination, and xenophobic violence in society.

As Table 7.4 shows, the institutional perspective is dominant in Britain (44.3 per cent of all claims), and virtually absent in Germany (4.9 per cent). The important issues of political contention in Britain are systematic unequal treatment of minorities by public and private bodies, and in social service provision, discrimination in recruitment and employment of labour, and police racism. None of which implies that British institutions are more racist and discriminatory than their German counterparts. Social movement literature tells us that levels of protest cannot be used as indicators for the extent of the social problems that underlie them. Social movements depend on external opportunities to act and need to mobilise material and discursive resources, the availability of which tends to be inversely related to levels of deprivation. The concentration of British claims-making on issues of institutional racism and discrimination is therefore better interpreted as a result of the nature of British race relations politics. First, the notion of racial equality is firmly established as a norm in British political discourse, to which all British institutions, including societal actors such as employers, are formally committed. This provides a legitimating framework that enables claimants to frame real or alleged institutional racism and discrimination as deviations from an uncontested norm. Second, the British racial equality and anti-discrimination legislation provides a legal framework which challenging groups can refer to and use as a channel for asserting their claims in the public sphere. Third, a number of state-sponsored institutions, such as the (national) CRE and equivalent bodies at the local level, who have been set up with an explicit mandate to monitor the implementation of racial equality and anti-discrimination legislation, provide support for claimants who feel they have suffered acts of discrimination. To use our conceptual language, the British system of race relations politics has created an institutional opportunity-structure that provides channels of access to decision-making as well as a discursive opportunity-structure that gives resonance and legitimacy to claims against discrimination and racism in institutional contexts.

Such a facilitating structure is virtually absent in Germany. On the contrary, as most immigrants in Germany lack citizenship and are thus foreigners, their unequal treatment in many domains is in fact legally and normatively sanctioned. Because citizenship is a requirement for access to certain positions, some issues that are important in Britain do not arise at all in Germany. As a result the lack of representation of minorities in German political institutions, in the police force, or in the judiciary, cannot be challenged as deviations from a norm of equal representation as in Britain, at least not as long as this is simply a result of migrants' formal and legal exclusion on the basis of nationality. As 'foreigners', most immigrants in Germany fall under the jurisdiction of the Foreigners' Law, which specifies several restrictions to access in the labour market and social services for foreigners, and which contains provisions for the loss of residence permits with the result of deportation in cases of involvement in criminal activities or prolonged dependence on social welfare. Certainly, after long-term residence, foreigners can obtain an increasingly secure legal status which does away with many, but not all, of these restrictions. However, even long-term residence, or in the case of migrant children the fact of being born in Germany, does not give an individual the legal or normative right to equal treatment.[11] The point here is not that Germany has special legislation for non-nationals—Britain has such legislation too, which is certainly no less restrictive than its German counterpart (Çinar, Hofinger and Waldrauch, 1995). What is crucial, however, is that due to Germany's restrictive conception of citizenship, virtually all immigrants and their descendants fall under this special legislation, whereas in Britain most migrants, and certainly those born or long-time resident in the country, have British citizenship.

Another consequence of this aspect of citizenship is that Germany has no anti-discrimination or equal opportunity legislation or institutions to which anti-racist or anti-discrimination claimants are able to refer their appeals. The group for which such legislation is meant in the British context—citizens legally and normatively entitled to equal treatment but nevertheless subjected to discrimination on the basis of ethnicity or race—is simply not a relevant social category in Germany. Due to the absence of a framework for institutionally sanctioned rights and norms of equality, anti-racist and anti-discrimination claims in Germany are made within a framework of humanitarian values, which emphasise the need for tolerance, solidarity, hospitality and acceptance of foreigners and their cultures. The single largest category of claims (general claims against societal discrimination and racism) did not refer to any specific political aim, but simply expressed moral rejection of *Ausländerfeindlichkeit* (hostility to foreigners), anti-Semitism, or xenophobic violence. Rather than emphasising the structural dimension, anti-racist claims-making in Germany focuses attention on the often violent activities of xenophobic groups. In as far as specific solutions to this problem are advanced, they call, in the large majority of cases, for repression of extreme right groups and organisations, and for tougher sentences for the perpetrators of xenophobic violence (20 per cent of all claims).

It is important to emphasise that anti-racist mobilisation of this type has been a particularly massive phenomenon in Germany in the 1990s, mobilising millions of people in candle-lit marches against violent attacks on foreigners.

Thus, the large majority of the German population strongly reject xenophobia, and many Germans were actively engaged in protecting foreigners against such attacks, for instance with nightly vigils at asylum seeker centres. These demonstrations of solidarity show that there is no basis for the alarmist stories that Germany is on the verge of falling victim to Neo-Nazism. The main point of our argument is not that German public discourse takes racism less seriously than the British. The difference is rather that in the British discourse racism and discrimination are predominantly seen as an institutional problem of rights and their implementation, whereas the typical anti-racist claims-making in Germany consists of humanitarian and moral appeals to the German public's tolerance, and demands to repress those extremist minorities who place themselves outside this moral order.

Next, we turn in Table 7.5 to the actors involved in claims-making in the anti-racism and anti-discrimination field. Generally, these results are very similar to those for the broad field of migration and ethnic relations in Tables 7.2a and 7.2b. In line with the expectations derived from the opportunity model, we again find that ethnic minorities are more important actors in Britain than in Germany (19.6 per cent compared to 9.6 per cent, respectively), although the German minorities' share of claims-making on anti-racism issues is somewhat greater than their involvement in overall claims-making on migration and ethnic relations (6.7 per cent, see Table 7.2a). A closer inspection of the minority organisations and groups involved shows that this result is primarily brought about by claims made by Jewish organisations and spokespersons. In Germany, this group is, of course, a highly legitimate moral authority on issues of racism and right wing extremism. However, it is important to note that this legitimacy derives from the Jews' position as victims of the Holocaust, and not, or far less, from a status as speakers for ethnic minorities or migrants in general.[12]

There are a number of smaller deviations from the overall pattern in Tables 7.2a and 7.2b to which we would like to draw attention. First, in both countries government actors are less strongly involved in anti-racist claims-making than in the overall field. More generally, institutional actors—with the understandable exception of the police and security agencies, and the judiciary in Germany—are relatively less important, and civil society actors relatively more important in the anti-racism field.[13] This is probably a result of the fact that issue-fields such as immigration, asylum and minority rights are more policy-oriented, while in the anti-racism field moral issues, on which civil society actors are generally considered more legitimate speakers, have a greater prominence.

In Table 7.6 we show the actors to whom claims and demands are directed. Actors can appear in claims as addressees, either as the object of criticism (e.g., 'the police are not doing enough to combat xenophobic violence'), or more neutrally, as actors who are called upon to take measures to solve the problem identified in the claim (e.g., 'local authorities should ban racist demonstrations'). We systematically excluded minority and xenophobic groups, as these are automatically implied in claims on migration and ethnic relations (e.g., we could have coded 'xenophobic groups' as the criticised actor in many of the anti-racist statements, but this would not have been very helpful from an analytical perspective). Before we discuss which actors were

Table 7.5   Actors Making Claims in the Anti-Racism and Anti-Discrimination Field, by Type, 1990–1995 (Per Cent)

	Germany	Britain
Supranational institutions (EU, UN)	0.2	0.5
Foreign governments	1.1	–
National government	7.0	4.2
Regional and local governments	11.2	1.2
National legislative	3.5	10.1
Regional and local legislative bodies	2.1	6.1
Judiciary	5.8	6.4
Police and security agencies	3.9	6.1
State institutions dealing with minorities and migrants	1.2	7.3
Other state institutions	0.7	1.7
National political parties	7.4	1.7
Regional and local parties	5.8	0.7
Total state and party actors	**49.9**	**46.0**
Unions and professional organisations	5.1	4.7
Employers and business organisations	1.4	0.5
Churches	3.2	0.9
Media	1.3	2.6
Scientific and cultural organisations	3.8	6.4
Anti-racist, human rights and pro-minority organisations	3.6	9.9
Radical left groups	5.8	–
Minority and migrant groups and organisations	9.6	19.6
Racist and extreme right organisations and groups	3.0	0.7
Other organisations and groups	4.9	5.4
Unknown actors	8.2	3.3
Total	**99.8***	**100.0**
N=	2,158	424

* Due to rounding error the figure for Germany is 99.8 per cent and not 100.0 per cent.

most frequently mentioned, we should note that an important number of claims did not mention an addressee at all. This is especially true for such claims that expressed little more than an expressive, moral rejection of xenophobia, without proposing any concrete solutions. In line with what we said above about the stronger moral focus of the German discourse on racism, compared to the more structural focus of British claims-making, we find that the share of claims which mentioned an actual addressee—and thus went beyond mere expressive claims—is much higher in Britain than in Germany (66 and 38 per cent, respectively; compare the N's in Tables 7.6 and 7.5).

Clearly, institutional actors are by far the dominant focus of claims-making on racism and discrimination, either because they are criticised

Table 7.6   Actors Addressed by Claims in the Anti-Racism and Anti-Discrimination Field: Addressees, 1990–1995 (Per Cent)

	Germany	Britain
Supranational institutions (EU, UN)	–	0.4
Foreign governments	0.7	–
National government	13.7	7.2
Regional and local governments	11.2	6.8
National legislative	9.4	4.7
Regional and local legislative bodies	1.9	6.8
Judiciary	6.8	9.7
Police and security agencies	17.6	30.6
State institutions dealing with minorities and migrants	0.2	3.6
Other state institutions	1.1	7.9
National political parties	11.7	3.2
Regional and local parties	5.8	0.4
'Politicians' unspecified	0.7	1.4
Total state and party actors	**80.8**	**82.7**
Unions and professional organisations	4.7	4.0
Employers and business organisations	0.6	2.5
Churches	1.0	0.7
Media	3.3	1.4
Scientific and cultural organisations	2.9	2.5
Anti-racist, human rights and pro-minority organisations	0.4	3.2
Radical left groups	0.5	–
Other organisations and groups	5.8	3.0
Total	**100.0**	**100.0**
N=	822	278

themselves for discriminating, or because they are called upon to act against racism and discrimination by societal actors. The single most important addressee in both countries is the police and security agencies, particularly in Britain, where 30.6 per cent of all claims that mentioned an addressee were directed at this actor. For the British case, next come the judiciary (9.7 per cent) and the category of 'other state institutions' (7.9 per cent), which comprises for instance health and social service agencies. In Germany, the most important addressees after the police and security agencies are governments, both national (13.7 per cent) and regional and local (11.2 per cent), as well as the national political parties (11.7 per cent). Civil society organisations are mentioned as addressees in only twenty per cent or less in both countries, with unions and professional organisations being most frequently mentioned within this category.

Conclusions

Political decisions in the field of migration and ethnic relations may at times remain hidden from the public agenda, as politicians are often keen to 'manage' potentially divisive or coalition-threatening issues away from the scrutiny of public debate. Experience tells us, however, that the many different national attempts to provide institutional solutions to the problems relating to migration and ethnic relations have tended to produce more rather than less public reactions. Cleavages over cultural, ethnic and religious difference and the policy fields which are designed to manage them resonate constantly as issues in the public spheres of all European countries. As yet, however, there have been surprisingly few academic attempts to systematically deal with the public dimension of this important topic.

In this chapter, we have suggested that our understanding of the political process relating to issues of migration and ethnic relations can profit from the adoption of theoretical perspectives and methodological tools that have been developed in research on social movements, collective action, and political discourse. Theoretically, we have emphasised the importance of what we call institutional and discursive opportunity-structures in shaping the chances for accessibility of different actors and specific types of claims to the public and political domain. Methodologically, we have shown how an analysis of acts drawn from news coverage of events may be used to identify nationally specific patterns of claims-making on migration and ethnic relations.

In the empirical part of the paper, we devoted particular attention to claims-making within the anti-racism and anti-discrimination field in Britain and Germany. On the surface, this field seemed to be equally as important in both countries. However, as we have demonstrated, the broad category of 'anti-racism and anti-discrimination' refers to different things in the two countries.

In Britain, the field is dominated by demands that focus on structural forms of racism and discrimination, originating in the workings of institutions such as the police and the judiciary, the social services, or in the labour market. Such claims are sustained by the tension between the legally sanctioned norms of non-discrimination and equal opportunity embedded in British race relations politics, and—actual or perceived—deviations from this norm in the form of continued institutional discrimination against minorities. The British multicultural mode of incorporation not only gives resonance and legitimacy to these forms of claims-making, but also facilitates the mobilisation of minorities and pro-minority groups by providing resources and some channels of access to the policy process.

By contrast, in Germany this structural, institutional focus is almost entirely absent. As the large majority of immigrants in Germany are not citizens, but foreigners, there are no legal norms of equal treatment or institutional targets to which such claims-making could refer. On the contrary, various forms of unequal treatment of migrants are legally sanctioned on the basis of their status as non-citizens. As a result, anti-racist claims-making in Germany does not have the emphasis on rights of minorities and their implementation that is typical for Britain, but has a strong moral, humanitarian focus which stresses the duties of Germans to be tolerant and hospitable. Such claims are often very general and do not refer to any specific policy solutions. In as far as concrete demands are made, in the majority of cases they aim to increase the repression of those extremist and xenophobic groups, who place themselves outside this moral order.

That we are often talking about very different phenomena in comparing the politics of migration and ethnic relations in different countries will not surprise many readers. However, by introducing a methodological tool that allows us to pinpoint more precisely where the cross-national similarities and differences are, we think that we are able to move beyond the paralysing emphasis on national idiosyncratic stereotypes that permeates many descriptive cross-national studies. Moreover, by linking patterns of claims-making systematically to institutional and discursive opportunity-structures, we are able to situate national 'peculiarities' in a broader theoretical framework, that may help to advance our knowledge about how specific modes of migrant and minority incorporation affect levels and types of political conflict relating to ethnic and racial difference.

Notes

1 More detailed and systematic overviews of recent approaches to social movement literature are given in McAdam, McCarthy, and Zald (1988) and Tarrow (1994).

2 For a critical overview of this perspective in social movement research, see Donati (1992).

3 A more elaborate version of this approach appears in Koopmans and Statham (2000).

4 In addition, multicultural pluralism tends to maintain a relative hierarchy between the different cultures that are included within nationhood. British Muslims discovered through the Salman Rushdie controversy that the nation's blasphemy laws did not extend to their religion.

5 A more detailed exposition on the theoretical underpinning to our method appears in Koopmans and Statham (1999b). The British data for this project was collected with the assistance of a grant from the British Economic and Social Research Council (R000236558) held at the Institiute of Communcations Studies, University of Leeds. The German project was internally funded by the Wissenschaftszentrum Berlin (WZB).

6 In the British case, *The Times*, the *Sun*, the *Daily Express*, the *Mail*, and the *Mirror* have been coded in addition to the *Guardian* for 1995. In all cases except the *Mirror*—where there were too few cases—similar overall proportions of actors appear in the other samples, as in the *Guardian*. This vindicates the method by showing that the political affiliation and even genre (broad-sheet/tabloid) of the source does not significantly affect the proportion of recorded collective actions by different actor types. For example, in the *Guardian* sample for 1995, 21.1 per cent of the acts were by government actors; 18.6 per cent by ethnic minority actors; and 1.7 per cent by the extreme right; whereas for the *Sun*, a populist right wing tabloid, the respective proportions were similar, 23.3 per cent government actors, 16.3 per cent ethnic minority actors, and 2.3 per cent extreme right. For the German case, comparisons between the *Frankfurter Rundschau* and the right wing tabloid *Bild* give similar findings. The number of reported claims in the whole field is 4.6 times higher in the *Rundschau* than in *Bild*, but distributions across different issues (asylum, integration, anti-racism, etc.) hardly differs among the two papers, nor does the representation of different actors.

7 The same conclusion holds if we were to look at transnational and international actors as addressees of demands. Only 4.2 per cent of all claims in Britain and 1.4 per cent in Germany were directed at such actors. For a detailed elaboration on this topic see Koopmans and Statham (1999c).

8 Of course, one has to take into account here that the measure employed is relatively crude and does not distinguish between individual claims with regard to the degree to which they are anti-minority. Nevertheless, our measure does indicate that the CSU's interventions in the public debate are as often negative with regard to the position and rights of minorities as those of the *Republikaner* party.

9 The xenophobic politics field has, of course, a score of –1.00 by definition.

10 If Germany were to grant equal citizenship rights to its immigrant population, this would create a dilemma that is not easily resolvable. In order to promote equality, and especially if one wants to introduce forms of positive action, it is often necessary to have some form of registration of people's ethnic or racial background. While this is routinely done in the Anglo-Saxon context, it is clear that this type of labelling does not fit easily into the German context.

11 A spectacular recent case was that of a fourteen-year-old Turkish boy born and raised in Munich, who had committed a series of serious crimes and was deported 'back' to Turkey. The Bavarian government originally wanted also to deport his parents, residents for thirty years with no criminal record whatsoever, but this was ultimately prevented by a ruling of the Constitutional Court, which nonetheless did sanction the deportation of the child.

12 Without the Jewish groups, the share of ethnic minorities in overall claims-making (Table 7.2a) drops from 6.7 to 4.2 per cent and in anti-racist claims-making from 9.6 to 4.3 per cent, making the contrast with Britain regarding the representation of ethnic minorities and migrants even clearer than it appears in the Tables 7.2a and 7.2b, and 7.5.

13 In Britain, institutional (state and party) actors constitute 51 per cent of the whole field, and 46 per cent of the anti-racism and discrimination field. In Germany the respective figures are 56 per cent and 50 per cent.

References

Benford, R.D. (1997), 'An insider's critique of the social movement framing perspective', *Sociological Inquiry*, vol. 67, no. 4, pp. 409–430.

Brubaker, R. (1992), *Citizenship and Nationhood in France and Germany*, Cambridge, MA, Harvard University Press.

Castells, S. and Miller, M. (1993), *The Age of Migration. International Population Movements in the Modern World*, London, Macmillan.

Castles, S. (1995), 'How nation-states respond to immigration and ethnic diversity', *New Community*, vol. 21, no. 3, pp. 293–308.

Çinar, D., Hofinger, C. and Waldrauch, H. (1995), 'Intergrationsindex. Zur rechlichten Integration von AusländerInnen in aus gewählten europäischen Ländern', *Political Science Series*, no. 25, Institute for Advanced Studies, Vienna.

Diani, M. (1996), 'Linking mobilization frames and political opportunities: insights from regional populism in Italy', *American Sociological Review*, vol. 61, no. 6, pp. 1053–1069.

Donati, P. (1992), 'Political Discourse Analysis', in R. Eyerman and M. Diani (eds), *Studying Collective Actors*, London, Sage Publications, pp. 138–167.

Duyvendak, J.W. (1995), *The Power of Politics. New Social Movements in France*, Boulder, Westview Press.

Favell, A. (1998), *Philosophies of Integration. Immigration and the Idea of Citizenship in France and Britain*, Houndmills, Basingstoke, Macmillan.

Gamson, W.A., and Modigliani, A. (1989), 'Media discourse and public opinion on nuclear power. A constructionist approach', *American Journal of Sociology*, no. 95, pp. 1–38.

Goffman, E. (1974), *Frame Analysis. An Essay on the Organization of Experience*, Cambridge Mass., Harvard University Press.

Hailbronner, K. and Renner, G. (1998), *Staatsangehörigkeitsrecht*, München, C.H. Beck'sche.

Hilgartner, S. and Bosk, C.L. (1988), 'The rise and fall of social problems: a public arenas model', *American Journal of Sociology*, no. 94, pp.53–78.

Ireland, P. (1994), *The Policy Challenge of Ethnic Diversity. Immigrant Politics in France and Switzerland*, Cambridge, MA, Harvard University Press.

Kitschelt, H. (1986), 'Political opportunity structures and political protest. Anti-nuclear movements in four democracies', *British Journal of Political Science*, no. 16, pp. 57–85.

Koopmans, R. (1996a), 'New social movements and changes in political participation in Western Europe', *West European Politics*, vol. 19, no. 1, pp. 28–50.

Koopmans, R. (1996b), 'Asyl: Die Karriere eines politischen Konfliktes', in Wolfgang van den Daele and Friedhelm Neidhardt (eds), *Kommunikation und Entscheidung. Politische Funktionen öffentlicher Meinungsbildung und diskursiver Verfahren*, Berlin, Edition Sigma, pp. 167–192.

Koopmans, R. and J.W. Duyvendak (1995), 'The political construction of the nuclear energy issue and its impact on the mobilization of anti-nuclear movements in Western Europe', *Social Problems*, no. 42, pp. 235–251.

Koopmans, R., and Kriesi, H. (1997), 'Citoyenneté, identité nationale et mobilisation de l'extrême droite. Une comparaison entre la France, l'Allemagne, les Pays-Bas et la Suisse', in P. Birnbaum (ed.), *Sociologie des nationalismes* Paris, Presses Universitaires de France, pp. 273–294.

Koopmans, R. and Statham, P. (1999a), 'Ethnic and civic conceptions of nationhood and the differential success of the extreme right, in Germany and Italy', in M. Giugni, D.McAdam and C. Tilly, (eds), *How Social Movements Matter. Theoretical and Comparative Studies on the Consequences of Social Movements*, Minneapolis, University of Minnesota Press.

Koopmans, R. and Statham, P. (1999b), 'Political claims analysis: Integrating protest Event and Political Discourse Approaches', *Mobilization. The International Journal of Research and Theory about Social Movements, Protest and Collective Behavior*, vol. 4, no. 2.

Koopmans, R. and Statham, P. (1999c), 'Challenging the liberal nation-state? Postnationalism, multiculturalism, and the collective claims-making of migrants and ethnic minorities in Britain and Germany', *Discussion Paper Series*, Wissenschaftszentrum Berlin (WZB), FS III 98–105, pp. 1–52.

Koopmans, R. and Statham, P. (2000), 'The Contentious politics of migration, ethnic relations and xenophobia: An opportunity structure approach', in R. Koopmans and P. Statham (eds), *Challenging Immigration and Ethnic Relations Politics: Comparative European Perspectives*, Oxford, Oxford University Press.

Kornhauser, W. (1959), *The Politics of Mass Society*, Glencoe, III, Free Press.

Kriesi, H., Koopmans, R. Duyvendak, J.W. and Giugni, M.G. (1995), *New social movements in Western Europe: a comparative analysis*, Minneapolis, University of Minnesota Press.

Le Bon, G. (1960), *The Crowd: A Study of the Popular Mind*, New York, Viking Press.

McAdam, D. (1982), *Political Process and the Development of Black Insurgency*, Chicago, Unversity of Chicago Press.

McAdam, D., McCarthy, J.D. and Zald, M.N. (1988), 'Social movements', in Neil J. Smelser, (ed.), *Handbook of Sociology*, London, Sage, pp. 695–738.

McAdam, D., McCarthy, J.D. and Zald, M. N. (eds) (1996), *Comparative Perspectives on Social Movements*, Cambridge, Cambridge University Press.

McCarthy, J.D. and Zald, M. N. (1977), 'Resource mobilization and social movements: a partial theory', *American Journal of Sociology*, no. 82, pp. 1212–1241.

Moscovici, S. (1985), *The Age of the Crowd. A Historical Treatise on Mass Psychology*, Cambridge, Cambridge University Press.

Nelkin, D. and Pollak, M. (1981), *The Atom Besieged Extraparliamentary Dissent in France and Germany*, Cambridge, Mass., MIT Press.

Oberschall, A. (1973), *Social Conflict and Social Movements*, Engelwood Cliffs, New Jersey,

Prentice-Hall.

Rath, J. (1991), *Minorisering: De Sociale Constructie van Ethnische Minderheden*, PhD Thesis, University of Utrecht, Netherlands.

Rex, J. (1994), 'Introduction', in John Rex and Beatrice Drury (eds), *Ethnic Mobilisation in a Multi-Cultural Europe*, Aldershot, Avebury, pp. 3–12.

Rucht, D., Koopmans, R. and Neidhardt, F. (eds) (1998), *Acts of Dissent. New Developments in the Study of Protest*, Berlin, Edition Sigma.

Shorter, E. and Tilly, C. (1971), *Strikes in France, 1830–1968*, Cambridge, Cambridge University Press.

Smith, D.M. and Blanc, M. (1996), 'Citizenship, nationality and ethnic minorities in three European nations', *International Journal of Urban and Regional Research*, vol. 20, no. 1, pp. 66–82.

Snow, D. A. and Benford, R. (1992), 'Master frames and cycles of protest', in Aldon Morris and Carol Clurgh Mueller (eds), *Frontiers in Social Movement Theory*, New Haven, Yale University Press, pp.133–155.

Snow, D.A., Burke Rochford, E., Wordon, S.K. and Benford, R. (1986), 'Frame alignment processes, micromobilization, and movement participation', *American Sociological Review*, no. 51, pp. 464–481.

Solomos, J. and Back, L. (1995), *Race, Politics and Social Change*, London, Routledge.

Statham, P. (1998), 'The political construction of immigration politics in Italy: opportunities, mobilisation and outcomes', *Discussion Paper Series*, Wissenschaftszentrum Berlin (WZB), FS III 98–102, pp. 1–60.

Tarrow, S., (1994), *Power in Movement. Social Movements, Collective Action and Politics*, Cambridge, Cambridge University Press.

Tilly, C. (1978), *From Mobilization to Revolution*, Reading, MA, Addison-Wesley.

Tilly, C., Tilly, L. and Tilly, R. (1975), *The Rebellious Century. 1830–1930*, Cambridge, Mass., Harvard University Press.

Wieviorka, M. (ed.) (1996), *La société fragmentée? Le multi-culturalisme en débat*, Paris, La Decouverte.

Zald, M.N. and Ash, R. (1966), 'Social Movement Organizations: Growth Decay and Change' *Social Forces*, no. 44, pp. 327–41.

8 Group Goal Attributions and Stereotypes in Five Former Soviet States

LOUK HAGENDOORN & HUB LINSSEN

Introduction

In this chapter we will analyse negative inter-group stereotypes in five former Soviet states. The stereotypes refer to assumed negative traits—such as hostility and lack of reliability—of outgroup members. Such negative trait attributions can be considered as prejudice in so far as they reflect individual concerns that are unrelated to the negatively evaluated outgroups. However, negative trait attributions can also result from a realistic appraisal of outgroup characteristics, for example in the case of a real conflict over material or symbolic resources. The factors leading to biased or realistic negative evaluations of outgroups have received much attention in the literature on stereotypes and prejudice (Forbes, 1997). Yet, another source of negative trait attributions to outgroups, that negative goals attributed to outgroups as a collective may reinforce these stereotypes, has received less attention in the literature. Such attributed goals may be inferred from the positions outgroups have in society, from their organisational structure and actions, or from the history of the inter-group relations. Our hypothesis is that the attribution of outgroup goals will reinforce the attribution of negative traits to outgroup members if such goals are perceived as a threat to the ingroup. The effect will be tested across different countries, hence as a general cross-national effect. However, whereas the reasons groups have for attributing negative goals to outgroups may differ across countries, the nature and intensity of the effect will vary. The effect is expected to be particularly strong in countries with a recent history of violent conflict between the groups. This will be tested as well. We will first elaborate the concepts and then present the results of the research.

Aggregate Stereotypes and the Attribution of Group Goals

Usually stereotypes are conceived of as physical and psychological characterisations of ingroup or outgroup members (Brown, 1988). Stereotypes have been measured as traits characterising the majority (Katz and Braly, 1933), or the typical representatives (Brigham, 1971) of the stereotyped group, or characterising the stereotyped group more than comparison groups (McCauley and Stitt, 1978). Apart from the differences in determining what makes the attributed traits typical, these approaches have in common that the group to which the traits are attributed is defined as an aggregate of individuals (Devine, 1989; Augoustinos, Ahrens and Innes, 1994). The question is, however, whether or not people do indeed have only aggregates of individuals in mind when they think of social groups? Often social groups appear not only as categories of individuals but also as organised wholes trying to realise common goals. It is therefore plausible that the cognitive representation of groups also includes notions about the structure and goal orientations of these groups. The difference between these two aspects of group representations, that is, the attribution of traits to an aggregate of group members versus attributions of goals to a group as a whole, can be made clear by a simple example. Imagine a group of soldiers saluting their officer in command. All of them—as an aggregate of individuals—will appear as obedient. Next, imagine that a command to attack is shouted. Now they will appear as an aggressive collective, a machine prepared to fight. The difference is that the first representation focuses on typical traits shared by individual members of the group, while the second representation captures what the group as a whole is aiming at. In the second representation the group is not an aggregate but, rather, an entity with a will of its own. Campbell (1958) refers to this as 'entitativity'. A group is perceived as a group because it is an entity bound by a common fate, which extends from the past into the future. Group members are assumed to have a common history in the past and a common goal in the future.

Several authors have suggested that notions about group goals relate to stereotypes (Bar-Tal, 1990; Blumer, 1958; Horowitz, 1985; Kofta, 1994). Blumer (1958), for example, conceives prejudice basically as a sense of group-position rather than a set of individual feelings about outgroup members. Sense of group-position is in Blumer's view a social representation of the superiority or inferiority of the ingroup vis-à-vis outgroups. For dominant groups this sense of group-position consists of feelings of superiority, a proprietary claim to certain areas of privilege, and the idea that outgroups are intrinsically alien and harbour designs to claim the prerogatives of the ingroup. Bar-Tal has made an inventory of many different beliefs that people can have about the attributes and goals of groups, be it dominant or subordinate, majority or minority groups. Kofta (1994) considers the attribution of specific goals to outgroups as a separate aspect—or 'module'—of stereotypes, which he suggestively labels 'group-soul stereotypes'. Horowitz (1985) implicitly refers to the same aspect of stereotypes when claiming that negative intergroup relations almost always refer to groups differing in power and resources.

Although stereotypes have often been analysed in the context of inter-group relations (Mackie and Smith, 1998), the way in which group members incorporate the internal structure of outgroups in their stereotypes has generally not been taken into account. The suggestion of the above mentioned authors, to take into account the goals and internal structure attributed to outgroups in studying inter-group stereotypes, has not stimulated empirical research. Yet, the analysis of the intentions attributed to outgroups as a whole, instead of only to individual representatives of outgroups, seems vital to understanding the content of mutual stereotypes in contexts of inter-group antagonism and conflict. The analysis may reveal which features of the structure and position of outgroups lead to attributions of outgroup goals and how these features and goals are related. It may also show whether or not different goals and intentions are associated with the group as a whole or only with particular representatives, for example the leaders. And it may indicate whether or not the goals and intentions of outgroups affect all ingroup members or only challenge those who are directly threatened by them.

Outgroup Features Triggering Attributions of Outgroup Goals

If the attribution of goals to outgroups is a relevant factor affecting the attribution of specific traits to outgroup members, which then are the features of groups from which these attributed goals are inferred? A general hypothesis is that such goal attributions are inferred from the actions of outgroups and the context of their relative positions in society. The positions of groups are generally defined by a small number of significant dimensions and their actions are constrained by these positions. For example, the dimensions defining the position of ethnic and national groups in society are their relative group size and dispersion; social status and economic, political and cultural power; memory of past dominance and subordination relations; and ties that groups have with other groups, for example with foreign nations (Hagendoorn, Phalet, Henke and Drogendijk, 1995). In this respect the Hungarian minority in Slovakia can be characterised as a small national minority, concentrated in southern Slovakia close to the border with Hungary, having little control over the national economy and political system, and having been dominant in the past and tied to Hungary. Such features may invoke Slovaks to attribute potential lack of loyalty and irredentist aspirations to Hungarians in Slovakia. The attributed lack of loyalty belongs to the category of traditional trait attributions while the attributed irredentism is a goal or intention attributed to the group as an organised collective.

Group goal attributions clarify why groups perceive other groups as a threat. However, the perception of threat often results from impending changes in the inter-group-positions than from the existing group-positions per se. A threat of changing group-positions may be inferred from changes in the demography of groups, economic competition, and territorial claims of outgroups. Threat may also be evoked by memories of former domination, or by feelings of relative deprivation in comparison to outgroups. The violent conflict between Azeris and Armenians in Nagorno Karabach in the former Soviet Union in the 1980s, for example, arose from the Armenian fear of Azeri population growth, economic competition between Armenians and Azeris, historical enmity between the two populations, and feelings of relative deprivation of Armenians in Nagorno Karabach in comparison to Armenians in Armenia. The Armenians were afraid to lose their titular status in Nagorno Karabach and their autonomy within Azerbaidzjan (Yamskov, 1991). Hence, it was actually an impending change of group-positions that triggered the conflict. Political leaders activate fear of such changes when rallying support. The kernel of the evoked threat is that outgroups intend to harm the interests of the ingroup.

Types of Minority Groups and Typical Stereotypes

If the relative positions of groups govern the pattern and content of goal attributions to outgroups and thereby the content of mutual group stereotypes, what then is the match between positional features and attributions of harmful goals? A consideration of types of groups manifest in the ethnic composition of European countries may suggest which types of goal attributions are relevant. Many countries have *diasporic* goups of post-colonial migrants, guest workers, Jews and Gypsies. Generally these groups are not strongly concentrated but are, rather, dispersed mainly across urban areas. Yet there are also territorially concentrated ethnic and national minorities in many countries, such as Basques, Scots, Germans in Belgium etc., hence with or without a foreign homeland. In Central and Eastern European countries national minorities can be differentiated into specific subtypes, such as of former ruling groups (e.g., Russians in Ukraine, Hungarians in Slovakia) and minorities that were in the past dominated groups (e.g., Ukrainians in Russia, Slovaks in Hungary). These characteristics suggest the possible content of mutual stereotypes in terms of specific goal attributions. Diasporic groups (e.g., Gypsies in Hungary) can be perceived as parasites (Verdery, 1992). In some cases they are depicted as agents of hostile international networks (e.g., Zionism). Stereotypes of minorities that were once former rulers of the now dominant ingroup may, in contrast, accentuate the ingroup's intention to dominate and exploit, or the fear of potential betrayal by these groups because they will act as an agent (fifth column) of their foreign homeland. Stereotypes of minorities ruled by the ingroup in the past (e.g., Ukrainians perceived by Russians) will, rather, reflect the ungratefulness and disloyalty of such newly independent groups. Not just a single feature but the whole complex of historical and current data defining the position of groups within a country's ethnic composition, determines which harmful traits and goals are attributed to outgroups.

Conditions Evoking the Perception of Threat

The perception of an outgroup as a threat mirrors the attribution of harmful goals to outgroups. However, the reason for the perception of threat lies elsewhere. It is located in the emerging interpretation of contemporary inter-group relations. Typical inter-group relations activating such attribution processes are: (a) unequal economic, cultural, or political positions of ethnic groups (Gellner, 1983), (b) different citizenship of ethnic groups (Brubaker, 1992), and (c) the feeling that groups have weaker positions than they deserve (relative deprivation). Moreover, (d) active attempts by outgroups to limit the socio-economic opportunities of the ingroup by barriers to upward mobility, economic competition, and by rising outgroup educational levels and mobility (Gellner, 1994; Kaiser, 1994) have the same effect. Finally, (e) political extremism, violence and nationalism of outgroups are signals confirming the perceived threat because they are an explicit message of the intention to change the existing inter-group-positions.

In summary, negative stereotypes evolve from negative aspects of the inter-group relations (inequality, competition, relative deprivation). They are strongly reinforced by the attribution of harmful goals to outgroups. Such attributed goal orientations are derived from the position outgroups have relative to the ingroup in the ethnic composition of the respective society.

Context of the Research and Hypotheses

In this chapter a specific type of goal attributions to outgroups will be studied, that is *fifth column* attributions. Fifth column attributions are particularly relevant in the context of triangular inter-group relations. A prototypical triangular relation exists between a national majority group and a national minority having ties with a neighbouring motherland (Brubaker, 1996).

To what extent fifth column attributions reinforce negative stereotypes of national minorities who associate with a foreign motherland will be tested in five former Soviet Republics. The stereotypes indigenous national groups hold of Russian minorities in Belarus, Ukraine, Moldova, Georgia and Kazakhstan—all, since 1991, new independent states with significant Russian minorities—will be surveyed. It is expected that the reinforcing effect of fifth column attributions occurs across all the countries, but that the nature and strength of the effect varies between countries due to differences in the ethnic composition and recent violent conflicts involving Russians. The nature of the effect regards which negative features of the inter-group relations, such as economic, political and educational competition, feelings of relative deprivation and so forth are reinforced in evoking negative stereotypes. The strength of the effect is expected to be most significant in Moldova and Georgia because Russians were involved in the violent conflicts following the secession of Transdniestria in Moldova and of Abchazia in Georgia.

Hence, our first hypothesis is that fifth column attributions reinforce the effect of negative aspects of the inter-group relations on negative stereotypes of Russians. The effect is expected to emerge across all countries, but to vary in strength and nature. The second hypothesis is that this effect only occurs for attributed outgroup goals and not for goals attributed to the ingroup. In other words, the attributed fifth column intentions to Russians will make the stereotypes the indigenous population has of Russian minorities more negative, but Russians' attribution of fifth column intentions to fellow Russians will not affect their stereotypes of the indigenous population. The explanation for this difference is that fifth column intentions of ingroup members will not be perceived as harmful to the interests of the ingroup and therefore will not be perceived as a threat.

Method

Data Collection

Surveys were held among indigenous nationals and Russian nationals in Belarus, Ukraine, Moldova, Georgia, and Kazakhstan. Samples were drawn in urban areas having at least ten per cent of Russian nationals. Cities were randomly drawn. always including the capital city. This resulted in 11 cities in Belarus, 19 in Ukraine, 5 in Moldova, 4 in Georgia and 20 in Kazakhstan. In each city a random route procedure was followed to locate the respondents. Street-names were randomly selected from an alpha-numerical pool, houses were selected at random and respondents over 15 years of age, having their birthday closest to the date of the interview, were interviewed.

Fifteen hundred (750 nationals and 750 Russians) respondents were approached in Belarus, Ukraine, and in Kazakhstan. Nine hundred (450 nationals and 450 Russians) were approached in Moldova and Georgia. The nationality of the respondent was determined by self-identification. If the respondent was not indigenous or Russian the interview was broken off. Respondents participated on a voluntary basis. The non-response was low: two per cent across all countries. Russian respondents were interviewed in Russian and indigenous respondents in their national language or in Russian depending on their preference. The interviewer read the questions and the answers were registered. The surveys took place in the autumn of 1995.

Assessed Variables

The predictors of negative stereotypes measured were: *estimated income level, occupation, age, level of education, gender, indigenous language competence* (incorporating five categories from excellent to none), *ambivalent ethnicity* (having three categories ranging from ethnically homogeneous family composition to mixed family with Russian language use), *civic identification* (using the question 'I am a citizen of [Republic]'), to be answered on a 5 point scale from disagree to agree such as in the following questions: *ethnic identification* ('I am a representative of the indigenous population'), *perceived political competition* ('The political interests of the Russians living in the Republic are in conflict with those of the indigenous people'), *perceived economic competition* ('The economic interests of the Russians living in the republic are in conflict with those of the indigenous people'), *perceived educational competition* ('The use of Russian language in schools and higher educational institutes reduces the educational opportunities of the indigenous people'), *experienced relative deprivation* ('Russians living in the republic have more opportunities to find a good job than indigenous people'), *personal economic deprivation* ('In the last two years my personal economic position became: better/worse'), *perceived collective economic deprivation* ('In the last two years the economic position of the Republic became: better/worse').

Country served as an independent categorical predictor in order to examine cross-national differences moderating the effects of the other continuous predictors.

Perception of Russians as a fifth column of Russia was assessed by three questions: 'Indicate on a scale of 0 to 100 per cent how many Russians, living in this Republic in your opinion: (a) feel more close to Russia than to the Republic?; (b) will serve the interests of Russia even if this is against the interests of the Republic?; (c) will support a Russian attempt to place the Republic under its control?'. *Threat posed by Russia* was measured by four questions: 'How do you think that Russia will respond if the rights of the Russian minority were to be limited: with diplomatic pressure or economic sanctions or military intervention?' (with a five point scale from 'likely' to 'unlikely' for each alternative), and: 'In the end the Russian Federation wants to bring the Republic under its control' (with the same answer categories). *Economic threat* was measured by two questions: 'In what way do you think your personal economic situation will change in the next two years?', and 'In what way do you think the economic situation in your Republic will change in the next two years.' (better to worse). Factor-analysis indicated that fifth column attributions, threat posed by Russia, and economic threat loaded on separate factors. Therefore the average scores for each of these types of threat were computed.

Stereotypes were assessed by trait attributions on a 0 to 100 per cent scale. The same question was asked for each of the characteristics, which were: 'Please indicate on a scale from 0 per cent to 100 per cent, how many Russians in your country posses the following characteristic', followed by the percentage scale for: peaceable, honest, polite, rude, hostile, and deceitful. Factor analysis indicated that the stereotypes loaded on two complementary factors. Separate averages were computed for items loading positively and negatively. The reliability (alpha) was .67 for negative stereotypes and .70 for positive stereotypes. Only results for negative stereotypes will be reported.

All the questions were asked to the indigenous samples as well as the Russian samples. In so doiing, the perception of Russians as a fifth column was measured among Russian respondents as an attribution of ingroup goals and among indigenous respondents as an attribution of outgroup goals. An additional question measuring *Russian identification* (disagree to agree to: 'I am a citizen of Russia, a Russian') was asked to Russian respondents as well.

Analysis

A partially saturated general linear model (GLM) was used to simultaneously test the effects of all the above mentioned predictors on the stereotypes. Significant effects therefore refer to pure effects (controlled for two-way and higher-order interactions between country and gender, country and education, and education and gender). The mediating role of fifth column attributions was determined by comparing the direct effect of the predictors on the stereotypes relative to the model in which fifth column attributions operated as a mediator. Mediation by fifth column attributions was indicated by a reduction of predictor effects compared to their initial direct effects (Baron and Kenny, 1986). General effects across countries and specific country effects were determined by inspection of the interactions between the continuous predictors and country. The nature, strength and reliability of significant country effects was determined by simple slope analysis.

Results

Profile of Negative Stereotypes of Russians

To indicate the negative stereotype the indigenous population has of Russians, the averaged sum-score of three stereotype attributions was used, that is: to what extent Russians are perceived as hostile, rude, and deceitful. The sum-score is indicated as 'hostility attributed to Russians'. It appeared that attributed hostility to Russians is lowest in Belarus, where 30 per cent of the Russians are perceived as hostile. These percentages are, on the other hand, higher in Ukraine, Moldova and Kazakhstan, where, repectively, 39, 39, and 38 per cent of the Russians are perceived as hostile. Russians are feared most in Georgia where 41 per cent of Russians are perceived as hostile (see Figure 8.1; differences of more than a few points or percentages are significant).

Another way to indicate the negative stereotypes of Russians is by the percentage of the indigenous population attributing hostility to more than 50 per cent of the Russians. This is 13 per cent of the sample in Belarus, 27 per cent in Ukraine, 29 per cent in Moldova, 30 per cent in Kazakhstan and 37 per cent in Georgia.

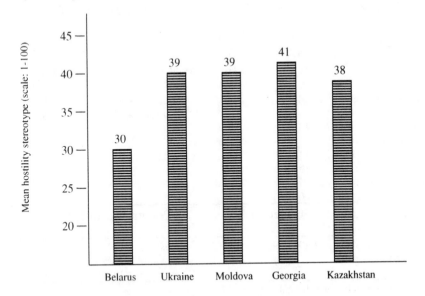

Figure 8.1   Percentages of Russians Stereotyped as Hostile by Indigenous Populations

The perception of Russians as a fifth column of Russia was indicated by the averaged sum-score of the three fifth column questions. The attributed percentages were substantial: 30 in Belarus, 43 in Ukraine, 50 in Moldova, 65 in Georgia and 60 in Kazakhstan.

Determinants of Negative Indigenous Stereotypes of Russians

The characteristics of the indigenous population contributing to negative stereotypes of Russians are indicated in the upper part of Table 8.1. There is a moderate effect of age, income and education: in all countries lower income categories, younger people and higher educated subjects have more negative stereotypes of Russians than higher income category, older and lower educated respondents. Perceived competition with Russians and feelings of being

Table 8.1   Effects of Predictors and Fifth Column Attributions on Negative Stereotypes of the Indigenous Populations about Russians[a][b]

Predictors	General Effects		Country-Specific Effects		
	with threat	without threat		with threat	without threat
Relative deprivation	+.17***	**+.10*****			
Political competition	+.16***	**+.09***	Moldova	+.21**	**n.s.**
			Georgia	+.33***	**+.21*****
Educational competition	+.14***	**+.11*****	Georgia	+.40**	**+.28*****
			Kazakhstan	+.12**	**n.s.**
Income	−.13**	−.10*			
Perceived collective					
Economic deprivation	+.11*	**n.s.**	Georgia	+.21**	**n.s.**
Education	−.10*	**n.s.**			
Economic competition	+.07*				
Age	−.06*				
Perceived Threat (mediator)	**General Effects**		**Country-Specific Effects**		
Perception of Russians as a fifth column	**+.14****		Belarus	+.13***	
			Moldova	+.28***	
			Georgia	+.19***	
Variance explained by the full model (R^2) = .274					

[a]Results are represented in <u>non-standardised</u> regression coefficients. Coefficients in **bold** represent GLM results for which the fifth column mediation effect is eliminated.
[b]* = p<.05;** = p<.01;*** = p<.001

deprived compared to Russians, substantially contribute to more negative stereotypes. In particular the effects of relative deprivation and perceived political and educational competition are strong. The effect of economic competition is weaker. Collective economic deprivation (perceived internal economic decline over the two years prior to the study, 1997–1999) moderately contributes to more negative stereotypes.

Simple slope analysis indicates that some of these effects are articulated in specific countries. In Georgia, perceived collective economic deprivation contributes more to the perception of Russians as hostile than in the other countries. The same is true for perceived political competition in Georgia and Moldova and for educational competition in Georgia and Kazakhstan.

The perception of the Russian minority as a Russian fifth column generally reinforced negative stereotypes of Russians greatly. The effect of fifth column attributions to Russians is, as was expected, strongest in Moldova and Georgia. Fifth column attributions also reinforce the effect of a number of predictors on the stereotypes of Russians, in particular those of relative deprivation, education, political competition and, less strongly also of income and educational competition. Hence the nature of the effect also varies. Perceived economic deprivation is not reinforced by fifth column attributions, except in Georgia where it is completely dependent on such attributions. In Moldova and Georgia the effect of political competition on negative stereotypes of Russians is strongly reinforced by fifth column attributions and the same is true in Georgia and Kazakhstan for the effect of educational competition. In Table 8.1, those effects in bold indicate what remains of the original effect if the reinforcing effect of fifth column attributions is eliminated.

Profile of Negative Russian Stereotypes of the Indigenous Populations

Hostility attributed by Russian respondents to the indigenous population (average sum-score of attributed hostility, rudeness and deceitfulness) is 27 per cent in Belarus, 37 per cent in Ukraine, 39 per cent in Georgia, 41 per cent in Kazakhstan and 44 per cent in Moldova (see Figure 8.2). The percentage of Russians perceiving 50 per cent or more of the indigenous population as being hostile is 6.8 per cent in Belarus, 28 per cent in Ukraine, 42 per cent in Moldova, 20 per cent in Georgia, and 33 per cent in Kazakhstan.

The perception that fellow Russians act as a fifth column of Russia was indicated by the averaged sum-score of the three fifth column questions. The attributed percentages were 25 per cent in Belarus, 40 per cent in Ukraine, 48 per cent in Moldova, 48 per cent in Georgia, and 55 per cent in Kazakhstan. These percentages are substantial, but lower than those indicated by the indigenous populations. The characteristics of the Russian respondents leading to negative stereotypes of the indigenous populations are: age, perceived economic and political competition, relative deprivation, and civic identification with the republic of residence (see Table 8.2). Younger Russians have more negative stereotypes of the indigenous population than older Russians. Perceived political competition and, in particular, economic competition and relative deprivation contribute to negative stereotypes. Russians who identify themselves as citizen of their republic of residence have less negative stereotypes of the indigenous population than Russians who do not. With hypothesis two we proposed that the Russians' attribution of fifth column intentions to fellow Russians would not affect their stereotypes of the indigenous population because such intentions of ingroup members would not be perceived as harmful to the interests of the Russian ingroup and thus would not perceived as a threat. It appears that the results do not support the hypothesis. Fifth column attributions to fellow Russians do contribute to more negative stereotypes and reinforce the effect of perceived political competition, relative deprivation and civic identification, as can be seen in Table 8.2. This suggests that hypothesis two should be rejected.

The effect of civic identification, however, suggests that there is also a possible alternative interpretation. Russians in the five countries can on the one hand identify with the republic of residence and on the other with Russia

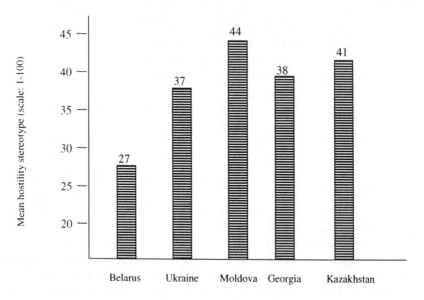

Figure 8.2   Percentages of the Indigenous Population Stereotyped as Hostile by Russians

or the Russian people (or with both). If they identify more with the republic of residence, then the idea that fellow Russians have the inclination to act as a a Russian fifth column may be felt as a threat. But why should this threat lead to more negative stereotypes of the indigenous population? Maybe it is not the reason at all and, instead, the logic works the opposite way. If many Russians are inclined to act as a fifth column for Russia, then the indigenous population may have reason to perceive Russians as hostile and thus may react in a hostile manner towards Russians in return. Hence, the idea that fellow Russians are a fifth column may, therefore, entail the expectation that the indigenous population will be hostile towards Russians. However, if Russians identify with Russia, the idea that fellow Russians may act as a Russian fifth column should not cause the stereotypes of the indigenous population to be more negative, as it presents no additional threat to the already present identification.

To test this interpretation, the determinants contributing to negative stereotypes of the indigenous populations were tested separately for Russian respondents identifying as citizens of Russia (agree and fully agree to the question 'I am a citizen of Russia, a Russian'; N = 353) and for those not identifying as citizens of Russia (neutral, disagree, fully disagree to the same question; N = 1759). The expectation is that hypothesis two will be confirmed for Russians identifying as a citizen of Russia and as a Russian.

Table 8.2   Effects of Predictors and Fifth Column Attributions on Negative Stereotypes of Russians about the Indigenous Populations[a][b]

Predictors	General Effects		Country-Specific Effects	
	with threat	*without threat*	*with threat*	*without threat*
Relative deprivation	+.15***	**+.13*****		
Economic competition	+.12***			
Civic identification	–.11***	**–.08****		
Age	–.09***			
Political competition	+.08**	**n.s.**		
Perceived Threat (mediator)	General Effects		Country-Specific Effects	
Perception of Russians as a fifth column	**+.10*****			
Variance explained by the full model (R²)= .313				

[a] Results are represented in <u>unstandardised</u> regression coefficients. Coefficients printed in bold script represent GLM results for which the threat mediation effect is eliminated.
[b] * = p<.05; ** = p<.01; *** = p<.001

It appears that fifth column attributions to fellow Russians indeed do not contribute to negative stereotypes of the indigenous population, as was predicted in hypothesis two (see Table 8.3: effect of fifth column attributions). Yet, for specific categories of Russians in specific countries the idea that fellow Russians are strongly orientated to Russia catalyses negative stereotypes of the indigenous population under conditions of perceived political competition or relative deprivation. The effect of political competition emerges among highly educated Russians in Ukraine and lowly educated Russians in Moldova. The effect of relative deprivation emerges for lowly educated Russians in Moldova (see Table 8.3).

The most plausible interpretation for this effect is that under these conditions Russians expect the indigenous population to react in a hostile manner towards any claim of political influence (competition) or improvement of position (deprivation) by Russians. Hence, although hypothesis two is generally confirmed for Russians identifying with Russia, even in this category goal attributions to the ingroup have under certain conditions an effect on stereotypes of the outgroup.

Table 8.3　Effects of Predictors and Fifth Column Attributions on Negative Stereotypes of the Indigenous Populations of Russians Identifying as Russians and Russian Citizens[a][b]

Predictors	Country and Education-Specific Effects			
			with threat	without threat
Relative deprivation	Kazakhstan	Highly educated	+ 2.00**	
	Moldova	Lowly educated	+ 0.73**	**n.s.**
Political competition	Ukraine	Highly educated	+ 1.91**	**n.s.**
	Moldova	Highly educated	− 1.12 ***	
		Lowly educated	+ 0.42*	**n.s.**
Economic competition	Ukraine	Highly educated	− 1.79 **	
	Moldova	Highly educated	+ 0.87***	

Perceived Threat (mediator)	General Effects	Country-Specific Effects
Perception of Russians as a fifth column	**n.s.**	
Variance explained by the full model (R^2) = .692		

[a] Results are represented in <u>unstandardised</u> regression coefficients. Coefficients printed in bold script represent GLM results for which the threat mediation effect is eliminated.
[b] * = p<.05;** = p<.01;*** = p<.001

Discussion

In this chapter we proposed to consider an aspect of stereotypes that has not yet received much attention: the attribution of goals to outgroups. It was assumed that if ingroup members attribute harmful goals to outgroups, negative stereotypes of outgroup members become reinforced. In addition it was assumed, on logical grounds, that goals attributed to the ingroup as a whole do not have the same effect, because such goals, in general, are not considered as harmful but, rather, as serving the interests of the ingroup. Outgroup goals were defined in the setting of five different countries in Eastern Europe and Asia with substantial new Russian minorities. These Russian minorities can be perceived by the indigenous populations as fifth columns of Russia, that is, inclined to serve the interests of Russia more than those of the newly independent republics. The test was for a general effect across countries. Yet, country specific effects were also tested because the relations between Russians and the indigenous populations might differ across the countries. The model tested, using GLM analysis, the effect of aspects of the perceived inter-group relations and other background factors on negative stereotypes of the outgroup, while fifth column attributions were considered to mediate these factors. Differences between countries in the effect of perceived inter-group relations and background factors on the negative stereotypes and of the relation between negative stereotypes and fifth column attributions, were determined by simple slope analysis. Hence a combined test of general effects across countries and specific cross-national differences was performed.

The results indicated that the attribution of fifth column intentions to Russians reinforce negative stereotypes held by the indigenous populations of Russians. The effect was in general not strong, but it was substantial compared to the direct effects of the other aspects of the inter-group relations. In Georgia and Moldova, however, a much stronger effect of fifth column attributions emerged. This can be related to the military conflicts in these countries in which Russians, or even the Russian army, played a role. In Moldova the Russian army intervened in the conflict arising from the secession of Transdniestria, the most industrialised part of the country in which Russians and Ukrainians are concentrated. In Georgia the internal war following the secession of Abchazia was partially attributed to Russian interference and was later contained by Russian peace keeping troops. Comparable conflict involving Russia was absent in the other countries.

Fifth column attributions to Russians also reinforced the effect of feelings of relative deprivation, perceived political and economic competition, and income in comparison to Russians, as well as completely explaining the additional effects of education and perceived collective economic deprivation.

In other words, relative deprivation, political and economic competition and lower income levels lead to negative stereotypes of Russians, but more strongly so if Russians are perceived as a Russian fifth column. And a high level of education and perceived collective economic deprivation lead to negative stereotypes of Russians if and only if Russians are perceived as a fifth column. In Moldova the effect of perceived political competition on negative stereotypes of Russians was not only stronger than in other countries but also completely determined by the idea that Russians in Moldova form a Russian fifth column. In Georgia the exceptionally strong effects of perceived educational and political competition on negative stereotypes were also reinforced to a large degree by attributed fifth column intentions while the negative effect of perceived collective economic deprivation was completely dependent on fifth column attributions. In Kazakhstan the same was true for perceived educational competition. Hence it appears that threat, that is the idea that Russians are politically not loyal to the new independent state, contributes to negative stereotypes of Russians. However, this threat is felt more strongly in some of these states than in others and therefore accordingly contributes more to the emergence of negative stereotypes of Russians, either in general or in interaction with specific features of the inter-group relations of the two groups.

The results of the complementary second hypothesis seemed less straightforward. It appeared that fifth column attributions by Russians to their fellow Russians have a similar effect on their stereotypes of the indigenous populations as they had, in reverse, on the stereotypes of Russians among the indigenous populations. However, in the case of the Russians the fifth column attributions refer to the ingroup and therefore should not be associated with perceived threat. Hence the outcome was contradictory. But the situation of Russians in the former Soviet republics is completely different from that of the indigenous populations. Russians have become minorities of a former dominant foreign power. Yet many of them have been residing in the new independent states for a long time or even for generations. These Russians may feel more loyal to the new republic than Russians who immigrated more recently. Therefore Russians should be divided into those who identify with the republic and those who identify with Russia and the Russian people. In particular the latter category of Russians should be considered as the Russian ingroup with regard to fifth column attributions. For these Russians fifth column intentions of fellow Russians are not a threat but are, rather, an indication of their shared loyalty to the original Russian ingroup. It appeared that when the test of the second hypothesis was confined to Russians identifying with Russia and the Russian people a consistent picture emerged. The negative effect of fifth column attributions on stereotypes of the outgroup was indeed insignificant for this subgroup. It was also interesting to note that this pro-Russia orientated subgroup of Russians was rather small across all countries, about ten per cent of all the Russian respondents, while consisting predominantly of new immigrants having settled in the country during the last ten years.

Yet, although the second hypothesis thus seemed to be confirmed, some details of the outcome of the analysis remained inconsistent. Fifth column attributions did not affect stereotypes of the indigenous populations across the countries, yet in some countries negative stereotypes of the indigenous population are triggered off by fifth column attributions to fellow Russians under specific conditions. More specifically, more highly educated Russians in Ukraine—identifying as Russian citizens—who feel the pressure of political competition with the indigenous population did perceive the indigenous population as more hostile if they thought that fellow Russians would engage in fifth column activities. The same is true for less highly educated Russians feeling the pressure of political competition in Moldova or perceiving themselves relatively deprived in comparison to Moldovans. These interactions explain more than two-thirds of the variance of the negative stereotypes of the indigenous population (see Table 8.3).

On the surface this result could be considered to refute hypothesis two for this subgroup of Russians among those identifying as Russian citizens. However, there is also an interpretation that does more justice to the complexity of the situation of Russians in the new republics. This interpretation is, as was said earlier, that if many Russians are inclined to act as a fifth column of Russia then the indigenous population may have a reason to perceive Russians as hostile and thus may react in a hostile way towards Russians in return. Russians who attribute fifth column attitudes to many of their fellow Russians may therefore fear hostile reactions of the indigenous population and perceive the indigenous population as hostile for that reason. This effect may in particular emerge for Russians who perceive that they are in a struggle for political influence in the country or who feel deprived in comparison to the indigenous population. The weakness of this post hoc interpretation is of course that the causal chain is reversed: negative stereotypes of the outgroup are not perceived as a direct expression of negative feelings about the outgroup among ingroup members but as a reaction to expected negative feelings among outgroup members. This is, however, not unrealistic. If Russians who are orientated to Russia have the idea that many other Russians have the same orientation and if they also assume that the indigenous population is aware of these orientations, then they are in a vulnerable position. This is even more true for Russians not identifying as Russian citizens or Russians, which explains the results found for all Russian respondents together, as presented in Table 8.2. After all, post independence it is the indigenous population that is in control in the republic not the Russians.

If we accept this interpretation two problems remain. First, why is it that in Ukraine more highly educated Russians have this fear, while in Moldova less highly educated Russians have these feelings about the indigenous population. A definitive answer is difficult to offer. Russians in Ukraine have generally higher levels of education than the indigenous Ukrainians (according to the 1989 Census the number of Russians with a high level of education was 213 per 1000 in urban regions against 154 per 1000 among Ukrainians and 66 against 41 per 1000 in rural regions in 1989). So, in particular those Russians among the more highly educated who strongly identify with Russia yet want to maintain political influence in Ukraine may feel vulnerable to negative reactions from the Ukrainian population. But in Moldova Russians are also more highly educated than the rest of the population (in 1989 the number of Russians per thousand with a high level of education was 241 against 158 Moldovans in urban areas and 94 against 43 in the rural areas). However, in management functions Moldovans exceeded Russians by 72 to 62. And although Russians were always over-represented in the higher economic strata Moldovans had comparable strong positions in the political institutions of the country, which contributed to the conflict in Transdniestria were Moldova's industrial base is located. Finally, the law declaring Moldovan the national language after the independence of Moldova undermined the economic position of the Russians because not many Russians speak Moldovan. So there was and is strong economic and political competition between Russians and Moldovans and maybe lower educated Russians are afraid to pay the price for the higher educated Russians having their base in semi-independent Transdniestria. Therefore they might fear the reaction of Moldovans if they and their fellow Russians are orientated towards Russia.

The interpretation of the results found for Russians who are not orientated towards Russia and yet assume that many Russians may act as a fifth column of Russia, as well as for those who are orientated towards Russia and assume that many fellow Russians share this orientation, indicates that more than just the attribution of antagonistic goals to outgroups reinforces negative stereotypes. The attribution of goals to the ingroup may have the same effect if ingroup members assume that outgroups may react in a hostile manner to these shared ingroup goals. In this sense reality is more complex than we assumed in our simple hypotheses. Further research has to show whether or not evidence supports this more complex interpretation of inter-group processes in stereotyping.

References

Augoustinos, M., Ahrens, C. and Innes, J. (1994), Stereotypes and prejudice: The Australian case, *British Journal of Social Psychology*, 33, pp. 125-141.

Baron, R. and Kenny, D. (1986), The moderator-mediator variable distinction in social psychological research: conceptual, strategic, and statistical considerations, *Journal of Personality and Social Psychology*, 51, pp. 1173–1182.

Bar-Tal, D. (1990), *Group beliefs: a conception for analyzing group structure, processes and behavior*, New York, Springer.

Blumer, H. (1958), Race prejudice as a sense of S, *The Pacific Sociological Review*, 1, pp. 3-7.

Brigham, J. (1971), Ethnic stereotypes, *Psychological Bulletin*, 76, pp. 15-33.

Brown, R. (1988), *Group processes, dynamics within and between groups*, Oxford, Basil Blackwell.

Brubaker, R. (1992), *Citizenship and nationhood in France and Germany*, Cambridge Mass., Harvard University Press.

Brubaker, R. (1996), *Nationalism reframed, nationhood and the national question in the New Europe*, Cambridge, Cambridge University Press.

Campbell, D. (1958), Common fate, similarity and other indices of the status of aggregates of persons as social entities, *Behavioral Science*, 3, pp. 14–25.

Clark, S. (1998), International competition and the treatment of minorities: seventeenth-century cases and general propositions, *American Journal of Sociology*, 103, pp. 1267–1308.

Devine, P. (1989), Stereotypes and prejudice: their automatic and controlled components, *Journal of Personality and Social Psychology*, 56, pp. 5-18.

Forbes, H. (1997), *Ethnic conflict*, New Haven, Yale University Press.

Furtado, C. and Hechter, M. (1992), The emergence of nationalist policies in the USSR: A comparison of Estonia and the Ukraine, in *Thinking theoretically about Soviet Nationalities*, by A. Motyl (ed.), New York, Colombia University Press, pp. 169-204.

Gellner, E. (1983), *Nations and Nationalism*, Oxford, UK, Basil Blackwell.

Gellner, E. (1994), Nationalism and modernisation, in J. Hutchinson and A. Smith (eds) *Nationalism*, Oxford, Oxford University Press.

Hagendoorn, L., Phalet, K., Henke, R. en Drogendijk, R. (1995), *Etnische verhoudingen in Midden en Oost Europa* (Ethnic relations in Central and Eastern Europe) Den Haag, WRR.

Horowitz, D. (1985), *Ethnic groups in conflict*, Berkely, University of California Press.

Jonas, K. and Hewstone, M. (1986), The assessment of national stereotypes, *The Journal of Social Psychology*, 126, pp. 745-754.

Kaiser, R. (1994), *The Geography of Nationalism in Russia and the USSR*, Princeton, Princeton University Press.

Katz, D. and Braly, K. (1933), Racial stereotypes in one hundred college students, *Journal of Abnormal and Social Psychology*, 28, pp. 280-290.

Kofta, M. (1994), Group stereotypes, prejudice and political attitudes, *Project proposal for NIAS Trends in Scholarship*, Netherlands.

Mackie, D. and Smith, E. (1998), Intergroup relations: Insights from a theoretically integrative approach, *Psychological Review*, 105, pp. 499–529.

McCauley, C. and Stitt, C. (1978), An individual and quantitative measure of stereotypes, *Journal of Personality and Social Psychology*, 36, pp. 929-940.

Verdery, K. (1992), Comment: Hobsbawn in the East, *Anthropology Today*, 8, pp. 8-10.

Yamskov, A. (1991), Ethnic conflict in the Transcaucasus: the case of Nagorno Karabach, *Theory and Society*, 20, pp. 631-660.

9 Changes in National and Ethnic Stereotypes in Central and Eastern Europe

EDWIN POPPE

Introduction

An advantage of cross-national research is that more or less general theoretical notions can be tested in a broader context than a single country and that possible differences between countries can be investigated as well. The present chapter examines changes in stereotypes of national and ethnic groups among adolescents from six Central and Eastern European countries using explanations derived from self-categorisation theory, social identity theory, relative deprivation theory, and scapegoat theory. The comparative nature of the study is twofold: national and ethnic stereotypes across countries and over time. The economic transformation processes in Central and Eastern Europe offer an opportunity to investigate whether the improved or deteriorated macro-economic circumstances of the perceivers affect national and ethnic stereotypes. Before proceeding to the study proper, I will discuss the concept of stereotypes, which forms the main comparative variable of this study, followed by an introduction of the countries involved in the cross-national comparison. I will then pay attention to the group of participants specific to this study, previous studies and theoretical explanations of changes in stereotypes, and, finally, I will outline the hypotheses to be tested.

Stereotypes

Since the 1980s, stereotypes have been predominantly defined as characteristics descriptive of, attributed to, or associated with members of a social group (Stangor and Lange, 1994). They are measured by various methods such as the adjective-checklist procedure (Katz and Braly, 1933) and percentage estimates (Brigham, 1971). The present study follows on from those of researchers who describe stereotypes as a comparative concept by using the estimated percentage of a particular trait adjective attributed to a particular target group in relation to the estimated percentage of this trait

191

adjective attributed to multiple target groups (McCauley, Stitt and Segal, 1980; Linssen and Hagendoorn, 1994). More specifically, the study focuses on two evaluative dimensions underlying stereotypes labelled as competence and morality and therefore does not describe or explain changes in a multitude of typical or atypical traits attributed to national or ethnic groups. Previous studies have indicated that the administered traits can be subsumed into these two dimensions, which are cross-nationally comparable. (Phalet and Poppe, 1997; Poppe and Linssen, 1999). The competence dimension involves traits such as intelligent and efficient on the positive side, and clumsy and slow on the negative. While the morality dimension is made up from traits such as honest and tolerant on the positive side, and aggressive and rude on the negative. This finding is in line with prior research indicating that competence (or 'ability') and morality (or 'sociability') constitute the two main evaluative dimensions by which groups and people are judged (Rosenberg and Sedlak, 1972). Hence, the focus of investigation in this chapter concern the content and changes in attributed competence and morality to national and ethnic groups.

Six Central and Eastern European Countries

The six countries across which the comparison was made were: Russia, Belarus, Bulgaria, Hungary, Poland and the Czech Republic. The description of the ethnic composition of the major ethnic groups in each of the countries is based on sources which deal with this in greater depth (Szajkowski, 1993; Hagendoorn, Phalet, Henke and Drogendijk, 1995; Hagendoorn, Çsepeli, Dekker and Farnen, 2000). Table 9.1 gives the four largest ethnic groups in each country.

The approximately 148 million inhabitants of the Russian Federation (Russia) belong to 101 identifiable ethnic groups, with Russians accounting for 82.6 per cent of the total population in the 1989 census. The Russian Federation is a complex multi-ethnic state with national minorities residing in Russia itself, and in 21 autonomous republics, where indigenous national groups live together with Russians, minorities from other titular republics, and minorities without a republic. Numerically significant ethnic minority groups include Tatars (3.6 per cent), Ukrainians (2.7 per cent), Jews (1.4 per cent), and Belarusians (1.2 per cent). Religious adherence varies, and many religions are closely connected to ethnic groups: Russian Orthodox for Russians and other Slavs, Islam for the indigenous people of the northern Caucasus (e.g., Chechen and Kabardinians) and Buddhism for the titular groups of the Central Asian autonomous republics (e.g., Tuvans and Buryats). Russians represent the largest ethnic group in most of the 21 republics in the Russian Federation, the exceptions being Tatarstan, Chuvash, Tuva and most of the republics in the Caucasus where the indigenous groups are in the majority.

Table 9.1   The Four Largest Groups in Six Central and Eastern European Countries: by Percentage of Total Population [a]

Country	Majority	Largest Minority		Second Minority		Third Minority	
Russia	82.6	Tatars	3.6	Ukrainians	2.7	Jews	1.4
Belarus	77.8	Russians	13.2	Poles	4.1	Ukrainians	2.9
Bulgaria	85.8	Turks	9.7	Gypsies	3.4	Pomaks	< 1.0
Hungary*	88.9	Gypsies	5.8	Germans	1.9	Slovaks	< 1.0
Poland*	96.0	Germans	< 1.0	Belarus'ns	< 1.0	Ukrainians	< 1.0
Czh Rep.	94.9	Slovaks	3.1	Poles	< 1.0	Germans	< 1.0

[a] 1989/1991 census data.
[b] 1993 estimate (Szajkowski, 1993).

Belarus (Byelorussia) became independent in 1991 after having being part of the Soviet Union, the Russian Empire and the Polish-Lithuanian Kingdom. Belarus has about 10.3 million inhabitants of whom 79 per cent are Belarusian (Byelorussian), 12 per cent Russian, 4 per cent Polish, 3 per cent Ukrainian, and 1 per cent Jewish, according to the census of 1989. The Belarusians are Eastern Slavonic people adhering mostly to the Eastern Orthodox Church. Although the official state language is Belarusian, the majority of the inhabitants prefer the Russian language. The large Russian community is concentrated in the capital, Minsk, and are mainly blue collar workers. Poles and Ukrainians live in the rural and agricultural north-west and south-west regions, neighbouring their countries of origin.

Bulgaria has approximately nine million inhabitants of which 86 per cent is Bulgarian. Eastern Orthodox Christianity is the major religion. Bulgarians are considered to be a mix of Slavonic and Finno-Ugric peoples. Turks represent the largest minority group, constituting about ten per cent of the total population according to the census of 1991, while reported estimations are closer to 15 per cent.[1] The Turkish people are concentrated in the eastern region of the country and live predominantly in villages. They are Muslim and Turkish is their first language. Gypsies (Roma) are the second largest minority group, forming about three per cent of the population (1991 census). They live dispersed throughout the country, often in separate ghetto-like neighbourhoods in cities. About 250 000 Pomaks, or 'Bulgarian Muslims', live in the southern Rhodope mountains, these are the descendants of Bulgarians who converted to the Islam during the centuries of Ottoman rule. They describe themselves as either Bulgarians of Muslim faith or as Turks and are therefore not listed as a separate ethnic group in the census data.

Hungary has about 10.3 million inhabitants. According to the census of 1990, the Hungarians (Magyars), a Finno-Ugric people, constitute 98 per cent of the population. A more realistic estimate made in 1993 (see Szajkowski, 1993), however, indicates that the Hungarians form 89 per cent, while Gypsies constitute about 6 per cent and Germans about 2 per cent. Roman Catholicism is the predominant religion among Hungarians. Gypsies live predominantly in the eastern regions of the country, while the Germans are concentrated in the western regions. Due to deportation during World War II and the later emigration to Israel, only a small number of the large pre-World War II population of Hungarian Jews remain (estimated at 10 000, see e.g., Çsepeli and Zavecz, 1992).

Today, Poland is relatively ethnically homogenous with Poles constituting about 96 per cent of a total population of 38.3 million based on a 1993 estimate (or 98 per cent according to the 1990 census; Szajkowski, 1993). Poles are Slavonic people of which an estimated 95 per cent are Roman Catholics. The three largest minority groups are Germans, Belarusians and Ukrainians who all form less than one per cent of the population and are predominantly concentrated in clearly defined regions of Poland. The Germans in the south-west (Silesia), the Belarusians in the east, and, surprisingly, two thirds of the Ukrainian population, are still in the west of Poland, where they were deported to after rioting against Polish rulers in 1947. In pre-World War II Poland substantial numbers of Ukrainians (4.5 million, 1931 census) and Belarusians (1.5 million) lived predominantly in rural areas, while most Jewish people lived in urban areas (some 3.5 million, 1931 census); they either fled the country or were killed during the Nazi occupation.

After the 1992 division of Czechoslovakia, the Czech Republic appeared to be relatively ethnically homogenous with Czechs comprising about 95 per cent of a total population of 10.3 million. Roman Catholicism is the major religion. Slovaks form the largest minority group in the Czech Republic constituting about three per cent (1991 census), but since then an estimated 40 000 have left the Czech Republic as a consequence of the removal of Slovaks from positions in government institutions. The Czech and Slovak languages are mutually comprehensible (western) Slavonic languages. Most of the numerous pre-WW II German community (about 2.5 million) were deported after the war, leaving the current German population at 0.5 per cent of the total national population. The Czech Republic's Gypsy population was 0.3 per cent according to the census of 1991, but estimates put the figure much higher at up to three per cent (see Szajkowski, 1993). Recently, the dominant role of

Bohemia within the Czech Republic, has led to the rise of regionalism, particularly in the region of Moravia.

In summary, the Russian Federation, Belarus and Bulgaria possess numerically substantial ethnic minorities concentrated in specific regions, while the Central European countries, Hungary, Poland and the Czech Republic are relatively ethnically homogeneous. In addition, various Central and Eastern countries have ethnic minorities originating from neighbouring countries. The Central and Eastern European intergroup context makes it particularly interesting to examine (changes in) ethnic minority stereotypes in conjunction with (changes in) national stereotypes.

Adolescents

This study examines stereotypes among a specific group of participants, namely adolescents in the highest level of secondary school in capital cities. The results are not intended to be generalised, for instance, to all adolescents or to the national populations. The participants, however, belong to a group who may be influential to the future of their countries. The focus on this specific group facilitates cross-national comparisons, as it may be assumed that the participants have similar relevant background variables such as education, urbanisation, and socioeconomic status (Van de Vijver and Leung, 1997). It is important to note that many cross-national studies ignore sample differences across countries and fail to assess the impact of such differences on their results. Socio-economic status may be the real explanatory variable of many cross-national differences because cross-national relations are often marked by differences in this status domain (Van de Vijver and Leung, 1997). Hence, an advantage of selecting secondary school students only, next to that of relatively low costs and effort, is the comparability across nationalities: it is not necessary to correct for unequal demographic characteristics.

Determinants of Changes in National and Ethnic Stereotypes

The transformation from a centrally planned economy to a liberal market economy in Central and Eastern Europe created economic uncertainty and dissatisfaction due to the loss of jobs and income, inflation, and new forms of competition for resources. In line with a number of theories, it may be suggested that a deterioration in the economic circumstances of the perceiving group's country influenced individuals' stereotypes of outgroups negatively (see e.g., Duckitt, 1994). The theoretical rationale behind this change may be the displacement of aggression caused by frustration (i.e., frustration-aggression-displacement theory, Dollard, Doob, Miller, Mowrer and Sears,

1939), or feelings of deprivation relative to outgroups (i.e., relative deprivation theory, Runciman, 1966; Brown, 1988), or outgroup blaming in order to maintain social identity (i.e., social identity theory, Tajfel, 1981). An interesting question is who is blamed for economic deterioration. Scapegoats are usually socially distinctive and politically or numerically weaker than the ingroup (Ashmore, 1970; Berkowitz and Green, 1962). Ethnic minorities engaged in trade and commerce have been frequently scapegoated, for instance the Jews in Europe (Simpson and Yinger, 1972) and the Chinese in South East Asia (LeVine and Campbell, 1972). In the context of Central and Eastern Europe, it may be that Western European nationalities are blamed (cf. Verdery, 1992), for instance, due to lack of expected economic aid, or fellow Central and Eastern European countries due to relative deprivation or lack of (previous) economic co-operation. Therefore, with this study I examine whether economic deterioration leads to changes in stereotypes of various national and ethnic groups. Stereotypes of ten target groups were assessed in each country. The target groups were the national ingroup, eight foreign national groups of which five were Central and Eastern European and three were major Western European nationalities (Germans, English, and Italians), and a major local ethnic minority group. The numerically most significant ethnic minority group (see Table 9.1) with a history of being the target of ethnic antagonism (see e.g., Szajkowski, 1993) was chosen for each of the six countries: Turks in Bulgaria, Gypsies[2] in Hungary, Germans in Poland, Russians in Belarus, Slovaks in the Czech Republic and Jews in Russia.[3] To summarise, what is to be examined is whether changing macroeconomic circumstances (a decrease or increase in gross national product) in Central and Eastern European countries are related to changing stereotypes of minority groups and foreign outgroups.

Apart from changing circumstances of perceivers, the present study will also focus on perceived changes in characteristics of target groups to explain shifts in national and ethnic stereotypes. Many studies suggest that the content of stereotypes change as a result of changing political and economic relationships between groups (e.g., Karlins, Coffman and Walters, 1969). For instance, a study in the United States indicated that stereotypes of Russians changed considerably between 1942 and 1948 in the context of deteriorating post-war relations, such that Russians came to be perceived as less 'brave' and 'hardworking' and more 'cruel' and 'conceited' (Buchanan, 1951). Another illustrative example is a recent study by Linssen (1995) which showed that stereotypes about Germans held by other West European groups changed in accordance with the increased size of the unified Germany. These studies confirm self-categorisation theory (Turner, Hogg, Oakes, Reicher and Wetherell, 1987) and realistic conflict theory (Sherif, 1967) by showing that changing stereotypes reflect changing features of targets and intergroup relations such as the increasing size of the target country, as well as political and economic conflicts (Brewer and Campbell, 1976; LeVine and Campbell, 1972). Almost all of the previous studies examined changes in stereotypes between cohorts (i.e., different participants were used at each time of measurement) and did not explicitly measure (perceived) changes in the characteristics of targets. The present research examines the relationship between changes in the stereotypes and changes in the perceived characteristics of targets (including relational features) by surveying the same participants twice, in 1994 and 1995 (i.e., a panel survey with two measurements). Previous analyses have indicated which target features and individual perceiver characteristics were related to the content of national and ethnic stereotypes in 1994 (Poppe and Linssen, 1999). It was found that national stereotypes in terms of competence correspond strongly with the perceived economic power of the nation-state and that morality attributed to nationalities is related to the small size, small degree of perceived conflicts, and small degree of perceived nationalism of the nation-states (Poppe and Linssen, 1999). The present study goes further by examining whether changes in these determinants affect stereotypes. Before examining the determinants of changes in stereotypes, I will look at whether the stereotypes changed at all or were stable over time. Given earlier findings that ingroup stereotypes are relatively stable over time (e.g., Linssen, 1995), it is expected that the competence and morality ratings of the own national group's have not altered between 1994 and 1995. Although it may be expected that the outgroup stereotypes have changed due to the perceivers' changing macroeconomic circumstances and the, possible, changing characteristics of targets, only small changes in absolute terms are expected because of the relatively short time-span between the two measurements taken.

Hypotheses

1. National and ethnic stereotypes will remain relatively stable over time (1994/1995); in particular, stereotypes of the national ingroup will remain stable, while stereotypes of national and ethnic outgroups will change slightly over time.

2. Stereotypes of national and ethnic outgroups change as a function of a worsening macroeconomic situation in the perceivers' country.

3. Stereotypes of foreign national groups reflect changes in perceived economic and relational features of nation-states, in particular, changes in

perceived economic power affect the content in terms of competence, while changes in the degree of perceived conflicts and nationalism of nation-states affect the content in terms of morality.

Procedures and Methods to Enhance the Validity of Cross-National Comparisons

There are various procedures and methods which can be applied in surveys carried out in more than one country to enhance the validity of cross-national comparisons or, in other words, to prevent bias due to in-equivalence (Van de Vijver and Poortinga, 1997; Hui and Triandis, 1985). There are three types of bias, or nuisance factors threatening the validity of cross-national comparisons: item-bias, method-bias and construct-bias. The first type of bias refers to measurement artefacts at item level and results from poor translation or complex wording of the item. The second type of bias arises from particular characteristics of the research instrument or its administration. The sources for method-bias, or measurement-bias, are: differences in administration of the instrument (e.g., physical condition), differential instruments (e.g., quality of the paper used for the questionnaire), sample in-equivalence (e.g., differences in educational background or age), and differential response styles (e.g., extremity scoring, social desirability). Construct-bias, the third type, will occur when the measured construct is not identical across countries due to incomplete overlap of definitions or incomplete coverage of the construct. These types of bias are related to each other. Item and method-bias may contribute to construct-bias, which is the most problematic one. Dissimilar constructs across countries imply that it is not allowed to make any cross-national comparisons.

Several methods were used to circumvent or detect these three types of bias in the study. The translation-backtranslation procedure (Werner and Campbell, 1970; Brislin, 1986) was used to circumvent item-bias. The questionnaires, with short uncomplicated sentences (i.e., the stereotype traits are just short words), were translated from English into the six Central and Eastern European languages and then back by native speakers in each instance. The author discussed the few discrepancies between the original English version and the translated version with the translators whereupon the most appropriate translation was chosen. The translators who worked independently on the translation, were all familiar with social science.

In order to circumvent method-bias, we attempted to get equivalent samples of participants, next to equivalent administration and content of the questionnaires across countries (Hui and Triandis, 1985; Van de Vijver and Leung, 1997). The equivalence of the sample with respect to age, urbanisation, social status and education level has been discussed earlier. Moreover, only adolescents who answered that they belonged to the country's national majority group were selected for the study. In other words, the questionnaires completed by participants who had answered that they belonged to an ethnic minority group (e.g., Russians in Belarus) were not used. The administration of the questionnaire was similar across the countries. After they listened to a standardised introduction and instruction (in their native language), the adolescents completed the questionnaire on a voluntary basis in their classrooms during a lesson of one hour. The cross-national data-collection took place within a restricted period, of approximately two months. The lay-out of the administered questionnaires was also equivalent across countries; all were printed on similar paper in the Netherlands. Furthermore, the order of the questions was similar: in each country four versions were used, in which the order of the target groups differed in order to distribute possible fatigue-effects on the last target groups to be judged. At the end of the questionnaire, participants were invited to comment in writing on the questionnaire. A measurement of social desirability was not included in the questionnaire because of time limits and our assumption that a possible bias from this source (and other differential response styles) can be detected by comparing the frequencies and also the structures of answers across countries with factor analysis, a method also used for detecting construct-bias.

Although the large number of cross-national and cross-cultural studies on stereotypes (see e.g., Oakes, Haslam and Turner, 1994) already suggest the comparability of the stereotype construct, each study should detect construct-bias by examining the factor-structure, reliability, and explained-variance of stereotypes composed by multiple items (cf. Van de Vijver and Leung, 1997). We used a special kind of factor analysis, simultaneous component analysis (Kiers, 1990), that indicated that the stereotype dimensions were comparable across countries in the underlying structure of traits, the degree of explained variance and reliability (see Poppe, 1999 for details).

Procedures and Methods to Enhance the Validity of Comparisons over Time

The three types of bias may also disturb the validity of comparisons over time. In the present study, item-bias was circumvented by using identical items at the first and second measurement. In order to prevent method-bias the data-collection in 1995 was similar compared to that of 1994 in content and lay-out of questionnaire, the voluntary completion in the classroom, the time of year and period (from March to May), and the participants. Almost all of the previous mentioned studies on changes in stereotypes examined stereotypes among two different groups of participants (i.e., cohorts), and therefore cannot convincingly claim that stereotypes changed over time because it may also be that the cohorts differed as to the stereotypes they had of groups. The present study is surveying the same adolescents twice (i.e., a panel study with two measurements). The data of adolescents who participated in the first and second measurement were matched by birthdate, these were filled in on both occasions. To prevent mismatching of participants with the same birthday, we checked for gender and class-number. This resulted in a total of 625 pupils: 108 Russian, 155 Belarusian, 61 Bulgarian, 127 Polish, 109 Hungarian, and 65 Czechs. In 1995, the composition in the classes was slightly different than in 1994 because some pupils had had to remain in the year below or had moved to another secondary school. Analysis indicated that the adolescents who dropped out of the survey did not differ significantly on the main variables, at the first measurement, from the participants (see Poppe, 1999, Chapter 5). Although it might be expected that construct-bias found in comparisons over time is improbable with such a short time-span, a separate factor analysis was conducted on each year's data, to indicate that the structure of the traits, the reliability, and the explained variance of stereotype-dimensions competence and morality were comparable (across countries and) over time (see for details, Poppe, 1999).

Results

Stability and Changes in Stereotypes over Time

First, competence and morality stereotypes attributed to the ingroup appeared to be identical in 1994 and 1995 (for details of the analysis of variance see Poppe, 1999). Table 9.2 presents these unchanged ingroup stereotypes. It can be seen that some of the Central and Eastern European nationalities are more positive about their ingroup in terms of competence (Russians, Czechs) or morality (Belarusians) than other nationalities (e.g., Belarusians on competence and Russians on morality) and this hierarchy is stable over time.

Second, competence and morality stereotypes attributed to ethnic minority groups also appeared to be unchanged between 1994 and 1995. Hence, irrespective of the type of ethnic minority group and the degree to which they are derogated in terms of competence or morality, ethnic minority stereotypes remain unchanged (see Table 9.3).

Third, stereotypes of foreign outgroups altered in some of the Central and Eastern European countries, as can be seen in Tables 9.4 and 9.5. Examining changes in competence attributions, it appeared that Bulgarians and Hungarians perceived some outgroups less positively in 1995 than in 1994 (see Table 9.4). Bulgarians perceived the English, Germans and Italians (i.e. the three

Table 9.2   Mean Competence and Morality Attributed to the National Ingroup in 1995[a]

	Trait-Dimension (%)		
Competence		Morality	
Russians	61	Belarusians	58
Czechs	60	Czechs	53
Poles	58	Hungarians	50
Hungarians	57	Poles	49
Bulgarians	57	Bulgarians	48
Belarusians	55	Russians	47

[a] These scores do not differ from the corresponding scores in 1994.

Table 9.3   Mean Competence and Morality Attributed to Ethnic Minority Groups in 1995[a]

	Trait-Dimension (%)		
Competence		Morality	
Jews in Russia	66	Slovaks in the Czech Republic	59
Germans in Poland	64	Russians in Belarus	52
Slovaks in the Czech Republic	57	Jews in Russia	46
Russians in Belarus	56	Germans in Poland	45
Gypsies in Hungary	46	Turks in Bulgaria	40
Turks in Bulgaria	45	Gypsies in Hungary	30

[a] These scores do not differ from the corresponding scores in 1994.

Western European groups) as less competent in 1995 than in 1994, while the Hungarians perceived the English and Italians as less competent. The competence stereotypes of fellow Central and Eastern European nationalities did not change. Hence, foreign outgroup stereotypes in terms of competence were relatively stable, as only Bulgarians and Hungarians perceive Western European nationalities to be less competent in 1995 than in 1994. The results with respect to the morality dimension indicated changes over time in four countries (see Table 9.5). In Russia, Belarus and Bulgaria, stereotypes of foreign outgroups became less positive irrespective of the target group (i.e., both Western, Central and Eastern European nationalities). In contrast the Czechs perceived the morality of foreign outgroups more positively in 1995 than in 1994 (see Table 9.5). Hence, foreign outgroup stereotypes in terms of morality are not very stable, as there are changes in four out of the six countries. As expected, all the changes are rather small (see Poppe, 1999 for details).

In summary, stereotypes of the national ingroup and the ethnic minority group did not alter in any country. Stereotypes of foreign outgroups changed in some of the countries. Stereotypes of competence altered among Hungarians and Bulgarians, but were target-specific: Western European nationalities were perceived as less competent in 1995 than in the previous year. Furthermore, Russians, Belarusians, and Bulgarians perceived the morality of all target groups less positively, while Czechs perceived foreign outgroups as more moral in 1995 than in 1994. Hence, Hypothesis one is confirmed, stereotypes attributed to the ingroup are stable over time and stereotypes attributed to foreign outgroups changed slightly in some cases, as expected, while stereotypes of minority groups appeared more stable than expected.

Table 9.4   Mean Competence Attributed to Foreign Nationalities: 1995 [a]

Participant Country	Target-Nationality								
	Rus	Blr	Bul	Hun	Pol	Cze	Eng	Ger	Ita
Russian	x	51	53	54	53	53	66	68	63
Berlarus	58	x	58	58	57	57	68	70	64
Bulgaria	54	49	x	56	53	57	**63**	**68**	**63**
Hungary	49	47	49	x	50	54	**66**	70	**62**
Poland	56	49	52	56	x	53	60	71	65
Czech Rep	44	49	48	54	52	x	65	70	60

[a] Scores significantly lower than in 1994 are bold, those the same are not highlighted. Rus = Russians; Blr = Belarusians; Bul = Bulgarians; Pol = Poles; Hun = Hungarians; Cze = Czechs; Eng = English; Ger = Germans; Ita = Italians.

Table 9.5   Mean Morality Attributed to Foreign Nationalities: 1995 [a]

Participant Country	Target-Nationality								
	Rus	Blr	Bul	Hun	Pol	Cze	Eng	Ger	Ita
Russian	x	**51**	**54**	**54**	**46**	**56**	**58**	**48**	**44**
Belarus	**47**	x	**55**	**56**	**51**	**57**	**60**	**53**	**54**
Bulgaria	**44**	**51**	x	**49**	**49**	**55**	**47**	**44**	**44**
Hungary	46	50	51	x	55	51	55	43	48
Poland	34	47	50	55	x	56	53	37	50
Czech Rep	*46*	*55*	*51*	*53*	*54*	x	*61*	42	*48*

[a] Scores significantly lower than in 1994 are bold, those significantly higher are italic, those the same are not highlighted. Rus = Russians; Blr = Belarusians; Bul = Bulgarians; Pol = Poles; Hun = Hungarians; Cze = Czechs; Eng = English; Ger = Germans; Ita = Italians.

Changes in Stereotypes as a Function of Growth in Gross National Product

Now that it is known in which of the countries the stereotypes changed, it is interesting to investigate whether differential macroeconomic changes can explain these cross-national differences (Hypothesis two). Gross national product (GNP), based on exchange rates and on purchasing power parities per capita of 1994 and 1995, was used to calculate GNP growth-figures and subsequently these figures were related to the changes or stability in stereotypes (see Poppe, 1999). Competence attributions did not change as a function of GNP growth. However, GNP growth in terms of both exchange rates and purchasing power parities significantly reflected changes in morality attributed to foreign nationalities. This indicates that morality attributed to foreign outgroups decreases as a function of a decline in the GNP of the perceiver's country. In other words, the tendency to perceive foreign outgroups as less moral than the previous year increases as a function of a decrease in GNP in the perceiver's country. This finding reflects the already mentioned result that in Belarus, Russia and Bulgaria (i.e., countries in which the macroeconomic situation deteriorated considerably relative to other countries in the study) stereotypes of foreign nationalities became more negative, whereas they became more positive in the Czech Republic (whose GNP grew relatively well). Hence, Hypothesis two is partly corroborated: stereotypes of foreign nationalities in terms of morality changed as a function of macroeconomic changes in participant countries. However, competence attributed to ethnic minority groups and foreign nationalities did not change as a function of macroeconomic changes in participant countries. We have seen that these stereotypes barely changed at all (see Tables 9.2–9.4).

Changes in Stereotypes Reflect Changes in Perceived Characteristics of Targets

The last Hypothesis to be tested refers to the relationship between changes in stereotypes and changes in perceived characteristics of target groups (as asked in the survey: economic power, nationalistic, conflicts of interest). It appeared that changes in terms of competence correspond to changes in the perceived economic power of nation-states. Hence, nationalities whose nation-states are perceived as less economically powerful than the year before, are perceived as less competent than they were the year before (see Poppe, 1999). Note that competence stereotypes changed only for Western European groups, and only in Hungary and Bulgaria. Apparently, Hungarians and Bulgarians perceive the West Europeans countries as less economically powerful and therefore the national populations as less competent **than years before**. Changes in terms of morality appeared to be related to changes in perceived economic power, nationalism and conflicts. Nationalities whose nation-states are perceived as less economically powerful, more nationalistic, and experiencing more intergroup conflicts compared to the previous year, are perceived as less moral than the year before. It should be noted that these effects are not very strong (see for details Poppe, 1999).

These results corroborate Hypothesis three. Additionally, it appears that changes in the perceived economic power of the nation-states are not only related to changes in terms of competence but also to changes in terms of morality.

Discussion

This study examined changes in national and ethnic stereotypes between 1994 and 1995 among adolescents in six Central and Eastern European countries. The findings corroborate the first hypothesis by indicating that stereotypes of the national ingroup and ethnic minority groups were stable between 1994 and 1995, while stereotypes of specific national outgroups changed slightly in some of the countries. Among Hungarians and Bulgarians, competence stereotypes changed only for Western European nationalities: they were perceived as less competent in 1995 compared to the year before. Morality stereotypes changed negatively among Russians, Belarusians, and Bulgarians and, did so irrespective of outgroup target, whereas the Czechs perceive foreign outgroups as more moral in 1995 than in 1994.

The second hypothesis was partly corroborated. It appeared that stereotypes of the morality of foreign national groups do indeed change as a function of the macroeconomic deterioration in the perceivers' country, which was determined by growth figures of GNP per capita both in terms of exchange rates and purchasing power parities. This finding delimits the finding that foreign outgroup stereotypes changed negatively in terms of morality in Russia, Belarus and Bulgaria (i.e., the countries which did relatively worse macroeconomically), did not change in Poland and Hungary (in which GNP per capita remained approximately similar), and became more positive in the Czech Republic (which did relatively well in macroeconomic terms). The hypothesis is not corroborated with respect to stereotypes of the competence of foreign national groups and stereotypes of ethnic minority groups.

The analysis confirmed the third hypothesis that posits that stereotypes of foreign national groups are affected by changes in perceived economic and relational features of nation-states. It appeared that a change in competence corresponds to changes in the economic power of nation-states and that a change in morality is related to changes in perceived nationalism, conflicts and also to the nation-states' economic power. Nationalities whose nation state is perceived as less economically powerful, more nationalistic and more conflict prone compared to the year before, are likely to be perceived as less moral. This illustrates that stereotypes of particular foreign nationalities change over time, namely about those nationalities whose nation states are perceived as less economically powerful (i.e., competence stereotypes of Western European nationalities held by Hungarians and Bulgarians) and more nationalistic and conflict prone (e.g., morality stereotypes of foreign nationalities held by Russians and Belarusians).

The present study supports and extends previous findings which showed that the content of stereotypes is not rigid but may change due to transformations in social reality (see e.g., Oakes et al., 1994). The focus on the two aspects of social reality investigated, the objective macroeconomic circumstances of perceivers and the perceived features of the targets, was useful for explaining why stereotypes changed in particular countries and why stereotypes of particular target groups changed in some of these countries. The cross-national effect of changing macroeconomic circumstances of perceivers on their attributions of morality is a new contribution to the existing research literature.

The results are in line with theoretical explanations of changes in stereotypes. The finding that stereotypes reflect changing features of targets and intergroup relations such as conflicts between the perceiver's group and the target group support self-categorisation theory (Turner et al., 1987; Oakes and Turner, 1990) and realistic conflict theory (Sherif, 1967). The findings on the effects of macro-level changes among perceivers may have some interesting implications for relative deprivation theory (Runciman, 1966) and social identity theory (Tajfel, 1981). First, the finding that stereotypes of the morality of foreign national groups changed negatively as a function of the economic deprivation in the perceiver's country relative to other countries, fits relative deprivation theory. However, changes in GNP did not affect stereotypes of the competence of foreign national groups, while this dimension reflects the socioeconomic power of targets (Poppe and Linssen, 1999). Hence, it seems that foreign outgroups are blamed for the deteriorated internal economic situation not because they are less competent than expected but because they are less moral than expected. This may be interpreted as disappointment about the lack of expected aid from more wealthy countries (e.g., Western Europe) or about the lack of cooperation from some countries in similar circumstances (e.g., Central and Eastern Europe). Although some results support relative deprivation theory, conclusive support for it was not found because the results did not clearly indicate that especially the nationality targets who did better than the national ingroup were deprived in terms of more negative stereotypes. Hence, although there seems to be an outgroup blaming mechanism behind the negative changes in stereotypes of the morality of outgroups, it was not directed at specific scapegoats. No evidence was obtained for scapegoating of ethnic minorities when the economic situation in a country worsened over time, a result in line with a recent study by Postma (1996) among Hungarians and their stereotypes of Jews and Gypsies. Interestingly, stereotypes of ethnic minorities originating from neighbouring countries (e.g., Russians residing in Belarus) also did not change while stereotypes of the national population of these neighbouring countries (e.g., Russians) changed. Whether stereotypes of ethnic minorities are generally stable and relatively hard to change is a topic for further investigation.

Several procedures and methods were followed to overcome the various types of bias which may otherwise threaten the validity of comparisons across countries and over time. The translation-backtranslation procedure, standardisation of questionnaire and data-collection, and the standardisation of constructs (i.e., dependent and independent variables) as a results of factor analysis, all attest to the comparability across countries and over time. The focus on a particular group of participants (i.e., adolescents in highest grade of secondary schools in capital cities) contributes to the validity of the cross-national comparisons. It would have been more difficult to explain cross-national differences in a comparative study across national representative samples because the comparison across countries may be confounded with inequivalent demographic characteristics which should then be corrected in analyses by complicated weighting procedures. Yet, secondary school students from different countries are often compared, and it is assumed that their demographic characteristics are similar across countries (Van de Vijver and Leung, 1997).

However, the procedures and methods taken to facilitate comparisons across countries and over time imply some limitations. First, potential particularities in the content and meaning of variables across countries are lost as a result of standardisation of constructs by means of factor analyses. For instance, Poppe (1999), found that of 19 administred items reflecting nationalistic beliefs, only seven were adequately scalable across countries. Some of the remaining items appeared to be related to nationalism in only some of the countries involved but not in all and were therefore not included in the nationalism scale which had to be comparable and reliable across countries. Second, the generalisation of the results is limited. The focus on a particular group of participants means that it is not possible to generalise by extension to other groups in the countries such as adults or even adolescents from other cities or rural areas. The results are also not generalisable to a different intergroup context, of (partly) other target groups and participant countries.

The possible generalisations of the findings on changes in stereotypes are also limited because there are only two measurements separated by a relatively short time-span. Although the Central and Eastern European countries are undergoing a period of rapid political and economic transitions, a study of changes in stereotypes over a longer time-span with more variation in the determinants (e.g., the degree of economic growth or decline) is necessary to determine if a lack of economic success relative to other nation-states may reinforce negative foreign nationality stereotypes. This negative effect of the unequal transformation processes in Central and Eastern European countries needs further confirmation, for instance, in a longitudinal design involving measurements at several points in time. In this way it may also be possible to determine whether, at the beginning of the twenty-first century the stereotypes of Central European nationalities have become more positive due to economic growth and a decrease in (economic) conflicts.

Acknowledgments

This research was supported by the Foundation for Economic, Socio-Cultural, and Environmental Sciences (ESR), of the Dutch Organisation for Scientific Research (NWO; grant number 510-81-504). I also wish to express gratitude to György Çsepeli, Jannes Hartkamp and Timea Venczel (Eötvös Lóránd University, Budapest); Yulian Konstantinov, Todor Shopov and Alexander Kolev (University of Sofia); Zdenka Pechacová and Maria Koutková (Agriculture University, Prague), David Rotman and Irina Ukhvanova (Belarus State University, Minsk), Sergey Tumanov and Vyacheslav Ryazantsev (Moscow State University) and Krystyna Skarzynska (Polish Academy of Science, Warsaw) for assistance with the data collection, and to the many people involved in translations, language correction and data entry.

Notes

1 In Bulgaria, as in many other Central and Eastern European countries, reported figures for minority populations are often larger than the official figures (e.g., Szjakowski, 1993).

2 Even though 'Gypsies' usually call themselves 'Roma', the term 'Gypsy' will be used in this Chapter to be consistent with the questionnaire.

3   The Jews are selected as a target group in the Russian Federation instead of the larger
    Tatar or Ukrainian group due to history of antagonism.

References

Ashmore, R. (1970), 'The problem of intergroup prejudice', in B.E. Collins (ed.), *Social Psychology*, Addison-Wesley, Reading, pp. 245–297.

Berkowitz, L. and Green, J.A. (1962), 'The stimulus quality of the scapegoat', *Journal of Abnormal Psychology*, vol. 64, pp.293–301.

Brewer, M.B. and Campbell, D.T. (1976), *Ethnocentrism and intergroup attitudes: East African evidence*, Halsted/Wiley, New York.

Brigham, J.C. (1971), 'Ethnic stereotypes', *Psychological Bulletin*, vol. 76, pp. 15–38.

Brislin, R.W. (1970), 'Back translation for cross-cultural research', *Journal of Cross-Cultural Psychology*, vol 1, pp. 185–216.

Brislin, R.W. (1986), 'The wording and translation of research instruments', in W.J. Lonner and J.W. Berry (eds), *Fieldmethods in cross-cultural research*, Sage, Beverly Hills, pp. 137–164.

Brown, R. (1988), *Group processes*, Blackwell, Oxford.

Buchanan, W. (1951), 'Stereotypes and tensions as revealed by the UNESCO International Poll', *International Social Science Bulletin*, vol. 3, pp. 515–528.

Çsepeli, G., & Zavecz, T. (1992), Conflicting bonds of nationality in Hungary; National identity, minority status, and ethnicity. *Innovation*, 5, 77–94.

Dollard, J., Doob, L., Miller, N.E., Mowrer, O. and Sears, R. (1939), *Frustration and aggression*, Yale University Press, New Haven.

Duckitt, J. (1994), *The social psychology of prejudice*, Praeger Publishers, Westport.

Hagendoorn, L., Çsepeli, G., Dekker, H. and Farnen, R. (eds) (2000), *European nations and nationalism in a historical perspective*, Ashgate, Aldershot.

Hagendoorn, L., Phalet, K., Henke, R. and Drogendijk, R. (1995), *Etnische verhoudingen in Midden- en Oost-Europa* (Ethnic Relations in Central and Eastern Europe), WRR, The Hague.

Hui, C.H. and Triandis, H.C. (1985), 'Measurement in cross-cultural psychology, a review and comparison of strategies', *Journal of Cross-Cultural Psychology*, vol. 16, pp. 131–152.

Karlins, M., Coffmann, T.L. and Walters, G. (1969), 'On the fading of social stereotypes: Studies in three generations of college students', *Journal of Personality and Social Psychology*, vol. 13, pp. 1–16.

Katz, D. and Braly, K.W. (1933), 'Racial stereotypes of one hundred college students', *Journal of Abnormal and Social Psychology*, vol. 28, pp. 280–290.

Kiers, H.A. (1990), *SCA: A program for simultaneous component analysis of variabeles measured in two or more populations*, ProGRAMMA, Groningen.

LeVine, R. A. and Campbell, D. T. (1972), *Ethnocentrism: Theories and conflict, ethnic attitudes and group behaviour*, Wiley, New York.

Linssen, H. (1995), *Nationality stereotypes in Europe: Content and change*, Unpublished doctoral dissertation, Utrecht University, NL.

Linssen, H. and Hagendoorn, L. (1994), 'Social and geographical factors in the explanation of the context of European nationality stereotypes', *British Journal of Social Psychology*, vol. 33, pp. 165–182.

McCauley, C., Stitt, C.L. and Segal, M. (1980), 'Stereotyping: From prejudice to prediction', *Psychological Bulletin*, vol. 87, pp. 195–208.

Oakes, P.J. and Turner, J.C. (1990), 'Is limited information processing the cause of social stereotyping?', in W. Stroebe and M. Hewstone (eds), *European review of Social Psychology*, Wiley, Chicester, pp. 111–135.

Oakes, P.J., Haslam, S.A. and Turner, J.C. (1994), *Stereotyping and social reality*, Blackwell, Oxford.

Phalet, K. and Poppe, E. (1997), 'Competence and morality dimensions of national and ethnic stereotypes: A study in six Eastern European countries', *European Journal of Social Psychology*, vol. 27, pp. 703–723.

Poppe, E. (1999), *National and ethnic stereotypes in Central and Eastern Europe; a study among adolescents in six countries*, Thela Thesis Publishers, Amsterdam.

Poppe, E. and Linssen, H. (1999), 'Ingroup favouritism and the reflection of realistic dimensions of difference between national states in Central and Eastern European nationality stereotypes', *British Journal of Social Psychology*, vol. 38, pp. 85–102.

Postma, K. (1996), *Changing prejudice in Hungary: A study on the collapse of state socialism and its impact on prejudice against Gypsies and Jews*, Thesis Publishers, Amsterdam.

Rosenberg, S. and Sedlak, A. (1972), 'Structural representations of implicit personality theory', in L. Berkowitz (ed), *Advances in Experimental Social Psychology*, Academic Press, New York, pp. 235–297.

Runciman, W.G. (1966), *Relative deprivation and social justice*, Routledge and Kegan Paul, London.

Sherif, M. (1967), *Groups conflict and cooperation: Their social psychology*, Routledge and Kegan Paul, London.

Simpson, G.E. and Yinger, J.M. (1972), *Racial and cultural minorities: An analysis of prejudice and discrimination*, Plenum, New York.

Stangor, C. and Lange, J.E. (1994), 'Mental representations of social groups: Advances in understanding stereotypes and stereotyping', *Advances in Experimental Social Psychology*, vol. 26, pp. 357–415.

Szajkowski, B. (1993), *Encyclopaedia of conflicts, diputes and flashpoints in Eastern Europe, Russia and the successor states*, Longman, London.

Tajfel, H. (1981), *Human groups and social categories*, Cambridge University Press, Cambridge.

Turner, J.C., Hogg, M.A., Oakes, P.J., Reicher, S.D. and Wetherell, M.S. (1987), *Rediscovering the social group: A self-categorization theory*, Blackwell, Oxford.

Van de Vijver, F.J.R. and Leung, K. (1997), *Methods and data analysis for cross-cultural research*, Sage, Thousand Oaks, CA.

Van de Vijver, F.J.R. and Poortinga, Y.H. (1997), 'Towards an integrated analysis of bias in cross-cultural assessment', *European Journal of Psychological Assessment*, vol. 13, pp. 21–29

Verdery, K. (1992), 'Comment: Hobsbawn in the East', *Antropology Today*, vol. 8, pp. 8–10.

Werner, O. and Campbell, D.T. (1970), 'Translating, working through interpreters, and the problem of decentring', in R. Naroll and R. Cohen (eds), *A handbook of cultural antropology*, American Museum of Natural History, New York, pp. 398–419.

10 Jewish Identity, Discrimination and Anti-Semitism in Three Countries

MONICA SAVULESCU-VOUDOURIS & CAMIL FUCHS

Social experience seems to confirm the thesis that while people who live in their own country are treated as individuals, in many cases, those living in a foreign country are treated as a group. For the local population, the foreigners are *Other,* and to be Other becomes a stigma (the well known sociological concept of 'group stigma'). The traditions and norms of the foreigners differ from those of the locals. They, the foreigners, have a different identity and the level of stigmatisation seems to be directly proportional to the strength of the definition and the level of active preservation of that identity.

Jews are considered to be a people with the longest history of living in foreign countries. The Jewish diaspora is spread all over the world, in traditional national, multi-national and multi-racial countries. In all those countries, their identity has been strongly defined and preserved. Group stigma against them has led to appalling tragedies, of which the Nazi Holocaust represents the most unimmaginable for its scale alone.

Half a century after the Holocaust the need for comparative research on the relationship betwenn the existence of a Jewish identity and anti-Semitism is as pressing as ever. Have the features of the Jewish identity remained intact and are they stigmatised in the same way as they were prior to the Holocaust? In other words is 'the Jewish Question' an eternal one for which 'anti-Semitism' as a form of racism is still a ubiquitous response?

The issue has a special relevance to contemporary post-modernist debates on integration, given that new ethnic communities are formed in the Diaspora. The old models of integration are no longer operational as the millennium draws to a close; and, in the immigration files, we witness a recrudescence of racism and xenophobia. But this racism has no unique form, and its particular characteristics come forth out of the specific social conditions in each country.

In a recent attempt to define the fundamentals of racism, Wieviorka (1991) geographically locates two basic poles around which the various forms of racism evolve, and defines their specific characteristics: the North American experience (the racism of whites against blacks) and the European experience (the racism of non-Jews against Jews). By including a non-European multi-racial country in this study, we try to assess whether this anti-Jewish racism really is a purely European phenomenon.

The considerations in our research differ from those of the theoretical outsider-analysts who measure and weigh, 'objectively', the empirical conditions and draw-up models with which to explain them. This is not the task we set ourselves nor did we intend to analyse how the majority population perceives the various minorities and the xenos. Instead, we set out to assess the *minorities' perceptions*, their subjective impressions about the way they are treated and how they view the discrimination they experience. Whether their perceptions are completely objective or are somewhat distorted is irrelevant. These perceptions are the only 'real thing' for the victims of racism.

Our findings on 'xenophobia' are thus based on the testimony of minority Jews who live as a 'xenos'. We compared their identity problems, the reaction of the majority population to this identity, and the perceived discrimination and anti-Semitism in European and non-European countries.

This comparison provides a special understanding of the frequency and the forms of racism in the countries. While theoretically we could have objectively assessed the anti-Semitism at the national level, in the political arena and the media, those who experience this form of racism are the only ones who can provide trustworthy information about the day to day experience of this form of racism—at school, on the street, in the work place etc. Even in an analysis of anti-Semitism at a national level, data on the perceptions of the minorities provides a fuller view than that of the outsider-analyst.

The experience of victims provides a good point of comparison for the study of anti-Semitic attitudes in national, multi-national and multi-racial countries. Their perceptions are affected by those historical factors and contemporary conditions specific to their communities. From within this framework we compare those countries with national, multi-national and multi-racial structures, in which anti-Semitism, as a form of racist attitude, can be assessed within white communities, in mixed (predominantly white) communities, and in mixed (predominantly black) communities.

This study allowed us to empirically verify the extent of the validity of Paxton and Marrus' (1981) 'three concentric circles' theory on the nature of present day anti-Semitism. This theory has been adopted by Wieviorka under the name 'tri-dimensional racism': a view in which racism develops from prejudice to segregation and then to an institutionalised doctrine of racism, adopted as an ideology (1991). We study the characteristics and manifestations of discrimination and racism with respect to the categories defined by Wieviorka: humiliating (or repressessive) racism, racism expressed by differentiation, and institutionalised racism, i.e., that adopted as ideology.

By extending the scope of the study to a non-European country, we were able to empirically assess Lévi-Strauss' 'cultural distance' theory (1983) which states that racism diminishes where groups intermingle to a lesser extent. We tried to locate the site of anti-Semitism within a less intermingled society to that of a special form of xenophobia. Our study of Jewish identity also permitted us to assess whether Sartre's remark on the essence of being Jewish is still valid for the contemporary world. The theory formulated famously as: 'It is the anti-Semitism that creates the Jew' assumes that Jews are primarily defined by non-Jews (Sartre, 1954).

The Target Countries

The three countries selected for the study were Romania, the Netherlands and Curaçao. Each has roughly the same proportion of Jewish to non-Jewish population (9:14 000). The selected countries differ in their location—Western Europe, Eastern Europe and the Caribbean respectively; the history and contemporary political and socioeconomic situation of their Jewish communities; in the way the communities were affected by the Holocaust (while the European countries suffered, Curaçao was unaffected, and in the national political and racial outlook.

Romania is a post-communist, traditionalist and nationalist country, which experienced a degree of multiculturalism after 1918, and which after WWII suffered from being a satellite of the then Soviet Union. The Netherlands on the other hand, has a century-old democratic system, and is a cosmopolitan post-colonial country. Curaçao is characterised by a multi-ethnic and multi-racial population formed by the vagaries of the slave trade. The country is situated in the Caribbean, close to the dominating influence of the multicultural United States.

The differences between the three countries affect the attitudes of their non-Jewish towards their Jewish population. Furthermore, as we shall see, the history of each country in general, and the specific political and racial hegemony at the institutional and national level in particular, seems to have a significant effect on the Jewish population's perceptions as well.

Anti-Semitism as Part of the Jewish Identity

Recent sociological theories regard the concept of identity as fluid; endlessly mutable in relation to place, time, the person(s) or group(s) involved, and the political orientation of the society (see e.g., Wieviorka, 1998). Therefore we looked for the most recent definition of Jewish identity originating from one of the target countries. Consequently, the analysis of the components of the Jewish identity in this study are based on Ido Abram's (1993) definition. Ido Abram uses five aspects to define Jewish identity: religion, culture, and tradition; direct or indirect experience of anti-Semitism and xenophobia; relationship with Israel; relationship with non-Jewish culture and people; and individual (personal) life experience.

This definition of identity contains an important aspect not to be found among those who live in their own country: the Jewish self-image is shaped by the attitude non-Jews express towards them, the direct and indirect experience, mentioned above, of anti-Semitism and xenophobia. We tried to assess the similarities and the differences in the way this attitude is perceived by the Jews with whom we spoke in the three countries. Thus assessing whether the same definition could be applied across all three countries.

The Post-War Jewish Generation

The respondents in our study are the first generation in the history of the Jews to live contemporaneous with the existence of an own country—the state of Israel—to which they could emigrate should they choose to do so. Their reasons for remaining in the country of their birth differ from country to country. These are influenced by historical factors that affected the formation, development and contemporary basis of their communities; here discrimination and xenophobia should be considered among the most relevant factors. In a comparative study on these two elements, we must take account of the historical circumstances which brought the Jewish population to each of these three selected countries, as well as the mass extermination of the Holocaust, and present-day policies affecting the Jewish population in each country.

A brief comparative analysis is given below. This chapter is by no means an exhaustive presentation of the difficulties experienced by the various Jewish communities throughout their history in these countries, nor are those discussed here necessarily the most significant ones. However, they do shed light on the situation, when referring to discrimination and xenophobia.

Rights, Citizenship and Regulations Prior to the Second World War

During the nineteenth century a large wave of Jewish emigration arrived in Romania, triggered by pogroms in Ukraine and Poland (the Askenazi Jews). Due to their commercial skills, the Jewish community soon became a serious economic competitor to the Romanians, who responded with restrictive laws. Jewish people did not have the right to own land or to receive Romanian citizenship. In 1877, those Jews who fought in the war against the Turks received the right to become citizens. In 1918 all Jews gained the right to receive Romanian citizenship, but this did not automatically mean integration. During the Second World War and the dictatorship of General Antonescu, Romania fought on the side of fascist Germany, the discriminatory rules of which became legislation in Romania as well.

Unlike the situation in Romania, the Jews in the Netherlands had received not only citizenship but full political rights by the end of the eighteenth century. The history of the Jews in the Netherlands starts in the seventeenth century when they arrived from Spain and Portugal (the Sephardic Jews) and from Poland (the Askenazi Jews). At that time, they received the right to religious freedom and were considered a seperate nation. During the eighteenth century the influence of the Enlightenment was felt in the Netherlands. Emancipation movements appeared, an example of which was 'the Patriots' movement (*de Patrioten*). Some Jews alligned themselves with such movements, while others supported the prince of Orange, partly due to the apprehension that religious emancipation might lead to a loss of power and prestige for the Jewish community. In 1795 the French army entered the Netherlands and in 1796 the National Assembly, the first elected body of the Netherlands, issued the 'Decree of Emancipation' in which the Jewish community were no longer viewed as a nation, but as a religion. This was also the year in which the community won two places in the National Assembly, the first Jewish members of a parliament in the world. Towards the end of the eighteenth century, they received full political rights. During the nineteenth century, the Jews integrated further and made significant contributions to Dutch society: there was a Jewish Minister of Justice, Jewish architects altered the face of Amsterdam, and the first Dutch trade union was that of the Jewish diamond crafters. Nevertheless, the Jewish community was segregated from the Dutch population. In the middle of the nineteenth century, 40 per cent of the Jewish community subsidised the other 60 per cent. Among them, socialist ideas started to emerge. In 1896 the Dreyfuss case, in France, proved to the world that assimilation is far from being an answer to anti-Semitism; Hertzl, a journalist at the trial, was later to found Zionism. But the movement never gained as many followers in the Netherlands as in Eastern Europe.

In Curaçao the status of the Jewish community was influenced early on by the composition of the local population as well as by the rule of the Dutch colonisers. In 1643, when the Dutch captured Curaçao from Spain, the majority of the population were Spanish or Indian. Curaçao represented a strategic point for the West India Company—an ideal halt between Brazil and the Netherlands. The Sephardic Jewish emigrants started businesses with Brazil, and became involved in tobacco trading and in the sugar industries. In 1648 the import of slaves from terriorties in Africa started and continued until 1863, when slavery was abolished. Until this time slaves represented about 90 per cent of the population. To posess slaves was a status symbol for the white inhabitants. The children in the houses of wealthy Jewish families were brought up by a 'Jaja', the 'Negro mammy', who enriched their culture with Afro-Caribbean influences. Children born of liasons between the free men and the slave women on their plantations bore the name of the father but were not considered Jewish under Jewish religious law.

In 1824 Roman-Catholic missionaries arrived on the island and began to convert most of the Negro population. Catholicism is now the main religion of the Afro-Caribbean population. The Sephardic Jews spoke Spanish, English and Dutch. Their multi-lingual status aided the Dutch in the trade wars with Latin America and North America. In 1825, the granting of civil rights, by royal degree, gave the Jewish community political power. At the same time Curaçao was undergoing a period of industrialisation. While most of the Dutch remained in the agriculture sector, the Jewish community were one step ahead, thanks to their cosmopolitanism and financial power.

At the beginning of the twentieth century most of the Jews were in a blossoming economic position. Their children were educated in Europe and North America. The discovery of oil in Venezuela led to the emergence of processing and transportation industries in Curaçao. The First World War was hardly felt on the island. However, European economic crises as well as the Depression of the 1930s led to a second substantial wave of emigrants, among which the Ashkenazi Jews from Germany, Poland and the Balkans. The level of economic competition on the island affected traditional behaviour, ships, for example, docked and were loaded and unloaded on the Sabbath days. The community began to divide between orthodox and liberal.

During the Second World War

The Romanian facist party, *Garda de Fier* (Iron Guard), conducted numerous anti-Semitic activities between 1938 and 1944. Seven thousand Jews were killed in the town of Jassy between June 29 and July 6, 1940. The pretext for the massacre being the alleged cooperation of Jews with the enemy. The 1941 crossing of the Russian border by the Romanian-German army was followed by the deportation of Jews to the camps of Transdniestria. Thirty per cent of the population of these camps died due to organised as well as random criminal acts, **and from deprivation combined with forced labour.** General

Antonescu, the ruler of Romania at the time, had a two-sided role in the deportation of the Jews. Initially he took no action against the deportations. Then from 1942 onwards, when confronted with a worsening situation on the front, he distanced himself from the mass deportation policy practiced in other occupied European countries. At the time of his execution in 1946, some considered him the rescuer of more than 300 000 Jews, while others saw him as the one mainly responsible for the death of almost 125 000 Jews.

Unlike in Romania, in the Netherlands there were no organised anti-Semitic activities following Hitler's rise to power in Germany. Furthermore, the Netherlands provided refuge to Jewish refugees fleeing Hitler's Germany. However in 1938 an economic crisis and rising unemployment led to the borders being closed. Those who had already entered were granted the right to remain in the Westerbork refugee center (15 000 persons), which within two years was to become known as the dreaded Kamp Westerbork—a concentration camp.

Deprivations and restrictions for the Jewish population followed the invasion of the Netherlands in 1940 by the German army. From 1942 onwards the Jews were obliged to wear the yellow star of David; random arrests took place. Many of the non-Jewish population organised solidarity strikes and other forms of resistance, such as assiting or hiding Jews (adults and children), and falsifying identity documents. However, there were those Dutch citizens who collaborated with the Nazis. In 1944, when the Netherlands was liberated, out of 140 000 Jews, only 30 000 had survived. Eighty per cent had perished, one of the highest percentages of any European country.

Of the three countries in our study, Curaçao was the only one not directly affected by the Second World War, nor did its Jewish community suffer directly. During the war, the fear that the Germans might attack the island in order to capture the oil led to closer relations with the United States at an official as well as at a more personal level.

After the Second World War

During the Second World War, a substantial number of Jews from Romania joined the communist party, partly in order to contribute to the fight against Nazism. As a result, in 1944 many Jews gained prominent positions in the communist party, leading in turn to a form of anti-Semitism specific to communist countries, 'Red anti-Semitism'.

Zionism appealed to a different segment of the Jewish population to that attracted to communism. In 1947 the communist party officially denounced Zionism as 'a phenomenon of the Jewish bourgeoisie supported by the

Americans'. In 1952 emigration to Israel was forbidden. Nevertheless, there were exceptions to the rule. From 1964 , under Ceausescu's rule, emigration was encouraged for a price: $US5 000 per person.

After the 1989 revolution, public expressions of anti-Semitism increased. This post-communist rise in anti-Semitism, common to all the former communist countries, occured despite the small size of the mostly aged Jewish population. However, evidence that some political parties encouraged anti-Semitic feelings in order to divert attention from Romanians poor economic situation is to be found in official party sources.

In the Netherlands, Jews received full political and social rights in/from 1945, and anti-Semitism was officially banned. Dutch citizenship brought with it the right to immigrate to the country of their choice. Many young professionals immigrated to Canada and the US, while among the more religious Jews, a larger proportion opted for Israel. The foundation of the state of Israel in 1948 gave moral support to those Jews spread all over the world, but some remaining in the Netherlands chose to distance themselves from the new Jewish state. We may speculate that in some cases the fear of what the future might bring, or the need for oblivion, may have played a role here.

As for Curaçao, after the Second World War, relations with the United States grew closer. The Jewish community was not immune to the ensuing Americanisation, a result of which was a new openess towards the other ethnic groups. Mixed marriages occured, and in most cases the woman converted, primarily due to economic reasons. The phenomenon strengthened the cosmopolitan inclination on the island.

The Samples

The respondents were selected from those with a contemporary awareness of the problems of Judaism and xenophobia. In each of the three countries we interviewed a group of 20 young Jewish people, between the ages of 18 and 35 years, whose level of education indicated that they should be capable of a self-reflexive conceptualisation of the issues involved. They were selected haphazardly using the snowball technique. Hence, this is not a probability sample and its representativeness is limited to the population from which the respondents were drawn. As a result of the sampling technique and of the age of the target group(s), the majority of the respondents from Romania and the Netherlands were either students or recent graduates. In Curaçao the professional and socioeconomic position of the respondents was higher than those in the European sample: managers in the family business, bank managers, marketing professionals, management consultants, students studying in Europe or the United States, account managers, political representatives. Their parents also held high socioeconomic positions: bankers, surgeons, entrepreneurs, restaurant owners, and businessmen. Most of the children and parents were born on the island, but the generation prior to theirs came from Argentina, the United States, Panama, St. Mauritius, Costa Rica, and to a lesser extent from the Netherlands, Mexico, and Egypt.

The Questionnaire and Sampling Technique

The study was carried out by face-to-face interviews. The same questionnaire was used in each of the three countries, except in Curaçao where three sections were added to the basic questionnaire. The extra sections dealt with specific historical, geographical, and other local characteristics.

The basic questionnaire included about 170 questions divided into six sections corresponding to specific areas of interest, drawing upon Ido Abraham's definition of Jewish identity: (a) general and demographic; (b) Jewish identity of the respondent and his/her family; (c) personal and general feelings related to Jewish identity; (d) discrimination and anti-Semitism; (e) Jewish and non-Jewish organisations; (f) relations with Israel.

The extra sections in the Curaçao questionnaire related to the indirect influence of the Holocaust; to the direct influence of the multicultural mix of Curaçao (Spanish/Portuguese, Afro-Caribbean, Dutch, Jewish, multicultural American), and to the relations with Europe and the United States. Aside from these obvious differences, empirical field work experiences indicated that in this country the local factors might carry more weight than the general factors of Jewish identity and of specific forms of anti-Semitism. The evidence seems to indicate that, unlike the experience of being a Jew in Europe, in Curaçao being a Jew does not necessarily mean that one bears a stigma. Rather, one has status. As an anecdotal example, we mention here an encounter between the student doing the interviews and a black cleaning lady on her way to work. When the student told the woman that she was there to interview Jewish people living in Curaçao, the black woman proudly told the student: 'Look at my skin' 'isn't it so that I look whiter than the other blacks on the island? And do you know why? One of my grandfathers was a Jew'.

We set out to analyse all the aspects of Jewish identity mentioned above. To this end, within the six areas analysed in this study, we focus here on issues of discrimination and anti-Semitism. We were interested to find out the reasons why the members of each group remained in the Diaspora; the communication structures within each ethnic group—relationship between generations, and ethnic organisations—and those of other (non-Jewish) ethnic groups—feelings of isolation, or solidarity and loyalty; their participation in activities against anti-Semitism and xenophobia—etc.

Closed- and Open-Ended Questions

All the questions had an initial closed part, in which the respondents selected the most appropriate response from those offered. Additionally, for many issues, the respondents were given the opportunity to supplement their responses with open ended replies. The closed questions were usually formulated as statements, for which the reply to each question reflected the respondent's degree of agreement with the statement. Alternate positive and negative formulations were used to allow us to assess the consistency of the replies obtained (e.g., 'Feel proud', 'Feel isolated'). In addition to the replies to the individual questions, we also constructed indices, weighted averages of the responses to several questions, for which, the coefficients of the participating variables were used to account for the meaning of the specific questions (negative or positive).

Data Analysis: the Closed Questions

With the statistical analysis we aimed primarily to assesses the differences between the various aspects of Jewish identity in the three countries in general, and between the forms of discrimination and anti-Semitism in particular.

Items relating to discrimination are concerned with the subject's perception of both its general and specific forms. The general form was assessed by two questions, which refer to the respondent's perception of the discrimination towards the Jews in his/her country in general, and in comparison with other countries. The specific forms of discrimination were assessed by questions formulated with the following perceived reasons in mind: their wealth, their left wing opinions, their right wing opinions, their perceived bigotry, their history, and the politics of Israel. The items relating to anti-Semitism are concerned with the subject's perception of the level of anti-Semitic attitudes in his/her country, in the political arena, in the media, at school, at work, on the street and in the family. Subjects were also asked to answer 'yes/no' questions on their personal experience of direct and indirect anti-Semitism.

The questions related to discrimination and those related to anti-Semitic attitudes were formulated in two versions. In the first, the subject was asked to assess (on a scale of 1 to 6) his/her feeling about the existence of the stated phenomenon in the country (1=No, never; 6=Yes, always). In the second version, they were asked to assess (on a scale of 1 to 3) how often the stated phenomenon occurs (1=Never, 2=Sometimes, 3=Always). With minor exceptions, the two versions yielded very similar results, thus for the sake of brevity we give only the means based on the results from the first version.

Tables 10.1 and 10.2 show the means of the responses in each of the three countries, on a scale ranging from 1 to 100. Table 10.1 is devoted to discrimination issues, and Table 10.2 to anti-Semitic attitudes. The percentage of subjects who had personally experienced anti-Semitic attitudes, is presented for each country in Table 10.3. The Tables also give the *p*-values of the chi-square tests, which assess the statistical significance of the differences in the response distributions (on the original scale), both among the three countries as well as between the pairs of countries. A small *p*-value (e.g., less than .05) is indicative of a significant difference between the compared groups.

The results from Table 10.1 present compelling evidence of the influence exerted by the country specific characteristics on the various aspects of discrimination. We first observe that, overall, the Romanian respondents have the strongest sense that in their country Jews experience more discrimination than in the Netherlands and Curaçao (means of 36.7 versus 20.8 and 19.2, respectively). The Curaçaoan and Romanian subjects perceive a considerably higher level of general discrimination than the Dutch subjects (means of 48.3, and 48.3 respectively versus 34.2).

The analysis of the levels of discrimination caused by the various perceived-reasons yielded subsets of questions related to the conditions in the countries. Thus, the level of discrimination perceived by the respondents to be due to their left wing opinions and cosmopolitan outlook is highest in Romania, the post-communist and most traditional and nationalistic country. On the other hand, the subjects from Curaçao feel more strongly that the Jews in their country experience discrimination because of their wealth, as well as due to perceived bigotry, and that too in relation to the socioeconomic conditions of the population in Curaçao in general, and of the Jewish population in particular. Interestingly, Jews in the Netherlands feel that the politics of Israel influences the discrimination they experience. The Jewish communities in the other two countries are less affected, due to a lower level of media coverage on Israel and being more distant in their relations with Israel, either geographically or politically. Out of the three countries, the Jews in the Netherlands feel the least discrimination stemming from the historical conditions specific to the Netherlands.

The responses of the subjects were also aggregated into indices, which are weighted averages of the results on the various items in the two versions of the questions: 'Do you think that the Jews experience discrimination...?' and

'How often...?'. The means for the discrimination index are given at the bottom of Table 10.1 and they are 43.5, 35.8 and 42.4, for Romania, the Netherlands and Curaçao respectively.

The analysis of the anti-Semitic attitudes (Tables 10.2 and 10.3) reveals a much more clear-cut division between the countries. The relevant areas are anti-Semitic attitudes in politics, in the media, at school, at work and on the street (excluding the issue of anti-Semitic attitudes in the family, which turned out to be irrelevant). In all these areas, the highest levels of perceived anti-Semitic attitudes were found in the sample from Romania. The differences

Table 10.1   Means and Levels of Significance for Discrimination: 'Do You Think that the Jews are Discriminated against in this Country?'

p-Values for Comparisons				Means			
NvsC	RvsC	RvsN	All 3	Curaçao	Netherlands	Romania	
0.63	0.14	0.07	0.10	19.2	20.8	36.7	More discriminated here: than in other countries
0.30	0.21	0.04	0.11	48.3	34.2	48.3	Discriminated, in general
							Discriminated because of:
0.48	0.10	0.09	0.13	25.4	25.0	39.2	their leftist opinions
0.32	0.13	0.17	0.12	40.8	36.7	45.0	their cosmopolitanism
0.02	0.06	0.43	0.08	78.3	47.5	47.5	their wealth
0.11	0.02	0.41	0.06	67.5	32.4	33.3	their perceived bigotry
0.01	0.22	0.02	0.01	41.2	55.0	38.3	the politics of Israel
0.50	0.43	0.24	0.42	31.6	33.3	23.3	their rightist opinions
0.04	0.09	0.20	0.10	54.2	44.2	54.2	their history
				42.4	35.8	43.5	Discrimination Index

between the means for the Netherlands and Curaçao were not statistically significant. In most cases, the means in the sample from Curaçao were higher than those from the Netherlands. The means for the anti-Semitism indices are 54.0, 27.5 and 31.5, which reflect the results regarding the specific items.

The analysis of the actual distributions of indices for discrimination and anti-Semitism (not shown here) provide additional indications beyond those found in the analysis of the means. For example, in the Dutch sample, in both indices there were no subjects whose calculated index exceeded 60. Unfortunately, in the Romanian sample we found subjects with indices of 80 for both issues, suggesting that they feel, either personally or in general, that there are strong indications of discrimination and anti-Semitic attitudes.

An interesting aside to the Romanian sample is observable in the response rate for the various questions. Only 55 per cent responded to the question on anti-Semitic attitudes in the workplace, while the response rate to all other questions was 90–100 per cent. This high non-response rate, may be related to specific Romanian conditions, and may be correlated to the fact that the mean for this question is lower than those obtained for the others. However, we cannot exclude the possibility that this particular high non-response rate may be due to the irrelevance of the question for the non-responding subjects.

Table 10.2 Means and Levels of Significance for Differences: Anti-Semitism: 'Did You Experienced Anti-Semitism in the Following Areas?'

p-Values for Comparisons				Means			
NvsC	RvsC	RvsN	All 3	Curaçao	Netherlands	Romania	
0.74	0.00	0.00	0.00	26.7	25.0	60.8	In politics
0.53	0.01	0.01	0.00	35.0	28.3	69.2	In the media
0.26	0.75	0.03	0.12	43.3	29.2	53.3	At school
0.60	0.16	0.14	0.06	25.0	22.5	33.3	At work
0.60	0.02	0.03	0.00	27.5	32.5	44.2	On the street
0.80	0.32	0.30	0.12	19.2	19.2	17.5	In the family
				31.5	27.5	54.0	Anti-Semitism Index

The subjects were also asked to state whether they suffered personally from anti-Semitic attitudes, directly or indirectly. The results from Table 10.3 present a similar picture to that obtained from Table 2, i.e., the percentage who suffered personally from anti-Semitic attitudes was highest in the Romanian sample (75 per cent directly and 95 per cent indirectly). The smallest percentage was found in the Dutch sample (30 per cent, both directly and indirectly). While in the sample from Curaçao the percentage of those who suffered from direct anti-Semitic attitudes was the same as in the Netherlands (30 per cent), although a higher percentage suffered from indirect anti-Semitic attitudes (70 per cent versus 30 per cent). All the differences in the percentages are statistically significant (see Table 10.3).

Table 10.3   Personally Experienced Anti-Semitic Attitudes: 'Have You Personally Experienced Anti-Semitism?'

p-Values for Comparisons				Percentages			
NvsC	RvsC	RvsN	All 3	Curaçao	Netherlands	Romania	
1.00	0.01	0.01	0.00	30	30	75	Directly
0.00	0.01	0.00	0.00	70	30	95	Indirectly

Curaçaoan Jewish Identity

Because the sample of Curaçaoan Jews is somewhat special, we give here some results based on the questions related to their identity: half of our respondents stated that the main reason for their staying in Curaçao is the economic, political and religious safety they have. The effect of being Jewish on their career is minor: 95 per cent of them stated that being a Jew hindered their career in no way. The great majority (90 per cent) stated that they feel solidarity with the non-Jews of Curaçao, most of them also feel solidarity with the Jewish people of Israel; none of them has definite plans to immigrate to Israel, and none feel any great sense of isolation in Curaçao.

Most of the subjects' relatives were in Panama, Venezuela, Egypt, and the United States at the time of the Holocaust and so there were none for whom both parents had suffered indirectly or directly in the Holocaust. They had heard about the Holocaust from their families (90 per cent), but also from school and from reading material about European anti-Semitism. However the Holocaust influenced both their identity as well as their perspective about other events of the Second World War (e.g., they stated that the bombing of Hiroshima also played an important role; 30 per cent stated that it was of equivalent importance, 70 per cent that it had a less important role).

The Afro-Caribbean and North American cultures have an significant impact on their daily life, but their traditions and their customs are more influenced by the Spanish/Portuguese culture (the language in the synagogue). At the same time, they unanimously declare that their identity has not been superseded by any of these groups.

All the subjects have been to the United States more than once, whereas less have been to Europe, and have done so less often. They have little intention of immigrating to Europe, even though they have more confidence in Europe's political, economic and social future than that of the United States or Curaçao; the opposite is true with respect to the religious future (70 per cent trust the United States more in this respect). This could explain the greater tendency to immigrate to North America than to Europe.

Data Analysis: the Open-Ended Questions

On many issues, in addition to the closed questions the respondents also provided open-ended replies. Interpreting these individual replies with all due caution, we can observe some characteristics particular to each country. We focus here on the replies relating to issues of racism, xenophobia and extremism.

Individually, the respondents in this study exhibited no forms of religious extremism ('I respect any kind of religion', 'All religions are interesting for me') or political extremism. They seem to be well anchored in the present-day political reality of their countries, including any racist manifestations. This is evident from the frequent negative references to media, and other personalities who express anti-Semitic opinions (Corneliu Vadim Tudor in Romania and his Dutch equivalents, Theo van Gogh and Jan Maat), about recent activities of extremist groups from Romania (such as those from the town of Campulung Moldovenesc, and the discourses and party-documents of the Romanian *Mare* Party) and about other events (such as the Jewish abandonment declaration in Romania of the well known political figure Petre Roman, the ex-prime minister, the 'non-Jewish Jew', who hid his Jewish identity to be able to take on this position).

We found a strong correlation between the respondents' perception of anti-Semitic attitudes, as reflected in the replies to the closed questions, and racist manifestations in the country. More remarks about current racist activities are to be found in the sample from Romania, which also has the highest levels overall of perceived discrimination and anti-Semitism.

The respondents in this study displayed an openness towards the society in which they live. They seem to be idealistic and tolerant both towards the majority ethnic group as well as towards other minority groups. At the same time, they take their Jewish identity as given. They do so with more detachment and less pathos in the Netherlands and Curaçao (where came across replies like: 'I accept it', 'I was born Jewish' etc.), and more dramatically and consciously in Romania ('I consider any form of denial cowardy'), where they are confronted with greater levels of discrimination and anti-Semitism.

The respondents declare that the ethnic organisations are important to the preservation of the Jewish identity and in the fight against racism and xenophobia, but only a few of them are involved in these organisations—for personal, and individualistic reasons in the Netherlands, such as 'I don't have enough time', 'I have other priorities', and with some awkward justifications in Romania like 'I don't have enough power', 'Because of smugness', 'I hadn't thought about it', 'It is something for men only'.

Although respondents in both Romania and the Netherlands noticed an increasing level of racism and xenophobia in their countries, they don't have an active attitude about this. It is possible that anti-Semitism is viewed as a separate phenomena to xenophobia in general.

The Curaçaoan respondents, also exhibited no forms of religious or political extremism. Moreover, although the Holocaust was in Europe, its lessons are obvious in Curaçao: it alerts the people of the island to the forms that racism and xenophobia might take in their daily lives. The open-ended questions contain several interesting references to this issue: 'I've got more respect for people from other religious backgrounds because there wasn't any respect for Jews in World War II'; 'I am more aware of what might constitute discrimination against people from other cultures'; 'Never look down on other people from a different background'; 'We learn from our past. If something bad happened in the past, we try to not let it happen again'; 'Hiroshima and the Holocaust represent for me the same thing: discrimination against minorities'; 'It makes me conscious of my identity and also of the identity of other minorities'; 'It has increased my awareness and made me more active against xenophobia and racism'. All the subjects mention more than one of their co-national cultures (Spanish/Portuguese, Afro-Caribbean, Dutch, American etc.) to which they feel an affinity and which influences his or her daily life. At the same time, all of them agree that none of these additional cultural identities suppresses their Jewish identity.

The Curaçaoan responses to the open-ended questions regarding the forms of xenophobia and anti-Semitic manifestations, are closely related both to their replies to the closed questions and to socioeconomic factors. Among them, the issue of wealth, and the anti-Semitism this seems to instigate, is frequently mentioned: 'some people —a small frustrated group—make the connection between Jews and being rich (take the right wing politician, Stanley Brown)'; 'I've heard a teacher saying: Oh, you rich Jews!'; 'because we've got a lot of money and we let it be seen'; 'it has to do with money and the financial ability to travel'; 'the non-Jews think the Jews use their money to gain influence over all the people of Curaçao'; 'there are a few really anti-Semitic persons on Curaçao; they surfaced during the 30th of May rebellion of 1969—a rebellion between black and white, rich and poor. Many Jews became victims of this rebellion. Not because they were Jews, but because they owned lots of shops'.

It appears that the respondents distinguish between the issues of discrimination and anti-Semitism instigated by national and religious reasons (which are probably less frequent), versus the frustration and possible envy caused by economic factors, which in this case, take the form of a group stigma against the Jewish community. Indeed, some respondents reply with: 'there is not much anti-Semitism over here'; 'it's only in a joking way, nothing serious'.

Conclusions

This comparative sociological study revealed that vastly general concepts like Jewish identity or anti-Semitism are not fixed, standard concepts. They are influenced by the geographical location—the proximity of a dominant country, the United States for Curaçao, the former Soviet Union for Romania; by historical factors—the peculiarities of the formation of the Jewish community particular to each of the three countries, and the experience of the Holocaust in the Netherlands and Romania; by local political factors—'the Red Jew' and 'Red anti-Semitism' in post–communist Eastern Europe; by the current socioeconomic situation of the country—the relationship between anti-Semitism and class in Curaçao; by each society's ethnic composition— the relationship between anti-Semitism and multi-ethnicity in the Netherlands, and in Curaçao where the multi-racial mix also plays a role etc.

Generally, discrimination as well as anti-Semitic attitudes manifest themselves within an empirical space in all three countries. They all exhibit the first two stages as defined in Wieviorka's tri-dimensional theory without reaching the third stage of an institutionalised and doctrinal racism. Symbolic racism exists in all three countries (subtle prejudices instead of violent responses), despite the fact that sometimes political actors display a tendency to briefly enter the limelight, and use the mass media to engender a consensus in the nation.

The results of the analysis of the anti-Semitic attitudes strongly suggest that in the various areas of life, there are higher levels of anti-Semitism in Romania, while the levels in the Netherlands and in Curaçao are comparable to each other and not statistically different.

Today's racism in Romania is a racism of a country in crisis and lacking a clear national purpose, where the society finds in the Jews a scapegoat to be blamed for the political, economic and social difficulties. The analyses of the anti-Semitic aspects in the Netherlands proves that here one finds mainly an instrumental racism, based on prejudices, while in Curaçao the racism is mainly of a differential form. The socioeconomic background of the Jewish population in Curaçao seems to be stronger than the ethnic or religious identity. In Curaçao anti-Semitism is mainly engendered by economic reasons. The Jews are envied for their wealth, which brings them political power as well as enabling a cosmopolitan way of life.

In the case of Curaçao, the differential racism can be described as an inverted Marxism, where the social roles are swapped; here we cannot speak about a humiliation or repression of the Jews as an underclass, but of the segregation of the society into black and white, poor or rich communities. Curaçao also reminds us of the old theories of the Chicago school, such as Robert E. Park's (1950) suggestion that those groups constructed on the basis of race and colour are strictly regulated by an etiquette. However, the data from our empirical study did not support Lévi-Strauss' theory of 'cultural distance', which anticipated the lowest levels of racism and anti-Semitism in Curaçao. We found, indeed, that the levels of anti-Semitism in Curaçao are much lower than in Romania, but they are not lower than in the Netherlands. Additionally, the empirical results of this comparative study did not support the Huntington's (1997) recent theory about the clash of civilisations along fault-lines. Anti-Semitism and xenophobia are not more severe in Curaçao, where very different civilisations 'clash', than in the European countries, where we can speak about only one civilisation (Judeo-Christian). In the same study, Huntington warns of the currently restrictive and temporary meaning of the word 'anti-Semitism' by writing: 'In Western Europe the anti-Semitism directed towards Arabs replaced the one directed towards Jews on quite a large scale.'

The overall empirical conclusion on discrimination, is that the highest levels were found in Romania and the lowest in the Netherlands. But the overall result reveals only a partial picture and indeed the picture presented by the analysis of the discrimination issue is less complex than the analysis of the anti-Semitic attitudes. The analysis illustrates the profound effect exerted by the specific conditions of each selected country on the level of discrimination and its forms of manifestation: discrimination because of left wing opinions and cosmopolitanism in Romania, discrimination because of their wealth in Curaçao, and discrimination because of the politics of Israel in the Netherlands. These features indicate that undesirable situations in the various countries are attributed to Jews as a group and become a pretext for a group stigma. The specific conditions affect not only the levels of discrimination against the Jewish community but also the characteristics of the agenda of the Jewish minority and its identity. The analysis of the relations with Israel offers an example of this. Indeed, the Dutch were more critical of Israel than were the Romanians, while the Jews in Curaçao are more indifferent. Their attention is focused more on North America than on Israel. Unlike Romania, from which most of the Jews wanted to immigrate to Israel for a better life, in Curaçao Israel does not seem as attractive.

The research allowed us to perceive the paradigmatic aspect presented by the preservation of Jewish identity and by xenophobia in the contemporary world. In the last decades, immigration has become a mass phenomenon. In almost every European country second and even third generation 'immigrants' are born (Turks, Moroccans, Italians, Greeks, etc.). In all these populations, the preservation of identity under the various circumstances created by immigration and the recrudescence of racism is of significant importance. A study in several countries of an ethnic group may provide evidence on the general factors contributing to the preservation of identity and xenophobia as well as on the specific characteristics of the minority studied. The same approach exposes the national policies concerning minorities in the involved countries.

Such a comparative study of one generation of an ethnic group which obtained a national state in its lifetime and opted to remain in the Diaspora despite the various forms of xenophobia, may have again a paradigmatic value for contemporary history. There are reasons to believe that this process may continue in the case of other peoples such as, for example, the Palestinians and the Kurds.

The various aspects of acculturation (both intercultural and interracial) mentioned by the group from Curaçao ('All other cultures influence us, no culture suppresses us') underline the validity of Wieviorka's warning: not to fall for ethnocentrism while studying the identities of populations. As this study has shown these are arguments for the idea that one of the strictest identities is less strict in a multicultural and multi-racial world; the flexible aspects of the identity in this modern process of acculturation give us an encouraging view of the way out from isolationism.

Acknowledgments

We wish to thank Studia Interetnica Research, Utrecht, and the University of Amsterdam, the Netherlands, for their support of this study. Special thanks are due to Professor H. Heeren and Dr. W. Campbell from Studia Interetnica Research, and to Professor H. Lamur from the University of Amsterdam, for very fruitful discussions and for the fieldwork of their students in the Netherlands and Curaçao. We are also pleased to thank Dr. Mihai Razvan Ungureanu and his students from the Alexander Ioan Cuza University of Iassy, Romania, for the sampling and interviews of the respondents in Romania.

References

Aarts, I.B.M.(1991), *De joodse na oorlogse generatie [The Jewish Generation after the War]*, Van Loghum.

Abram, I.B.H. (1993), *Joodse identiteit [The Jewish Identity]*, Kok.

Bacon, J. (1991), *De geilustreerde atlas van de Joodse beschaving [The Illustrated Atlas of the Jewish Culture]*, Amsterdam.

Cohen, R. (1982), *The Jewish Nation in Suriname*, Amsterdam.

Eckhuis-Leyh, B. (1979), *A Survey of the Position of Sephardic Jews* (m.a.t.), Amsterdam.

Eland J. (1990), *Twee generatiea Joodse Nederlanders [The Second Generation of Dutch Jews]*, Van Loghum.

Fischer-Galatzi, S.T. (1974), *Fascism, Comunism and the Jewish Question in Romania*.

Hass, A. (1991), *In the Shadow of the Holocaust*, Tauris.

Herzberg, A. (1982), *Is Anti-Semitism Dying out?*, Van Gennep.

Hoeting H. (1966), *Het patroon van de oude Curaçaose samenleving [The Paterrn of the Old Curaçaoan]*, The Hague.

Huntington, S. (1997), *The Clash of Civilization and the Remaking of World Order*, Simon & Schuster.

Karner, F.P. (1969), *The Sephardics of Curacao*, Amsterdam.

Kesler, E.K. (1939), *De Joden en de Holandshe colonizatie [The Jews and the Dutch Colonies]*, Historia V.

Knight, Fr. (1990), *The Caribbean-The genesis of a Fragmented Nationalism*.

Lévi-Strauss, C. (1983), *Le Regard Eloigné [The Distant View]*, Plon, Paris.

Manuila, S. and Friedman, W. (1994), *The Jewish Population In Romania*, F.C.R.

Marrus, R.M. and Paxton, R.D. (1981), *Vichy et les Juifs [Vichy and the Jews]*, Calmann-Levy, Paris.

Mungiu, A. (1995), *Romanii dupa 1989. Istoria unei neintelegeri [The Romanians after 1989, The History of a misunderstanding]*, Humanitas.

Park, R.E. (1950), *Race and Culture*, The Free Press (vol. 1).

Ped. (1992), *Geschidenis van Joodse gemeenschap in Nederland [The Separation within the Jewish Community in the Netherlands]*, Enschede.

Sartre, J.P. (1954), *Reflexions sur la Question Juive [Reflections on the Jewish Question]*, Gallimard, Paris.

Vago, R. (1991), *Anti-Semitism in the New Romania*, SICSA.

Volovici, L. (1991), *Nationalist Ideology and Anti-Semitism: the Case of Romanian Intellectuals in the 30s*, Pergamon Press, Oxford.

Volovici, L. (**1994**), *Anti-Semitism in Post Communist Eastern Europe: A marginal or central Issue?*, SICSA.

Wieviorka, M. (1991), *L'espace du racism [The Space of Racism]*, Edition du Seuil, Paris.

Wieviorka, M. (1998), 'The double challenge for democracy: individualism and cultural differences', Public Lectures Series, ERCOMER, Utrecht University, NL.

11 A Typology of Racist Violence: Implications for Comparative Research and Intervention

CLAUDIO BOLZMAN, ANNE-CATHERINE SALBERG MENDOZA,
MONIQUE ECKMANN & KARL GRÜNBERG

Introduction

This article deals with racism as the victims experience it. Many scholars have concentrated on the causes of racism and the relationship between this phenomenon and economic, social, cultural, political, and social factors. They have also explored the transformations of racism throughout history, especially by analysing its more extreme manifestations. However, less attention has been granted to the victims. We intend to demonstrate why a victim oriented perspective provides a better understanding of racist deeds, leading, in turn, to more accurate forms of intervention against racism. Such an approach may also encourage comparative research on less visible forms of racism.

General Research Frame

Our research[1] focuses on outward expressions of racist violence, as well as on proposed penal and preventive responses. The study described here, defines what the victims and the witnesses consider as a racist deed, through a systematic analysis of the calls received by ACOR (the Association romande contre le racisme[*]), over a three-year period (1995–1998), on their '0800 SOS Racism' hot line.

Working from primary sources allows us to collect information on racist violence in French-speaking Switzerland and, in so doing, to gain a more accurate picture of the less visible forms of violence. It also allows us to consider the victims' point of view and to record the facts as reported by them and/or the witnesses to such acts. With this study we aim to establish a better understanding of what racist acts are, the victims, and the perpetrators, and to evaluate the potential scope of a range of innovative actions. The study forms part of the Swiss National Research Program on everyday violence.

Research Questions

For this study we use two complementary approaches: (1) a quantitative analysis of the forms completed for each call received by '0800 SOS Racism', and (2) a qualitative analysis of selected cases followed up by '0800 SOS Racism' over an extended period, usually several weeks or months. The research questions were:

- What type of acts are reported as racist?
  How do the victims define them?

- How can we relate racist acts committed at an individual level with those committed at the collective level?

- What is the relationship between the victims and the perpetrators? Do racist acts take place between strangers or, on the contrary, are the perpetrators known to the victims, through work, their local community, or family?

- Does an antiracist hot line promote awareness of 'new' racist acts, not yet acknowledged as such by legislation or public opinion?

- How do victims perceive the racist act and what forms of assistance to do they request?

- What is the relationship between the type of racist acts described by the people who call the hot line and the type of action proposed by the hot line?

Definitions

This study uses a broad definition of racist violence encompassing more than solely physical violence. In a situation of violence, people or organisations influence and steer the behaviour of others in order to make them comply with their priorities. They act directly or indirectly, harming one or many, in a variable sequence of actions. They cause harm by attacking a person or group's physical or mental integrity, or by hindering their symbolic or cultural participation, or by causing damage to property (Michaud, 1996).

In doing so, they inflict serious harm or injury, the effects of which can be prolonged or irreparable. In acts of racist violence the offence is justified because the Other is perceived to be biologically or culturally inferior. Exclusion of this Other is seen as normal because they have been classified as not belonging to the same human category. Memmi (1964) defined racism as the general and permanent valorisation of imaginary or real biological differences, within a context of power, in a way beneficial to the accuser and prejudicial to the victim. The current acceptability of invoking 'cultural' differences, instead of the now less acceptable biological ones (Taguieff, 1991; Guillaumin, 1992), adds weight to the idea that empirical cultural differences do exist, leading to 'postulation[s] of inassimilability' (Taguieff,1991).

We differentiate between the notions of *racist violence* (also referred to as: 'racist act' or 'racist deed') and of *racial discrimination*. Racist violence, although difficult to define, relates here to 'violence in which victims are 'selected' not in their capacity as individuals, but as representatives of imagined minority communities based on phenotypic characteristics, and/or religious, national or cultural origin' (Witte, 1996). Here direct and indirect violence includes that which causes physical, social, economic, or psychological damage to people, whether intentional or not. Racial discrimination is unequal treatment and is defined by international agreements[2] as the denial of equal access to goods, rights or services based on illegal distinctions of race, colour, religion, or national or ethnic origin. Despite these differences, we use both terms because the callers to the hot line do not always differentiate between the two.

Introducing a Typology

Without underestimating the gravity of the physical violence and ideological hatred advanced by the extreme right, it is important to emphasise that racist behaviour is not confined to the members of these organisations alone. It is, rather, widespread throughout society and its form and magnitude is context dependent. Here, the victim's viewpoint can be a clarifying one with which to broaden the definition of everyday racist violence because for the victims the experience is not confined to physical violence alone, it may include molestation, harassment, insults, threats, and the denial of civil rights. Thus, forms of behaviour usually considered 'normal' and construed as such by state institutions or the media can be considered as forms of racist violence.

In our study, those submitted to racist violence define it. For them, it is a real situation and they are looking for help, advice, and understanding. Here, we draw upon William Thomas' (1966) classic interactionist perspective: 'If the actors define a situation as a real one, it is a real situation.'

Knowledge of racist behaviour is based mostly on police and media reports. Yet, victims rarely inform either the police nor the media. Moreover, the police only record a complaint if it conforms to already recognised forms of racist aggression. Thus, a considerable number of racist incidents do not show up in statistics because they are not defined as such by the police (Willems, 1994). However, using this data, as well as that from the media, is still informative, even if it is limited to the most visible forms of violence, and to that generally agreed to be racist by the offenders. Police data usually contains records of violent offences or crimes such as racist murders, assaults and arson, vandalism, distribution of propaganda, the use of signs and symbols of unconstitutional organisations, and of disturbing the peace.

This leads us to present a *typology* of forms of racist violence based on the first report of each incident to the hot line. We deliberately chose not to do so from the perspective of belonging to a minority-group, because in Switzerland this question is simply not at stake, neither socially nor politically. Swiss minorities are language-minorities, congruent with fixed territories, and there are no significant ethnic-minorities because Switzerland's colonial experience was limited to the financial and commercial elites' economic involvement in the colonial interests of other countries. (See also the section on institutional violence below.)

The innovative potential of the victim perspective to unearth 'other' racist social actors to those already considered as such is often overlooked simply because it is not made the focus of most studies. A more precise distinction made between the different forms of racist acts and the different actors may lead to more accurate forms of comparative research and thus to more appropriate and interventions, adaptable to a broad range of situations.

Research Design

The research team is composed of two partners: ACOR undertakes fieldwork, while the Institut d'Etudes sociales, IES** concentrates on research and training. Together they pursue the principles of action-research with the three-fold objective of improving our knowledge about racism, as well as testing and evaluating innovative actions with which to counter it.

The Association Romande Contre le Racisme

The fieldwork partner, a non-governmental organisation (NGO), manages the toll-free hot line, '0800 SOS Racism', as well as a social service and educational centre. The hot line offers active-listening by professionals trained in empathetic listening as well as assistance to persons who are victims or witnesses of racist acts. It is very often the first opportunity the caller has had in years to talk about the racist acts to which they have been subjected, or have witnessed. In many cases, the situation they describe occured at work, within their family or local community, or in dealing with the authorities.

Deciding to call ACOR is an important step for these people, and one with implications. As a result of the 1994 anti-racist law, article 261 bis of

Swiss Penal Code, people in Switzerland now feel able to seek a legal response to the racist discrimination they have experienced (Message, 1992). The victims often know their aggressor and expect reparation, which a legal proceeding alone would not fulfil. Legal action is often an inadequate response against preconceived ideas that often arise from ignorance and fear. Added to which, in many cases, the incident does not meet the conditions required to file a complaint, and when it does, a counter-complaint is frequently made. Even when such cases are heard, the parties involved seldom make amends, and damages are rarely awarded.

An approach favouring legal measures frequently finds itself powerless in the face of latent racism. This is pernicious as the degree of humiliation already experienced is often only heightened by the apparent denial of justice of a courtroom failure. Indeed, the legal system's inability to recognise latent racism can aggravate racial tensions making reconciliation even harder to achieve. In order to respond to such situations, ACOR has established an intervention strategy that allows a restorative solution for the victim.

The first step in ACOR's strategy is to always favour dialogue and to restore communication. This goal can be achieved through mediation or through contact with a respected member of the offender's community, who can appeal to offender's ethical principles. However, it is often necessary to create negotiation conditions by filing a complaint, informing the media or undertaking some form of political action.

ACOR is also working towards a shift in public opinion through training programmes for individuals and groups who are likely to commit, or are susceptible to, discrimination.

Data-Gathering

The benefit of an action-research approach is that researchers are in direct contact with the social reality being studied. This becomes a solid base from which to propose action when combined with data collection and analysis (Barbier, 1996). ACOR collects our data. The main information and requests made by each caller are recorded either during or just after each call. More information is added to the file if there are further calls or encounters with the person.

The testimonies we receive are indirect because ACOR refuses to record the phone calls, to protect the caller's anonymity. Moreover, such a procedure necessarily implies that the person receiving the call selects what is recorded. Hence, those working in the call-centre receive special training. When registering a call, they describe, as completely as possible, the reasons for that call, including the features of the incident (type of violence, place, time, etc.), the type of actors involved (perpetrators and victims), the requests made and, where appropriate, the feelings of the victims along with some basic data about them.

The quantitative part of the study involves making a systematic inventory of the calls received. The data recorded during each call is data-processed and then analysed statistically in order to describe various parameters.

In this chapter we focus on a typological, qualitative analysis of the registered calls. Each case given here was followed over an extended period, providing us with a better understanding of both the racist incidents and the victim's point of view.

This typological classification allows us to lay the basis for future comparison with other victim-oriented investigations, as well as to stress less visible forms of racism. Various antiracist hot lines operate across Europe but, to our knowledge, there is no published research about the calls made to these hot lines. We hope that this study will stimulate more data-gathering and comparative perspective in this field.

Typology

A Typology of Racist Violence

We constructed our typology using an ongoing process of interaction between the analysis of empirical data and the formulation of theory (Glaser and Strauss, 1966). Our starting point was the reports received by the hot line.[3] From there, we tried to distinguish different levels of racist violence based on the forms of interaction between the victim and the perpetrator. The typology is not constructed on an analysis of the types of racist act, but on an examination of the kind of relationships between the actors. What is important is that the perpetrator determines the nature of the interaction, even though the form of the racist acts may vary widely.

We have distinguished two dimensions crucial to the relationship between the perpetrators and victims: *power* and *organisation*. The question of power is always present in racist violence, and may be exerted from a position of either *formal* or *informal power*. Often, a perpetrator is someone with the opportunity to directly influence the victim's quality of life, by enforcing discriminatory laws, or by abusing their control over access to social or economic goods. Others may possess only *informal power* and, although lacking any formal means of coercion, may simply desire to inflict violence. They can, of course, threaten their victims, they may have guns or other means of intimidation. They are informal because they are neither representatives of the law nor holders of a position within an official body or organisation. From the point of view of the victim, the possibility of response is greatest in the second case.

The other dimension is the perpetrators' *level of organisation*. Racist violence can be expressed by people belonging to a *structured* institution or group with a more or less elaborated racist ideology. In this case, an offender represents an organisation that perceives racist violence (or at least some forms of it) as normal behaviour. *Non-aligned* individuals also commit racist violence simply out of personal prejudices linked to wider social prejudices. However, they do not do so in a structured way. Importantly, such people are, to varying degrees, aware that they are acting contrary to prevalent social norms of egalitarian behaviour. For this reason, it is probably easier to seek damages through various forms of negotiation in the latter than in the first situation, where legal avenues can be more useful. However, because both these forms of racist violence can be either spontaneous or premeditated, it is often difficult for a person to know which form of racist violence they are the victim of. By combining these two dimensions we constructed a typology (see Table 11.1) with which the four forms of racist violence can be outlined.

Table 11.1   Types of Racist Violence

	Formal Power	Informal Power
Organisational Violence	institutional violence	doctrinaire, organised violence
Individual Violence	power abuse	interpersonal violence

Institutional Violence

The first form, *institutional violence*, is that exerted by an organisation able to claim a 'monopoly of legitimate physical violence' (Weber, 1959) and to define legality. This is most often a state organisation, whose actions (identity controls in the street, expulsions) are not perceived as legitimate by those upon whom they are carried out. Moreover, a certain number of legal but discriminatory norms are implemented by government employees; who thus fail to ensure equality of treatment for all. For example, in Switzerland, immigration policy is based on 'cultural criteria': many immigrants from, mainly, the Third World or Eastern European countries have no right to a residence permit because they were born in or have a passport from one of these countries. Other laws, such as those regarding access to social security are, in certain instances, unfair to people coming from such countries or to immigrants because of restrictions relating to their class of residence permit.

This type of discrimination has been analysed by authors such as Radtke (1990), Bukow (1992), and Alund and Schierup (1991) who have concluded that it is the state's discursive and administrative practices which both create the new minorities and produce the discrimination they experience. According to Weill and Grünberg (1997) such practices were established at the turn of century in Switzerland by the then immigration authorities, and were founded on the concept of *Überfremdung*, in which foreigners were considered a threat to national cohesion, because their presence would 'excessively alter' the Swiss population.

In fact, most cases of institutional violence, reported by the victims, are related to the Swiss immigration policy, known as the 'three circles policy'. Implemented on May 15, 1991 on the basis of two articles dating from legislation enacted in 1931:

> art. 4. The civil authority is free to decide, within the boundaries of legal regulations and foreign treaties, about the granting of residence permits.

> art. 6. al. 1. The granting of a permit will be determined by the moral and economic interests of the country, as well as by the level of the excessive *Überfremdung* (population augmentation). (Authors' translation)

> (Loi fédéale, 1948)

the three circles policy selects the candidates for immigration according to their origin: first circle immigrants (EU and EFTA) obtain a work permit with relative ease. Second circle immigrants (i.e. other industrialised countries, such as the United States or Canada) are liable to certain conditions, but can obtain work permits. However, those from the third circle (the Third World and Eastern Europe) have almost no chance of gaining a Swiss work permit. Their only possibility for residence in Switzerland is as either a refugee (a very difficult status to obtain), or as the spouse of a legal resident.

Clearly, the policy contradicts the 1965 International Convention on the Elimination of all Forms of Racial Discrimination. Further, its implementation continues the same legal, administrative and cultural context that brought about the 'sui generis' anti-Semitism during the 1920s. Representing not only an affirmation of a racist law, which has been developing to this present day but also a concealment of the past that fertilises already extant racist ideas.

In this context, a state employee's impersonal, treatment of a foreigner— the implementation of institutionally 'routinised' practices—rests upon a legitimised ideology. The employee may not even have paused to consider the discriminatory character of the policy of which the practices form a part. The official may even, in some cases, disagree with the legislation, but is, or feels, powerless to do other than follow a particular procedure.

Those who experience this type of discrimination do not necessarily perceive it as the actions of an individual. Usually, this kind of treatment is not even considered racist, but as normal. As a foreigner, especially one from a Third World country, one must 'deserve' a permit. It is not seen as an individual right but as a conditional possibility. It is often an impersonal decision of the 'administration', and it becomes impossible to identify the author of the racist deed. Here, racism takes on an administrative form such as the refusal to grant or renew a residence permit, or the threat of refusal.

The victims often feel that they have been unjustly treated, but they do not know how to exercise their rights in dealing with the institution, all the more so because they find themselves in an extremely asymmetrical position. Moreover, due to the discriminatory legislation, those concerned often have an awkward legal status. They are asylum seekers, or are 'illegal' and so on. They feel as if they have 'their back to the wall' like prisoners with little recourse in the face of legislation that does not respect their 'right to have rights'. On the whole, they do not contest the general principles of the immigration policy, but are opposed to the lack of provision for individual circumstances within the legislation.

Such is the case of Mercedes Ruiz,[4] who came to Switzerland towards the end of 1981 with her two children (Clara aged five and Miguel aged one-and-a-half) to join her husband. He had arrived in 1980 from a South-American country as an asylum seeker. Asylum applications move slowly through most systems, and Switzerland is no exception to this rule. By 1989, the Ruiz Family has obtained a 'humanitarian' annually-renewable residence permit (a B-Permit). However, Mercedes Ruiz and her husband get divorced. She remains, with her children, in Switzerland. She works part time and receives welfare from the local authorities.

In 1994 Mrs. Ruiz enlists a lawyer to have her B-permit changed into a residence permit (C-permit). She is under the impression that having lived ten years in Switzerland, that this was now possible. She thinks this will improve her chances of employment and will allow her to be financially independent. Moreover, Switzerland has become her country and especially that of her children, who have even applied for Swiss citizenship.

The Swiss authorities inform the lawyer that a C-permit is only granted ten years after having obtained a humanitarian permit, therefore not before 1999 for Mrs Ruiz. Moreover, they add that she is not in permanent employment and is receiving financial assistance from the welfare system. The authorities decide that not only does she not meet the requirements for a C-permit but they temporarily suspend the B-permit. As of 1996, the B-permit must be renewed every six months, and then every four months. The social worker assigned to her case tells her that it would be better for her to return to her home country where it would be easier for her to find employment.

At this point Mrs. Ruiz phones ACOR. She thinks that after 15 years in Switzerland she has a right to a residence permit (C-permit). However, she is afraid that should she press her case her daughter may not obtain Swiss citizenship. She considers that the social worker acted in a racist manner in suggesting she should see a psychiatrist... 'I feel judged, scorned, I feel depressed, I am afraid', she concludes.

In some cases, institutional violence, especially in the case of permits, can have direct implications on private life and may alter the relationship between a couple, by granting one more *power* than the other. In such a case, institutional violence gives one person free reign to exert private-violence on an other, as shown by the next example.

Maria Sanchez is an illegal alien, and had to leave her beloved daughter, Ines, in her South American home country. She flies back to take care of Ines but her fiancé, Luis Garcia, a Spanish immigrant, wants to marry her. Therefore, Maria receives an airline ticket from Luis, with the promise that her daughter, Ines, will join them as soon as the Swiss immigration office permits her to come.

One and half years later, Ines eventually arrives in Switzerland. Unfortunately, Luis cannot bare the close and emotionally intense relationship between mother and daughter. He becomes violent, jealous, he asks Maria to pay for everything, for his own luxurious cars and even for the plane ticket he offered her. He retains family allowances, forbids Maria to learn French and tells her, she has no rights, and that he can throw her out of the country.

Maria calls the ACOR hot line. She wants to know about her legal rights. Is it correct that her husband can retain all her money, and that she can loose her work permit if she doesn't obey him?

Some time later, Maria calls again. Her husband has raped her, and she has sought asylum in a women's centre. However, she was told that she could not report the offence without risking her right to residence, so if she wants to stay in the country, she had better go back to her husband.

Power Abuse

The second form of racist violence is *power abuse*. In this case, individuals ignore legal guarantees of equality of treatment, and abuse their position in an institution to unfairly exclude other individuals from access to social goods (such as employment, social security, public transportation, restaurants, shops, etc.), or they use their position to exert violence against individuals who they view as inferior. The perpetrators feel legitimated and protected by their official function. Considering themselves to be protected by their position within the hierarchy, they carryout racist acts with impunity. In this case, the circumstances create the possibility for racist behaviour. The asymmetric character of the relationship between the perpetrators and the victims permits the former to translate subtle prejudice into openly racist behaviour. It is often expressed through verbal aggression[5]—'if you don't like it here, just return to your country'—threats, blackmail, in blatant or hidden discrimination in access to social goods and services. Few studies have been made of this form of violence. Either because the available data does not provide information on such incidents or because the distinction that we make between institutional violence and power abuse, is not one usually made.

Most victims who call ACOR have a stable place of residence as well as a high socio-professional level. These people tend to feel self-assured and respond in a more active manner. They ask that the institution, to which the offending party belongs, should disavow and condemn its actions. The following examples show how discrimination is exerted by a police patrol, and an apartment owner:

John Doe is in the second lane of a four-lane avenue, waiting for his wife. A police car stops next to his car and he is asked for his identity card. The policeman returns his Swiss identity card and drivers licence to Mr. Doe with the words 'anyway, you are not Swiss, you have no rights' and issues him with a 210 franc fine.

Very offended, Mr. Doe, calls the ACOR toll free number. He feels that he has been the victim of a racist act. The antiracist Convention does apply in Switzerland; this policeman should be disciplined if not charged. John Doe is angry, because this is not the first time that, just because of the colour of his skin, he has had to endure such discriminatory treatment at the hands of the police. He was so outraged that he lodged a complaint with the police and the United Nations. He wants ACOR to contest the fines and to accompany him to court.

Mr. Bamako moves out of his rented flat. He has an appointment with the manager. When the latter arrives, he insults and offends Mr. Bamako, telling him: 'we should enclose Europe in barbed wire; our planet is wrongly inhabited, it should turn upside down on the foreigner-shits like you and let the Swiss people be at the top'. Although Mr. Bamako is shocked and humiliated, he remains calm and polite. Even so, the manager tells Mr. Bamako that he will keep the three-month rental-bond Mr. Bamako paid him, in order to repair the apartment.

A few days later, the manager calls Mr. Bamako, apologises for saying that they were on welfare and that they behave like pigs. He also informs Mr. Bamako that the rental-bond money will be returned him.

Mr. Bamako calls the ACOR toll free number. He says how badly insulted he has been by the manager. He wants to file a complaint for racial discrimination, and doesn't want to go to the appointment to which the manager invited him, because it is too easy now to try and resolve the problem amicably.

Doctrinaire, Organised Violence

The third form of racist violence is *doctrinaire organised violence*. In this situation sustained violence is exercised by individuals or groups who have no formal power but act on the basis of a strong racist ideology as expressed by right wing extremist parties or in other group-discourses. The perpetrators are, or have been, members or sympathisers of such organisations. Here violence is often strategically directed against specific groups of victims in order to create a climate of prejudice and discrimination. It is a more conscious and strategic violence than in the other cases, and is exerted by heavily indoctrinated individuals.

This type of behaviour corresponds to the more classic analyses of right wing extremist parties or groups (Bähler, 1994; Kriesi and Altermatt, 1995). It is a form of violence usually considered illegitimate by the majority and condemned by law. It is not only denounced by its victims but also by those who have witnessed it. It is not often reported to ACOR. Most instances of it concern the distribution of racist propaganda in the press, on the internet or world-wide-web or through other forms.

Such is the case of an article—which was, in reality, thinly veiled anti-Semitic propaganda about the 'escheat funds'[6] affair—published in a village's local newspaper. The editor of the paper took the view that freedom of expression requires that everyone has the right to express his opinion. However, a reader called ACOR to find out if it is possible to file a complaint against the author of the article who is known for his position against refugees and aliens.

A witness calls the ACOR to question the possible racist meanings of an electoral flyer distributed by an extreme right wing party. The picture on the flyer shows a man 'murdering' the French language. He is wearing an armband with the word 'asylum' on it, a gold watch, a leather jacket, a cellular phone, a big car and plenty of money (the flyers look like welfare checks). The caller wants to know if a legal complaint can be filed.

Interpersonal Violence

The fourth form of violence is *interpersonal violence*. This is racism exerted by individuals or informal groups who posses no structural power over the victims nor do they have a strong racist ideology upon which their aggressive behaviour rests. Usually, they know the victims and interact with them in private or semi-private spaces. This is a kind of 'everyday' racism; the main perpetrators are neighbours, colleagues, acquaintances, and so on. They transform interpersonal conflicts into racist interactions, attributing 'racial' characteristics or other ethnic, religious or cultural stereotypes to the victim, thus making peaceful cohabitation impossible and legitimating their violent and/or discriminatory behaviour.

A possible, but by no means only, explanation for interpersonal violence is that perpetrators focus their dissatisfaction with their own life (living and/or working conditions, career opportunities, etc.) onto a scapegoat (Girard, 1972). They 'protest' against their everyday problems by blaming 'foreigners' (Oechste and Zoll, 1985). Some, threatened by an incomprehensible and uncontrollable world, represented by the Other, fantasise about the past or other form of idealised environment, (Adorno, Frenkel-Brunswick, Levinson and Sanford, 1950; Bell, 1964; Windisch, 1978; De Rham, Grandmousin and Bernasconi, 1986; Lalive d'Epinay, Bolzman and Modak, 1987). While others, resort to strategic racist behaviour in a conflict situation, in order to improve their position and disadvantage their adversary.

Interpersonal violence can occur at various levels and different intensities. It may be expressed as verbal aggression (insults and threats), but also in segregationist behaviour (contact avoidance, shunning objects of or places used by the Other, or not 'mixing' with them). It may include generalised harassment (anonymous telephone calls, noise and other behaviour aimed at ruining the victim's quality of life), and physical violence.

The victims of this form of racist behaviour seem to have no particular social characteristics other than belonging to a group considered a minority by the Swiss-majority-population. The victims feel offended, are filled with indignation, and react with the hope of receiving compensation and acknowledgement from the perpetrators for the acts.

The Singh family bought an apartment. Their two neighbours, the Dubois family and Mr. Pellet (Mrs. Dubois' brother) are openly racist. One day, as Mrs. Singh is wallking down the common stairway Mr. Pellet comes out of his apartment, grabs her by the chin and tells her 'you, "darky", you have no right to live here, I'll kill you'. His girlfriend and Mrs. Dubois arrive and join in. When another neighbour comes to help Mrs. Singh, she too receives similar treatment.

Mrs. Singh calls the ACOR hot line. She is hurt, afraid. She does not want to file a complaint because they have had very bad experiences with no results when doing so before. Moreover, Mr. Dubois is a police officer. The Singh family just wants to find solutions, which will allow them to live in peace in their home.

One evening, Mr. Kabula drives with two friends to the railway station. On the main station parking lot, Mr. Leclerc, a young Swiss man, questions them: 'in the jungle, do you listen to the music so loud?' The three friends get out of the car to talk to Leclerc, but as they see he is acting in a provocative manner, they leave their friend on the platform to catch the train, and drive home. Mr. Leclerc is furious; he calls the police and files a complaint for threat, insult, assault and battery. Although the police investigation finds no evidence of the charges, and despite Mr. Leclerc's friend, Marie's, statement that she remembers 'that the way Leclerc spoke did not sound correct to me. I wouldn't have ever talked like that. Anyway, there was neither assault nor battery'—the judge concludes that there is a case to be made and refers the case to court.

Mrs. Kabula calls the ACOR toll free line. She explains that her husband is unfairly accused. She worries about his Swiss naturalisation request, as he is having so much trouble with his work permit, a Swiss passport could help him to find a job, and to travel more easily. She requests legal help from ACOR for her husband.

Serial Racist Violence

The distinctions made here between the four types of racism are, of course, analytical. In reality the different types are often combined in specific cases, thus becoming more virulent. This is why, we observed, that many racist incidents display a cascading pattern, with the acts multiplying over a given period of time, especially when other actors intervene after the initial event. For example, when an apartment resident harasses a neighbour, and is then supported by the caretaker of the building. Or when, the police, without even having heard the victim's version, support the aggressors instead of the person filing the complaint. People who commit acts of racism often encounter support from officials, or justify their actions on the basis of immigration law or on using the ideological discourses of right wing political parties, thus legitimising their actions and rendering their victims powerless.

Often, we found that in cases of *abuse of power* and *interpersonal violence* without witnesses the racist aggressor accuses the victim of being the aggressor, thus forcing the victim to prove their version, rather than vice-versa. The idea being that the victims deserved what they got. This is similar to cases of sexual harassment or attacks against women, where the victim is blamed for what is inflicted upon them. In both cases, the victim is a victim twice: he or she has been victim of an aggression and, in addition, his or her suffering is ignored.

In most of the cases we analysed, the categories set up by Swiss immigration policy tended to legitimise the racist acts, and provided an ideological shelter which the racist aggressors use in their interpersonal contacts or abuses of power.

Types of Violence and Forms of Action against Racism

The procedures developed by ACOR are based on a model of restorative justice, and promote active-listening, renewed communication, dialogue, compensation, and reconciliation. Because it responds to actual, intended or suffered racist and violent incidents, ACOR initiates a dynamic process where mediation and socio-pedagogical interventions help to promote understanding of these acts; enabling appropriate responses which avoid stigmatising the perpetrators.

Distinguishing between different types of racist violence can be useful when choosing adequate forms of response. As mentioned, antiracist legislation was passed in Switzerland in 1994, thus making it possible to file a legal complaint. However, in many cases an incident is difficult to prove, especially in cases of interpersonal racism, which usually occur within the private sphere and without the presence of witnesses. In addition, victims often know their aggressor and hope that they will recognise and acknowledge the damage caused; something legal action may not provide. However, the existence of antiracist legislation is an essential foundation on which to base negotiation or mediation between the author and the victim.

Disciplinary measures do not always guarantee adequate compensation, nor does it always decrease public prejudices, which are most often the by-products of ignorance and fear.

In order to respond to cases of interpersonal racism, ACOR encourages the re-establishment of communication, mediation and negotiation. Under-takings which may offer the injured party an emotional compensation and which encourage perpetrators to accept responsibility for their actions. ACOR always attempts to find adequate forms of compensation and promotes, where possible, changes in the attitude of the aggressor.

In situations of institutional racism, the goal is to find concrete solutions for the victims, such as obtaining a residence permit, and, at the same time, to work towards modifying discriminatory legislation. In 1996 and 1997, ACOR conducted a national and international (UN) campaign against the 'three circles policy'. It included media coverage and was aimed at exposing the contradictions between Swiss antiracist legislation and immigration policy.

In cases of individual violence, whether interpersonal or not, ACOR can resort to other means: reminding perpetrators of ethical principles and of the existence of the antiracist laws, instigating legal action, or informing the persons local community or place of work or their actions.

The type of intervention used will depend on the level of violence and on the role played by other participants (persons of influence with the person's community, lawyers, etc.). In the case of the traffic-fine issued with racist abuse, ACOR provided legal advice which resulted in the cancellation of the fine. ACOR also met with the police to complain formally about the racist act by the police officers. Although the police did not take any internal action, the solution satisfied the victim who felt relieved.

Filing charges led, in the case with the landlord, to a legal conciliation between the parties. The defendant made a public apology and the claimant dropped the charges, for him it was more important to have a legal condemnation than a fine that would 'fix the price of a racist offence'. Here ACOR pressed for court-based mediation because it permits such restorative solutions (Zehr, 1995; Faget, 1997).

In the case of Mrs. Singh, mediation between the two parties was attempted. However, a different strategy was required because the neighbour refused mediation and threatened to file a complaint for slander. A person of standing in the man's community was approached to intervene and mediate.

With doctrinaire racism, where the chances of changing the perpetrator's mentality are slight, it is all the more important that society is seen to condemn acts such as the publication of thinly veiled racist propaganda. In the case of the article in the village local paper, ACOR asked the Press Ethical Committee for advice. The committee condemned the article for racial hatred. Because the newspaper did not publish this opinion, ACOR filed a criminal complaint against the author and the editor. The journalist was found guilty of racial discrimination and fined 200 francs. This was also, supplemented with socio-pedagogical work with different target groups.

Conclusion: Prospects for Comparative Research

Using a qualitative approach we have determined certain forms of racist violence and different possible modes of intervention. The quantitative aspect of the study provides important information on the frequency of each form of violence described by the callers. Proceeding this way is more interesting, especially if systematically maintained over an extended period of time. Together these approaches allow the analysis of the different forms of racism as they alter over time, and of adopting the means of intervention accordingly.

A systematic observation of racist manifestations in the French speaking part of Switzerland enables comparison of data gathered by other Swiss and European antiracist hot lines. Our typology offers a starting point to help standardise such comparisons, providing another source of information with which to analyse the question of racism in Europe; a complementary tool if used with other established sources, such as police and media records, publications and databases. In addition, this type of primary source will allow cross-national comparison of antiracist measures. Therefore, what we report here will only gain its full significance when placed within the context of all forms of racist acts reported to antiracist hot lines across Europe.

Notes

1 'Violence raciste en Suisse romande: analyse des actes, des acteurs et de nouvelles formes d'intervention', Swiss National Research Fund, Project 40440-45202. PNR 40.

* The French-speaking Swiss Association against Racism, FSAR.

2 Agreements such as the International Convention for the Elimination of all Forms of Racial Discrimination and article 261 bis of the Swiss Penal Code.

** The Institute for Social Studies, IES.

3 Acts of racist violence and racist discrimination are reported to '0800 SOS Racism'. Both of which have direct consequences on the victim's situation and emotional state. This is why these two levels sometimes seem to overlap in our typology.

4 The facts are true but names and dates have been changed in order to preserve the anonymity of the real persons.

5 Because our typology is based upon interaction between actors, forms of behavior may be classed under more than one form of racist violence. For example, this form, is also to be found under *interpersonal violence*.

6 Recently the United States authorities and the Jewish World Congress accused the Swiss banks of retaining funds deposited by victims of the Holocaust. Most of this money has been refunded to the descendants of the victims, even those who had made no claim until recently.

References

Adorno, T.W., Frenkel-Brunswik, E., Levinson, D. and Sanford, R. (1950), *The Authoritarian Personality*, Harper and Row, New York.
Allport, G.W. (1958), 'The Nature of the Prejudice', Anchor Books, New York.
Alund, A. and Schierup, C.-U. (1991), *Paradoxes of multiculturalism*, Avebury, Aldershot.
Bähler, R. (1994), 'Die rechtsradikale Szene der Schweiz [Radical Right Wing Scene in

Switzerland]', éd. Gesellschaft für Minderheiten in *der Schweiz und Stiftung gegen Rassismus und Antisemitismus*, Zürich.

Barbier, R. (1996), *La recherche-action [Action-Research]*, Anthropos, Paris.

Bell, D.(ed.) (1964), *The Radical Right*, Anchor Books, New York.

Bonafé-Schmitt, J.-P. (1992), *La médiation : une justice douce [Mediation: a Soft Justice]*, éd. Syros Alternative, Paris.

Bukow, W.-D. (1992), 'Ethnisierung und nationale Identität [Ethnicisation and National Identity]', in Institut für Migrations- und Rassismusforschung (eds), *Rassismus und Migration in Europa*, Argument Verlag, Hamburg, pp.133–146.

De Rham, G., Grandmousin, C. and Bernasconi, M. (1986), *L'asile dans notre quotidien. Discours populaire sur les réfugiés [Asylum in our Everyday Life: People Speeches on Refugees]*, Publicetim, Genève.

Faget, J. (1997), *La médiation, essai de politique pénale [Mediation: Essay on Penal Policy]*, Erès, Ramonville Saint-Agne.

Girard, R. (1972), *La violence et le sacré [Violence and Sacredness]*, Grasset, Paris.

Glaser, B. & Strauss, A. (1967), *The Discovery of Grounded Theory*, Aldine, Chicago.

Guillaumin, C. (1992), *Sexe, Race et Pratique du pouvoir [Sex, Race and Power Practice]*, Côté-femmes, Paris.

Kriesi, H.-P. and Altermatt, U. (eds) (1995) *L'extrême-droite en Suisse. Organisations et radicalisation au cours des années quatre-vingt et quatre-vingt-dix [Extreme Right Wing in Switzerland. Organisations and Radicalisation in the 80s and 90s]*, (ed.) Universitaires Fribourg.

Lalive d'Epinay, C., Bolzman, C., Modak, M. (1986), 'L'ethos totalitaire chez les petits possedants', in *Cahiers Internationaux de Sociologie*, vol. 36, pp.325–344.

Loi fédérale (1948), 'Loi fédérale sur le séjour et l'établissement des étrangers du 26.3.1931', in Feuille Fédérale, Bern, no.12, pp.1277ss.

Memmi, A. (1964), 'Le racisme: essai de définition', in *La Nef*, no. 19–20. [Racism: Definition Essay].

Message (1992) 'concernant l'adhésion de la Suisse à la Convention internationale sur l'élimination de toutes les formes de discrimination raciale et la révision y relative du droit pénal' [Message on Swiss Membership to International Convention for the Elimination of all Forms of Racial Discrimination and the Relating Penal Law Revision], Berne, 2 March 1992.

Michaud, Y. (1996), *La violence [Violence]*, Presses Universitaires de France, Paris.

Oechsle, M. and Zoll, R. (1988), 'La classe ouvrière en Allemagne et le racisme' [Working Class in Germany and Racism], in *Les Temps Modernes*, no. 466, pp. 2095–2119.

Radtke, Franz-Olaf (1990), 'Multikulturell-Das Gesellschaftdesign der 90er Jahre?' [Multicultural-Society Design of the 90s?] in *Informationsdienst zur Ausländerarbeit*, no. 4, pp. 27–34.

Taguieff, P.-A. (ed), (1991) *Face au racisme [Facing Racism]*, éd. la Découverte, coll. Points, Paris.

Thomas, W.I. (1966), *On social organisation and social personalitiy: selected papers*, University of Chicago Press, Chicago, London.

Weber, M. (1959), *Le savant et le politique [The Scholar and the Politic]*, Plon, 10/18, Paris.

Weill, A. and Grünberg, K. (1997), *La police des étrangers, de l'Ueberfremdung à la politique de trois cercles ou la métamorphose d'une idée fixe [Foreigners' Police: from 'Ueberfremdung' to 3 Circles Policy or the Metamorphosis of a Fixed Idea]*, Cahier no. 2, Association romande contre le racisme, Lausanne.

Willems, H. (1994), 'Youth Violence against Foreigners in Germany: Biographical Traits, Generational Aspects and Escalation Process', Paper presented at the *6th Annual International Conference on Socio-Economics of the Society for the Advancement of*

Socio-Economics, Jouy en Josas, France.

Windisch, U., Jaeggi, J.-M., de Rham, G. (1978), *Xénophobie ? Logique de la pensée populaire [Xenophobia? Logic of Popular Thinking]*, L'Age d'Homme, Lausanne.

Witte, R. (1996), *Racist Violence and the State*, Longman, London & New York.

Zehr, H. (1995) 'Justice Paradigm Shift? Values and Visions in the Reform Process', in *Mediation Quarterly*, vol. 12, no. 3.

12 Monitoring Ethnic Relations in Western and Eastern Europe

CRISTIANO CODAGNONE

Introduction

The large majority of existing states exercise their authority over ethnically diverse populations. In contrast to the *nation-building* and *national integration* narratives of the 1950s and 1960s, already in the early 1970s a global survey of political developments suggested that ethnic identity was on the rise as a tool for political mobilisation (Connor, 1972, p. 327). The crucial importance assumed since the late eighties by ethnic politics is not a new phenomenon, but rather one which has acquired new relevance and attracted more coverage in the post-Cold War international context. While the post-1989 scenario promised the vision of a new peaceful world order, we have in fact witnessed an upsurge of violent ethnic wars and latent tensions of an ethnopolitical nature.

Europe in particular, here intended in its broadest geographical meaning stretching from the shores of Portugal to the Ural mountains, has been the theatre of regional ethnic wars and of increasing and widespread feeling and manifestations of xenophobia.

The escalation of such conflicts and tensions and their, at times dire, humanitarian consequences render of crucial importance the capability to use existing knowledge, to gather and systematise relevant information to monitor and, consequently, better respond to ethnopolitical crises. In the last years several monitoring and/or early-warning systems on broadly defined ethnopolitical developments have been set up to respond to meet this need for preventive information. According to a recent survey, there are currently more than 40 operational monitoring and early warning operations established by a range of different institutions such as NGOs, academic research centres, governmental bodies, and international organisations (for example see http://www.yorku.ca/research/crs/prevent/eweffort.htm). One of which, the European Observatory on Racism and Xenophobia, was established in 1998 by the European Commission in Vienna to run the Ethnobarometer Project (henceforth the EP). The EP is a continuous monitoring and reporting system on the state of ethnic relations in ten countries in Western and Eastern Europe, for which I am responsible for the design of the supporting conceptual/ terminological and methodological framework.[1]

While comparative monitoring is not exactly the same as comparative research, establishing its supporting framework entails addressing many of the same issues and problems that are the object of conceptual and theoretical discussion in the scholarly literature, and that must be 'solved' before undertaking comparative empirical research. Here I will raise some of these issues as I encountered them in the process of designing the EP's general framework and co-ordinating the reporting activity of correspondents in 12 different countries. Though I will refer at times to experiences specific to the EP, the discussion I develop aims to be more general.

In the first section, I outline the basic features that differentiate early warning and monitoring from research. In the second, I discuss conceptual/ terminological issues, while in the third I analyse the choice of the indicators selected for monitoring. Then in the fourth section I consider problems of sources and data, while in the conclusive paragraph some preliminary considerations are presented on issues relevant from a comparative perspective.

The Monitoring and Early Warning Field

New primary field research is of crucial importance and will always improve the understanding of broadly defined ethnic phenomena, on the other hand the implicit assumption of a monitoring system is that a great deal of relevant data already exist. Therefore, the benefit of such a system resides in the analytical capacity of those doing the research to use existing data and efficiently disseminate the resulting analyses to a broad audience. An audience including, besides researchers, policy makers, international organisations, human rights activists and the media.

Data on any topic is today easier and cheaper to access and, borrowing the language of the media and business experts, not having data is certainly a cost but simply having it is not *per se* an advantage. Large corporations and bureaucracies cannot help but amass all the data relevant to their operation, but they often find themselves in the position of not knowing what they know and/ or being overloaded by the data they possess and process. This business discourse, often referred to as 'knowledge management', is based on a distinction between tacit inert data and explicit information, that is data transformed into easy to retrieve and use informative material. With some modification, this idea can be applied to the monitoring of ethnic phenomena. Some modification is necessary because such monitoring is linked to the enterprise of academic research, a different activity from data gathering in corporations and bureaucracies.

Most material accumulated on ethnic phenomena over decades of research activity has been produced precisely by turning raw data into intelligible and insightful information. This, however, has been mostly done in an idiosyncratic fashion, due to sharp differences in the conceptual/ terminological apparatuses, theoretical and methodological perspectives, disciplinary focus, national coloration, and political engagement of each research study. This is not necessarily a drawback, but it does mean that the body of accumulated research does not add up to explicit and easy to use information. Because, for a monitoring operation aiming at cross-national comparison and at the widest possible intelligibility across disciplines, national borders, and, last but not least, across professions, it still represents raw data.

Most European countries already posses a considerable amount of data on ethnic and migration issues, though with some variation with respect to accuracy. This consists of material such as census and large national survey data, published empirical research, media coverage, legislation and policy documents. To gather and use this data in a way that adds value to them, a monitoring system must do a number of things, at three different stages:

- the design of its supporting framework;
- the implementation of this design;
- the re-elaboration of the gathered data, and the drafting of the final periodic report to be disseminated.

In the first stage, leaving aside each country's peculiarities, the design must establish a general blueprint of its activity, which will determine the quality of the final output. This entails selecting and delimiting the object to be monitored, choosing a precise, yet abstract, conceptual/terminological apparatus, surveying major theoretical approaches and their respective methodologies and levels of analysis to extract an exhaustive template of indicators.

In the second stage, the initial choices made in designing the supporting framework have to be tailored to each of the chosen country's peculiarities, as conveyed in preliminary meetings by the selected correspondents. The aim is to find the most suitable cross-national common denominator, in terms of concepts, terminology, and indicators with which to guide the correspondents' gathering and reporting of information. One should avoid imposing a general and rigid framework and allow instead some flexibility to accommodate each country's peculiarities. This, however, does not entail surrendering to these peculiarities, as, ultimately, this would hinder the comparative power of the whole operation. Even at this stage one should aim at some basic level of standardisation. Had we listened to all of the correspondents' objections to our initial framework, during the first meeting, the operation would never have got off the ground. Instead, successive meetings allowed us to reach a satisfactory common platform from which to begin. This involved a continuous fine-tuning effort, which is still going on and will go on in the future.

Finally, in the third stage the circle must be drawn to a close and the finished product distributed, which, assuming stage one and two have been successful, should reflect the initial design ameliorated by the input arising from the second stage.

Peculiarities and Differences of Early Warning and Monitoring Systems

Before proceeding to the analysis of the major conceptual, theoretical, and methodological issues involved in all of the three stages outlined above, a brief discussion is in order on the detectable peculiarities and differences between early warning and monitoring systems.

The survey mentioned earlier[2] shows that most of current projects are early warning systems (EWS). The most characteristic element of EWS is that their focus is on the 'extra-ordinary', that is on situations of acute crisis which can lead to humanitarian disasters. Another is their theoretical and, I would say, epistemological perspective, as can be seen in the ambition to anticipate and forecast events. EWS, in fact, were originally devised and have being used for decades to forecast ecological disasters such as flood, drought, storms and famine. This has been done and is done by relying on long-term historical series of data on weather patterns or on other easy to measure variables, which are used as predictors of such disasters.[3] Although EWS only began to be applied to man made disasters and humanitarian crises in the late 1970s, their application has proliferated since the late 1980s and there is now a consistent body of academic research and theoretical literature on the topic.[4] The application of EWS to conflicts and humanitarian emergencies, aiming to reproduce the hard scientific facts of the EWS of ecological disaster, rests on the strong premise that theory can incorporate the lessons of a large number of historical cases into a general analytical framework which in turn will be used for future assessment and prediction. Accordingly, the templates of indicators constructed for such studies follow well-defined and rigid predictive models.

A good example of an early warning system is EAWARN, established and directed by Professor Valery Tishkov at the Russian Academy of Sciences' Institute of Ethnology and Anthropology, in Moscow. EAWARN relies on a network of correspondents covering the entire Russian Federation and most of the former Soviet republics and uses a sophisticated template consisting of seven blocks of large questions (from environmental conditions to state policies and international aspects) for a total of about 50 indicators. Each indicator is periodically given a score (within an established scale) on a combined basis of objective data and experts evaluation, thus providing a total score on an area/issue of potential ethnic conflict.

Another project which deserves a separate mention is the Minority at Risk Project (MARP), directed by Professor Ted Gurr of the Center for International Development and Conflict Management (CIDCM), Maryland University in the USA. MARP, lies somewhere in between EWS and monitoring, and resulted in the compilation and analyses of detailed information on the status of 270 ethnopolitically active groups in the period 1990–1995.[5] The major aim of this project has been the building a global database to formulate and test general causal models explaining the causes and dynamics of ethnopolitical conflicts. MARP is not however a system of continuous monitoring and reporting and the data available on each of the 270 groups are to great extent historical and static, ending with the updating which stopped in 1995.

As anticipated, the EP is a continuous monitoring and reporting system on the state of ethnic relations in countries of Western, Eastern, and Central Europe and of the post-Soviet space.[6] Ethnic relations are here broadly defined as the ensemble of situations and events involving individual and group-level interaction to political effect between the different ethnic communities of a state, as well as interactions between state authorities and individuals or organised community level groups. I will discuss objectives and content of the EP monitoring and reporting in detail below in 'Theory Informed Monitoring'.

It must be stressed that, since reporting will be on the general state of ethnic relations, such situations and events may be indicative not only of ethnic tensions and conflicts but also of instances of successful accommodation of ethnic diversity. This is one of a number of differences between continuous monitoring and reporting systems (CMRS) such as the EP and early warning systems. CMRS do not focus exclusively on extra-ordinary instances of crisis, but produce a more systematic and continuous reporting. This means that they include also the more mundane, 'everyday' unfolding of events regarding the area/issues chosen for reporting, whether or not there is an acute condition of crisis. Hence they are more inclusive in two ways: a) they must also try and report on less open and intense cases of tension and conflicts; b) they are also interested in positive developments indicating successful accommodation of ethnic diversity. In this sense monitoring and reporting, at least as it is intended by the EP, present some analogies with the annual SOPEMI report on migration produced by the OECD. Finally, again specifically concerning the EP, the epistemology behind the operation is substantially different from that informing most early warning systems, since there is no ambition to objectively forecast events. If on the one hand, standard indicators and the analytical elaboration of current and historical information helps a great deal in understanding better the issue at stake and in spreading such information and knowledge, it is, however, doubtful that general formalised models can, to any practical extent, predict what in the last instance is ontologically unpredictable human behaviour.

Terminological/Conceptual Problems

> *Basic terms/concepts: nation, nation-state, nationality, citizenship, ethno-nation,sub-nation, national minority, ethnicity, ethnie, ethnic group, ethnic minority, race, racial group, racial minority, ethnoracial group...*
>
> *Derivative terms/concepts: nationalism, civic nationalism, patriotism, ethno-nationalism, ethnic nationalism, nationalising states, separatism, secessionism, irredentism, autonomism, ethnicism, ethnic antagonism, ethnocentrism, xenophobia, racism, cultural racism...*

The terms/concepts listed above in no order other than that in which they came to mind, are but some of what one can find in the broadly defined field of nationalism, ethnic, and migration studies. At the time of writing it is exactly twenty years since the journal *Ethnic and Racial Studies* published Walker Connor's article 'A Nation is a Nation, is a State, is an Ethnic Group, is a...' (1978), which recently reappeared in a collection of essays by the same author re-titled 'Terminological Chaos' (Connor, 1994, pp. 90–117). Connor lamented how, for instance, words as important as nation, state, nationalism were '...shrouded in ambiguity due to their imprecise, inconsistent, and often totally erroneous usage' (Connor, 1994, p. 91). Time has not dated Connors' essay, and the literature on nationalism, ethnic, and migration studies is still plagued by a conceptual and terminological impasse which forces the reader, especially if he/she moves across disciplines and national research traditions, to engage repeatedly in conceptual translation in order to relate one study to the other and make some generalised sense out of different research findings.

After few brief examples of the major ambiguities characterising key basic and derivative terms/concepts—'basic' meaning those used to identify broadly defined ethnic collectivities, while 'derivative' refers to actions and/or ideologies and/or attitudes of which members of ethnic collectivities are either active or passive subjects—I will focus on the question of why clear definitions of concepts are necessary to monitoring, how definite and clear they should be, and how to achieve such a goal.

In a way the 'mother' of all definitions and, accordingly, of most ambiguities is the 'nation' which, as a result of the fusion that occurred in the eighteenth and nineteenth centuries between nation and state, became the main ordering criteria according by which human groupings are identified, classified and accorded collective rights. On the one hand, various scholars have shown that ethnicity also characterises the 'nation' (Connor, 1994, pp. 100–103; Smith, 1994, pp. 382–383; Weber, 1968, p. 923), which in its pristine and more appropriate meaning refers to an ethnically defined community of origin and descent enjoying or aspiring to self-government. While, on the other hand, the use of the root 'nation' in expressions or names such as 'United *Nations*', '*inter*national relations', '*nation*al bank', 'industry *nation*alisation' seems to equate its meaning to that of the word 'state'. In the nation-building and national integration literature of the 1950s and 1960s 'nation' is intended as all citizenry regardless of individual ethnic origins and identities.[7] Thus the major ambiguity inherent in the concept of the 'nation' is derived from and linked to the tension between a political and an ethnic characterisation.

Another noticeable ambiguity concerns the concept of 'ethnic group'. As remarked upon by several authors (Connor, 1994, p. 101; Jackson, 1984, pp. 221–222; Riggs, 1991b, pp. 448–449), especially in North American sociology, the use and definition of 'ethnic group'—generically characterised as a group with a common tradition and sense of identity living as a sub-group in a larger society—makes it synonymous with minority. So in some contexts it is used as a synonym for 'minority group' (ethnic, and migration studies) while in others it refers to a dominant element in a state (nationalism studies).

The ambiguity surrounding basic terms/concepts is inevitably reflected in the definitions and usage of derivative terms/concepts, and the best example is how the ambiguity of the concept of the 'nation' is directly translated in that surrounding 'nationalism'. Nationalism is used at times to indicate a universal sense of loyalty toward a state (which should be better termed as patriotism or civic nationalism), at others to refer to the radical ideology and mobilisation in the name of ethnically defined nations.

Another problematic couple of terms/concepts are racism/xenophobia. In the first place both terms refer to an individual attitude, or better to an a priori negative attitude, namely a prejudice directed toward a group and its members. In social psychology textbooks (see for instance Myers, 1996, Chap. 11), an attitude is a combination of feelings (affection), inclination to act (behaviour tendency) and beliefs (cognition). Racist/xenophobic feelings/inclinations/beliefs are the result of categorisations of self and others into ingroup and outgroup members. In principle one could easily distinguish them according to the criteria used in the categorisation of others as ingroups or outgroups. In practice this is not so, precisely because of the lack of clear-cut and generally accepted distinctions in the use of the concepts of 'race' and 'ethnicity'. Nowadays hostile distinctions are overwhelmingly based on ethnicity/culture and much less on strictly defined 'race' (Crowley, 1998). Building on such quite established empirical facts, Banton argues that from the perspective of conceptual clarity the idiom of race and racism have lost any merit (1994, p. 7). Yet he recognises that they cannot be abandoned because '...we need the word race as part of the rationale for all the legislation, international and national, which has been designed to combat discrimination based on the idea of race' (Banton, 1994, p. 7)). The new concept of 'cultural racism' can be considered in part a response to the problem of keeping the idiom of racism despite changes in the criteria used in the categorisation process. But how can one distinguish clearly 'racism' or 'cultural racism' from 'xenophobia'? Baumgartl and Favell's (1994) minimal definition of xenophobia, for instance, is 'dread of 'foreigners' as a group, whether defined legally, as 'immigrants', or by their strangeness as a visible group' (1994, p. 379). It goes without saying, that visible strangeness does not necessarily coincide with the legal condition of being foreigner. Thus, if a negative attitude or behaviour targets individuals who are categorised as outgroup members neither on the basis of strictly defined race, nor on the basis of their legal status as foreigners, but simply because of their allegedly detectable strangeness (including not only physical features but also behaviour and practices seen as deriving from alien culture), are we confronted with a manifestation of 'xenophobia' or 'cultural racism'?

The examples discussed above represent only a very selective sample of the terminological/conceptual problems characterising the literature of nationalism, ethnic, and migration studies. Given such a context, the first question I posed myself when starting the design of the Ethnobarometer project monitoring framework was whether clear definitions of concepts are necessary for monitoring ethnic relations in a cross-national comparative perspective. The answer to which is not a neutral matter of methodological choice, and depends on the basic theoretical underpinning to how concepts such as ethnicity, ethnic group, and nation are conceived.

The ambition to give externally objective definitions of such concepts presupposes, in fact, a substantialist approach, conceiving 'ethnic groups' or 'nations' as *res extensa* with immutable and identifiable objective attributes as well as viewing humanity as consisting of discontinuous and clearly separate groups. My view is that *ethnie* or *nation* are, on the contrary, nothing but variable social constructions used for the definition of the 'collective self' and 'collective other'. The difficulty encountered, for instance, in reaching a consensus on an external and objective definition of the nation depends, as Conversi has acutely observed (1995, p. 77), precisely on the impossibility of defining from without what is itself an operative tool of self-definition from within. According to Tishkov (1997, p.33) the nation cannot be defined as a scientific category because it is primarily and above all a category of social and political practice. More generally Banton argues that, to start from any prior conception of ethnic or national entities before looking at individual and group behaviour, amounts to a sort of 'methodological collectivism' (1994, p.1). Brubaker lists several developments in social theory that have in recent years challenged the treatment of social groups as real and substantial entities,[8] and considers the persistence of realist, substantialist concepts a flaw in the literature on nation and nationalism (1996, p.13).

This criticism of substantialist notions of ethnic collectivities does not, in my view, imply that it is not worth bothering with clear definitions, but is, rather, a warning against what I call 'ethnic nominalism', namely the automatic treatment of all individuals as members of ethnic collectivites simply because they share some of the allegedly 'objective and ascriptive markers' with which such collectivities are identified. While at the first level of approximation, membership in a group should, and can, be estimated using the widest official demographic definition available, at the same time information should be supplied, as far as is possible, on the actual extent to which nominal members of a group actually identify with it. Too often, in fact, when discussing issues related to an ethnic collectivity, implicitly or explicitly it is assumed that it actually coincides with its broadest demographic definition as this is offered by, for instance, official census data. This at times may result in reifying individuals into an ethnic collectivity who, though they share some elements that could be used to group them together, in fact do not demonstrate a strong sense of identity nor any form of mobilisation.

Going back to the question of whether clear definitions of concepts are necessary at all for cross-national monitoring of ethnic relations, the answer cannot but be affirmative, as was probably already clear from the discussion presented in the first section on what the added value of monitoring is and which steps are necessary when designing the monitoring system to ensure that such value is produced.

It is an established rule in comparative research that a meaningful comparison and interpretation of data coming from different national contexts is only possible if comparable definitions and operationalisations of key concepts guides the data gathering and generating process. Though cross-national monitoring is not exactly the same as cross-national research, its goal is the widest possible intelligibility of its output across disciplines, national borders and professional fields, which is possible only if, after selecting and delimiting the object to be monitored, the following conditions are met:

- a blueprint of the monitoring activity, including a general theory-informed conceptual apparatus, must be designed, which in the end will determine the quality of the final output;
- the widest possible cross-national common denominator in terms of concepts and terminology must be achieved to guide the actual gathering and reporting of information by the correspondents.

Therefore, in the first place, it is the same logic of cross-national comparison, as well as the practical requirement to organise the gathering and reporting of information by country correspondents, that requires establishing some clear definitions of basic and derivative concepts.

Moreover, no matter how arbitrarily constructed and variable ethnic collectivities might be, once individuals display feelings of belonging to them and mobilise in their name or are targeted by others because they are perceived and categorised as members of such collectivities, the consequences of ethnically motivated social action can be as concrete as the bloodshed at times produced by ethnic conflicts. Since the phenomena to be monitored occurs on the basis of internally or externally perceived belonging, a minimal set of concepts are needed to select on which groups and manifestations of ethnically inspired social actions country correspondents must report.

Having established that clear definitions are necessary, the next step is to discuss how to achieve them and how precise they must be. Following Sartori (1984, p.82), I will refer to the ensemble of terms/concepts used in nationalism/ethnic/migration studies as a *semantic field*, that is a co-varying set of associated and neighbouring terms cutting across several disciplinary boundaries which should, in principle, hang together in some coherent and consistent way.

Conceptual ambiguity arises in any field when keywords accumulate several meanings, a phenomena particularly widespread in the social sciences where, unlike in the natural sciences, there is a tendency to avoid the creation of new words (*neologism*) and to resort instead to *neosemanticism*, namely the establishment of a new meaning for already existing terms or expressions (Riggs, 1991a, pp. 283–284). In the social sciences this is further complicated by the fact that, given the general public and political relevance of most of the issues studied, terms with an originally precise meaning loose their conceptual clarity for they become popularised and/or politicised and/or assigned a different meaning in legislation. Though neosemanticism is widespread across all the fields of the social sciences, the problems of popularisation, politicisation and legislative redefinition of key terms is particularly acute in nationalism, ethnic, and migration studies.

The collective ambiguity of any semantic field is not the same thing as the ambiguities of a particular author. It is produced when the accumulated body of literature, as well as the popular and political/legal usage of key terms, result in a widespread presence of both homonymy, *the use of one word for different meanings*, and synonymy, *the use of different words for the same meaning*. The clearest example of homonymy in our semantic field of interest is evident in ambivalent and confusing usage of 'nation' and 'nationalism' to refer to two substantially different entities and ideologies.

While at first glance synonymy might seem less unsettling of a semantic field than homonymy it is, in fact, a source of both terminological waste and conceptual ambiguity (Sartori, 1984, pp. 38–40). From the perspective of the economics of terminology, widespread usage of synonymies does nothing to reduce the number of terms burdened by several meanings. More dangerous is the practice of using conceptual synonymies, which is something substantially different from lexical synonymies. The existence of lexical synonyms is a given and, though it is a terminological waste, one can clearly deal with them choosing to use consistently only one of the available synonyms to express a concept. Conceptual synonyms are instead stipulated, even between terms which lexically are not synonyms, when it is claimed that A is the same as B or, more strongly, that the correct meaning of A is B. If the stipulation is intentionally made on the basis of interpretation, then conceptual synonymy does not contribute to the ambiguity of a field. The problem arises when conceptual synonymy is either arbitrarily established or is the implicit result of terminological usage and definitions. The clearest example of a conceptual synonymy not grounded in interpretation and resulting simply from erroneous practice is that between 'ethnic group' and 'minority group'. Besides being a waste of language, what is a conceptual synonymy within the conceptual/ terminological practice of a single country or area of countries, can become an even more confusing homonymy when another country, or area of countries, with similar conceptual/terminological practices is included in the analysis. The example here is the ambiguity arising in the European East–West comparative perspective when using the concept of 'nationality', a conceptual synonym for citizenship in Western Europe and for 'ethnicity' in Eastern Europe and post-Soviet space.

From the above discussion one could extract a rule of thumb to be followed in the design of the conceptual/terminological framework: *rule out homonymies and avoid as much as possible synonymies*. This rule, however, raises a number of problems potentially constraining the drive toward terminological/conceptual clarity. First, because the audience to which the results of monitoring should be disseminated is likely to have been heavily influenced by the most popularised terminological usage, excessive purity might lead to further misunderstandings. A possible additional rule of thumb is then the following: *avoid unnecessary neologism and neosemanticism.*

A second and more intractable problem concerns terms left with little analytical credibility but politically and legally loaded. Personally, for instance, I am convinced that the concept of race has been emptied of any analytical power, yet the idiom of racism is the rationale of positive political action and legal provisions to fight certain types of aggressive and discriminatory behaviour. Ruling out, on the basis of an analytical critique, race and racism from the terminological apparatus of a monitoring system, the results of which are intended to be as public as possible, will most probably result in political controversy and radical accusations. Here it is very difficult to establish a general rule and the choice one makes unfortunately cannot be inspired only by analytical considerations.

The third, fortunately, is more an analytical problem related to the question of the comparative use of terms/concepts across the different countries monitored. In doing this, one must deal with the trade off existing between general standardised conceptual clarity/precision and consistency, and the necessity to reflect countries' peculiarities. It is well known that cross-national comparisons that include an elevated number of countries inevitably face the problems of the limits of general theoretically constructed concepts. Stated differently, theoretically sound and precise concepts can fall into what is known as 'conceptual overstretching' with respect to relevant empirical characteristics that the analysed phenomena might have in different countries. Though the trade-off between achieving general standardised conceptual clarity and reflecting countries' specificities does not have any optimal solution, a useful rule to follow is: *use minimal definitions of basic concepts which include only the most relevant defining characteristics and leave out accompanying properties.* The parsimony of minimal definitions ensures the establishment of widely applicable concepts, which integrated by more contingent accompanying properties can be adapted to countries' peculiarities.[9]

Finally, a good practice with which to establish a terminological/conceptual apparatus is to follow what is often referred as the 'ladder of abstraction'. This means starting with the most basic and abstract concept, identified by the least possible number of defining characteristics, then descending the ladder by adding the number of characteristics to define more specific, but still generic, concepts. Further descent implies adding contingent properties, an operation that should be limited to include countries' peculiarities.

Though I will not outline all the concepts' definitions elaborated and used for the Ethnobarometer monitoring system, I will now discuss briefly some of the basic choices that have inspired such definitions. Following the rule of minimal definitions and of the ladder of abstraction, the starting point is the concept of ethnicity defined as: *a subjective belief of belonging to a community of presumed common cultural-historical origins and descent.* Accordingly, at the most abstract and general level, an ethnic collectivity is: *any form of community, regardless of its political status in a given state, consisting of individuals consciously sharing a sense of ethnicity.* Though both these definitions are given from the within-perspective, ethnicity and ethnic collectivity are also defined and constructed from without, in certain cases even when the internal sense of ethnicity is weak. Further distinctions among different types of ethnic collectivities down the ladder of abstraction and the definitions of derivative concepts have been inspired by a basic hypothesis about the nation-state and its effects.

As stated earlier, the fusion of the eighteenth and nineteenth centuries between nation and state has made of the 'nation' the main ordering criteria according to which other human groups are identified. Whether this practice is correct or not it is of little relevance compared to its concrete empirical detectable consequences. Despite the recognised empirical evidence that self-aware and organised ethnic communities are by far more numerous than sovereign states, the idea of the nation-state remains in practice the major ordering principle by which populations are classified, granted rights and it is also the object of discussion, tension, conflict. The strong hypothesis underlying my analysis is that, political organised action, pre-political social action, and mere social prejudices and attitudes with a broadly defined ethnic basis are, directly or indirectly, related to such an ordering principle.

Most states exercise their authority over ethnically diverse populations which include not only the nationally dominant group but also other communities as a result of two processes:

- the incorporation of territorially concentrated communities which in most cases had previously experienced some forms of political or **pre-political** self-rule;
- the reception of **individual and familial immigration** which over time give rise to non territorialised but culturally linked communities.

This is the most basic distinction, used by the state to accord collective rights to different ethnic communities and to a certain extent determine the type of claim these communities may raise or the action of which they may become the passive subject on the side of state agencies or of members of other ethnic communities (most often of the dominant national group). One might criticise this distinction as a way of legitimising a hierarchy of human collectivities according to their political statuses. In fact, there is no intention to defend and legitimise such a hierarchy of political statuses. The choice aims to avoid substantialist definitions of each collectivity, and a pragmatic way to do so is to look at the different claims and forms of mobilisation to which each of them most often gives rise. Whether good or bad, it is a matter of fact that such political statuses shape to a large extent the type of claims different communities make or the external action to which they are subjected. Again without any intention of legitimising such practice, it is a fact that some states recognise certain collective rights and even territorial autonomy to territorially concentrated communities, while they do not to communities resulting from immigration (Bauböck, 1994, p. 8).

Theory Informed Monitoring

Monitoring cannot be reduced to a mere registration of events, but must be informed by theory in the choice of the object to be monitored and of the indicators used. For the EP, the basic hypothesis illustrated above about the relevance of the nation-state has naturally influenced the choice of what will be the object of monitoring and the content of annual reporting. Ethnic relations, as I defined them in the first section, are monitored only in so far as they have politically relevant effects. This means, for instance, that individual and group level processes and problems of identity formation and/or maintenance are considered an event or situation to monitor not in and of themselves, but only if they are the basis of political claims and/or are addressed as an issue by state policy. A corollary is also that monitoring should focus only on ethnopolitically relevant groups, that is: *groups which, as a result of a high level of internal identity and organisation or of being categorised as outgroups from without, are at the centre of politically relevant events and situations as either active or passive subjects.*

Political relevance must be defined very broadly to include not only organised political mobilisation, but also pre-political social action such as grass-roots riots or individual attacks with generically defined ethnic motivations, as well as the consequences of the administration of state power. From this definition it follows that groups with a weak identity and little internal organisation become politically relevant when they are the object of hostile behaviour on the part of other groups or by the state.

Naturally monitoring and reporting should focus on the relevant events and situations developed in a given year. Though the distinction has the usual limits with respect to the complexity of empirical reality, these events and situations can be distinguished at three levels:

- non organised pre-political individual or group level;
- organised political group level;
- state level decisions and action.

Without listing all the possible events and situations identified for the EP monitoring and reporting, I briefly mention some of them as examples. At the first level are instances of non organised inter-ethnic tension and conflicts which may or may not imply the actual use of violence in its different forms (verbal, physical, etc.), as well as cases of individual discrimination. At the second level are cases of group-level politically organised mobilisation, which may be limited to the level of discourses and debates, or may take more concrete but not violent political forms (petitions, protests etc.), or openly violent organised forms (this is most likely for ethnoterritorial conflicts). It is important to stress that this level includes articulated public discourses of the political representative of a given ethnic community and/or those constructed from without on such community (this implies media coverage). The third level is that of the state and concerns new legislation, change in policies, implementation of specific policies, landmark court decisions, instances of institutional discrimination.

If monitoring and reporting were limited to simply registering and briefly describing events and situations such as those mentioned above, the final product (annual report) would amount to nothing more than an annotated chronology of little interest and value. For this reason a very important component of monitoring and reporting consists in gathering data on, and providing interpretation of, background and short term indicators, the choice of which is crucial to the real added value and quality of the final output. These indicators are, in fact, selected as the possible root causes and/or precipitators of the events and situations which occurred in the given year, but are also the instruments by which the general state of ethnic relations is assessed with an appraisal of positive developments and warnings on areas of new potential tensions and conflicts. Looking at the activity of monitoring from the perspective of its policy relevance, it goes without saying that a list and brief description of key events and situations would be of no value without an interpretation of their causes and the consequent identification of possible solutions.

It is precisely in the selection of indicators that the design of the monitoring framework must take into account and rely on the various explanatory and interpretative hypotheses developed in the inter-disciplinary body of literature on nationalism, ethnic, and migration studies and on the relative empirical findings. The goal of monitoring, however, unlike that of many academic endeavours, is not to prove the superiority of one theoretical hypothesis over other competing ones, but rather to extract as much practical value as possible from all of such hypotheses. Though innovative thinking is naturally also important in designing a monitoring system, one must make sure not to try reinventing the wheel. For this reason, the establishment of the indicators selected for monitoring must be based on a widely representative overview of major approaches and hypotheses, which will most likely cover all of the four levels of analysis listed above.

It is beyond the scope of the present discussion to repeat here in detail such an extensive review of the literature as the one developed for the preparation of the the EP framework, it would require an entire separate chapter. Below, merely for exemplification's sake, selectively and without any claim to exhaustiveness, I will limit myself to identifying some clusters of related hypotheses from which one can derive different blocks of indicators.

A first cluster one can identify is that of several hypotheses explaining broadly defined ethnic and/or national phenomena (identity formation, mobilisation, conflicts, etc.) in terms of socioeconomic conditions and of their variations in a given society, such as the 'diffusion/erasure' or 'developmentalist' hypothesis, the 'internal colonialism/reactive ethnicity' hypothesis, the 'relative deprivation' hypothesis, and the 'ethnic competition' hypothesis.[10] Though these hypotheses are quite different from each other, they all refer us to a block of economic, demographic, and social indicators regarding both a given country or region as a whole and separately to each of the ethnic communities residing there, such as for instance:

- level of economic growth and per capita income;
- level of unemployment;
- presence of ethnically segmented labour markets;
- level of education among different ethnic communities;
- ethnic composition of a given area over time and rates of immigration;
- presence/lack of natural resources in regions inhabited by territorially concentrated ethnic communities;
- other.

A second cluster is that of culturalist hypotheses which, whether inspired by a primordialist conception of ethnicity or by a functionalist idea of societal integration, emphasise the cultural and historical 'differentness' of the ethnic communities studied as an explanation of the sociopolitical phenomena of which they become the active or passive subjects. I deemed, for instance, the explanation of violent separatist mobilisation in terms of the cultural and historical distinctiveness of ethnoterritorial community mobilising for independence as 'cultural primordialism' (Codagnone, 1998, p. 12). Wimmer, instead, defines as 'functionalist' the widespread thesis that the cultural 'differentness' of immigrants is the main reason for conflicts with the native born population and is the input fuelling the racism and xenophobia of the latter toward the former (1997, p. 22). Accordingly, from such approaches we can derive indicators of cultural and historical distinctiveness distinguishing various ethnic communities, and particularly immigrant and ethnoterritorial communities from the dominant ethnonational component of a given state. For any given ethnic community, for instance, one could construct a scale of cultural and historical distinctiveness using descriptive indicators such as:

- detectable 'strangeness';
- language;
- religion;
- customs and traditions;
- history of (this specifically for ethnoterritorial communities):
  - lost autonomy or independence;
  - rebellions;
  - repression;
  - deportations;
- other.

The two previous clusters of hypotheses, despite the important differences existing among them, have in common the fact that all of them establish a direct, non mediated link, between ethnic mobilisation/conflict and socioeconomic and/or ethnocultural and ethnohistorical conditions. While all of these hypotheses have some explanatory power, they nonetheless miss a crucial intermediate level existing between ethnic mobilisation/conflicts on the one hand, and ethnocultural and socioeconomic conditions on the other. This intermediate level is represented by the conditioning and precipitating effects of, respectively, the established institutional-political context and the short-term political dynamic in which such mobilisations and conflicts occur.

Borrowing from the literature on collective action and social movements the insights from approaches such as 'political opportunity structure' and 'frame analysis',[11] as well as and from neo-institutionalist approaches,[12] it is possible to develop an institutional-political framework for the study of broadly defined ethnic mobilisation and conflicts. The basic argument of such framework is that socioeconomic factors and social change influence collective action indirectly, by restructuring its political context. Disruptive events and deep crises weaken political authority and the cohesion of dominant elites, thus opening a space for collective action. Forms and levels of mobilisation will be, however, conditioned and shaped by a country's political institutional context and configuration of power. In the area of migration and citizenship politics, for instance this implies that mobilisation is likely when there is a crisis of political authority and when dominant elites are internally divided on such issues. The level and success of mobilisation will in turn depend on how opportunities are structured by institutional and political established arrangements such as: access to citizenship (if more established members of immigrant communities are citizens, they vote and might represent an electoral group to be considered in mainstream politics); electoral law (proportional representation may facilitate the success of radical ethnic nationalist parties); dominant cleavages, and models and policies of incorporation; division/unity of dominant elite; configuration of power (which political party or coalition is in power). Since this framework implies, with respect to the two previous clusters of hypotheses, a shift from socially and culturally determined causation toward institutional conditioning and political contingencies/uncertainties, it cannot be made explicit in a clear-cut hypotheses. Nonetheless, it still helps to extract qualitative indicators one might use in building a monitoring system, such as:

- citizenship and naturalisation regimes;
- prevailing definition of the nation;
- established minority and migration policy approach;
- level of polity openness/closure to ethnic based claims;
- dominant cleavages;
- strategies of conflict resolutions;
- unity/fragmentation of state level elites;
- other.

Finally, establishing the indicators for a monitoring system cannot but take into due consideration the insights deriving from the application of discourse analysis to the field of interest, particularly for what concerns dominant discourses and ethnic diversity and ethnic minorities. The basic thesis of this approach, as summarised by Wimmer (1997, pp. 25–27) , holds that concepts of distinctiveness and incompatibility are the crucial operator of exclusion and are discursively created by the official and semi-official power holders and then institutionalised in policies and practices. Though not easily translatable into discrete indicators, the implication of this thesis for a monitoring system is to include a coverage of discourses on broadly defined ethnic diversity issues as they are articulated in the media and parliamentary debates. One possibility is to analyse such discourses in order to identify constructions such as:

- dominant reproduced notions of nation and citizenship;
- evaluation of ethnic based mobilisation;
- placing of blame on differences;
- immigration viewed as invasion;
- securitisation of immigration;
- criminalisation of minorities;
- economic behaviour stereotypes;
- other.

Data and Sources

Having established a comparatively flexible but coherent and standardised conceptual/terminological apparatus, and a set of theory informed indicators, is not the final step in the complex task of a establishing a monitoring and reporting system. Another major area of concern is that of the data and sources to be used which refer us to their level of reliability, validity and comparability, on which I will now discuss some brief considerations.

In discussing the data and sources I will here follow the distinction made in the previous paragraph between actual phenomena occurring in a given year to be monitored and reported on the one hand, and the background and short term indicators, which are considered as possible root causes and/or precipitators of such phenomena.

Group-level organised ethnopolitical developments most likely result from mobilisation and are characterised by being publicly very visible. Moreover, they tend to be discrete (concentrated in time, at least as they initially emerge) and can be considered relatively extra-ordinary, in the original sense of not being an ordinary everyday occurrence. Hence, they are easily detected and reported by relying on most traditional media.[13] Simply by using basic news reports that various forms of such events occurred, one might even construct a scale, for instance, of protest (0=none, 1=petitions, 2= hunger strikes, 3= rallies/demonstrations...). Relevant state decisions and action, with the exception of discrimination exercised by specific state agency which is at times hard to detect, are also public and therefore do not present a major problem as an object of monitoring and reporting.

It is moving to the individual level manifestations—more continuous, ordinary, subtle and, at times, less overt and evident—that the same availability of data, their empirical validity and reliability, and their comparability becomes problematic. For attitudes and perceptions one could rely on the periodic Eurobarometer surveys, which do not, however, cover Eastern Europe and the former Soviet Union (included in the EP). More substantially, even assuming that the questions used in a survey are framed in such a way as to yield both valid and comparatively sound results, their reliability is dubious, i.e., repeating the same survey at different times might produce different results. This is mainly because the answers provided by the respondents at a precise point in time might be influenced by a particular recent event and thus differ from those provided some time earlier or which will be given in the future.

On pre-political non organised ethnic violence, suffered by individuals as a result of the action of other individuals, there are some source of data available (not for all countries), which are also problematic. First, as pointed out by Witte (1995, pp. 492–494), courts and police statistics are compiled according to country specific criteria which make cross-national comparison almost impossible. Second, leaving aside comparability, even within the country these data presents problems of validity, as they do not reflect all crucial aspects of the phenomena. In Great Britain, one of the countries where official ethnic monitoring is well developed, it has been showed that official statistics (police statistics and the British Crime Survey) under-report ethnic offences (Virdee, 1997, p. 262). This is particularly so for less overt forms of ethnic violence (in British terminology 'low-level racial harassment'), such as insulting and threatening behaviours which are not seen as criminal events and are therefore not recorded by the police (Virdee, p. 263). The results of 'victimisation surveys' are more reliable, but are available only for a limited number of countries.

Another source is the reports that the states joining the 'International Convention for the Elimination of all Forms of Racial Discrimination' periodically make to the United Nation, available for consultation on the website of United Nations High Commissioner for Human Rights (http://www.unhchr.ch).[14] Besides the fact that they are produced by the governments of the country under report, a first preliminary reading of some of them suggests a low level of comparability. Very informative and well articulated are the studies on racial discrimination in employment promoted by the International Labour Organisation. They are, however, limited to only one specific aspect and available only for a few countries.

An alternative way of gathering information is the scrutiny of a representative number of newspapers used, not for the analysis of media representational effects, but as a source on cases of ethnic violence. Resorting to press reports for individual-level ethnic violence is, however, more problematic than in the case of group level forms of mobilisation discussed above. The incidents of more or less open individual-level violence are many and occur with high frequency. The data obtained by press reports will not completely reflect the phenomena, because not all acts are reported in newspapers and resources do not allow scrutiny of more than a limited number of them (problem of validity). Besides, the same acts may be reported in different ways in different newspapers (problem of reliability). A recent report from a research following this method conducted in Italy in 1996,[15] shows that the information provided by journalists often do not allow the type of violence to be defined nor the perpetrators to be clearly identified. I noticed a tendency, in the Italian papers, that when *'extra-comunitari'* (the widespread Italian expression for all non-EU immigrants) fall victim to violence perpetrated by Italians, to define such cases as pertaining to the realm of ordinary criminality or as a result of drunkenness to reassure the readers that this is not a matter of racism or xenophobia. In such cases a scrutiniser is left to choose, rely on the journalist's account or make their own deduction and classify such acts as expression of ethnic violence despite the journalist's description.

Fortunately the situation is relatively less problematic for data on background and short term indicators, taken as possible root causes and/or precipitators of the phenomena to be monitored. For most of the early warning and monitoring systems reviewed it is a common practice to use existing secondary sources as background indicators, such as:

- census data;
- official statistics;
- published research based on primary fieldwork data.

The possible problems arising from the use of official data is corrected by resorting to the published result of most recent primary research. Moreover, if the correspondents are well chosen, their experience and expertise, as well as those of the academic colleagues whose opinions they should easily obtain, are the source of 'expert judgement', also widely used in early warning and monitoring.

Reporting on short-term developments creates somewhat more problems and in the case of the the EP we instructed the correspondent to integrate information obtained from the media, with interviews with key informants.

Finally, it must be stressed that an increasing amount of information is available on the world wide web, in electronic newsletters, and the like. The EP has compiled such information on a closed on-line site (Intranet), and the information is used by staff of the directorate to integrate (and to a certain extent check) the periodic reports received from the country correspondents.

Conclusive Considerations

I will use this final section to focus briefly on two questions which, although they are implied already by the comparative focus used in establishing the concepts and indicators, I still consider it important to stress their strong national and political hue with respect to broadly defined issues of nationalism/ethnicity/migration, and to emphasise the difficulty when using them to compare Western and Eastern Europe.

One thing to keep in mind is that the 'national' political context and the established discourses related to ethnic diversity shape and influence not only all the aspects to be monitored, but also the social scientists and thus the research and information they produce. They (the social scientists and their production) constitute/reproduce and are influenced by context and discourses, in the same way as other actors (ordinary people, politicians, policymakers, journalists and activists). As Favell has clearly shown (1997), in France and Britain, for instance, the responses offered by researchers and intellectuals to the post-war immigration crisis were more or less a modified reimposition of the nationally specific idioms of incorporation: French universal republican assimilation and British multicultural race relations. Favell has also stressed how, the symbolic and political salience of the issues involved, often result in research that is not only limited by its very peculiar and nationally bounded repertoire, but is also a reflection of local political struggles.

All of the correspondents and the academic sources they will use for reporting, as well as myself and the other staff members of the the EP directorate who will interpret and re-elaborate such reports, will be influenced by their respective 'national context'. In the same way that there are political, value loaded principles within each one of us. This is unavoidable and cannot be completely eradicated. Actually, national traditions and ongoing local political struggles reflected in research cannot be overlooked, but a monitoring system, just as comparative research, must try and reduce, or control for, national parochialism and excessive political engagement.

One wants to avoid positions that, implicitly or explicitly, try to prove the relative merits and superiority of one tradition over the other; positions that most of us have probably had occasion to listen during international conferences.[16] Allowing some flexibility for national peculiarities, the EP has striven towards a framework and rationale that ensures a break away from the local coloration and political content of research in the field. Difficult as it might be, non-partisan objectivity and cross-national validity are two supreme standards to struggle for. A goal, required of any European comparative research, and one which inspired the EP framework, is what I call 'breaking the East–West divide'. This effort implies avoiding acritical use of what appear to be more or less implicit stereotypical assumptions on the cultural-historical and sociopolitical peculiarities of Eastern Europe.

It was in the 1940s that Kohn, in his study on the idea of nationalism, established the influential distinction between Western 'territorialism' and Eastern 'ethnicism' (1945, pp. 329–351). Up until then the argument was that in Western Europe,[17] because the rise of 'nations' and 'nationalism' followed or was contemporary to the establishment of modern centralised sovereign states, they (nation and nationalism) took a territorial and political form, spreading a sense of belonging that could be shared by the masses in a rational association of common law over a given territory. On the contrary, according to Kohn, nationalism emerged later in Eastern Europe and as a result of its backward sociopolitical context—in which the frontiers of existing state formations (none of which are comparable to the modern centralised states of Western Europe) and of emerging potential nations seldom coincided—evolved in opposition to existing state authority, not to transform it into the power of the people but to redraw the boundaries in conformity to strictly ethnic criteria. The idea of nationalism in Eastern Europe, constructed by intellectual elites but not shared by the masses, was based on a 'folk community'. The conclusion is that, while Western nationalism was originally and strictly linked to individual liberty and rational cosmopolitanism (universalism), Eastern nationalism fostered a more organic and potentially authoritarian sense of community (particularism).

A second distinction, sharing with the first an emphasis on the historical differences in the process of modernisation, is between Western individualism and Eastern collectivism. Eastern collectivism, originating during the East's late and peculiar transition to a bourgeois industrial society, has been allegedly reinforced by the experience of Soviet type state socialism. The general distinction between individualism and collectivism as value orientations has been widely operationalised and tested in social psychology. The main idea is that individualistic cultures stress more individual rights and achievements, while collectivistic ones place great value on loyalty and obligation to one's ingroup. The implication is that collectivism fosters stronger ethnic identification and group level ethnic competition and antagonism, and is thus more likely to characterise Eastern Europe, even more so after the fall of communism. Without completely denying the empirical validity to these two distinctions, they seem to be overdrawn and, if acritically accepted, can mislead or make the comparison worthless.

With respect to the first, even accepting that Eastern nationalism was mainly ethnic, it is false that Western nationalism was always political and universalist. Further, in Western Europe most nationalism after 1789 increasingly adopted an ethnic model because, to achieve integration and legitimate borders, '...myths of descent were needed, not only for external consumption, but for internal mobilisation and co-ordination' (Smith, 1986, p. 148). But even without going back to history and simply looking at the current situation in Western Europe, it is easy to see that ethnic national identities are widespread, not only in the ideology of radical right wing xenophobic parties. Castilian, Catalan, and Basque identifications, for instance, have not been obliterated by the construction and discourses of a political Spanish nation. The same applies to British and Belgian identities and, despite official denial, in France with respect to Bretons and Corsicans.

As far as individualism and collectivism are concerned, it is a question of empirical research, the result's of which are heavily dependent on how these two concepts are operationalised and measured and on the specific timing of when answers to survey questionnaires are given. Even conceding that history contributed to forging more collectivistic orientations in Eastern Europe, one should also take into account that things change and, in fact, recent studies in social psychology show that collectivism has been declining since the collapse of Communism (Phalet, 1995).

The observable difference between Eastern and Western Europe is that, in the first the number of territorially concentrated ethnic communities is higher than in the latter, while the ethnic diversity arising from immigration is more pronounced in the latter. This, however, does not support separating the two areas to concentrate only on ethnoterritorial conflicts in Eastern Europe and on the politics of migration and citizenship in Western Europe. First, ethnoterritorial communities are more widely acknowledged as a problem of Eastern Europe and the former Soviet Union and not of Western Europe. This is to some extent a result of a tacit international double standard which leads, for instance, a large number of actors (including institutional) to be interested in the self-determination rights of the Chechens while very few are concerned with groups such as the Basques or Corsicans. Second, issues of migration are increasingly becoming relevant in the East. And third, though the aftermath of Communism's collapse was followed in many countries by a wave of ethnic nationalising policies, more recently an increasing attention to the question of citizenship and an effort to re-conceptualise the national community in a less ethnicised and more political fashion is detectable.

All of these considerations suggest that a real East–West comparison, like the one attempted by the EP, requires a framework based on the assumption that the two areas can be analysed and monitored in terms of the same general concepts and indicators, without any predetermined distinctions. Eastern European countries should not be analysed as isolated cases as if the problems linked to territorial and immigrant communities could not in anyway be approached in the same way as those of Western Europe.

Notes

1   The *Ethnobarometer Project* is a collaboration between 12 EU countries. It is co-directed

by Dr. Alessandro Silj, director of the Italian Social Science Council (CSS) and Prof. Malcolm Cross, chairperson of the UK based Centre for European Migration and Ethnic Studies (CEMES).

2 See http://www.yorku.ca/research/crs/prevent/eweffort.htm.

3 A good example is the models used by the US Food and Agricultural Organisation (FAO) to predict and assess local and global food needs.

4 See among others Clark (1989), Davies and Gurr (1998), Gurr (1993, 1994), Harff (1994), Harff and Gurr (1997), Homer-Dixon (1994), Jenkins and Schmeidl (1995), Jongman (1994), Schmeidl (1997).

5 A previous phase of the project had done the same for 227 groups in the period 1945–1989 (the clear division being before and after the end of the Cold War). The data gathered, the methodology and several papers analysing the project results are available on-line at http://www.bsos.umd.edu/cidcm/mar.

6 The countries selected for monitoring in the first year of operation were: Belgium, Bulgaria, France, Germany Greece, Hungary, Italy, Rumania, Russia, Slovakia, Turkey, and Ukraine. More countries will be added for monitoring in the coming years.

7 According to Connor (1972, 1978) this conception, which created confusion in the field, derives from the work of authors (he quotes Deutsch, Almond and Coleman; Almond and Verba; Apter),who worked within a modernisation perspective. The underlying model is the so-called 'diffusion/erasure' according to which socioeconomic, cultural, and political modernisation processes would have inevitably weakened ethnic particularism, and historical left-over to leave the space for a birth of a new civic sense of national belonging.

8 The theoretical developments mentioned by Brubaker are: (a) network theory; (b) rational choice theory; (c) the shift from structuralism to constructivism; (d) the emergence of the post-modernist theoretical perspective stressing fragmentary and shifting rather than fixed boundaries and **identities.**

9 It must be stressed that minimal definitions, in the sense I have taken from Sartori (1984, p.79), are not the same thing as operational definitions, which are definitions aimed at measurement, establishing the meaning of a definiendum in terms of observable/measurable indicators (Sartori 1984, p. 80).

10 For a good review of these hypothesis see Nielsen (1985) and Ragin (1986).

11 A good review of the literature on collective action and social movements and of its possible application to the field of ethnic and migration studies is presented by Koopmans and Statham as a preliminary to their analysis of mobilisation over migration and citizenship (1998).

12 See for instance Brubaker's institutionalist account of nationhood and the national question in the post-Soviet space (1994).

13 While the way they are reported and interpreted by the media is in itself an object of

monitoring, the simple news of their occurrence can be used as an objective indicator.

14 The actual country reports are not easy to find starting from the home page, so I give here the url where all of the reports are listed: (http://www.unhchr.ch/tbs/doc.nsf/c12 563e7005d936d4125611e00445ea9?OpenView&Start=1&Count=30&Expand=1.3#1.3).

15 The research was conducted by the Sociology Department, Faculty of Communication Sciences, University 'La Sapienza' in Rome (the title of the research report from which the information commented on here is taken from: *Più di uno al giorno. Atti di violenza contro gli stranieri nel corso del 1996: analisi di 20 quotidiani italiani*). The research represents a census of all acts of violence perpetrated against foreigners in Italy through an examination of 20 Italian newspapers.

16 I have in mind a particular plenary session, that of the 1995 European Sociological Association conference held in Budapest, where John Rex and Dominique Schnapper engaged in fruitless contest on Anglo-Saxon differentialism versus French republican universalism. A written example of a nationally biased comparison on the same topic can be found in Todd (1994, pp. 312-313).

17 It must be noted that Kohn does not include the German case with other cases of Western European nationalism, but it treats together with Eastern European ones.

References

Bauböck, R. (1994), *The Integration of Immigrants*, Council of Europe, Strasbourg.

Baumgartle, B. and Favell A. (1994) 'Introduction', in Baumgartle, B. and Favell, A. (eds), *New Xenophobia in Europe*, Kluwer Law International, London.

Brubaker, R. (1994), 'Nationhood and the National Question in Post-Soviet Eurasia: An Institutionalist Account', *Theory and Society*, vol. 23, pp. 47–78.

Brubaker, R. (1996), *Nationalism Reframed: Nationhood and the National question in the New Europe*, Cambridge University Press, Cambridge.

Clark, L. (1989), *Early Warning of Refugees Flows*, Refugees Policy Group, Washington, D.C.

Codagnone, C. (1998), 'Explaining Degrees and Outcomes of Ethnoterritorial Nationalism: A Comparative Analysis of Autonomous Nations Mobilisation in Russia, 1990–1994,' paper presented at the II ERCOMER Summer School , Barcelona May 22nd .

Connor, W. (1972), 'Nation-Building or Nation-Destroying ?', *World Politics,* vol. 24, pp. 319–355.

Connor, W. (1978), 'A Nation Is a Nation, Is a State, Is an Ethnic Group, Is a...', *Ethnic and Racial Studies*, vol. 1, pp. 377–400.

Connor, W. (1990), 'When is a Nation?', *Ethnic and Racial Studies*, vol. 13, pp. 92–103.

Connor, W. (1994), *Ethnonationalism: The Quest for Understanding*, Princeton University Press, Princeton.

Conversi D. (1995), 'Reassessing Current Theories of Nationalism: Nationalism as Boundary Maintenance and Creation', *Nationalism and Ethnic Politics*, vol. 1, pp. 73–85.

Crowley, J. (1998), 'Does the Idea of Cultural Racism Make Sense?' Paper presented at the III ERCOMER International Conference 'New Directions In Comparative Research on Racism and Xenophobia', Utrecht, 23–25 April.

Davies, J. L. and Gurr, T.R. (eds), (1998), *Preventive Measures: Building Risk Assessment and Crisis early Warning Systems*, Rowan and Littlefield, Lanham, MD.

Favell, A. (1997), 'Citizenship and Immigration: Pathologies of a Progressive Philosophy,' *New Community*, vol. 23.

Gurr, T.R. (1993), *Minorities at Risk: A Global View of Ethnopolitical Conflict*, United States Institute of Peace Press, Washington, D.C.

Gurr, T.R. (1994), 'Testing and Using a Model of Communal Conflict for Early Warning', *The Journal of Ethno-Development*, vol. 4, pp. 20–25.

Harff, B. (1994), 'A Theoretical Model of Genocide and Politicides', *The Journal of Ethno-Development*, vol. 4, pp. 25–31.

Harff, B. and Gurr, T.R. (1997), 'Systematic Early Warning of Humanitarian Emergencies', (http://www.bsos.umd.edu/cidcm/mar/pubs.htm).

Homer-Dixon, T. (1994), 'Environmental Scarcities and Violent Conflict: Evidence from Cases', *International Security*, vol. 19, pp. 5–140.

Jackson, R. (1984), 'Ethnicity', in Sartori (ed.), *Social Science Concepts*, Sage Publications Beverly Hills, pp. 206–233.

Jenkins, J. C. and Schmeidl, S. (1995), 'Flight from Violence: The Origins and Implications of the World Refugees Crisis', *Sociological Focus*, vol. 28, pp. 63–82.

Jongman, A.J. (1994), 'The PIOOM Program on Monitoring and Early Warning of Humanitarian Crises', *The Journal of Ethno-Development*, vol. 4, pp. 65–72.

Kohn, H. (1945), *The Idea of Nationalism*, Macmillan, New York.

Koopmans, R. and Statham, P. (1998), 'The Contentious Politics of Migration and Ethnic Relations in Britain and Germany: An Opportunity Approach for Studying Public Claims and Collective Mobilisation,' paper presented at the III ERCOMER International Conference 'New Directions In Comparative Research on Racism and Xenophobia', Utrecht, 23–25 April.

Myers, D. (1996), *Social Psychology*, 5th edition, McGraw-Hill, New York.

Nielsen, F. (1985), 'Toward a Theory of Ethnic Solidarity in Modern Societies', *American Sociological Review*, vol. 45, pp.133–149.

Phalet, K. (1995), 'Individualism-Collectivism: Concept and Measurement,' Utrecht, unpublished paper.

Ragin, C. (1986), 'The Impact of Celtic Nationalism on Class Politics in Scotland and Wales', in S. Olzak and J. Nagel (eds), *Competitive Ethnic Relations*, Academic Press, New York.

Riggs, F. (1991a), 'Ethnicity, Nationalism, Race, Minority: A Semantic/Onomantic Exercise (Part One)', *International Sociology*, vol. 6, pp. 281–305.

Riggs, F. (1991b), 'Ethnicity, Nationalism, Race, Minority: A Semantic/Onomantic Exercise (Part Two)', *International Sociology*, vol. 6, pp. 443–463.

Sartori, G. (1984), 'Guidelines for Concept Analysis', in Sartori, G. (ed.), *Social Science Concepts*, Sage Publications, Beverly Hills, pp. 15–85.

Schmeidl, S. (1997), 'Exploring the Causes of Forced Migration: A Pooled Analysis, 1971–1990', *Social Science Quarterly*, vol. 78, pp. 284–308.

Smith, A. (1986), *The Ethnic Origins of Nations*, Basic Blackwell, Oxford.

Smith, A. (1994), 'The Problem of National Identity: Ancient, Medieval and Modern?', *Ethnic and Racial Studies*, vol. 17, pp. 375–399.

Tishkov, V. (1997), *Ethnicity, Nationalism and Conflict in and after The Soviet Union: The Mind Aflame*, Sage, London.

Todd, E. (1994), *Le destin des immigrés: assimilation et ségregation dans les démocraties occidentales* [The Destiny of Immigrants: Assimilation and Segregation in the Western Democracies], Seuil, Paris.

Virdee, S. (1997), 'Racial Harrassment' in T. Modood and R. Berthoud (eds.), *Ethnic Minorities in Britain: Diversity and Disadvantage*, Policies Study Institute, London.

Weber, M. (1968), *Economy and Society*, edited by G. Roth and C. Wittich, Bedminster Press, New York.

Wimmer, A. (1997), 'Explaining Xenophobia and Racism: A Critical Review of Current Research Approaches', *Ethnic and Racial Studies*, vol. 20, pp. 17–41.

Witte, R. (1995), 'Racist Violence in Western Europe', *New Community*, vol. 21, pp. 489–500.

Author Index

Subject Index